The Protagonists
of Italian
Art

PIERO DELLA FRANCESCA

BOTTICELLI, LEONARDO

MICHELANGELO, RAPHAEL

TITIAN, CARAVAGGIO

CANALETTO
AND THE VEDUTISTI

D1531060

SCALA

© 2001 SCALA Group S.p.A.
Antella Florence

Photographs: SCALA Group Picture Archive, except pp. 12, 66b, 78, 79, 80a, 81, 128, 129, 130, 151, 152, 196b, 197, 222, 326, 337b, 343, 359, 408, 409, 414, 421, 432, 446, 447b, 462, 468, 469, 517, 518, 519, 541a, 592, 593, 605 (National Gallery, London); pp. 18, 139, 525 (Staatliche Museen, Berlin); pp. 64, 65a (Frick Collection, New York); pp. 67, 94c, 311, 461 (Gardner Museum, Boston); pp. 132-3, 134, 220, 334b, 339, 358a, 377, 442a, 444, 456b (National Gallery of Art, Washington); pp. 149, 488a (Metropolitan Museum of Art, New York); pp. 157, 586 (Fogg Art Museum, Cambridge, Mass.); pp. 176, 186, 264, 305, 321a (British Museum, London); p. 242 (Graphische Sammlungen, Munich); pp. 355, 358b, 386, 470 (Alte Pinakothek, Munich); p. 449 (Bayerische Staatsgemäldesammlungen, Munich); p. 243 (Albertina, Vienna); p. 394 (Royal Academy, London); p. 394 (Victoria and Albert Museum, London); pp. 266, 267, 268, 269, 270, 271, 272, 273, 274, 275, 306, 307, 308, 309 (Vatican Museums); pp. 348, 425a, 467, 475b, 537, 541b (Kunsthistorisches Museum, Vienna); pp. 378a, 425b (Gemäldegalerie, Dresden); pp. 413, 422a, 460 (Collection of the Duke of Sutherland on loan to the National Gallery of Edinburgh); p. 453b (Gemäldegalerie, Kassel); p. 464 (Patrimonio Nacional, El Escorial); p. 471a (Saint Louis Art Museum); p. 472a (Fitzwilliam Museum, Cambridge); p. 475a (Museum Boymans-van Beuningen, Rotterdam); p. 489 (Wadsworth Atheneum, Hartford, Conn.); p. 490 (Institute of Art, Detroit); pp. 494, 580, 581, 584 (Thyssen-Bornemisza Collection, Madrid); p. 520a (Bildarchiv Preussischer Kulturbesitz, Berlin); p. 529 (Nelson Gallery of Art, Kansas City); p. 539 (Museum of Art, Cleveland); p. 555a (Shickman Gallery, New York); 557 (Musée des Beaux-Arts, Nancy); 559 (Kimbell Art Museum, Fort Worth, Texas); p. 560 (Banca Commerciale Italiana S.p.A., Milan); pp. 569, 571, 578 (photos supplied by the author); p. 573 (Stiftung Preussische Schlösser und Gärten, Potsdam); pp. 574-5 (Artothek, Peissenberg); pp. 577, 625, 636b (Ashmolean Museum, Oxford); pp. 585, 587, 608-9 (The Royal Collection, Her Majesty Queen Elizabeth II); pp. 596-7, 598, 599 (by kind permission of the Marquess of Tavistock and Trustees of Bedford Estate); pp. 600-1 (Museum of Fine Arts, Boston); p. 606a (Toledo Museum of Arts); p. 610a (Roudnice Lobkowicz Collection, Prague); p. 610b (Dulwich College Picture Gallery, London); p. 611 (by courtesy of the Dean and Chapter of Westminster), p. 624a (Archivio Pedicini, Naples); pp. 636a, 637 (Calouste Gulbenkian Museum, Lisbon); the drawings from the Royal Library, Windsor, are reproduced by Fac-simile

Produced by SCALA Group
Printed by: Lito Terrazzi, Cascine del Riccio (Florence), 2001

This volume is a digital abridgment of the SCALA series "The Great Masters of Art"

CONTENTS

PIERO DELLA FRANCESCA

The Formative Years: Florence 1435-40

The scarcity of information about the painting of Piero della Francesca in the artistic literature of the time must not make us underestimate the importance of his art in the varied and complex context of Italian 15th-century painting. The fact that Piero was born and spent many years in Borgo San Sepolcro, and worked almost all his life far away from a literary and artistic centre such as Florence, certainly contributed to the lack of information about his activity. With a few exceptions, in fact, Piero was entirely ignored by his contemporaries. It was not until Vasari wrote his biography in 1550 that the literary sources began to pay any attention to Piero's painting. Until then the only interest had been shown by artists working at the same time as Piero, who had been in contact with his paintings and whose work showed his influence. But none of our literary sources, not even Vasari, realized that Piero della Francesca was more than any other Italian 15th-century painter responsible for the development of Florentine Renaissance painting and for the spreading of the principles of the new art throughout Italy. And nowhere in the artistic literature of the Renaissance is it recognized that Piero's work represents one of the highest moments of synthesis between Italian painting and its interest in perspective and space, on the one hand, and Netherlandish painting, on the other, with its study of light and natural phenomena. Here we shall see how Piero's painting can be examined in terms of the progressive development of his original style—a strictly Florentine perspective-based art—towards a more Northern kind of painting, which rapidly conquered the European art world of the late 15th century with its brightly coloured, almost enamel-like, surfaces. Vasari, with a remarkable critical intuition, seems to sense the co-existence of these two elements in Piero della Francesca's painting. In his biography of Piero, he stresses the 'perspective,' the 'measure' and the 'foreshortening' as essential characteristics of Piero's compositions. But at the same time, in his description of the frescoes in the church of San Francesco in Arezzo, he emphasizes the admirable play of light in the obscurity of a night scene, or the shining armour in the *Battle between Heraclius and Chosroes*. Vasari's keen eye even goes further in his understanding of Piero's style: while pointing out the

importance of Piero's 'sweet and new manner' in the artistic development of contemporary painters, he actually seems to be stressing that it also influenced a great deal of early 16th-century Venetian art. On the other hand, Vasari was a man of the 16th century, with a taste for 'grace,' 'feelings' and emotions; Piero's figures, with their aloof detachment, must have been more difficult for him to understand.

Whereas Vasari's biography of Piero is, from the critical point of view, so rich in penetrating observations on his paintings, as far as biographical information is concerned, the historian from Arezzo would seem to be rather confused and elusive: he does not mention Piero's formative period spent in Florence, nor does he appear to know that the young artist had been a pupil of Domenico Veneziano, a fact that is proved by contemporary documents as well as by the obvious influence of Domenico in Piero's early works. But Piero's painting, at the height of his artistic development, must have seemed culturally light years away from Florentine mid-15th-century art, and it would have been difficult for Vasari, who had no access to the documents of the time, to suggest that Piero had spent his formative years in Florence. In fact, even in modern times, the difficulty of finding historical explanations for Piero's initial stylistic development caused scholars to propose very different theories. It was not until the first decades of this century—primarily thanks to Roberto Longhi's research on Piero—that we were able to clarify the artist's basic cultural development. To this day, Longhi's study is still the most complete examination of the great art of Piero della Francesca. Early biographical information on the artist is scarce: we do not even know in what year he was born. Even later, as we shall see, we have very little definite information on his life, which was in any case lacking in memorable events, almost entirely consecrated to the art of painting. We know that Piero was born in Borgo San Sepolcro, in a family of artisans and merchants, probably sometime between 1415 and 1420.

The fact that he was born in a small town in the Tuscan countryside, with no established local traditions, and so different from the large cities such as Florence and Siena, is very significant. Piero did not have a cultural homeland or ancient artistic roots to follow and abide by; and very early on he moved away from his home town, embarking on his search for a new art.

The fundamental element in Piero's youth is his stay in Florence; he arrived in the city perhaps even before he was twenty years old. The only certain piece of information we have about this important formative period is that in September 1439 Piero was definitely in Florence, where he worked with Domenico Veneziano on the frescoes in the choir of the church of Sant'Egidio. This is where Piero della Francesca's career as a painter begins.

Florence in the 1430s was Italy's most lively and modern artistic centre. The fathers of the early Renaissance, Brunelleschi and Donatello, were at the height of their careers and their fame. The more modern and up-to-date painters were by this time all following the new ideas of Masaccio, trying to adapt the extraordinary and 'terrible' aspect of his figurative revolution to more traditional artforms. It was during this remarkable decade that Leon Battista Alberti returned to Florence, after the bitter years of exile he and his family had undergone; in 1436 with his *De Pictura* he had produced the first theoretical treatise on the new art 'created' by Brunelleschi and Donatello. Some passages of Alberti's treatise undoubtedly call to mind ideas realized in painting by Piero della Francesca. *De Pictura* is the result of Alberti's study of the works of Fra Angelico, Paolo Uccello and Domenico Veneziano, as well as the outcome of the lively scientific and artistic debate whose protagonists were not only Brunelleschi, Paolo Toscanelli and Alberti himself, but all the major scholarly figures of early Humanism in Florence.

In the field of painting this period was marked by an extremely rapid evolution of knowledge and by innumerable developments which soon were to transform the very concept of painting as a trade. Alberti's work, and later Piero's, were decisive in giving artists a new social standing, for artists now needed to have a theoretical background as well.

And it was also during Piero della Francesca's formative period spent in Florence that the first elements of Northern painting began to filter into Florentine and Italian figurative culture: they were destined to influence the most progressive Italian painters for the rest of the century.

Whether one is investigating the Northern origins of Piero's teacher, Domenico Veneziano, or one examines the frescoes by the Portuguese artist Giovanni di Consalvo in the Chiostro degli Aranci in the church of Badia (1436-39), which must have been so rich in transparent textures and colours, or one considers the translucid vase that Filippo Lippi placed in his *Annunciation* in San Lorenzo. . . in all these cases we are confronted with a civilization and a culture which is pro-

*1. Filippo Lippi
Annunciation
Florence, San Lorenzo*

*2. Nanni di Banco
Four Crowned Saints
Florence, Orsanmichele*

8

foundly different from the austere and heroic nature that characterizes Masaccio's apostles (1424-28), or from the classical Roman 'gravitas' of Nanni di Banco's *Four Crowned Saints* at Orsanmichele (1415-20). This new 'chromatic' art of the painters in the 1430s on the one hand adopts Donatello and Masaccio's linear perspective, while on the other attempting to rediscover all those values that late-Gothic use of colour had been based on, and which will be fundamental to the new vision of Netherlandish painting.

In Florence, probably as early as 1435, Piero della Francesca was able to study Fra Angelico's masterpieces, such as the *Coronation of the Virgin*, painted originally for the church of San Domenico in Fiesole and now in the Louvre, and the extraordinary San Marco polyptych: two great paintings created in the critical years of that decade. Here Fra Angelico placed his compositions in an airy spatial environment, even succeeding in making his figures monumental; he then covered the whole with brilliant colours, like a precious enamelled gem. And we must not forget the influence that Paolo Uccello's early works must have had on Piero: the frescoes in Prato Cathedral, the monument to *John Hawkwood* in Florence Cathedral (1436), and above all the three panels depicting the *Battle of San Romano,* painted for Cosimo de' Medici in 1438-40. Paolo Uccello, in fact, was primarily interested in perspective, in the study of the basic structure of shapes, in the almost geometrical simplification of volumes: his figures are like archaic prototypes of Piero's. Further evidence of common interests of Paolo Uccello and the young Piero is offered by a drawing, now in the Uffizi, showing a schematic geometrical representation of a vase. Traditionally attributed to Paolo Uccello, the drawing seems much closer to the static and imposing stance of figures and objects painted by Piero. All the more so since it fits the description of a vase made by Vasari in his biography of Piero: "a vase drawn in squares and faces, in such a way that one can see the front, the back, the sides, the bottom and the mouth."

Piero's study and research cannot have involved only the novelties of contemporary art; like all other great early 15th-century artists, he must also have studied those examples of 14th-century painting which, although painted a century earlier, were the true beginning of the Renaissance in the figurative arts. He would probably have had great interest in spacious and brightly coloured works, like Maso di Banco's frescoes in Santa Croce which, with their large figures of saints depicted in solemn poses, could almost be the work of a Giottesque Piero della Francesca.

But let us return to that document of 1439 that confirms Piero's presence, together with his master Domenico Veneziano, in Sant'Egidio, working on the choir. Unfortunately, this cycle of frescoes has not survived, but it must have been remarkably imposing,

3. Fra Angelico
Coronation of the Virgin
Paris, Louvre

4. Paolo Uccello
John Hawkwood
Florence, Cathedral

9

5. Paolo Uccello
Battle of San Romano
Florence, Uffizi

6. Paolo Uccello
Geometrical study
of a vase
Florence, Uffizi

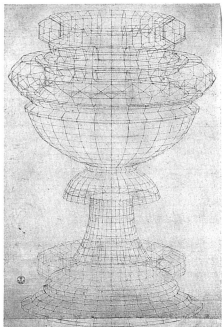

opment of the time, it will be enough to have a look at Veneziano's works dating from just after 1440, like the large altarpiece for the church of Santa Lucia de' Magnoli, now at the Uffizi. If we examine this painting, Veneziano's masterpiece, in comparison with his early works, painted probably before 1438, such as the fresco of Canto de' Carnesecchi or the *Madonna and Child* now in Bucharest, it will be obvious that his development was parallel to that of his young assistant. The altarpiece of Santa Lucia de' Magnoli is the Florentine painting that comes closest to the art of Piero. The compositional harmony between architecture and figures, achieved by following Alberti's theories, can be considered a prototype for so many of Piero's later works. Thanks primarily to the bright colours (as if the scene were taking place at midday), the artist places his figures in a realistic space, and makes them move in a graceful and balanced way. A very 'ornate' painting, in other words rich in colour, grace and texture, compared to the art of Masaccio, but which is nonetheless a logical development of the great message proposed by the Carmine frescoes.

The first work of Piero della Francesca's that we know probably belongs to this Florentine period: the *Madonna and Child* formerly in the Contini-Bonacossi Collection. The painting is unfortunately in very bad condition, but it is still clearly related to the work of Veneziano, so much so that it would seem likely that it was painted while Piero was in his workshop. Here the young artist already shows his interest in the study of perspective, with the Virgin fitting into the window frame. The open window replaces Veneziano's more usual background of rose bowers. Even the reverse side of the painting is of interest: within a square frame there is a monochrome vase with a simplified geometrical structure, which creates the effect of a wooden intarsia.

The relationship between Piero and the more exper-

comparable only to Masaccio's frescoes in the Brancacci Chapel or his *Sagra* among the paintings of the period. At the time it must have been the most modern synthesis between the new perspective theories elaborated in Florence and the Gothic tradition of use of colour, represented in those years by painters such as Fra Angelico and Masolino, who were anything but old-fashioned. To understand fully what the frescoes of Sant'Egidio must have meant to the artistic devel-

imental wood inlayers of the time will develop greatly in later years, as we shall see. Looking at this vase, we must bear in mind that in the 15th century perspective and intarsia witnessed a parallel development, and that it was in 1436 that work began on the intarsia in the Sacristy in Florence Cathedral where Brunelleschi's influence is very clear.

7. *Domenico Veneziano*
Altarpiece of Santa Lucia de' Magnoli
Florence, Uffizi

Piero's Early Works in Borgo San Sepolcro

In the early 1440s Piero returned to Borgo San Sepolcro, where he was recorded as town councillor in 1442. His first important commission dates from this period: the *Baptism of Christ*, now in the National Gallery in London, originally painted for the Chapel of San Giovanni in the Pieve. The most striking feature of this painting is the extraordinary lighting from above, creating delicate pastel colours, with pale shadows that surround the figures and enhance their three-dimensionality. At the centre, the figure of Christ is portrayed as a simple man, but his stance is so solemn as to make him look as majestic as a Greek god. His torso and his legs are circular and solid, like the tree on the left; the holy dove, like a little cloud, fits into a patch of sky amidst the foliage of the tree, rendered with almost Impressionistic strokes. Piero displays great originality in his interpretation of nature, reproducing its elements in simple and perfect shapes, as can be seen also in the small triangle of water that is the river Jordan, rather like a mirror reflecting the sky and the hills of the background. The formative years spent in Florence are still very evident, yet Piero succeeds already in this first work in going beyond them. The three angels on the left, with their pale but round faces, are reminiscent of the groups of children sculpted by Luca della Robbia for the Cantoria in Florence Cathedral (1432-38); and even their blonde hair, decorated with garlands, is clearly inspired by Luca's models. The face of the angel in the centre, with his

fixed gaze, brings to mind the *Madonna* painted in the mid-1430s by Domenico Veneziano for Canto de' Carnesecchi, today in the National Gallery in London. By using Veneziano's paintings of the 1430s as models, Piero seems to go back even further: the soft range of colours is very similar to Masolino's art. But the delicate, almost Gothic, textures of this group of angels are given such solidity and weight that they acquire the power of a sculptural group. In the same way, Veneziano's new techniques of drawing are clearly evident in the tense pose of John the Baptist and in the elegant figure in the background removing his clothes; but Piero had made the outlining of the figures invisible, as it is in reality, and it serves solely to delimit the patches of colour which, in the different light areas, give the bodies their depth.

In 1445 the Compagnia della Misericordia, a confraternity of Borgo San Sepolcro, commissioned Piero della Francesca to paint a polyptych for them, within three years; according to the taste of the time, the polyptych was to be painted with precious colours and have a solid gold background. Piero did not respect the time limits set down in the contract, for he was busy working on other, more important projects. The polyptych for the Misericordia was only finished after 1460, almost twenty years later. The oldest parts of the polyptych are undoubtedly the two panels with *St Sebastian* and *St John the Baptist*, to the left of the main panel. No other figure of Piero's, more than this

11

8. Baptism of Christ
167 x 116 cm
London, National Gallery

9. Polyptych of the Misericordia
273 x 323 cm
Sansepolcro, Museo Civico

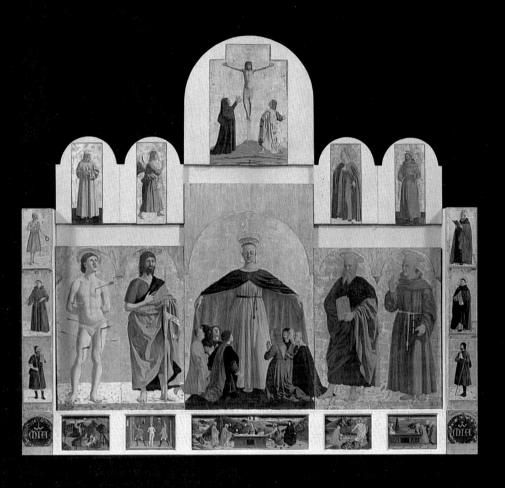

10-11. *Polyptych of the Misericordia*
detail of St Sebastian and St John the Baptist
108 x 90 cm
detail of the Crucifixion
81 x 52 cm
Sansepolcro, Museo Civico

12. *Masaccio*
Crucifixion
Naples, Museo di Capodimonte

St Sebastian, shows such close connection with Masaccio's nudes, even in his rather graceless but realistic pose. Before Piero, only Masaccio had over succeeded in creating a real space against the flat and abstract gold gold background, in which to place flesh and blood figures.

Piero goes even further: he foreshortens the saints' feet, as though burdened by the weight of the body, and places them on pedestals creating delicate shadows. A little later Piero painted the panels of the tympanum, with the *Crucifixion* in the centre and *St Benedict*, the *Angel* and the *Madonna of the Annunciation*, and *St Francis* at the sides. The *Crucifixion* reveals the influence of Masaccio's polyptych for San Francesco in Pisa. But Masaccio created a dramatic atmosphere both with the moving gestures of the characters and with the strong, almost violent, colours; Piero's composition, on the other hand, is orderly and symmetric and the gestures of the figures are solemn, almost ritualistic.

Even the strongest and most painful emotions appear to be overruled in Piero's art by a predetermined order, controlled by a sense of balance imposed from above. This sensation of great solemnity and order is the result of the complete absence of movement that characterizes Piero's work. Piero reproduces even the most dramatic action as though fixed at its culminating moment, in its absolute expression, placed in a unitary and scientifically constructed space, where there is no room for chance or for the changing movement of things.

The *Angel of the Annunciation* is similar to Fra Angelico's celestial beings, but it is as though a strong and heavy body contributed to making that model more alive and concrete. The *Virgin of the Annunciation*, with her billowing cloak, is depicted in an attitude of very realistic and anything but divine astonishment; her feet, barely visible under the cloak, help create the two planes on which she stands. During this period Piero was assisted by another painter who is responsible for the predella and for the six figures on the side pilasters: not an excellent artist, of obviously Florentine formation, who struggled to imitate Piero's style.

As we have mentioned above, Piero completed the polyptych much later than contracted. In January 1455 the confraternity of the Misericordia threatened to demand their money back from the artist's father unless the painting were completed within forty days. Towards 1450 Piero finished the figures of *St Andrew* and *St Bernardino*; the latter is given a round and smooth halo like a saint, instead of the small halo with rays that symbolized the blessed. This indicates that the painting cannot date from before 1450, the year Bernardino was canonized.

Even in the portrayal of this saint, usually represented as an emaciated old man by traditional Sienese painters, Piero does not abandon his ideal of a strong

and solid body. Bernardino stands erect, emphasizing the spatial depth with a calm gesture of the hand. *St Andrew*, like *St John*, is clad in a flowing cloak with deep folds, creating the effect of a painted statue.

13. Polyptych of the Misericordia detail of St Andrew and St Bernardino 108 x 90 cm Sansepolcro, Museo Civico

14. Polyptych of the Misericordia detail of the predella with the Deposition 23 x 70 cm Sansepolcro, Museo Civico

15. St Jerome and a donor 40 x 42 cm Venice, Gallerie dell'Accademia

The Journey to Romagna: Piero's First Contact with Alberti's Architecture

While working on the Misericordia polyptych, in the late 1440s and early 1450s, Piero travelled to the Marches and to Emilia-Romagna. These journeys are documented by relatively reliable sources such as Pacioli and Vasari, by the traces of his influence on local painting and by one signed and dated painting. There is no reason to doubt Piero's presence in Pesaro and Ancona, even though nothing remains of the fresco of the *Marriage of the Virgin* in the church of San Ciriaco in Ancona, mentioned by Vasari. On the other hand, Piero's influence is unmistakeable in the fresco of the *Madonna with Saints Nicholas of Tolentino and Anthony Abbot*, painted by the painter from Camerino Girolamo di Giovanni in 1449, now in the Pinacoteca in Camerino.

Piero's presence in the major artistic centres of the Marches just before 1450 would explain the development of new perspective elements in much of the painting of this region around that period.

According to Vasari's reconstruction, it would appear that Piero della Francesca, by that time already quite famous, was called to Ferrara by the Duke of that city, Lionello d'Este. Here, too, however, we have no trace of any works painted by Piero in Ferrara, although the sources do mention a cycle of frescoes in

the church of Sant'Agostino and another in Duke Borso's palace, which have since been destroyed. In any case, the most concrete evidence of Piero's presence in Ferrara certainly lies in the strong influence of his art on later Ferrarese painting.

In 1451 the artist was in Rimini, where he signed and dated the fresco of *St. Sigismund and Sigismondo Malatesta* in the church of San Francesco. But before that he had painted two small panels: *St Jerome and a donor*, in the Gallerie dell'Accademia in Venice, and the *Penance of St Jerome*, in the Gemäldegalerie Dahlem in Berlin. We do not know exactly when or for whom these were painted, but they are probably to be included amongst the 'many paintings of small figures' mentioned by Vasari as being commissioned by several rulers during the artist's journeys in the Marches and Emilia-Romagna.

In the small panel in Venice we can see for the first time Piero's signature, on the tree trunk that forms the base of the Crucifix in the lefthand corner. On the ground, in the foreground, there is also an inscription indicating that the panel was commissioned by Gerolamo Amadi 'veneziano,' who is shown kneeling in prayer before the saint. The donor and his protecting saint appear to be conversing as equals, for it was ob-

16. *Penance of St Jerome*
51 x 38 cm
Berlin, Gemäldegalerie Dahlem

17. *St Sigismund and Sigismondo*
Malatesta
257 x 345 cm
Rimini, San Francesco (Tempio
Malatestiano)

18. *St Sigismund and Sigismondo*
Malatesta
detail of St Sigismund
Rimini, San Francesco (Tempio
Malatestiano)

viously Piero's intention to exalt the human dignity of his patron, as he was to do again in the case of Sigismondo Malatesta in Rimini. The bright hues of colour are similar to the clear sunlit atmosphere of the London *Baptism of Christ*, and even the background, with its rolling hills and steep country paths, confirms a vision of landscape that was first anticipated in the London painting. Compared to Paolo Uccello's nighttime, rather abstract and fairytale landscapes, or Fra Angelico's gentle and precious ones, Piero's are closer to Veneziano's, or even Masaccio's, with bare hills, partially covered with vegetation. And Piero makes his landscapes even more real and alive, for the vegetation is burnt out by a Mediterranean sun, the city walls are made of white lime and the water of the river is transparent.

The Berlin *St Jerome* is one of the two paintings by Piero that is dated; the landscape composition is even more closely connected to the London *Baptism of Christ*. Recently this panel has been restored, and all the later additions have been removed from the back-

ground and the sky: it is as though we now had a new and hitherto unknown painting by Piero. We can now see, in the crystal-clear lighting, behind the hermit saint, a receding background with the perfectly straight tree trunks reflected in the winding river. The clear sky is barely dotted with little white pointed clouds, finer and smaller than in the *Baptism*. It may seem strange that this painting, so lacking in colour (to the extent that it was added by others not long afterwards) and basically so similar to Piero's earliest works, is dated 1450. Yet the incredible attention to detail shown by the artist in his depiction of the foreshortened books, for example, or the houses and villages painted in the background between the slender trees, clearly show the development Piero's art had undergone during his journey to Ferrara.

We know that Lionello d'Este possessed a triptych by Rogier van der Weyden before 1449, and surely the presence in Ferrara of this Netherlandish painting must have aroused Piero's interest immediately. After 1450, Piero's panel paintings begin to show a new fea-

18

ture of his pictorial vision which will gradually develop into the extreme attention to even the tiniest details—a feature of the artist's mature work.

And so we come to 1451, the year in which Piero painted the fresco of *St Sigismund and Sigismondo Malatesta* in the church of San Francesco in Rimini. With its monumental composition and the studied placing of the figures within the environment, it is the painting that most resembles the cycle in the church of San Francesco in Arezzo. In few other works of Piero's is Alberti's influence so evident, and in fact Alberti was working at the same time in the same church in Rimini, which he was transforming into the Tempio Malatestiano. The scene is enclosed by an architectural frame, reminiscent of bas-relief decorations, and is seen as though from an 'open window, through which I can see what will be painted here,' as Alberti describes the best point of view for a pictorial composition. Also influenced by Alberti is the decoration of the room with slabs of coloured marble; and Piero's interiors in later paintings all use the same decoration, enriching the colours even further. St Sigismund sits on a throne like a majestic and wise sovereign; he is depicted from below so as to make his appearance more monumental. At his feet, Sigismondo Malatesta, seen

19

19. Sigismondo
Malatesta
44 x 34 cm
Paris, Louvre

20. Bartolomeo
Bonascia
Pietà
Modena, Galleria
Estense

in profile, pays homage to his patron saint. A profane atmosphere is created by the ostentation of the
symbols of temporal power: the heraldic portrait, the
coat-of-arms and the castle that is visible in the distance through the small round window, like the engraving on a medallion. The pair of greyhounds, lying
on the ground behind Sigismondo, is portrayed with
magnificent simplicity: their intelligent expressions reveal an attentive study of nature—like a Pisanello
drawing—while the roundness of their bodies confirms
once more the artist's interest in the study of three-
dimensionality.

Also dating from Piero's period in Rimini is the portrait of *Sigismondo Malatesta*, today in the Louvre. As
in the case of the portrait in the fresco in the church of

San Francesco, this portrait is also taken from a medal
made by Pisanello in 1445 for Sigismondo. Yet, even
though he was working within a context of traditional
International Gothic iconography, Piero succeeds in
giving it new depth: what was just an emblem on a
coin becomes a fully-rounded, almost sculptural portrait, with a proud expression of unrelenting cruelty.
The three-dimensional effect is achieved also by a
most realistic skin tonality, created with the technique
of oil paints.

Piero della Francesca's brief period spent in Romagna is of fundamental importance not only for the
development of an exceptional school of painters like
the Ferrarese, as we have mentioned above, but also
for the gradual spreading of the study of perspective to

other cities in Emilia and the Po Valley, dominated until the second half of the century by a pictorial style that was still basically late Gothic. Luca Pacioli claims that Piero spent some time in Bologna, although this is not documented. But there were two artists active in Modena who were closely connected to Piero, as well as being his friends: the wood inlayers Cristoforo and Lorenzo Lendinara. It is thanks to their ability in reproducing Piero's ideas on perspective in wood that we now have the choirstalls of Modena Cathedral. Here we can see how the technique of intarsia, placing different coloured woods next to each other, is the perfect medium for the reproduction of different planes seen in perspective. In Emilia, the innovations brought by Piero only really take hold in the 1460s, but they are still present in the work of the Modenese brothers Agnolo and Bartolomeo degli Erri, of Marco Zoppo in his large polyptych for the Collegio di Spagna in Bologna, and even in the unique *Pietà* by Bartolomeo Bonascia, now in the gallery in Modena.

Before returning to Borgo San Sepolcro in 1453, Piero must have stopped in Urbino. It is almost certainly during this first visit to Urbino that Piero painted one of his most famous panel paintings: the *Flagellation* now in the National Gallery in Urbino. This painting contains subtle references to the situation of the time, which are very difficult for us to understand today.

From the point of view of composition and perspective it is very rigorously planned. His interest in spatial depth, which had been evident from his earliest works, is here developed to such an extent as to suggest that Piero had already embarked on theoretical studies as well. The composition appears to be divided into two scenes, separated by the column supporting the temple in which the Flagellation of Christ is taking place. On the right are three figures, arranged in a semi-circle; their identity is not certain. They are probably well-known characters of the time and, as such, they would be portrayed with their real features. The

importance of the architecture in this painting, with the elegant classical temple, would suggest again that Piero was in touch with Alberti's contemporary writings. During the 15th century every great painter interested in perspective appears to have had an architect whose work on the measuring of volumes and space he studied. Just as Masaccio's concept of space would be inconceivable to us without Brunelleschi's architecture, if it were not for Alberti's work we would not be able to understand Piero's scientific methods of arranging his figures within his compositions. The onlooker must stand directly in the centre of the painting, for the composition is strictly unitarian, and this unity is achieved by the rigorous use of a single vanishing point. The organization of space in 14th-century art, even in Giotto's paintings, was fragmentary and the laws of perspective were only hinted at, for there was not a single vanishing point. The Urbino *Flagellation* is the ultimate example of Quattrocento linear perspective. And yet there is nothing aridly theoretical about this painting. The distance between the figures is suggested by the reflection of light on the pure colours, by the crystal-clear atmosphere of the morning light. A clear light surrounds the figures in the background, watching the Flagellation, with effects that anticipate Venetian painting from Antonello da Messina to Giovanni Bellini. Even though he is working within a unitary space, Piero does not give up his interest in detail, such as the ceiling of the temple or the bronze sculpture on the column with its splendid reflection of the light. These effects are obtained by a subtle technique, certainly deriving from Piero's acquaintance with Netherlandish paintings, like the Van Eyck that belonged to the Duke of Urbino (now lost); but his style is so original that his sources are barely recognizable. Even the magnificent damask garment worn by the character on the far right, with its contrast between blue and gold, reveals Piero's love for luxurious clothing and for the most fashionable styles, which many Florentine painters, following Masaccio's austere example, had eliminated entirely from their work. This is another element that Piero had acquired from the late Gothic tradition and which he had also found in the latest paintings by Netherlandish artists, where the brightness of the coloured fabrics was further enhanced and given a velvet-like softness by the use of oil paints.

We mentioned earlier the difficulty of interpreting the more hidden meaning of the painting. In recent years, the theory that seems to be proposed most frequently is that the painting was commissioned as an attempt to favour the reconciliation between the two Christian churches, of the East and of the West, in view of the imminent Turkish attack on Constantinople. Both the presence of the character in the centre, dressed after the Greek fashion, and the in-

scription 'convenerunt in unum' which could be read on the frame until the last century, would seem to support this interpretation. But, as in the case of many other paintings commissioned by patrons who were deeply involved in the Humanist culture of the times, the meaning of these two separate yet related scenes is still to a great extent unexplained.

Piero's work in Ferrara, Rimini and Urbino stimulated the artistic development of these towns; thanks to his innovations they became artistic centres of great importance, rivalling the traditional art capitals of the time, such as Florence and Siena. Piero left Florence as soon as work on the frescoes in Sant'Egidio was finished and never returned; the Florentine trends in painting, based as they were on drawing rather than on perspective and colour, could not possibly attract him. His travels coincided several times with those of Alberti, also a Florentine but, like Piero, only as far as his basic training was concerned. The parallel development of these two artists is responsible for the spread of the great 're-born' art in Florence in the early 15th century; later it was in part rejected by the Florentine heirs of Brunelleschi and Masaccio. Piero della Francesca's painting, made up of so many complex and varied elements yet blended together in a single expression, was welcomed much more favourably in

21. Flagellation
59 x 81 cm
Urbino, Galleria Nazionale

22. Flagellation, detail
Urbino, Galleria Nazionale

the smaller centres. Here the new rulers, such as the Malatesta and the Montefeltro, who had only recently acquired their positions of power fighting in the battlefields at the head of their armies, were attempting to legitimize their fortunes, from the cultural point of view as well, by becoming the intelligent patrons of a profoundly new art.

Piero's perfect synthesis of a progressive instrument such as linear perspective, with some of the elements of the Gothic tradition and the attention to even the tiniest details derived from Netherlandish art was undoubtedly the most important artistic product created thanks to the patronage of the new rulers of Central Italy as an alternative to contemporary Florentine trends.

23. Cappella Maggiore in the church of San Francesco, Arezzo
The 13th-century Crucifix with St Francis, formerly attributed to Margarito d'Arezzo and now attributed *to the Maestro di San Francesco, was already in the church when Piero della Francesca frescoed the chapel; it has recently been placed above the main altar.*

The Fresco Cycle in the Church of San Francesco in Arezzo

In the years immediately following his travels through Romagna, Piero della Francesca is recorded in Borgo San Sepolcro (1435-55), but the artist had probably been to Arezzo several times during 1452 as well, where work on the fresco cycle in the Cappella Maggiore of the church of San Francesco had already begun. The contract awarding the commission of these famous paintings to Piero has not survived, so that we cannot be absolutely certain as to the identity of the patron nor do we know the exact chronology of the project. We know that the chapel belonged to the Bacci, a family of rich Arezzo merchants, who had had it decorated with a stained-glass window in 1417 and had planned to commission a fresco cycle. In 1447 Francesco Bacci sold a vineyard to pay the Florentine painter Bicci di Lorenzo who was working in the chapel. Bicci was one of the last representatives of the Florentine Gothic tradition; he died in 1452, leaving the decoration of the chapel barely begun, for he had only painted the vaulted ceiling and the two Doctors of the Church on the underside of the entrance arch. Piero probably began to work for the Bacci family right after Bicci's death, covering in a few years the walls of the Gothic chapel with the most modern and most advanced—in terms of perspective—frescoes that the Italian 15th century could have created.

The subject-matter of the stories illustrated by Piero is drawn from Jacopo de Voragine's *Golden Legend*, a 13th-century text that recounts the miraculous story of the wood of Christ's Cross. This popular text, typical of the medieval love for accounts of miraculous events, inspired several other fresco cycles in the 14th and 15th centuries in churches belonging to the Franciscans, an order that was in close contact with the people. The most famous iconographical precedents for Piero's stories are Agnolo Gaddi's frescoes painted for the Franciscans of Santa Croce in Florence, Cenni di Francesco's painted for the church of San Francesco in Volterra and Masolino's *Stories of the Cross* painted in 1424 in the church of Sant'Agostino in Empoli.

This traditional subject-matter was undoubtedly proposed to Piero—and probably to Bicci di Lorenzo

24. *Scenes from the fresco cycle of the Cappella Maggiore in San Francesco, Arezzo*
Death of Adam (25)
Exaltation of the Cross (30)
The Queen of Sheba in adoration of the Wood and the Meeting of Solomon and the Queen of Sheba (34)
Angel (38)
Angel (39)
Prophet (40)
Prophet (41)
Torture of the Jew (43)
Burial of the Wood (44)
Discovery and Proof of the True Cross (45)
Battle between Constantine and Maxentius (49)
Constantine's Dream (52)
Annunciation (53)
Battle between Heraclius and Chosroes (54)
Angel (59)

before him—by the Franciscan order of Arezzo, while some variations on the traditional account, presumably prompted by contemporary events, must have been suggested to the artist by a scholarly Humanist. Although we have no documents to prove Piero's contact with Giovanni Bacci, it has recently been suggested that this Humanist, a member of the rich family who owned the chapel, was responsible for commissioning the frescoes. If that is case, the learned Giovanni was probably also responsible for guiding Piero in choice of episodes to represent. Briefly, the story tells how Adam, on his deathbed, sends his son Seth to Archangel Michael, who gives him some seedlings from the tree of original sin to be placed in his father's mouth at the moment of his death. The tree that grows on the patriarch's grave is chopped down by King Solomon and its wood, which could not be used for anything else, is thrown across a stream to serve as a bridge. The Queen of Sheba, on her journey to see Solomon and hear his words of wisdom, is about to cross the stream, when by a miracle she learns that the Saviour will be crucified on that wood. She kneels in devout adoration. When Solomon discovers the nature of the divine message received by the Queen of Sheba, he orders that the bridge be removed and the wood, which will cause the end of the kingdom of the Jews, be buried. But the wood is found and, after a second premonitory message, becomes the instrument of the Passion. Three centuries later, just before the battle of Ponte Milvio against Maxentius, Emperor Constantine is told in a dream that he must fight in the name of the Cross to overcome his enemy. After Constantine's victory, his mother Helena travels to Jerusalem to recover the miraculous wood. No one knows where the relic of the Cross is, except a Jew called Judas, who refuses to reveal the secret. Judas is tortured in a well and finally confesses that he knows of a temple dedicated to Venus where the three crosses of Calvary are hidden. Helena orders that the temple be destroyed; the three crosses are found and the True Cross is recognized because it causes the miraculous resurrection of a dead youth. In the year 615, the Persian King Chosroes steals the wood, setting it up as an object of worship amidst idolatrous symbols. The Eastern Emperor Heraclius wages war on the Persian King and, having defeated him, returns to Jerusalem with the Holy Wood. But a divine power prevents the Emperor from making his triumphal entry into Jerusalem. So Heraclius, setting aside all pomp and magnificence, enters the city carrying the Cross in a gesture of humility, following Jesus Christ's example.

Very briefly, this is the basic narrative account of the Story of the Cross. It is hardly surprising that this rather naive tale was used so frequently as a source in late 14th-century Tuscan painting, especially by those painters whose work was essentially anecdotal.

At a first glance, nothing could seem more far removed from Piero's solemnly constructed compositions than this medieval and colourful folktale; nothing could have been more foreign to his sobre and classical painting than the naive atmosphere of the miracles of the Golden Legend. And yet we shall see how the stylistic interpretation that Piero gives these events raises the story to a level of solemnity and gravity that almost makes it an epic poem.

The first large scaffolding was probably built in 1452; it was used to reach the lunettes at the top on the two side walls, where the first two stories were painted. The first fresco, in the righthand lunette, illustrates the story of the Adamites in three separate episodes. On the right, the ancient Adam, seated on the ground and surrounded by his children, sends Seth to Archangel Michael. In the background, we see the meeting between Seth and Michael, while on the left, in the shadow of a huge tree, Adam's body is buried in the presence of his family. By placing all three stages of the story within the same background landscape, Piero is abiding by traditional narrative schemes already used by Masaccio in his fresco of the Tribute Money in the Brancacci Chapel. The meeting between Seth and the Archangel (which, for example, in Agnolo Gaddi's fresco had been given a prominent position) takes place in the distance, as though it were of secondary importance; in the foreground Piero has placed his splendid group of Adam's sons. These are the representatives of a new mankind, whose ideal beauty is somewhat reminiscent of certain examples of classical sculpture. But there is no feeling of a return to antiquity in Piero's paintings: his inspiration rests almost entirely on contemporary pictorial developments and he introduces a new vision of man and nature, studied, for the first time, down to the magical changing of lighting. A clear, bluish light envelops men and objects, while delicate shadows run across the bodies revealing their three-dimensionality. In these first scenes of the Arezzo cycle, in the strong sense of drawing shown in the anatomy of the figures, in the depiction of their solid yet elegant limbs, Piero's Florentine

25. Death of Adam
390 x 747 cm
Arezzo, San Francesco

26. Death of Adam
detail of Adam and his children
Arezzo, San Francesco

27. *Death of Adam*
detail of Adam's burial
Arezzo, San Francesco

29. *Death of Adam*
detail of Adam's burial
Arezzo, San Francesco

28. *Masaccio*
Tribute Money
Florence, Santa Maria del Carmine, Brancacci Chapel

training is still evident. See, for example, the almost naturalistic depiction of Eve's ancient and wrinkled features, or Adam's rigid body, lying lifeless surrounded on all sides by the straight and muscular legs of his descendants. As in the *Crucifixion* of the Borgo San Sepolcro polyptych, here, too, the profound feeling of grief, masterfully expressed by the woman with outstretched arms, does not give rise to movement; everything is frozen in that fixed gesture and subordinated to the unmoving laws of perspective. As in an allegory of human life, in this fresco the young stand next to the old; the two youths on the left, who witness with dismay the first death in the history of man, are undoubtedly among the most noble and natural creations of the painting of all time.

Piero della Francesca's work continues in the lefthand lunette with the scene showing the *Exaltation of the Cross*, the last episode of the cycle. Evidence that this scene was painted just after the righthand lunette is offered by the almost reluctant modelling that Piero uses in his depiction of Heraclius's followers, marching outside the walls of Jerusalem. The figure of the Emperor himself, on the other hand, is almost entirely illegible now. The Oriental noblemen wear splendid

30. Exaltation of the Cross
390 x 747 cm
Arezzo, San Francesco

31. Exaltation of the Cross, detail
Arezzo, San Francesco

30

*32. Exaltation of the Cross
detail of Heraclius's followers
Arezzo, San Francesco*

33. Exaltation of the Cross
detail of the inhabitants of Jerusalem in adoration
of the Cross
Arezzo, San Francesco

34

34. *The Queen of Sheba in adoration of the Wood and the Meeting of Solomon and the Queen of Sheba*
336 x 747 cm
Arezzo, San Francesco

35. *Adoration of the Holy Wood*
Arezzo, San Francesco

36. *Lorenzo Ghiberti*
Meeting of Solomon and the Queen of Sheba
Florence, Baptistry

37. *Meeting of Solomon and the Queen of Sheba*
Arezzo, San Francesco

Greek headdresses, like the ones that Piero must have seen in Florence in 1439 during the 'Council of the Greeks.' The exotic elegance of those headdresses had been admired by all the Florentines at the time.

Piero's interest in these enormous hats, cylidrical or pyramidal in shape, is dictated by the same motives which had driven Paolo Uccello to concentrate on the complex armour of contemporary warriors—the study of shapes and perspective.

And the colours of the garments are more lively, too. In the midday light and under the blue sky, they vary from pale blue to violet, from bottle-green to pearl-white. This scene is the confirmation that Piero wishes to depict an ideal mankind, healthy and strong, with a peaceful expression, characterized by calm, measured gestures. He conveys the impression of a race of mature men, rationally at peace with themselves, far removed from the dramatic emotions of Masaccio's heroic apostles or his realistic Florentine beggars, with their menacing expressions and their abrupt, urgent gestures.

We do not know how much time after he had begun work on the cycle Piero della Francesca had the scaffolding lowered so that he could start painting the scenes directly below the lunettes. But it must have been before his journey to Rome in 1458. The two following episodes, *The Queen of Sheba in adoration of the Wood* and the *Meeting of Solomon and the Queen of Sheba*, are shown in the same fresco, separated from each other by the column of the royal palace, re-

peating the composition scheme used in the *Flagellation*. Here, too, the architectural element (the column) is the centre of the composition and the vanishing point for the whole fresco. The episode on the left, with the Queen of Sheba shown in adoration of the little bridge, is drawn from the *Golden Legend*, while the *Meeting of Solomon and the Queen of Sheba* is an iconographical element added by Piero. The subject, quite rare in artistic iconography, also appears in one of the panels of Lorenzo Ghiberti's *Doors of Paradise*, produced at more or less the same time for the Florence Baptistry. This scene is probably intended to suggest the meeting between Gentiles and Christians, more particularly, in the 1450s, the hoped-for reunification of the Church of Rome with the Eastern Church, to fight against the Turks who had conquered Constantinople (1453). It seems quite likely that this addition was suggested to Piero by Giovanni Bacci, who together with his friend Ambrogio Traversari and several other Florentine Humanists had been one of the most ardent supporters of the unity of the two churches, both during and after the 1439 Council.

Behind the Queen of Sheba, kneeling in adoration, is her retinue of aristocratic ladies in waiting, with their high foreheads (according to the fashion of the times) emphasizing the round shape of their heads and the cylindrical form of the neck. Their velvet cloaks softly envelop their bodies, reaching all the way to the ground. The almost perfect regularity of the composition is underlined by the two trees in the background,

38. *Angel*
Arezzo, San Francesco

39. *Angel*
Arezzo, San Francesco

40. *Prophet*
Arezzo, San Francesco

41. *Prophet*
Arezzo, San Francesco

whose leaves hover like umbrellas above the two groups of the women and of the grooms holding the horses. And yet Piero's constant attention to the regularity of proportions and the construction according to perspective never gives way to artificially sophisticated compositions, schematic symmetries or anything forced. Thanks to his invention of creating two separate scenes, whose single vanishing point is placed between them, on the central column, each of the two stories gives the impression of being slightly irregular in composition. The famous scene of the *Meeting of Solomon and the Queen of Sheba* takes place within a typically Albertian architectural structure, enlivened by decorations of coloured marble. Everything seems created according to architectural principles: even the three ladies standing behind the Queen are placed so as to form a sort of open church apse behind her. There is a real sense of spatial depth between the characters witnessing the event; and their heads, one behind the other, are placed on different planes. This distinction of spatial planes is emphasized also by the different colour tonalities, with which Piero has by this stage in his career entirely replaced his technique of

outlining the shapes used in previous frescoes. There is an overall feeling of solemn rituality, rather like a lay ceremony: from Solomon's priestly gravity to the ladies' aristocratic dignity. Each figure, thanks to the slightly lowered viewpoint, becomes more imposing and graceful; Piero even succeeds in making the characteristic figure of the fat courtier on the left, dressed in red, look dignified. In this fresco we truly feel that man for Piero della Francesca, as indeed for Alberti, is the 'means and measure of all things.'

Work on the fresco cycle continued on the end wall, where the size of the scenes was smaller because of the space occupied by the window. Piero painted the heads of angels inside the quatrefoils along the ribbing. Around the stained-glass window the artist painted two young prophets at the top, who look out like two solid guardians. In the lefthand prophet one can recognize the hand of an assistant, who painted the figure following Piero's cartoon, achieving however a rather arid result. The much higher quality of the righthand prophet proves that it was certainly painted by Piero himself: see, for example, the compact and luminous red drapery, or the modelling of the face with its large eyes, gazing out proudly. Also on the sides of the window, but lower down, Piero placed on the left the *Burial of the Wood* and on the right the *Torture of the*

42. Giovanni da Piamonte
Madonna delle Grazie
Città di Castello, Santa Maria delle Grazie

43. *Torture of the Jew*
356 x 193 cm
Arezzo, San Francesco

44. *Burial of the Wood*
356 x 190 cm
Arezzo, San Francesco

38

Jew. These two stories were painted by Piero's main assistant, the Florentine Giovanni da Piamonte, whose only other certain work is the panel of the *Madonna delle Grazie* in the church of the same name in Città di Castello (1456). He was an artist of considerable talent who managed to follow Piero's style remarkably well in the frescoes in Arezzo, executing the cartoons designed by the master. His heavier hand gives the figures a more 'peasant' look, with pronounced features, fleshy lips, almost Negroid, as in the figure of Judas in the *Torture.* In this fresco, despite the dramatic nature of the subject, which should give rise to a great sense of movement, once again we find the contrary. Piero's world is governed by measured perspective, eliminating all unplanned movement. If we forget for a moment the subject of the story, the scene could appear to be taking place in a peaceful princely court.

In the *Burial of the Wood*, Giovanni da Piamonte's heavy modelling draws the stiff folds of the bearers' garments and their hair, rather mechanically tied in bunches. On the Cross the vein of the wood, like an elegant decorative element, forms a halo above the head of the first bearer, who thus appears as a prefiguration of Christ on the way to Calvary. The sky covers half the surface of the fresco and the irregular white clouds are as though inlaid in the expanse of blue.

On the wall opposite the *Meeting of Solomon and the Queen of Sheba* is the large scene of the *Discovery and Proof of the True Cross*, one of Piero's most complex and monumental compositions. The artist depicts on the left the discovery of the three crosses in a ploughed field, outside the walls of the city of Jerusalem, while on the right, taking place in a street in the city, is the *Proof of the True Cross.* His great genius which enables him to draw inspiration from the simple world of the countryside, from the sophisticated courtly atmosphere, as well as from the urban structure of cities like Florence or Arezzo, reaches in this fresco the height of its visual variety. The scene on the left is portrayed as a scene of work in the fields, and his interpretation of man's labours as acts of epic heroism is further emphasized by the figures' solemn gestures, immobilized in their ritual toil.

At the edge of the hills, bathed in a soft afternoon light, Piero has depicted the city of Jerusalem. It is in fact one of the most unforgettable views of Arezzo, enclosed by its walls and embellished by its varied coloured buildings, from stone grey to brick red. This sense of colour, which enabled Piero to convey the different textures of materials, with his use of different tonalities intended to distinguish between seasons and times of day, reaches its height in these frescoes in Arezzo, confirming the break away from contemporary Florentine painting. To the right, below the temple to Minerva, whose facade in marble of various colours

is so similar to buildings designed by Alberti, Empress Helena and her retinue stand around the stretcher where the dead youth lies; suddenly, touched by the Sacred Wood, he is resurrected. The sloping Cross, the foreshortened bust of the youth with his barely visible profile, the semi-circle created by the Helena's ladies-in-waiting, and even the shadows projecting on the ground—every single element is carefully studied in order to build a depth of space which, never before in the history of painting, had been rendered with such strict three-dimensionality.

Between 1458 and 1459, during the papacy of Pius II, Piero della Francesca is recorded in Rome. The Arezzo fresco cycle was probably completed on his return to Tuscany. The last stories painted by Piero on the walls of the Bacci Chapel, while still fitting into the stylistic unity of the whole, display an even greater sense of light and colour, suggesting that the artist had further developed his techniques in the field. Many Spanish and Netherlandish artists had spent time in

45. *Discovery and Proof of the True Cross*
356 x 747 cm
Arezzo, San Francesco

46. *Discovery of the True Cross*
detail of the city of Jerusalem (view of Arezzo)
Arezzo, San Francesco

47. *Discovery of the True Cross*
Arezzo, San Francesco

48. *Proof of the True Cross*
Arezzo, San Francesco

Rome, especially during the rule of Nicholas V and Calixtus III Borgia, and in that city Piero had been able to study again the contents of their painting which had interested him so much in his Florentine period.

It is certainly not by chance that the young Antonello da Messina painted a panel around 1460, showing the *Madonna Reading*, today in the Walters Art Gallery in Baltimore: under the luminous Flemish-style skin, the features might almost have been traced from a drawing by Piero.

It seems very likely that the two great artists met in Rome, where, around the middle of the 15th century, painters of so many different schools were coming together and exchanging experiences. The results of this meeting were extraordinary, especially as far as the younger of the two painters was concerned.

The *Battle between Constantine and Maxentius*, painted on the lower register of the righthand wall, is an episode that certainly carried an important idealistic hidden meaning and also touched on contemporary events, at a time when Pius II was planning a crusade against the Turks. All attempts to reconcile the two churches had in fact failed, so that, after the Turkish conquest of Constantinople, the only solution appeared to be to unite all Christians in the struggle against the Infidel. In Piero della Francesca's fresco, Constantine's face is a portrait of John VIII Palaeologus, former Eastern Emperor. And just as Constantine had gone into battle, leading his troops carrying the symbol of the Cross, so his modern Emperor can defeat the Infidel by leading all Christian armies into battle. But beyond this symbolism—probably suggested to Piero by Giovanni Bacci—the battle between Constantine and Maxentius is depicted as a splendid parade, from which the crashing of arms has definitely been eliminated. The absence of movement immortalizes

the horses with raised hoofs in the act of jumping, the shouting warriors with open mouths, all fixed once again by the unbending rules of construction according to linear perspective. Compared to the *Battle of San Romano*, painted by Paolo Uccello about twenty years earlier and which was one of the highest achievements of that Florentine pictorial perspective that inspired the young Piero, in the Arezzo fresco there is a totally new depth of space between the figures. A realistic atmosphere, conveyed by the bright lighting, emphasizes the various spatial planes. Within this composition, Piero della Francesca has succeeded in reproducing, thanks to his highly refined use of bright colours, all the visual aspects of reality, even the most fleeting and immaterial ones. From the reflections of the light on the armour, to the shadows of the horses' hoofs on the ground, to the wide open sky with its spring clouds tossed by the wind, the reality of nature is reproduced exactly, down to its most ephemeral details.

And, once again, in the centre is the same landscape, like a recurring memory: a view of Borgo San Sepolcro with the Tiber running through it, with the houses, trees and bushes reflected in the water.

So far we have seen how Piero della Francesca, thanks to his subtle use of colour tonalities, was able to reproduce the lighting conditions of the various times of day and of different seasons. But in the fresco of *Constantine's Dream*, on the lower righthand side of the end wall, he takes his experiments with light and colour one step further, setting the scene in the middle of the night. Inside his large tent, the Emperor lies asleep. Seated on a bench bathed in light, a servant watches over him and gazes dreamily out towards the onlooker, as though in silent conversation. With a daring innovation, that almost seems to anticipate Cara-

49. *Battle between Constantine and Maxentius*
322 x 764 cm
Arezzo, San Francesco

50. *Battle between Constantine and Maxentius*
detail of Constantine's army
Arezzo, San Francesco

51. *Battle between Constantine and Maxentius*
detail of Constantine
Arezzo, San Francesco

52. *Constantine's Dream*
329 x 190 cm
Arezzo, San Francesco

53. *Annunciation*
329 x 193 cm
Arezzo, San Francesco

vaggio's modern concept of light, the two sentries in the foreground stand out from the darkness, lit only from the sides by the light projected from the angel above.

Piero's work on the cycle continued with the *Annunciation*, a subject that has nothing to do with the *Golden Legend* and was added by Piero. Alberti's classical architecture is present once again with the elegant column in the centre, echoed on the right by the statuesque solemnity of the young Mary. And here again the symmetry of the proportions is broken by vanishing point, placed not in the centre but to the right, behind the Virgin. As in all the other later stories, there is great attention to even the smallest detail, brought out by the reflections of the light. From the transparent veil that covers Mary's head, to the pearls that decorate her dress, from the wood intarsia on the door, to the shadows that are projected on the white marble surfaces, there are many new elements that will be further developed in Piero's later works.

The last scene Piero painted is almost certainly the *Battle between Heraclius and Chosroes*, on the left wall opposite the *Battle of Ponte Milvio*. Compared to Constantine's battle, depicted as an elegant military parade, this battle is violent and dramatic. Movement is hinted at in this composition which, at least in some parts, suffers slightly from lack of space: the bodies are crammed together in their violent struggle, the drawing that models the mass of limbs is constantly broken and interrupted, and the huge horses, rearing in fright, fill much of the scene.

Yet, despite the allusion, the dynamics of movement have no place in this universe governed *a priori* by thousands of invisible perspective lines. A large part of the actual painting of this last story is undoubtedly the work of an assistant, probably Lorentino d'Arezzo, Piero's most loyal, even though rather mediocre, disci-

ple. The weakness of some parts, painted probably by Lorentino, stands out against the master's powerful art, expressed in a few elements of absolute beauty. Among these, the most famous is certainly the figure of the trumpeter on the left who, in the midst of this dramatic battle, continues to play his instrument. On either side of this figure, the two warriors in their shining armour, with their imposing presence, recall the warriors that Masaccio had painted in Masolino's fresco of the *Crucifixion* in the church of San Clemente in Rome. And this is another element which goes to prove that the last episodes of the *Golden Legend* cycle were painted after Piero's journey to Rome in 1459.

54. Battle between Heraclius and Chosroes
329 x 747 cm
Arezzo, San Francesco

55. Battle between Heraclius and Chosroes, detail
Arezzo, San Francesco

56. Battle between Heraclius and Chosroes, detail
Arezzo, San Francesco

57. Battle between Heraclius and Chosroes, detail
Arezzo, San Francesco

58. Battle between
Heraclius and Chosroes,
detail of the decapitation
of Chosroes
Arezzo, San Francesco

59. Angel
Arezzo, San Francesco

On the far right, under a canopy decorated with idolatrous symbols, the Persian King Chosroes is about to be decapitated. Around the kneeling sovereign, ready to receive the final blow, are the portraits of three members of the Bacci family. The only one actually painted by Piero, the one on the left shown in profile, is probably the Humanist Giovanni.

Piero was also certainly responsible for painting some now very badly damaged figures that decorate the surrounds of the fresco cycle, such as the bust of *St Peter Martyr*, on the left above the entrance pilaster, and the head of an *Angel*, on the right of the entrance. The solid colour values that are still evident in these fragmentary remains appear to go beyond even the developments in use of colour we have observed in the later stories of the cycle, so that it seems justified to date these works at around the mid-1460s.

The only document we have that gives any indication of when the fresco cycle was finished is a contract, dated December 1466, in which the Arezzo confraternity of the Misericordia commissioned Piero to paint them a standard, qualifying the artist as 'he who painted the Cappella Maggiore in San Francesco in Arezzo.' So we know that by 1466 the frescoes were certainly finished; on stylistic grounds, though, we can say that they were finished several years earlier.

Rome, Perugia and Urbino

During the period in which he was painting the fresco cycle in Arezzo, Piero della Francesca was also involved with several other commissions in various towns of central Italy. The fresco of the *Madonna del Parto*, painted in the chapel of the cemetery of Monterchi, dates from the same period as the earlier frescoes in Arezzo. The figure of this Madonna, the protector of pregnant women, with her austere expression and natural stance of a woman heavy with child, stands out against the damask canopy, held open at the sides by two angels. The sacred and ritual nature of the image is further emphasized by the fact that the angels are drawn from the same cartoon, repeated in mirror image.

Dating from just a few years later is the only fragment that has survived of Piero's fresco decoration of the church of Sant'Agostino in Borgo San Sepolcro: a bust of *St Julian*. The solidity of his features, and the use of soft colours, relate this proud Christian knight to the young *Prophet* in the Bacci Chapel.

Another one of Piero della Francesca's greatest masterpieces, again painted for his native city, probably just before his journey to Rome in 1458, is the *Resurrection of Christ* in the Palazzo Comunale. This is one of the paintings that best exemplifies Piero's ability

60. Madonna del Parto
260 x 203 cm
Monterchi, chapel of the cemetery

61. St Julian
130 x 105 cm
Sansepolcro, Museo Civico

62. *St Ludovic*
123 x 90 cm
Sansepolcro, Museo
Civico

63. *Resurrection*
225 x 200 cm
Sansepolcro, Museo
Civico

to use archaic iconographical elements, belonging to the repertory of popular sacred images, yet placing them in an entirely new cultural and stylistic context. In this particular case, the splendid transformation of the traditional subject-matter was probably inspired also by the 14th-century polyptych of the *Resurrection* in the Cathedral of Borgo San Sepolcro. Piero takes the construction of his scene from the central panel of this polyptych. Within a framework, formed at the sides by two fake marble columns, Piero's composition is divided into two separate perspective zones. The lower area, where the artist has placed the sleeping guards, has a very low vanishing point. Piero frequently used this technique of lowering the vanishing point.

Alberti, in his theoretical writings, suggests that the vanishing point should be at the same level as the figures' eyes. By placing it on a lower level, Piero foreshortens his figures, thus making them more imposing in their monumental solidity. Above the figures of the sleeping sentries, Piero has placed the watchful Christ, no longer seen from below, but perfectly frontally. The resurrected Christ, portrayed with solid peasant features, is nonetheless a perfect representative of Piero's human ideal: concrete, restrained and hieratic as well. The splendid landscape also belongs to the repertory of popular sacred images: Piero has symbolically depicted it as half still immersed in the barenness of winter, and half already brought back to life—

Misericordia
detail of the Madonna of
Mercy
134 x 91 cm
Sansepolcro, Museo
Civico

resurrected—by springtime.

Unfortunately nothing remains of the work Piero della Francesca did in Rome, where he worked in the Vatican for Pius II between 1458 and 1459. His frescoes, which were probably as grandiose as those of the Arezzo cycle, were soon destroyed and the importance of this Roman period is confirmed only by the profound influence his perspective vision left in the works of artists such as Antoniazzo Romano, Lorenzo da Viterbo and Melozzo da Forlì. The few fragments of a fresco showing St Luke the Evangelist in the chapel of Cardinal d'Estouteville in the church of Santa Maria Maggiore are the work of one of these Roman artists, who painted the figure following a cartoon designed by Piero himself. It seems likely that Piero visited Rome several times after he left Florence. In fact it is very probable, as Vasari suggests, that Piero first went to Rome, perhaps even accompanied by Alberti, as early as the 1440s, during the papacy of Eugene IV or Nicholas V. Here he would have contributed to setting up in the Vatican, where Fra Angelico and Jean Fouquet were already active, an alternative to Florentine artistic trends. But unfortunately all evidence of these important cultural developments is lost.

early 1460s, is the central panel, showing the Madonna della Misericordia (Madonna of Mercy).

The difficulty of dealing with a solid gold background, requested by the patrons, is solved here by Piero by placing the kneeling members of the confraternity in the realistic space created by the Madonna's mantle, held open around the figures like the apse of a church. The perfectly central positioning of the Virgin and the fact that she is seen frontally are reminiscent of the same atmosphere of hieratic solemnity in the Resurrection. But there are several new elements in the kneeling figures, and in their garments, that suggest a slightly later date: there is, for example, a greater attention to the light reflections on the characters' hair, and there is a more refined technical ability in rendering the various textures and patterns of the fabric.

More or less at the same time as he was working on the final scenes of the San Francesco cycle, Piero was given another important commission in Arezzo: the fresco of Mary Magdalen in the Cathedral. This monumental figure is created entirely by large patches of bright colours, rather like an early 16th-century Venetian painting. Yet even with this new use of colour,

66. Mary Magdalen
190 x 105 cm
Arezzo, Cathedral

67. Polyptych of St
Anthony
338 x 230 cm
Perugia, Galleria
Nazionale

68. *Polyptych of St Anthony*
detail of the Madonna and
Child
141 x 65 cm
Perugia, Galleria Nazionale

69. *Polyptych of St Anthony*
detail of St Anthony and St
John the Baptist
124 x 62 cm
Perugia, Galleria Nazionale

70. *Polyptych of St Anthony*
detail of St Francis and
St Elizabeth
124 x 64 cm
Perugia, Galleria Nazionale

Among the many works that, according to Vasari, Piero painted in Perugia, the historian describes with great admiration the polyptych commissioned by the nuns of the convent of Sant'Antonio da Padova. This complex painting, today in the Pinacoteca Nazionale in Perugia, was begun shortly after Piero's return from Rome, but was not completed for several years. The central part of the composition, the *Madonna and Child with Saints Anthony, John the Baptist, Francis and Elizabeth*, reveals in its unusual damask-like background the artist's acquaintance with a trend of contemporary Spanish painting, which Piero would have had the opportunity to see in Rome. We can therefore date the panel at around 1460. The polyptych is also made up of three predella panels showing *St Anthony of Padua resurrecting a child*, the *Stigmatization of St Francis* and *St Elizabeth saving a boy who had fallen down a well*, as well as two roundels placed between the main panel and the predella. The quality of this predella is extraordinary: Piero's characteristic spatial

and light values are achieved here, on a small scale, by emphasizing the white walls of the interiors, the splashes of light and the deep shadows of the night scene in the open countryside. These scenes, where the bodies and even the shadows are fully three-dimensional, were to set an example for predella panels which was widely followed by Italian artists of the second half of the 15th-century, from the young Perugino to Bartolomeo della Gatta and, via Antonello da Messina, to the Neapolitan 'Master of Saints Severino and Sossio.' A few years later, Piero della Francesca completed the Perugia polyptych: above the ornate and still basically Gothic frame, he painted his extraordinary *Annunciation*.

The lack of compositional unity with the central part of the polyptych has led some scholars to suggest that Piero simply added this *Annunciation* to the altarpiece, much later.

But, on the contrary, the whole polyptych has a structural unity; Piero simply cut out the top part, orig-

71-75. Polyptych of St
Anthony
details of the predella:
St Clare (71)
St Agatha (72)
St Anthony of Padua
resurrects a child (73)
36 x 49 cm
St Elizabeth saves
a boy who has fallen
down a well (74)
36 x 49 cm
The Stigmatization o
St Francis (75)
36 x 51 cm

Perugia, Galleria
Nazionale

76. Polyptych of St
Anthony
detail of the
Annunciation
122 x 194 cm
Perugia, Galleria
Nazionale

inally intended to be rectangular, and transformed it into a sort of cusped crowning. Once again Piero has succeeded in overcoming the limitations imposed by patrons with old-fashioned artistic taste, giving us one of the most perfect examples of his use of perspective. Thanks also to his use of oil paints, Piero della Francesca achieves the extraordinarily detailed depiction of the series of capitals, running towards the vanishing point. Each architrave, and each column as well, projects a thin strip of shadow into the splendid cloister arcade, which appears to go beyond any inspiration derived from Alberti's architecture. The subtle analysis of the decorations painted on the walls reaches an unprecedented level; yet everything is contained in a single and organic space. Distances, so perfectly calculated, are neither forced nor artificial: they

are conveyed by the realistic light and atmosphere, as had been the case almost twenty years earlier in the Urbino *Flagellation*.

In 1454 Piero della Francesca agreed to paint a polyptych for the Augustinians of Borgo San Sepolcro; the painting was to be finished within eight years and was intended for their monastery. As usual, the work was not completed until much later; the final payment for the painting was not made until 1469. Due to the historical events concerning the monastery in Borgo San Sepolcro, the polyptych was later replaced and dismembered. It was only in this century that scholars succeeded in reconstructing this work, Piero's last surviving polyptych. None of the panels that survive appear to have been painted in the 1450s, in other words at the time the contract was signed. The

oldest parts date from the early 1460s, and are contemporaneous with the last frescoes in Arezzo and with the central panel of the Perugia polyptych.

The panels that originally formed the predella—*St Monica*, an *Augustinian Saint* and the *Crucifixion*, all in the Frick Collection in New York—are clearly reminiscent of Piero's synthetic style adopted for a small scale, which characterized the predella and the outer decorations of the polyptych of Perugia. *St John the Evangelist*, also in the Frick Collection in New York, and *St Nicholas of Tolentino*, in the Poldi-Pezzoli Museum in Milan, date from the mid-1460s, the busiest period in Piero's career.

Against a background, which is neither made of gold, like the Misericordia polyptych, nor of damask, like the Perugia polyptych, but which is finally a realistically constructed space with a marble balustrade, stands the figure of *St John*, whose features anticipate those of the saints of the Brera altarpiece. Compared to the full and solid bodies of the Misericordia altarpiece, this figure of the Evangelist expresses more movement; he is dynamic yet elegant. His lined face,

surrounded by white hair, his bony hand weighted down by the heavy book, even the ornate borders of the garment that unexpectedly shows through under the wide cloak, are elements that stand out and appear to force their way through Piero's earlier sense of measure. *St Nicholas of Tolentino* is a more original figure: the austere and calm features of his round face almost create the effect of a portrait. But all elements of realism are, as usual, absorbed by the aristocratic sense of regularity; each detail of this painting is rendered with a unity of lighting that anticipates certain trends in 17th-century painting. The two panels with *St Augustine*, now in the Lisbon museum, and *Archangel Michael*, in the National Gallery of London, belong to Piero's late period (1469-70). *St Augustine*, portrayed with a mitre and a splendid bishop's cope, is one of the high points of Piero's painting, for here he achieves perfect harmony between the imposing solidity of his three-dimensional forms and his miniaturistic attention to detail, observed down to the subtlest aspects of reflected light.

Since the art of Gentile da Fabriano, no Italian

painter had succeeded, at such a high qualitative level, in giving such a detailed reproduction of a saint's vestments. Having fully mastered the secrets of Netherlandish art, Piero della Francesca paints every single scene depicted on this precious cope as though he were painting a small predella panel, using, for the soft decorations of the fabric, a 'dot' technique worthy of a miniature by Fouquet. And yet it is still the monumental values that prevail in the figure of this severe saint. *Archangel Michael* is portrayed as an ancient warrior, his athletic limbs made more elegant by his precious armour, by the graceful tunic and by his beautiful boots decorated with tiny pearls. There is nothing violent nor dramatic in the killing of the dragon, who is shown as a snake, its decapitated body lying on the ground. The usual absence of movement, that characterizes all Piero's compositions, is here enhanced by the feeling of graceful elegance conveyed by the saint's gesture, for he holds the severed snake's head with the same delicacy with which one would touch a precious gem.

Among the parts of the polyptych that have unfortunately not survived, there is also the central panel, which almost certainly showed the *Madonna and Child*. The panel with *St Apollonia*, now in the National Gallery in Washington, although it is exactly the same size as the two saints in the Frick Collection, was

probably not part of this polyptych, but of another one also painted for Borgo San Sepolcro. In fact, the source of light in the *St Apollonia* panel is on the opposite side compared to the Frick paintings, and Piero della Francesca was always extremely careful not to alter the lighting or the spatial construction within a single composition.

Towards the middle of the decade, the artist also painted for Borgo San Sepolcro the fresco of *Hercules*, later removed and now in the Gardner Museum in Boston. This Hercules was probably originally part of a series of mythological characters or famous men. Looking at this nude, which more than any other of Piero's subjects could have lent itself to the imitation of examples from classical art, we can see how the artist always refused borrowings from antiquity, unlike other artists who followed the 'archeological' trend of the time. As in the case of many of his Florentine contemporaries, classical art was for Piero a stimulus in the literary sense, which fuelled his imagination and suggested images to him, but was never a source of direct inspiration. This tall, strong figure, with his modern hairstyle, portrayed in a 15th-century room, is totally unrelated to the sculptures from classical antiquity that Piero had become acquainted with in particular during his stay in Rome.

Towards 1465, the artist resumed his contacts with

77. St Monica
39 x 28 cm
New York, Frick Collection

78. Augustinian Saint
39 x 28 cm
New York, Frick Collection

79. St John the Evangelist
131.5 x 57.5 cm
New York, Frick Collection

80. St Nicholas of Tolentino
133 x 60 cm
Milan, Museo Poldi Pezzoli
One notes the difference in colour between this panel and the one to the left, which has recently been restored.

the Montefeltro family in Urbino, who became his most generous patrons. The famous diptych with the portraits of *Battista Sforza* and *Federico da Montefeltro*, today in the Uffizi in Florence, can be dated at the very beginning of this period. In these two relatively small panels, Piero attempts a very difficult compositional construction, that had never been attempted before. Behind the profile portrait of the two rulers, which is iconographically related to the heraldic tradi-

tion of medallion portraits, the artist adds an extraordinary landscape that extends so far that its boundaries are lost in the misty distance. Yet the relationship between the landscape and the portraits in the foreground is very close, also in meaning: for the portraits, with the imposing hieratic profiles, dominate the painting just as the power of the rulers portrayed dominates over the expanse of their territories. The daringness of the composition lies in this sudden switch between

81. St Augustine
133 x 60 cm
Lisbon, Museu de Arte Antigua

82. Archangel Michael
133 x 59 cm
London, National Gallery

83. Hercules
151 x 126 cm
Boston, Isabella Stewart Gardner Museum

84. *Battista Sforza*
47 x 33 cm
Florence, Uffizi

85. *Federico da*
Montefeltro
47 x 33 cm
Florence, Uffizi

86. *Jan Van Eyck*
Madonna of Chancellor
Rolin
Paris, Louvre

87. *Allegorical Triumph*
of Federico da
Montefeltro
47 x 33 cm
Florence, Uffizi

88. *Allegorical Triumph*
of Battista Sforza
47 x 33 cm
Florence, Uffizi

such distant perspective planes. Even Jan Van Eyck, for example, in his large painting of the *Madonna of Chancellor Rolin*, had felt the need to place an architectural balustrade between his figures in the foregound and his landscape in the background, to bridge the gap. In the portraits of the Duke and Duchess, Piero reveals once again his great ability to simplify shapes and to convey three-dimensionality; and Federico's aquiline profile almost becomes an image of abstract and geometric purity.

Piero's ability in rendering volumes is accompanied by his attention to detail, by now a constant in his art. Through his use of light, he gives us a miniaturistic description of Battista Sforza's jewels, of the wrinkles, moles and blemishes on Federico's olive-coloured skin. Apart from Antonello's slightly later works, in no other 15th-century European painting is such a remarkable synthesis achieved between the accurate depiction according to the rules of linear perspective, as elaborated by Italian art, and 'miniaturistic' painting obtained thanks to the technique of oil paints, developed to such an extraordinary degree by Netherlandish artists. The greatness of Piero's art, rather than in his radical break away from traditional patterns, lies in this unique ability to harmonize elements from such different cultures, and transform them into a universal language.

On the reverse of the two portraits Piero has depicted the *Allegorical Triumphs* of the rulers of Urbino. Here the landscape becomes more dominant, and almost acquires independent life. Before these two panels were placed in their modern frame, the two views of Federico's territorial domains formed a single composition. The expanse of peaceful, luminous water, like a mirror at the feet of Montefeltro's gently sloping hills, must have made this composition seem even more innovative compared to similar depictions of landscape by Florentine or Northern artists.

CLARVS INSIGNI VEHITVR TRIVMPHO ·
QVEM PAREM SVMMIS DVCIBVS PERHENNIS ·
FAMA VIRTVTVM CELEBRAT DECENTER ·
SCEPTRA TENENTEM ·

QVE MODVM REBVS TENVIT SECVNDIS ·
CONIVGIS MAGNI DECORATA RERVM ·
LAVDE GESTARVM VOLITAT PER ORA ·
CVNCTA VIRORVM ·

Piero's Late Works and the Development of Linear Perspective in Italian Painting

Piero della Francesca's connection with the artistic environment of Urbino is documented by several records proving the artist's presence in that city on several occasions during the last twenty years of his life. In 1469 he was in contact with the Urbino painter Giovanni Santi regarding the execution of a painting for the confraternity of Corpus Domini. The predella of the painting had already been carried out by Paolo Uccello; for some reason, in the end Piero did not paint the altarpiece, and the commission was passed on to the Netherlandish artist Justus van Ghent. This interchange between Italian and Netherlandish artists, who often replaced each other in commissions even in such a small centre as Urbino, is a further demonstration of what an artistic crossroads this town had become; it was the meeting ground of the most varied cultural trends, and was rapidly becoming one of the leading and most progressive Italian artistic centres of the time. Evidence of the highly important role played by Piero in Urbino in the 1470s is offered by the unmistakeable influence his art had on all the painters working in the city at the time, including those of Netherlandish background, such as Pedro Berruguete, who within a few years became entirely 'converted' to the fundamental scientific rules of perspective art. And even in the field of literature Piero's important role is recognized by the theoretical writers working in Urbino in the second half of the 15th century. There must have been theoretical discussions concerning the problems of perspective and of proportions, much as there had been in Florence in the early 15th century. In his *Cronaca rimata*, Giovanni Santi praises Piero, calling him one of the major artists of the century, and Luca Pacioli, a pupil of Piero's, wrote a theoretical treatise that was based entirely on the master's thoughts and ideas. All this is evidence of the fact the Piero della Francesca was admired not only for his paintings, but also for his theoretic ability.

Two small panels, the *Madonna and Child with Angels* in the Clark Institute in Williamstown and the *Madonna of Senigallia* in the National Gallery in Urbino, date from the early 1470s. The former is a masterpiece of study in proportions and in the subtle relationships between figures and architecture, as some of the frescoes in the church of San Francesco in Arezzo had been. This small panel is reminiscent of some of the Arezzo compositions also in the way it creates a sense of chance in the placing of the figures in semi-circles. It is from paintings like this one that Piero's faithful pupil, Luca Signorelli, was influenced at first, at least until 1475, when the novelties arriving from the Florentine artistic world entirely changed his original style. In fact, the young Luca Signorelli is undoubtedly the closest follower of Piero, as can readily be seen from his two versions of the *Madonna and Child with Angels*, one in Boston and one in Oxford, and from the *Madonna and Child* in the Cini Collection; these works are comparable, but at a far higher level of quality, to the imitations of Piero's work carried out by Lorentino d'Arezzo.

The *Madonna of Senigallia*, originally in the church of Santa Maria delle Grazie in Urbino, is quite different from Piero della Francesca's previous production, particularly in the type-casting of the figures. The faces still have an expression of aloofness and of superior rational wisdom, but they also convey a sense of precious, almost exotic, beauty. This is one of the paintings in which the artist most clearly reveals his interest in light values, both in terms of reflections and of magical transparencies. From Mary's veil, slightly puckered on her forehead with subtle light variations, to the coral necklace around the Child's neck, to the angels' shining pearls—these are all effects which, together with the light streaming in from the window, and forming a perfectly geometrical shape on the end wall, will appear again and again in Dutch painting of the 17th century.

The blonde hair of the angel on the left, because of the reflection of the light coming in from behind, acquires an almost magical golden glow, as though it were a natural halo.

As we mentioned earlier, in the Arezzo fresco of the *Burial of the Wood of the Cross*, Piero created a similar effect of a natural halo with the veins of the wood behind the head of one of the characters. With the use of these original inventions, the artist seems almost to be constructing his sacred image by making conventional mystical portents fit into the natural world, an idea that was first used by Masaccio and, before him, by Giotto. Giotto, in fact, had been the first artist to

89. Madonna and Child with Angels
106x78 cm
Williamstown, Clark Institute

paint saints' haloes according to the strict rules of perspective, showing them foreshortened as any real object would have been. Masaccio, in his polyptych for the Carmelites of Pisa, had painted the haloes as solid objects, with a definite spatial depth, with the result that they are almost like plates or bowls hovering behind his saints' heads. Piero della Francesca, as he gradually became more interested in the depiction of natural reality—although he never entirely abandoned the elements of popular tradition and of ritualistic sacred images, as we have seen in his paintings for Borgo San Sepolcro—tended to eliminate wherever possible the depiction of such an abstract object, so far removed from his visual knowledge. All elements of naive medieval tradition are banished from the solid and mature awareness of Piero's sacred figures; they have no need to resort to outward symbols to demonstrate their divine nature.

Shortly after the *Madonna of Senigallia*, Piero set to work on the most grandiose of his paintings dating from this period. This was the huge altarpiece showing the *Madonna and Child with Saints*, today in the Pinacoteca di Brera in Milan. Probably painted for the church of the Osservanti di San Donato in Urbino, this panel was transferred, after the death of Federico in 1482, to the church of San Bernardino, the modern mausoleum built for the deceased Duke. Federico da Montefeltro, shown kneeling at the foot of the Madonna's throne, is portrayed in his warrior's armour, but without the insignia awarded to him by Pope Sixtus IV in 1475.

The absence of these emblems, which Piero would certainly have included in an official portrait like this one, leads us to date the splendid Brera altarpiece, previously believed to be Piero's last work, at around 1472-74. The complex and majestic architectural background, against which the 'sacra conversazione' takes place, is clearly derived from designs very similar to the ones followed by Alberti in his construction of the church of Sant'Andrea in Mantua. Yet, at the same time, the architecture anticipates certain 'classical' elements which will be used by the young Bramante—another extraordinary artist from Urbino. In this painting, too, the artist's mastery of proportions is remarkable; it is almost symbolized by the large ostrich egg hanging from the shell in the apse. The shape of this symbolic element is echoed by the near perfect oval of the Madonna's head, placed in the absolute centre of the composition. In this painting Piero places his vanishing point at an unusually high level, more or less at the same height as the figures' hands, with the result that his sacred characters, placed in a semicircle, appear less monumental. Piero's extraordinary invention of an architectural apse echoed below by another apse, consisting in the figures of the saints gathered around the Madonna, was taken up time and

again by artists working at the end of the 15th century and at the beginning of the 16th, particularly in Venice, starting with the almost contemporary paintings of Antonello da Messina and Giovanni Bellini. This organized composition, typical of Piero's work, contained within a unity of space and lighting, seems however to have a new feel about it, as though the artist were taking part in the new currents being developed in Italian art after 1470. The new trends are dictated primarily by the great popularity that Netherlandish painting was enjoying, particularly in Urbino. The most descriptive and 'miniaturistic' aspects of Netherlandish painting are echoed in the Brera altarpiece in the Duke's shining armour, for example, and in the stylized decoration of the carpet. Netherlandish art was popular among the patrons of the period as well, as we can see by the rings on Federico's hands, which Piero had painted by Pedro Berruguete, a Spaniard with a Northern training.

The other aspect of this painting that must not be underestimated is its similarity with the new developments of Florentine painting, visible primarily in the work of Verrocchio and some of his young pupils. The angels' garments are decorated with jewels and in huge precious brooches, their hair is held back by elegant diadems: these elements, and even their melancholy expression, are certainly influenced by the recent developments in Florentine art. In the same way, St John the Baptist's and St Jerome's bony limbs, emaciated by deprivations in the wilderness, recall some of Verrocchio's studies; and the sleeping Child, in his extraordinary contorted position, anticipates some of the young Leonardo's drawings of putti.

Among Piero's surviving paintings, the last one in chronological order is the *Nativity* in the National Gallery in London. The missing patches of colour, which might almost indicate that the painting is unfinished, are in fact probably the result of overcleaning. The Child lies on the ground, on a corner of Mary's cloak, following traditional Northern iconography which is reflected also in the features of the Child. Other elements of Northern culture can be found in a few naturalistic details, interpreted in a highly original fashion by Piero, such as the strange figure of St Joseph, nonchalantly sitting on a saddle, or the two animals in the background, depicted with great realism. No landscape view of Piero's is as miniaturistic as the city depicted in the background at the right: even the streets and the windows of the buildings are visible, just like in a landscape by Petrus Christus. Even the composition of the painting is quite innovative compared to Piero's

90. Madonna of Senigallia
61 x 53 cm
Urbino, Galleria Nazionale

91. *Interior of the church of Sant'Andrea, Mantua*

92. *Madonna and Child with Saints*
248 x 170 cm
Milan, Brera

previous production. The wide expanse of ground, dotted with patches of grass, and the roofing of the hut, with its shadow projecting onto the ruined brick wall, seem to indicate an attempt by the artist to fragment the space of the picture, breaking the rule that he had always rigorously abided by. The vanishing point is slightly raised, as in the Brera altarpiece, and gives one an almost bird's-eye view of the spectacular river landscape, which extends into the distance with trees, bushes and sheer rockfaces that remind one of some of the young Leonardo's drawings.

These aspects of new perspective composition, of experimental naturalism and even of movement must be read as symptoms of the aging painter's incredible ability to update his art to the latest novelties being developed by Florentine and Netherlandish artists. But it is also clear that Piero could not have gone any further in this direction, for it would have meant abandoning the basic principles of his art. The directions that painters like Verrocchio and the young Leonardo were taking, with their almost scientific studies of action and movement, were leading too far away from the principles of spatial construction elaborated and developed by Piero and Alberti. Piero della Francesca's background culture, still very much alive in this last painting in the group of angels clearly inspired by Luca della Robbia's Cantoria in Florence Cathedral, was the 'heroic' environment of the early Renaissance, created in Florence by Brunelleschi and Donatello, by Leonardo Bruni and Paolo Toscanelli. Compared to the ideals of the earlier generation, the refined and courtly culture which was developing around the artistic patronage of Lorenzo the Magnificent, with its poetic Neo-Platonic abstractions and its archeological nostalgia for the romantic nature of classical antiquity, must have seemed superficial and ephemeral—almost a betrayal of its origins.

Over the following years, Piero accepted several commissions in Borgo San Sepolcro, but the works he produced have all been lost: a fresco cycle in the church of Badia (1474), and a *Madonna* painted for the confraternity of the Misericordia in 1478, the last of his paintings mentioned in the documents of the time. In 1482 the artist is recorded as travelling to Rimini, where he rented a house; but we do not know whether he went there in order to paint something or not. These documents and his will, dictated in 1487, in which he is described as 'sound of mind, intellect and body,' suggest that he only became blind in the last years of his life, as Vasari states, and that he did not completely lose his eyesight until the 1480s. But none of Piero's works painted after 1475—the year of the London *Nativity*—have survived, and we have no real explanation of why Piero gradually stopped painting almost twenty years before his death (October 12, 1492). Certainly one of the reasons would have been his ill health and his growing blindness; but it is also probable that he felt that he wanted to examine further the theories behind those laws of perspective and proportions that, with the addition of his original and inventive talent, had contributed to the creation of his extraordinary pictorial compositions. Faced with the birth and development of a modern art so different from his, Piero della Francesca responded with his treatises *De Prospectiva pingendi* and *De Corporibus regularibus*, in which he analyzed the theoretical and scientific foundations of his pictorial culture. It is from his drawings in *De Prospectiva pingendi* that the per-

spective construction of the panel of the so-called
Ideal City, in the National Gallery in Urbino, is born.
This painting is so closely connected to Piero's theoretical writings that it must have been painted by a very
close collaborator of his. This square, with its buildings
inspired by the architecture of Alberti, is perfectly in
harmony with Piero's ideals: the rational construction
and the depiction of Florentine palaces are both ideal
and realistic.

Piero della Francesca's two treatises, which, compared to some of Alberti's splenid passages, are com-

93. *Madonna and Child with Saints, detail*
Milan, Brera

94. *Nativity*
124 x 123 cm
London, National Gallery

posed of dry mathematical calculations, are among the most important scientific texts of the 15th century. Leonardo da Vinci and Albrecht Dürer, as well as Piero's pupil Luca Pacioli, will later base their own work on these studies. A third text by Piero, the *Tratta-to d'Abaco* (treatise on abacus), has recently been published; this text has no connection with painting, for it is an entirely mathematical and practical study. As well as being the great intellectual that we have seen, the aging Piero did not think it unworthy of his talents to write 'some questions of abacus necessary for merchants. . . some mercantile procedures such as trading, credit and companies.' Once again we find evidence of

the close connection between art, science and mathematics which, from Brunelleschi onward, was one of the main elements of Italian Humanism—and perhaps the one that is most difficult for us to understand.

No study of Piero della Francesca, however short, can be complete without a mention of the deep mark his work has left on all Italian art and, as a consequence, on European art. Piero's influence, direct or indirect, was the determining factor in the conversion of vast areas of the art world to a new form of painting, a new vision based on a fully Renaissance concept of spatial depth. Equalled only by the developments produced by Donatello's works in Florence and Padua, Piero's art succeeded more than any other in explaining and teaching the principles of linear perspective, conceived as the only valid construction technique of any figurative composition. After leaving Florence around 1440, Piero della Francesca had travelled widely through central Italy's minor centres, where he had found an

art that was still fundamentally Gothic and bound by the artistic traditions of the past. Towards the end of his life, the artist was able to observe how, thanks largely to his own work, art based on linear perspective had definitely spread beyond the city walls of Florence, to large cities and small towns alike.

The interpretation of figurative space offered by Piero is completely different to Donatello's expressed in his Florentine works and primarily in his Paduan ones. Donatello gives his compositions a sense of space that is suggested, or hinted at, made up of sudden daring foreshortenings that create dramatic effects. In his reliefs for the altar of the basilica of Sant'Antonio in Padua, the sculptor even uses materials such as gold and coloured stones to enrich, enliven and give movement to his bronze surfaces; in a few square centimetres of a relief he succeeds in conveying the idea of an almost boundless space. In Piero's work, on the contrary, the strict unity of space is matched by the regularity of the composition, by the exaltation of shapes in their volumes and their colours; nothing is suggested or hinted at, everything is fully depicted.

These substantial differences between Piero's art and the prevailing Florentine tradition, where Donatel-

95. *Nativity, detail*
London, National Gallery

96. *Luca della Robbia*
Cantoria
Florence, Museo dell'Opera del Duomo

97. *Nativity*
detail of the musician angels
London, National Gallery

98. *Ideal City*
60 x 200 cm
Urbino, Galleria Nazionale

lo's innovations also influenced painting towards the middle of the 15th century, largely explain why the artist left Florence so soon and why he never returned. The Florentine painters closest to Piero are Alesso Baldovinetti and Andrea del Castagno, but the similarities are due more to their common training in Domenico Veneziano's workshop rather than to actual contact. In this respect, Andrea del Castagno is particularly interesting: while some of his monumental compositions, such as the frescoes today in Sant'Apollonia in Florence, are definitely reminiscent of Piero's art, Andrea is profoundly different, for he paid little attention to the delicacy of the paintbrush and created rounded figures that at times appear to have been carved out of rock. The great pictorial developments of the 1430s, that reached their height in the frescoes in the church of Sant'Egidio, did not last long; by around 1450 the most successful artists in Florence were Lippi, Pesellino and Gozzoli, who concentrated on an art based on modelling and drawing that will later achieve such extraordinary results in the work of Pollaiolo and Leonardo.

But Piero's heritage is really to be found in Venice, where from the early 1470s Giovanni Bellini showed the influence of Piero's works which he had seen in Urbino.

At the same time, Antonello da Messina, with works such as the *San Cassiano Altarpiece*, the fragments of which are today in Vienna, brings to the Venetian lagoon that sense of colour and atmosphere that characterizes the last frescoes in the church of San Francesco in Arezzo and which seems to have been transferred directly to the work of Bellini and Carpaccio. And, beyond Venice, the whole of the Po Valley area appears to understand Piero's message. To the north of Emilia, which, as we have seen, was one of the first areas to be influenced by Piero, Milanese painters follow the trends set by Bramante, whose theories of mathematical perspective were learnt in Urbino.

The older and more established artistic centres of central Italy renounce their local traditions to follow Piero's concepts of colour and space, as happens in

Perugia with the young Perugino and in Siena with Francesco di Giorgio and Pietro Orioli. Large areas of the Marches and the major area of Piero's activity—Arezzo, Cortona, Borgo San Sepolcro—are conditioned by Piero's art, as can be seen by the work of Bartolomeo della Gatta and the young Signorelli. And further south, from Rome with the works of Antoniazzo Romano and Melozzo da Forlì, to the countryside of Abruzzi, to the large southern cities like Naples, or the great Antonello's Messina—the art-historical map of Italy is profoundly altered by the spread of Piero della Francesca's art, a painting conceived as a 'perspective synthesis of shape and colour.'

BOTTICELLI

1. Adoration of the Magi detail with the painter's self-portrait Florence, Uffizi

Sandro Filipepi, Florentine Painter

Alessandro, the youngest of four sons, was born in Florence to Mariano and Sm ralda Filipepi who lived on Via Nuova, today's Via del Porcellana, in the quarter of Santa Maria Novella not far from the Arno river. Alessandro's father, together with many other inhabitants of the area, was a tanner, and was aided in his trade by the proximity of the Arno and the Mugnone torrent which emptied into the Arno at Prato d'Ognissanti. The first written notice of Alessandro is found in the so-called 'portate al Catasto', the declarations of income for tax purposes which every head of family was ordered to make by decree of the Republic in 1427. In one of these, in 1458, Mariano Filipepi stated that he had four sons, Giovanni, Antonio, Simone and Sandro: the latter was thirteen years old and was 'studious and sickly'. This phrase of his father's casts a light on the introspective nature of the boy, possibly due to childhood illnesses, which certainly left its mark in the melancholy tones of many of his paintings.

Around 1464 Alessandro entered the workshop of Fra Filippo Lippi where he stayed until his twenty-second year in 1467. His first work may well have been on the last frescoes painted by Fra Filippo and his students for the Cathedral in Prato.

In 1469 he was working on his own because a declaration by Mariano stated that he was working at home. The careers of the four sons (Giovanni became a pawnbroker, a position corresponding to that of a government official, and earned the nickname of 'Botticella' which was to pass on to his more famous brother) brought money and position to the family. They owned houses, land, vineyards and shops. On 9 October 1469 Fra Filippo died in Spoleto. The following year Sandro began his own workshop: here, between the 18th of June and the 18th of August of that year, he completed a work which was to bring him both public acclaim and artistic prestige. This painting was *Fortitude* (one of a series depicting the seven Virtues) commissioned for the Tribunale di Mercatanzia (a court where crimes of an economic nature were judged), one of the most important local institutions. The other Virtues had been commissioned from a well established painter, Piero del Pollaiolo, which is an indication of the prestige enjoyed by Sandro in Florentine artistic circles. In 1472 he joined the Compagnia di San Luca (the painter's guild) and also had his dear friend and collaborator, the fifteen-year-old Filippino Lippi, son of his old teacher, registered in the guild. Botticelli's commissions were primarily for Florentines; the important painting of *St Sebastian* (now in Berlin) was done for the Church of Santa Maria Maggiore. However, in the year 1474 he was sent for outside of Florence. The Pisans needed his collaboration on a cycle of frescoes for the Camposanto Monumentale (Monumental Cemetery) and commissioned an altarpiece depicting the *Assumption of the Virgin* as a trial. Sandro — for unknown reasons — never finished the painting, nor did he work on the frescoes. It was during these years that the painter established his close relationship with the house of Medici, by then the recognized rulers of Florence. He painted banners for a famous tournament held in 1475 in Piazza Santa Croce in honor of the brother of Lorenzo the Magnificent, Giuliano. Giuliano was killed in 1478 as a result of a conspiracy conceived by Pope Sixtus IV and carried out by members of the Pazzi family against the Medici. Sandro painted effigies of the conspirators, both those who had been executed and those still at large, on the facade of Palazzo della Signoria by the side of the Porta di Dogana (Customs Gate). With this gesture Sandro embraced the cause of the house of Medici and the period of his greatest prestige and most intense activity began. By 1480 his workshop was large and well-known to judge by the number of students and assistants registered in the 'Catasto'. In the same year he painted the *St Augustine* for the Church of Ognissanti for the Vespucci family, one of the most important families of the city who were closely allied with the Medici.

The new cultural policy of Lorenzo the Magnificent, who sought a reconciliation with the Pope, led to Botticelli's departure for Rome (27 October 1480) together with Cosimo Rosselli, Domenico Ghirlandaio and Pietro Perugino, to fresco the walls of the Sistine Chapel. He left Rome towards the end of February 1482. The contract for the frescoes was settled on the 17th of the month and on the 20th his father died in Florence. The return to Florence was final and the Signoria gave him, together with the most qualified painters of the day, Ghirlandaio, Perugino, and Piero del Pollaiolo, the commission to fresco the Sala dei Gigli (Room of the Lilies) in the Palazzo dei Priori (now called Palazzo Vecchio) on 5 October 1482. Sandro, however, did not execute this work. The following year, with the assistance of his students, he painted for Lorenzo the Magnificent four panels of a chest with the story of Nastagio degli Onesti, a tale from Boccaccio's *Decameron*. 1487 saw Sandro at work on yet another civic commission: the Magistratura dei Massai di Camera (tax officials) ordered a *tondo* for their audience hall in the Palazzo della Signoria. This work is known today as the *Madonna of the Pomegranate*. The arrival of Savonarola on the Florentine political scene did not go unobserved by Botticelli; as we shall see, religious themes began to predominate in all his paintings. The years 1489-90 saw the completion of an *Annunciation* painted for the Cistercian monks (today at the Uffizi), while the restlessness of his nature led him to be fined for an unknown infraction of the law by the Ufficiali di Notte e Monasteri (a disciplinary commission). Meanwhile, commissions poured in. With Gherardo and Monte di Giovanni, famous mosaic artists, he was asked to create a mosaic decoration of two ceilings in the Chapel of St Zenobius in the Cathedral of Florence. He was also asked, together with Lorenzo di Credi, Ghirlandaio, Perugino and Alesso Baldovinetti, to form a committee with the purpose of deciding upon a facade for the Cathedral. Three years later Sandro's brother Giovanni died. In 1495 he carried out his last work for the Medici, painting for that branch of the family later known as 'the Medici of the people' several works for their villa at Trebbio.

In 1498, the year of the execution of Savonarola, his income declared in the 'Catasto' was considerable; he had a house in the Santa Maria Novella quarter and collected rent from a villa in Bellosguardo, outside the Porta San Frediano. But Botticelli was deeply disturbed by the Dominican's death. In Simone Filipepi's *Cronaca* (1499) there is a record of a conversation between Sandro and Doffo Spini, who was one of the judges at the trial that condemned Savonarola to death; Sandro's words voice his feelings of what to him seemed a grave injustice. The influence of the Dominican made a deep impression on Sandro, whose work became more visionary and more isolated from the general stream of Florentine artistic trends in those early years of the new century. In the year 1501 he painted the *Mystic Nativity* with its apocalyptic symbols and allusions to the present situation in Italy, and for the first time he signed and dated a painting. Although he was aging, his opinion still carried considerable weight and was sought after by his contemporaries. In 1504 he was part of a committee, along with Cosimo Rosselli, Giuliano da Sangallo, Leonardo da Vinci and Filippino Lippi, formed to decide where to place the newly executed *David* by Michelangelo. The opinion of Filippino Lippi prevailed and the marble 'giant' was

2. Madonna in Glory with Seraphim
120 x 65 cm
Florence, Uffizi

placed on the platform outside the Palazzo della Signoria.

The old painter, by now practically inactive and nearly forgotten in a Florence that had surrendered her leadership in the field of the figurative arts to Rome, died on 17 May 1510 and was buried in the family tomb in the church of Ognissanti.

3. Filippo Lippi
Madonna and Child with Angels
Florence, Uffizi

4. Madonna of the Rosegarden
124 x 65 cm
Florence, Uffizi

Early Development

Critics have found three basic trends in Botticelli's artistic development. These are evident from the very first works of the painter around the year 1470, that is as soon as he had finished his apprenticeship in the workshop of Fra Filippo Lippi. Lippi died in Spoleto in 1469 while engaged in frescoing the Cathedral.

The earliest influence on the young Botticelli was certainly Lippi, an influence seen most strongly in the facial characteristics of Sandro's figures, a style he continued even in the later works. The earliest Botticelli paintings are seen by critics as variations of the famous Lippi *Madonna and Child with Angels* of the Uffizi. The themes of the first Florentine Renaissance were still visible in the works of the Carmelite Lippi, who transformed the solid volume of Masaccio's work into relaxed and imaginative forms and changed the severe heroism of the figures of this first great Renaissance master into a colorful and lively down-to-earth representation. However, the artists of the third generation of the Renaissance — above all the Pollaiolo brothers, Piero and Antonio, as well as Andrea del Verrocchio — brought to perfection a new stylistic tendency, each according to his own temperament, transforming yet again the style of Masaccio that had already been changed in linearity and use of color by the greatest artists of the second generation of the Renaissance, that is by Lippi himself and Andrea del Castagno.

It is in the painting of Antonio del Pollaiolo and Andrea del Verrocchio that the other two currents in the style of Botticelli are to be found. The dynamic line and energy of the former, who was able to create figures with only the design of a profile and who changed completely the depiction of movement, was one influence; the capacity of the latter to elaborate on living forms and place them

5. *Piero Pollaiolo*
Temperance
Florence, Uffizi

6. *Antonio Pollaiolo*
Hercules and Antaeus
Florence, Uffizi

7. *Andrea Verrocchio*
Doubting Thomas
Florence, Church of Orsanmichele

8. *Fortitude*
167 x 87 cm
Florence, Uffizi

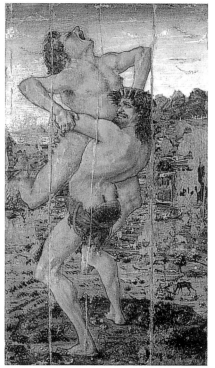

in their proper setting, shading the forms with light and color so as to put in play the tactile qualities of the subject (a direction in which the young Leonardo was moving), was the other.

The Botticellian style evolved from these three directions. Naturally — as with all great painters — Sandro's style was not a simple mechanical synthesis of the style of his masters, but an original and unique personal expression. Sandro, with his sensitivity, was able to take what he had learned from his teachers and add to it certain elements of his own: for example, the faces in his paintings with their slightly melancholy expression, characteristic of withdrawn and thoughtful natures. Also, his primary interest was in the human figure, not in the setting (a reason for considering him a precursor of the Mannerists even though the cultural foundations were quite different); and a linearity sometimes used to denote expression (forms that are modified depending on the sentiment to be expressed). These tendencies are particularly evident in his later work. Unlike many other artists, Sandro retained these elements, without any major change, throughout his entire artistic career. What did change was the subject matter and also every time the linear component, the color and the expressionistic elements were more accentuated. In some of the later paintings the colors are very pure, clear and nearly blinding in their intensity, as though the lessons of Verrocchio had been quite forgotten.

From his very earliest works he expressed clearly these stylistic qualities. In the tradition of Lippi, particularly in the faces, are the two Madonnas in the Uffizi: the one called *Madonna of the Rosegarden*, the other with its 'glory' of seraphim. Both are stylistically very recognizable, especially in the figure of the Virgin which is more elongated and articulated than in Lippi's paintings. The Child of the *Rosegarden* is in the style of Verrocchio, while the other Child is especially Botticellian, so aware is he of his sacred nature, and has a wistful melancholy expression. Sandro's most prestigious work of the 1470s, however, is the *Fortitude* of the Uffizi commissioned by Tommaso Soderini in May 1470 for the Tribunale della Mercatanzia. The painting was paid for on 18 August 1470. The entire series of Virtues had been ordered from Piero del Pollaiolo in 1469; Pollaiolo protested when he learned that Botticelli had been asked to do a second Virtue, a decision which led to a protest by other painters and the withdrawal of the commission to Botticelli. The figure of *Fortitude* is placed on a high throne with elaborately carved arms, a piece clearly traceable to Verrocchio, but the feeling of tension that this thoughtful figure gives off

surely comes from Antonio del Pollaiolo. The blue enamel work on the armour and the highlights on the metal are particularly interesting as they indicate a thorough knowledge of the goldsmith's art. The way in which cloth is portrayed comes from Verrocchio (see, for example, the heavy drapery in the *Doubting Thomas* at Orsanmichele). The energy and vitality of the girl in armour, expressed in her face and her pose, is an original creation of Botticelli's and shows clearly the very personal way in which he developed and enriched the styles of his contemporaries.

The *Madonna* at the Isabella Stewart Gardner Museum in Boston was the end product, showing the synthesis of trends that formed the style of Botticelli's painting. The composition of the painting resembles Lippi's art, but the figures are more delicately blended into the painting and their expressions and poses are more complicated. The figure of the Christ Child reaches from his mother's lap to bless the bunch of grapes and stalks of grain held out to him by the angel, symbolizing the sacrament of the Eucharist (the bread and wine that become the body and blood of Christ), in a more explicit manner than the traditional one of the pomegranate used by the Florentine painters of the early fifteenth century.

From Lippi, and through him from the iconography of Verrocchio, comes the composition of the landscape framed in the tall, open piece of furniture that forms the background of the scene. Botticelli then attempted to illustrate an episode from the Bible, painting two pictures of the Stories of Judith, believed by critics to be painted primarily in 1472. Though tiny in size, they are masterpieces because of the complexity of the composition, the attention to minute details and the atmosphere in each scene. Especially noteworthy is the atmosphere of tragedy in the *Discovery of the Body of Holofernes*, where the body of the Assyrian warrior-king — a nude created with the dynamic linearity of Pollaiolo — sprawls headless on his couch, surrounded by officers in various poses and with expressions showing despair, horror and shock. Even the material of the tent and the curtains, coarse and heavy, add to the overall impression of gloom, in spite of the reflections of light on the armour and the lavish harnesses of the horses. The atmosphere of *Judith's Return to Bethulia* on the other hand is free and serene; the colors themselves are lighter, the cloth is no longer coarse but

decorated with lace, and the landscape, animated with brilliant figures, is filled with the light of dawn. The two main figures, the Hebrew heroine and the lady-in-waiting, with their clothes blown by the wind, walk so lightly that they seem weightless. The iconography is classical and was also used by Donatello on the base of the statue of *St George*, originally placed in Orsanmichele, as well as in the 1452 *Bartolini Tondo* by Lippi.

Sandro then began painting portraits in the fifteenth-century Florentine tradition, but to the official, flattering portraits then in fashion he added a subtle psychological tension. In the *Portrait of a Man with the Medal of Cosimo the Elder*, a work that was an indication of the ties that were to bind Sandro to the Medici family, the man has never been definitely identified, notwithstanding the many suggestions made by scholars. The most plausible suggestion is that the man is Sandro's brother, Antonio (there is a marked family resemblance to Sandro's self-portrait in the *Adoration of the Magi* in the Uffizi), who according to certain documents was often commissioned to cast medals for the city's ruling family. The expression is intense, the features softened by an attempt at portraying classical beauty; the hands are agile and nervous as they hold the medal with pride. In the background is a vast landscape showing the winding course of the Arno, in keeping with the Florentine tradition of the period.

By 1470 Botticelli's style was completely formed. His work was enriched in the following years by the Humanistic themes found in the commissions given to him by members of the Medici family.

9. Portrait of a Young Man
51 x 33.7 cm
Florence, Galleria Palatina (Palazzo Pitti)

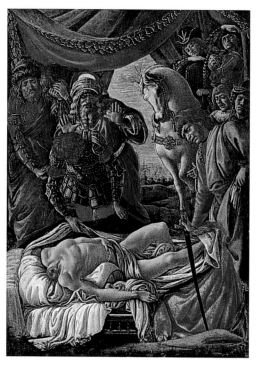

10. *Discovery of the Body of Holofernes*
31 x 25 cm
Florence, Uffizi

11. *Judith's Return to Bethulia*
31 x 25 cm
Florence, Uffizi

12. *Madonna and Child with an Angel*
85 x 64.5 cm
Boston, Isabella Stewart Gardner Museum

13. Portrait of a Man with the Medal of Cosimo the Elder
57.5 x 44 cm
Florence, Uffizi

14. *Scheme of the Adoration of the Magi. From left to right: 1) Lorenzo the Magnificent; 2) Agnolo Poliziano; 3) Giovanni Pico della Mirandola; 4) Gaspare Lami, who commissioned the work; 5) Cosimo the Elder; 6) Piero 'the Gouty'; 7) Giovanni de' Medici; 8) Giuliano de' Medici; 9) Filippo Strozzi; 10) Joannis Argiropulos; 11) Sandro Botticelli; 12) Lorenzo Tornabuoni.*

15. *Adoration of the Magi*
111 x 134 cm
Florence, Uffizi

Sandro Botticelli and the Neo-Platonism of the Medici

Sandro's most important paintings, the master-pieces that have won him acclaim not only from critics but from the entire museum-going public, were created almost completely within the sphere of the Medici family and reflect the cultural atmosphere which surrounded it. It seems appropriate to sketch briefly here the history of the family and of its most influential members. The founder of the family's fortunes was Cosimo, the son of Giovanni (called Cosimo the Elder by later historians to avoid confusion with Cosimo, the first Grand Duke) who in the third decade of the fifteenth century opposed the ruling regime led by his rivals, the Albizzi family. He was imprisoned in Palazzo della Signoria (now called Palazzo Vec-

chio) and then exiled in 1433. A year later he returned in triumph and with the full authority to put into practice his political plans for the city and make himself and his family the city's rulers. He used his vast fortune to these ends.

The great epoch of Medici patronage began with Cosimo the Elder. First there were buildings by the greatest architects of the period, Brunelleschi and Michelozzo di Bartolommeo. Then followed other cultural as well as ecclesiastical innovations. An example of the latter was the Council of Florence, which gathered together all the Bishops who had previously met in Ferrara and were attracted to Florence by Cosimo's generosity and his prestige (in 1439 he was made Gonfalonier, or Chancellor

of the city). Cosimo also established the Platonic Academy, which met in his villa at Careggi. The villa was restored by Cosimo and it was here that he died in 1464. The ends to which all Cosimo's efforts were directed were the strengthening of ties between the various members of his family, enhancing the family's prestige, and assuring its position of supremacy in the state. He had a plan in which, without widespread revolution or even disturbances, the government of the city would become a real Signoria (a government by one lord), at the same time preserving some of the republican institutions and placing trusted followers in charge of them.

When Cosimo died his plans had not been accomplished; although the family was rich and powerful, it was not numerous. The programs that Cosimo had outlined seemed far too ambitious for such a small family to carry out; his pronouncements from the palace in Via Larga seemed voiced with regret that no large group of heirs was available to continue his work. However, the family's fortunes and prestige prospered after its founder's death. Cosimo's son Piero (called 'the Gouty') was able to keep the power left to him by his father during his brief reign (1464-1469) and, despite his ill health, he carefully prepared for the succession of his sons, Lorenzo and Giuliano, using his personal authority to see that his heirs would be accepted as the city's rulers. In 1471, in fact, the most important men of the city asked Lorenzo to become ruler of the city, following in the footsteps of his father and grandfather; thus the dynastic succession was assured. Lorenzo used his powers with a great sense of duty, differing from Cosimo in that he put the interests of the state before those of his family. However, he did see to it that his son Giovanni was made a cardinal (Giovanni later became Pope Leo X). His policy of inviting (and paying for) artists and literary figures to come to Tuscany led to a wider cultural exchange and collaboration. The Pazzi conspiracy of 1478 (master-minded by Pope Sixtus IV, who looked with disfavor upon the rise of the house of Medici), although it cost the life of Giuliano, showed the consensus of the Florentine people in favor of the Medici. It was the population who fell upon the conspirators and executed them summarily. From 1478 until his death in 1492, Lorenzo was personally involved in political matters — uniting Italian princes in peace treaties that would keep foreign powers, notably France and Spain, from invading Italy — and artistic and cultural affairs. He surrounded himself with such important figures as Marsilio Ficino, Agnolo Poliziano, Pico della Mirandola, philosophers, poets and men of letters. The age of Humanism had begun:

the artists and intellectuals of the early fifteenth century were fascinated by the rediscovery of Greece and Rome. Florence had become the principal artistic center of Italy, not only in terms of quality, but also in terms of the large number of workshops throughout the city. The workshop of Verrocchio (where Leonardo was a student and where Botticelli, Perugino and a great many lesser artists worked) and that of Ghirlandaio (where Michelangelo studied) were the two most famous in the city. This then was the artistic climate of Florence, where the stimulating presence of the Medici family was felt by all artists, and where Sandro Botticelli's artistic expression developed.

The work which can most reasonably be considered as typifying the relationship between the Medici family and the artist is the *Adoration of the Magi*, now in the Uffizi Gallery. According to scholars, this was commissioned between 1475 and 1478 by Giovanni (or Gaspare) di Zanobi Lami, a banker with close ties to the Medici family who wanted it placed on his family altar in the Church of Santa Maria Novella. The main attraction of this painting, as far as critics are concerned, is the fact that it contains so many portraits of historical characters. But all this should not lead us to ignore the outstanding compositional accomplishments which show how much Botticelli was by this time master of his own art.

His art also unifies the elements taken from other painters and the expression of melancholy pride, to be seen even in the self-portrait in this painting, gives the entire work that sense of fairy-tale meditation which will be a constant feature of all his later work. We must also mention some of the identifications of characters in the painting with real historical figures (see caption).

As far as the painting itself is concerned, we can add that it is drawn with a striking fluency of line and that the golden coloring, rather like a beautifully calm dusk, is one of the most outstanding Botticelli was ever to achieve, recreating in a more complex but more spacious background the atmosphere of the two Stories of Judith.

Probably associated with the painting of the *Adoration of the Magi* is the frescoed lunette with the *Nativity*, now to be found on the internal facade of Santa Maria Novella above the entrance door. Its original location was on high, crowning the chapel (or altar) built by Gaspare Lami in the church's internal facade. It was a singular fate that caused both its position and form to change, since after its removal it was replaced by Masaccio's fresco of the *Trinity* which today we see back in its original position on the wall to the church's left nave.

The lunette, which was rounded, was detached

20. *Birth of Christ*
200 x 300 cm
Florence, Church of Santa Maria Novella

21. *Portrait of Giuliano de' Medici*
54 x 36 cm
Bergamo, Accademia Carrara

22. *Portrait of a Young Woman, called "Simonetta"*
61 x 40 cm
Florence, Galleria Palatina (Palazzo Pitti)

in the 19th century, fixed to a lathwork support and given an ogival shape to adapt it to the ogival frame of the ornamental panel above the door. Obscured by repaintings, it was carefully restored in 1982 by the Opificio delle Pietre Dure. It was revealed to be a simple composition, although one with extraordinary expressive force: the same enclosed space of crumbling squared stones that also appears — though in a broader perspective — in the Uffizi altarpiece. A light colouring, with golden ochres, dazzling azure blues and the vermilion of the young St John's fluttering cloak, constitues the fresco's chromatic *leit-motiv*. Although his pose is different, the physiognomy of the pensive St Joseph is reminiscent of the one in the painting with the *Adoration of the Magi*; the face of the Virgin still shows traces of the influence of Filippo Lippi, though with that vein of softness so peculiar to Botticelli. Even the ox and the ass — so masterfully juxtaposed — participate in the feeling of satisfied admiration present in the scene. The recent restoration has now made it possible to banish definitively the doubts of those critics who have questioned the painter's autography. Here (and it must be in the years 1476-78, the same years to which the altarpiece of the Lami chapel belongs), the artist reveals his talents as a fresco painter, the previous evidence of which had been scanty and inconsequential.

At about the same time, in the summer of 1478, the Republic, by now in the hands of the Medici, asked Botticelli to paint the portraits of the conspirators who had murdered Giuliano on the northern wall of Palazzo Vecchio. He also painted at least one portrait of Giuliano himself — one before Giuliano's death, and perhaps others later. There are many versions, none clearly identifiable as by

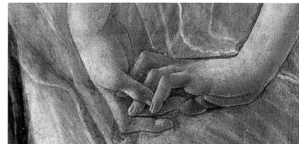

23, 24. *Primavera*
details of the Three Graces
Florence, Uffizi

25, 26. Primavera
details of the goddess
Florence, Uffizi

Botticelli. It is also difficult to establish which one of these is the earliest, because of their terrible state of preservation. What is certain is that it is around this time that Botticelli passed from group representations of people to individual portraits, while still maintaining that primary quality of melancholy which justifies the phrase 'sadness of exile', so often used to describe the characters in his paintings. There is another portrait which can be dated to around this period, that of *Simonetta* in the Pitti Palace. Although the identification with Simonetta, the young girl with whom Giuliano was in love, is probably only the result of legend and not of fact, the subtle melancholy which pervades this clearly-designed figure is undeniable proof that it is the work of Botticelli. It is this very uncertainty about the real identity of the figures in these portraits that increases their effect of mystery.

Sandro Botticelli's two most famous works, the so-called *Primavera* (Spring) and the *Birth of Venus*, were both commissioned by the Medici. The two paintings are admirable products of the cultural environment created by Medici patronage. The critics are all in agreement about the years in which they were painted: 1477-1478. They were painted for the brothers Giovanni and Lorenzo dei Medici, the sons of Pierfrancesco who was the first cousin of Piero 'the Gouty'. This branch of the family later rebelled against the absolute rule of Piero di Lorenzo and earned the nickname of 'the Medici of the people'. It was to this branch that the Grand Dukes belonged. Lorenzo, the son of Pierfrancesco, had been a pupil of Marsilio Ficino and he commissioned from Botticelli some frescoes for his villa of Castello, where he also wanted to place the two famous paintings. Lorenzo's Neo-Platonist training is important in attempting to explain the subject-matter of these paintings. Marsilio Ficino was the greatest representative in fifteenth-century Florence of this philosophy which followed the teachings of Plato, revised in such a way as to fit in with Christian doctrine. There have been many interpretations about the origins of the subjects of the two works, including some which see them as deriving from classical poetry, in particular from the work of Ovid and Horace. It also seems possible that the inspiration could have come from the work of Ficino himself, developed artistically by the poet Poliziano, and that Venus, instead of symbolizing the carnal nature of pagan love, might be the representation of the Humanist ideal of spiritual love, that is "those conscious, or semi-conscious, upward movements of the soul, through which all is eventually purified" (Chastel). It is therefore a cosmological-spiritual representation, in which Zephyrus and Flora give birth to Spring, the central symbol of the creative capacity of Nature. In the center of the *Primavera*, with blind-folded Love above her, is Venus, identified with *Humanitas* — the sum total of man's spiritual activities; with her are the three Graces, who represent these activities put into practice, while Mercury disperses the clouds with his staff. This mythological representation is given strength and life by Botticelli's style and by the mastery with which he was able to create in the background an orange grove moved by the same dance-like rhythms as the clothes of the figures stirring in the breeze. The figures stand

27-31. Primavera
203 x 314 cm
Florence, Uffizi

32-35. Birth of Venus
184.5 x 285.5 cm
Florence, Uffizi

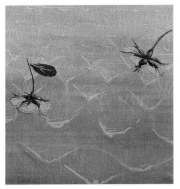

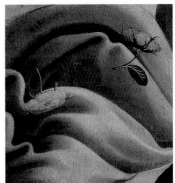

out clearly against the background of dark leaves, creating an effect similar to that of a tapestry. Some critics have seen in all this a return to Gothic fantasy, but it is more sensible to see it as the first successful attempt in the early Renaissance at placing figures freely in space.

The *Birth of Venus* also has the same basic setting and it portrays the preceding moment in the development of the Neo-Platonist myth: *Humanitas* is about to be created by Nature, while the lifegiving spirit, united with matter, gives it vital force and the Hour (or Time), symbolizing the historic moment of humanity, offers her the cloak which will make her 'modest' and able to distribute goodness. This painting is probably what Poliziano is referring to in the lines from his *Stanzas*: "A maiden not with a human face / pushed forward by lustful Zephyrs / stands on a shell; and the Heavens enjoy the sight". Remarkable is the way in which the delicate colors of dawn are portrayed in the flesh-tones of the figures rather than in the

36, 37. *Birth of Venus, details*
Florence, Uffizi

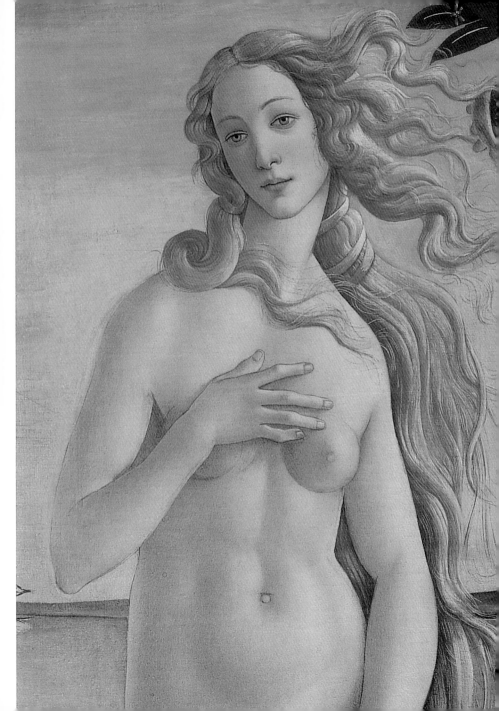

*38. Birth of Venus
detail of Hour
Florence, Uffizi*

*39. Nastagio degli Onesti
(first episode)
83 x 138 cm
Madrid, Prado*

background, and in the colors of the clothing, so delicate and enlivened by the decorations of cornflowers and daisies. The optimism of the Humanist myth is here blended harmoniously with the calm melancholy so typical of Botticelli's art. After two paintings, the conflict of conscience which had overtaken the cultural and figurative values of the Renaissance involved Botticelli as well in ways that we are about to see. The first traces of this can be noticed as early as the 1480s.

Lorenzo the Magnificent commissioned Sandro to paint four episodes from the story of Nastagio degli Onesti in Boccaccio's *Decameron*. The subject-matter of this story is at once fierce and chivalric, similar to the 'courtly' culture which centred around Lorenzo. The occasion for these paintings was the wedding of Giannozzo Pucci, Lorenzo's nephew, to Lucrezia Bini. The first three of these panels are now in the Prado in Madrid and the fourth is in the Watney Collection in Great Britain. Until the second half of the last century all four of them were still in the possession of the Pucci family.

The conception of these four panels is entirely Botticelli's, even though — as was quite frequent in those days — a large part of the actual painting was left to the workshop. The first three scenes show very clearly the hand of Bartolommeo di Giovanni and the last one that of Jacopo del Sellaio, both of whom were very close followers of Botticelli. The most pleasing effect of the works is produced by the harmonious background settings, both in the episodes that take place in the pine-woods of Ravenna and in the scene of the banquet for Nastagio's wedding to the daughter of Paolo Traversari. As was by this time customary in Botticelli's paintings, drama and formal elegance (exemplified in the agility of the figures and in the graceful movements of people and animals) blend together to give us the impression of a story half way between reality and fantasy, here enlivened by the pure colors of the architecture and by the subdued representation of nature.

In the spring of 1481 Botticelli frescoed on a wall of the Hospital of San Martino alla Scala an *Annunciation*, which is now in one of the vestibules of the Uffizi. The power of his art is here expressed at its best in the angel who arrives with his clothes billowing and the lily in his hand bent by the wind. Opposite the angel, the Virgin leans forward with that air of resigned submission which seems to foreshadow those figures prostrate with grief that recur in Botticelli's later work. The perspective is also used as a method of expression, so slanted in the

foreground and with the almost unending background.

As we have already mentioned, Botticelli was given the task of painting the members of the Pazzi conspiracy of 1478 on the walls of Palazzo Vecchio. It has been suggested that he was inspired in this by the paintings of hanged men by Andrea del Castagno in the Bargello: they were also members of a conspiracy against the Medici, the Albizzi conspiracy. After this work, of which there is no longer any trace, Castagno's influence on Botticelli can be

40. Nastagio degli Onesti (second episode)
82 x 138 cm
Madrid, Prado

41. Nastagio degli Onesti (third episode)
84 x 142 cm
Madrid, Prado

42. St Augustine
152 x 112 cm
Florence, Church of Ognissanti

119

seen in the powerful figure of *St Augustine* in the Church of Ognissanti, painted for the Vespucci family, who were close friends of the Medici. Since this figure stands together with the *St Jerome* painted by Ghirlandaio in 1480, we can deduce that they were part of a single commission and were painted in the same year. The outstanding energy of Andrea del Castagno's work is transformed by Botticelli into a prevailing mood which is full of restlessness and apprehension. One can begin to see in Sandro's work that tension which has been ascribed to a conflict of conscience after the bloody events of 1478, which certainly undermined the idyllic Humanist atmosphere created by the Medici. This work probably marked the height of Botticelli's fame as an artist and in 1480 he was called to Rome together with Cosimo Rosselli, Perugino and Ghirlandaio (and later also Pinturicchio, Piero di Cosimo and Signorelli) to paint stories from the lives of Moses and Christ on the walls of the Sistine Chapel. These were commissioned by Pope Sixtus IV, the traditional rival of Lorenzo the Magnificent; but there must have been a reconciliation between the two if so many Florentine painters, including Botticelli who could be called the official interpreter of Medici patronage, were summoned to Rome. In October 1482, as we have already mentioned, Sandro was again in Florence to decorate the Sala dei Gigli in Palazzo Vecchio.

There are still three enormous frescoes by Botticelli on the walls of the Sistine Chapel. These are *Scenes from the Life of Moses*, the *Temptation of Christ* and the *Destruction of the Children of Korah*. He also painted, with much help from his workshop, in the niches above the biblical scenes, some portraits of popes which have been considerably painted over. In all these works his painting appears weak and only in the first of the frescoes does he succeed in co-ordinating the formal with the narrative. In the rest he manages to express his usual vigor in the portraits only, whereas the whole appears fragmentary and lacks genuine quality. Probably the painter, working in a different environment, on subject-matters and in dimensions so unusual for him, felt lost and had difficulty in expressing his art to the full.

But when he returned to Florence he started working again with his customary sureness of hand, also incorporating some figurative elements acquired during his stay in Rome. The painting of *Venus and Mars*, today in the National Gallery in London, obviously derives from classical art and probably from the very same Roman sarcophagus which was also to provide the inspiration for the face of the centaur in *Pallas and the Centaur*. The painting of *Venus and Mars* can probably be dated

around 1482-1483, and like many of Botticelli's works has been subject to many different interpretations. Venus, calm and self-assured, watches the sleeping Mars, while little fauns playfully rush into the scene. This can all be connected with Humanist themes: Venus as the personification of love conquering Mars, who symbolizes discord. Despite the playful element of the fauns, the dominant mood of the painting is not serene: the sleeping god is fatigued and his body is almost too relaxed; Venus's expression is slightly restless and worried. This same feeling we can find again in the *Portrait of a Man*, probably painted around the same time (1483-1484), now also in the National Gallery. The face and the tense lines express a greater apprehension than in the *Portrait of a Man with the Medal of Cosimo the Elder*, mentioned above. Both portraits are typical of Florentine portraiture, but Botticelli's are different in mood from the celebrative portraits of the 1480s: they have another feel about them, something more subdued but at the same time more human. He seems to want to convey in this work a cautious analysis of his personal feelings.

In 1482 he painted for Lorenzo dei Medici, son of Pierfrancesco, *Pallas and the Centaur* — today in the Uffizi — perhaps intended as the third and concluding work of the trilogy begun by the *Primavera* and the *Birth of Venus*. For this painting too, many different interpretations have been put forward. That which is commonly regarded as most plausible again fits in with Humanist symbolism: wisdom (Pallas) overcomes instinct (the centaur), concluding the conceptual definition of *Humanitas* present in the other two allegories. The strong and vigorous figure of Pallas can be traced back to classical sculpture and, as we have said, the Roman sarcophagus which inspired the face of the centaur has been identified. The entire composition is characterized by great elegance, brought about by the rhythm of the line and by the physical relationship between the figures and the rocks "which form an orderly and solid architecture similar to the ruins of Rome" (Salvini). If we consider this painting the last of Botticelli's Medicean period, as is the general opinion of art-historians, we can see that from this point onwards the subject-matter of his paintings changes and becomes increasingly religious. The pictorial technique changes too: the colors become purer and more striking in order to accentuate even further the expressionism of the scenes; the contorted positions and shapes of the figures emphasize the exasperation of their movements and their gestures.

We must not underestimate the importance of the personal evolution of the painter's style, com-

43. *Annunciation*
243 x 550 cm
Florence, Uffizi

mon to many artists, in explaining away these transformations: that is to say, a development from the more tempered compositions, typical of the central phase of an artist's work, to the more elaborate and complicated forms, especially psychologically, of the later period. But personal artistic development, in Botticelli's case, was not the only reason for this evolution. The events of 1478 (the Pazzi conspiracy) certainly shook not only the Medici's power, but also the consciences of the most politically aware citizens of Florence. And even though until 1492 no internal force endangered the political stability of the Republic, certainly in the minds of more sensitive people, such as Botticelli, doubts concerning the contemporary situation must have begun to grow.

The painting of *Pallas and the Centaur*, as we were saying, marks the end of Botticelli's Medicean period. It is also the end of a very serene and prolific period in the artist's career, considering the variety and quantity of the works produced.

The policital situation changed with the death of Lorenzo the Magnificent in 1492 and the invasion of King Charles VIII of France in 1494. Piero di Lorenzo, son of the Magnificent, was forced to flee from Florence and the family temporarily lost power. The sentiments expressed in Botticelli's art also changed and this caused it to take on new directions and show new concerns. In the cultural atmosphere of declining Humanism, the complex personality of Fra Girolamo Savonarola appeared on the Florentine political scene.

44. Scenes from the Life of Moses
348 x 558 cm
Vatican, Sistine Chapel

45. Scenes from the Life of Moses
detail of Moses taking off his
shoes

*46. Scenes from the Life of Moses
detail of a young girl and a soldier*

*47. Scenes from the Life of Moses
detail of the daughters of Jethro*

48-52. Temptation of Christ
345.5 x 555 cm
Vatican, Sistine Chapel

53-56. Destruction of the
Children of Korah
348.5 x 570 cm
Vatican, Sistine Chapel

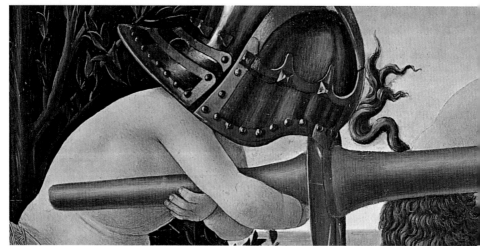

57-59. Venus and Mars
69 x 173.5 cm
London, National Gallery

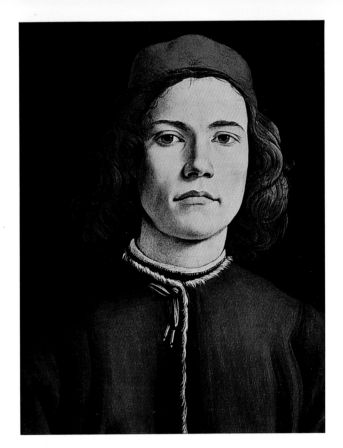

60. Portrait of a Young Man
37.5 x 28 cm
London, National Gallery

61. Pallas and the Centaur
205 x 147.5 cm
Florence, Uffizi

The Age of Savonarola: Pathos and Tragedy

Girolamo Savonarola was born in Ferrara in 1452. In 1475 he joined the Dominicans in Bologna, and very soon became famous for his preaching in the cities of northern Italy. In his impassioned sermons he stressed the need to reform the Church, to destroy its worldliness and nepotism, and to cleanse it of the corruption of the popes. His writings and sermons were full of prophetic tones which could quite well be adapted to present historical conditions. In 1489 he was summoned to Florence by Lorenzo the Magnificent and in 1491 he became Prior of the monastery of San Marco. Here his aversion to the power of dynastic Signorias, which he considered dangerous for the people, soon became obvious. He sponsored demonstrations against all forms of luxury, such as the famous 'burning of vanities', during which — with almost medieval fanaticism — precious objects, elaborate clothes and works of art of pagan content were destroyed by fire. With the invasion of Charles VIII his prophecies seemed to come true and, perhaps for this reason, he played quite an important rôle in the establishment of the Republican government after Piero dei Medici had been exiled. Very soon, however, he was called upon to take back his accusations against Pope Alexander VI Borgia who was well-known for his scandalous behaviour and his corrupt nature. Savonarola's refusal to go to Rome led to his excommunication in 1497. At first the Florentines supported him, but subsequently, out of fear that the entire city might be excommunicated and also because the friar had lost prestige by failing to prove his powers in a trial by fire to which he had been challenged by a rival Franciscan monk, they had him arrested. Then, after a plainly unfair trial, he was sentenced to be hanged and burnt at the stake in Piazza della Signoria, with two of his followers, on 23 May 1498.

Apart from the brief mention in Simone Filipepi's *Cronaca*, in which Sandro shows a certain interest in the fate of Savonarola, there is no other documentary evidence to prove whether or not he was one of the friar's militant followers. But we must note that there are certain themes in Sandro's later works, such as the *Mystic Nativity* and the *Mystic Crucifixion*, which are certainly derived from the sermons of the Dominican, which means that the artist was definitely attracted by that personality so central to the cultural and political events of the city during the last years of the century. And, in fact, it would be impossible to explain away the radical change of subject-matter and even of pic-

torial style which characterized Botticelli's activity from about 1490 to 1510, the year of his death, without taking into consideration the influence of the preaching of Savonarola. The tendency towards meditation, which ever since his earliest paintings had been an integral part of Sandro's personality and had enabled him to understand and therefore to express in figurative form the Humanist content of Ficino's Neo-Platonism, must have made him more open to Savonarola's principles. It is in this respect, culturally and at the same time psychologically, that Botticelli's acceptance of the Dominican's reform program must be viewed, even though it may not have implied a direct involvement or a political commitment to the Republic created after the Medici had been exiled.

We might consider the *Adoration of the Magi* today in Washington as a typical example of Botticelli's style after the dramatic events of 1478, both as

far as subject-matter is concerned and also because of some artistic innovations. This painting is usually dated immediately after Botticelli's return from Rome. But while the vaguely Umbrian landscape, with its tall slender trees, can be attributed to the influence of Perugino, the group of graceful figures have a more abstract air about them than, say, in the *Adoration* in Florence. The artist is working toward forms of greater expression which will be fully revealed in later works.

The *Madonna of the Book* in the Poldi-Pezzoli Museum in Milan belongs to the period around 1485. It is a small painting, dominated by the precise contours of the Virgin and Child, in whose faces one can see a relationship of deep affection coupled with the customary expression of serene melancholy. The dramatic intensity not expressed through the figures is suggested by the crown of thorns around the tender arm of the Christ Child. Of a different intonation is the well-known *Madonna of the Pomegranate*, painted in 1487 for the Florentine Magistratura dei Massai di Camera. The representation of figures is the dominant part of this work, so that even the special perspective is created by figures of angels who surround the Virgin and the blessing Child in a semi-circle. The probable link between these two paintings is the tondo called the *Madonna of the Magnificat*, now in the Uffizi, that critics have dated to around 1485. The slightly oval face of the Virgin is very similar to that of the *Madonna of the Book*. The scene is painted against the slightly unusual background of a round window, almost like the oculus of a church: this innovation, so typical of Botticelli's art, nevertheless bears a vague resemblance to Lippi's work, especially in the poses of the angels. The use of gold and the faraway landscape are wonderful examples of great artistry.

This painting was followed by the Madonna Enthroned with St John the Baptist and St John the Evangelist, commonly known as the *Bardi Madonna* because it was painted towards the end of 1485 for the Church of Santo Spirito on a commission by Agnolo Bardi. Today it is in the Staatliche Museen in Berlin. The composition is static and the only sense of movement is created by the elaborate

62. Adoration of the Magi
70 x 103 cm
Washington, National Gallery of Art

floral background, consisting of plants with symbolic meanings which refer to the incarnation and passion of Christ (lilies, olive branches, laurel leaves and palms). The figure of the Virgin is taller here, and her features are more ascetic. The painting is enlivened by the vivacious movements of the Child to which Mary responds with the instinctive maternal gesture of offering her breast. We can see through these figures a very definite tension, a prelude to some of Botticelli's later works. But in the meantime another very important organization in Florence, the Guild of Doctors and Apothecaries, commissioned from the artist a very grand altarpiece. It is the so-called *San Barnaba Altarpiece* (Madonna enthroned with St Catherine of Alexandria, St Augustine, St Barnabas, St John the Baptist, St Ignatius and St Michael), commissioned for the Church of San Barnaba of which the Guild was the patron. Scholars have dated this painting to 1486. Today it is in the Uffizi. The architecture, both concise and majestic, seems to point towards the art of the sixteenth century, and it is certainly the best example of Botticelli's mastery in this field. At the sides of the curtain, very finely drawn in little tondos, are the two figures of the Annunciation, the Virgin and the Angel. The angels on either side of the tall throne carry the crown of thorns and the nails of the cross, symbols which refer to the passion of Christ. The delicate figure of the Virgin is similar to that in the *Bardi Madonna*, but here the same type of features is also used for St John the

Baptist and for the young warrior Michael, without doubt the most beautiful part of the painting. It must be pointed out that, on the steps of the throne, there is for the first time in the history of painting an inscription in Italian. The line comes from Dante's *Divine Comedy* (Paradise, Canto 33, line 1): "Virgin mother, daughter of your son". This is the first evidence of Botticelli's interest in Dante's poetry, which culminates in his drawings of episodes from the *Divine Comedy*. The *San Marco Altarpiece* (Coronation of the Virgin with angels and St John the Evangelist, St Augustine, St Jerome and St Eligius) was painted around 1488-1490 for the chapel belonging to the Guild of the Goldsmiths in the Church of San Marco. The chapel was dedicated to St Eligius, called 'Alò' or 'Olò' in Florentine vernacular. The composition of the painting is rather archaic in structure, with different proportions used for the saints and for the angels and the imaginative niche where the coronation is taking place contrasted to the realistic space in which the four main figures stand. But the panels of the predella are exceptionally life-like: see, for example, the representation of St John the Evangelist amidst the rocks of the lonely island of Patmos, the figure of St Augustine in his bare study, the concise Annunciation, the rocky cave of the repenting St Jerome, the dynamic figure of St Eligius miraculously restoring his horse's leg, his body twisted in an unusual manner and his cloak billowing in the wind. Reminiscent of Leonardo's

134

64. Madonna of the Book
58 x 39.5 cm
Milan, Museo Poldi Pezzoli

work, and characteristic of Botticelli's ability to blend other artists' motifs into something quite personal, is the white horse. Throughout all these scenes Botticelli's intense emotions are predominant; he bends his figures into contorted positions to express more vividly their feelings.

And yet despite the considerable acclaim which it has received ever since shortly after its execution (it is referred to in Florentine art sources, like Albertini, the so-called "*Libro di Antonio Billi*", and the "*Anonimo Gaddiano*", and Vasari himself in both editions of the *Lives*), this large altarpiece has experienced a turbolent history, with numerous changes of location. From the altar of the Church of San Marco it passed to the chapter-house of the convent, from here to the Galleria dell'Accademia and finally to the Uffizi in 1919.

Only with the conclusion of the lengthy restoration, carried out in 1989 in the workshops of the Opificio delle Pietre Dure at the Fortezza da Basso,

can the work's physical and topographical vicissitudes be considered at an end. However, even the recent restoration only partly succeeded in putting to rights the damage caused by this stately painting's wandering through the various buildings that once housed it. The numerous transfers also witnessed the deprecatory loss of the superb original frame, which was subsequently replaced by another, meticulously carved, that came from the dissolved Church of the 'Battilani'. Restorations were made continuously necessary from 1830 (when, still at the Accademia, the painting was restored by Francesco Acciai) until 1921, at the end of the ten-year intervention by Fabrizio Lucarini, who completely repainted the color of the green clothing of the third left angel. In spite of this intervention, the lifting and losses in the painted surface continued, which led to the final and most complete restoration which seems to have definitively eliminated the shifting of the support.

65. *Madonna of the Pomegranate*
diam. 143.5 cm
Florence, Uffizi

66. *Madonna of the Magnificat*
diam. 115 cm
Florence, Uffizi

The charm of the painting resides essentially in the complex component organization of the heavenly vision, laden with elements drawn from the doctrinal and symbolic solicitations favoured by the apocalyptical meditations consequent upon Savonarola's presence in Florence, which shortly after would provoke the political and institutional upheavals that followed the first expulsion of the Medici from the city in 1494.

And in fact, the figure of the saint of visions and revelations contained in the last book of the Scriptures, John the Evangelist, is the medium, through

67. Madonna of the Magnificat, detail Florence, Uffizi

68. Madonna Enthroned with St John the Baptist and St John the Evangelist (Bardi Madonna) 185 x 180 cm Berlin, Gemäldegalerie Dahlem

the hand raised upward and the open book (white, because he still awaits the words which issue from the heavenly images), between the motionless figures of the onlookers (Augustine, Jerome and Eligius) and the fantastic caroussel of angels around the arc of cherubim and seraphim enclos-ing the Coronation of Mary. Amidst the dazzle of the gloria, the shower of roses, the apparition of the background angel between the screens of gold-en rays, the setting of the earthly landscape, bristling with desolate rocks and meadow on which the figures stand, the painting seems to affirm the

139

69-72. Predella of the
San Barnaba
Altarpiece
Florence, Uffizi

Vision of St Augustine
20 x 38 cm

Christ in the Sepulchre
21 x 41 cm

*Salome with the Head
of St John the Baptist*
21 x 40.5 cm

*Extraction of St
Ignatius' Heart*
21 x 40.5 cm

73. Madonna
Enthroned with Saints
(San Barnaba
Altarpiece)
268 x 280 cm
Florence, Uffizi

74. *San Barnaba Altarpiece, detail*
Florence, Uffizi

75. *Coronation of the Virgin (San Marco Altarpiece)*
378 x 258 cm
Florence, Uffizi

dialectic between the alluring phantasmagoria of heavenly reality and the scabrousness of worldly existence.

It is therefore evident in this painting that as a result of the splendid restoration the transcendence of that realistic and rational 15th-century figurative organization, towards ulterior compositional goals, is made to quiver with manifest clarity, making this painting one of the most important among those which mark the beginning of the artist's final period of activity.

The large *Annunciation* now in the Uffizi was commissioned in May 1489 by Benedetto Guardi for the convent of Cestello, which was then in Borgo Pinti, more or less where the Church of Santa Maria Maddalena dei Pazzi is now. This painting was rediscovered in 1870 in a villa in Fiesole which belonged to a group of nuns of that order. A recent restoration (1986), parallel with that of the *Birth of Venus*, has taken care of the damage wrought by a 19th-century intervention, which had partly abrased the original egg-white varnish, scratched the azurite of the sky in the background and worn down the gold of the elegant contemporary frame, decorated in the upper frieze with palmette motifs and angelical protoma, in the side pilaster strips with candelabra and — at the base of these — with

the coats-of-arms of the person who commissioned it. The predella — accompanied by lapidary inscriptions drawn from the Scriptures and the Magnificat — contains in the middle a touching image of Christ in pietà, from whose open sarcophagus, as a further theme of painful meditation, hangs the cloth of Veronica. The conservative intervention has restored richness and clarity to the composition, which presently reveals all the dramatic poignancy of the mature expression of Botticelli's art.

Scholars have pointed out the 'too elaborate' coloring of this painting, which it seems was the result of the collaboration of Filippino Lippi "whose artistic sensibility does not coincide with Botticelli's emotional research and who looks for expression in unnecessary luxury" (Bettini). But the conception of the two figures, with the angel almost bent

143

to the ground and the Virgin's reticent and contorted position, show how far Botticelli had come in his personal search for an artistic expression that would coincide with his spiritual tension. And, in fact, his purely Renaissance style is here enriched with forms that remind us of an archaic, almost Gothic kind of painting (the unreal folds in the angel's clothing and the Virgin's body almost twisted into a spiral). But at the same time the extremely modern elements of Botticelli's painting, already present in the *San Barnaba Altarpiece*, reappear in the architecture. Notice in particular the door which opens onto the background landscape.

This monumentality of architecture can be found again in the little *St Augustine in his Study* in the Uffizi, to be dated around 1490-1500 and mentioned in the records of the Vecchietti family, one of the most important Florentine families. The element of movement, which Botticelli never forgot in any painting, is given here by the opening curtain which reveals the saint and which hangs from a metal rung that coincides with the base of the arch

76-80. Predella of the San Marco Altarpiece
21 x 268 cm
Florence, Uffizi

St John on the Island of Patmos

Annunciation

ugustine in his Study

A Miracle of St Eligius

rome in the Wilderness

81, 82. Annunciation
150 x 156 cm
Florence, Uffizi

83. Annunciation
detail of the predella
with Christ in the
Sepulchre

84. St Augustine in his Study
41 x 27 cm
Florence, Uffizi

85. Communion of St Jerome
34 x 25.5 cm
New York, Metropolitan Museum
of Art

above St Augustine's chair. The synthesis of Humanism and Christianity — that is, the two poles of Botticelli's cultural and artistic development — is symbolized in the medallions with classical profiles above the columns and in the lunette at the back with the Madonna and Child. Another detail of Botticelli's expressionism is given by the bits of paper strewn carelessly on the floor.

The *Communion of St Jerome* in the Metropolitan Museum in New York was also painted around this time. The symbolism and the hyperbolic proportions, so common in Botticelli's later work, are present here. See, for example, the crucifix with palm fronds which seems to refer to St Jer-

ome's imminent death, while he receives communion in his hermitage. Even the figures of the acolytes, unrealistically bent in the hermit's hut, are by this time quite common features of Botticelli's painting and they reveal his interest in figurative research, very different from the naturalistic and narrative trends of the late fifteenth century in Florence (consider the work of his pupil Filippino and of Domenico Ghirlandaio).

This innovation, both in subject-matter and in representation, is carried further in the famous painting of *Calumny*, which reproduces the subject of a painting by the Greek painter Apelles, described in classical times by Lucian and men-

*86. Madonna
Adoring the Child
with Angels
('Madonna del
Padiglione')
diam. 65 cm
Milan, Pinacoteca
Ambrosiana*

*87. Lamentation
Over the Dead
Christ
107 x 71 cm
Milan, Museo Poldi
Pezzoli*

*88. Mystic Nativity
108.5 x 75 cm
London, National
Gallery*

89, 90. Mystic Nativity,
details
London, National Gallery

91. Calumny
detail of Truth and
Remorse
Florence, Uffizi

92. *Calumny*
62 x 91 cm
Florence, Uffizi

93. *Calumny*
detail of Malice, Calumny, Envy and Fraud

94. *Calumny*
detail of King Midas between Ignorance and
Suspicion

tioned in the Renaissance by Leon Battista Alberti in his treatise *De Pictura*. In this painting there is a representation of King Midas, with ass's ears, listening to the false words of Ignorance and Suspicion. In front of them, standing, is Malice who precedes Calumny. Calumny is accompanied by Envy and Fraud, dragging Innocence by the hair. Behind this group is the hooded figure of Remorse, who turns to look at the naked figure of Truth. This is the allegory of the painting which is set in a large hall with archways that are fully sixteenth-century in style. Through these we can see a clear faraway landscape of sky and completely barren countryside and along the walls of the room are niches with figures from classical antiquity and from the Scriptures. Also of similar subject-matter are the monochrome reliefs that decorate the arches and the bases of the columns. The blending of classical and biblical elements takes us back to the Humanist meditations on the possibility of reconciling pagan thought and Christian tradition. But the figures, as though tossed about by a strong wind that dies in the face of the monumental image of Truth, reveal how Botticelli's restlessness releases itself in the meditation on the mystery of man face to face with the two greatest spiritual movements of the West, classical culture and Christianity. This painting is essentially conceptual and its figures bear no relationship to reality. *Calumny* is today at the Uffizi and has been dated between 1490 and 1495.

Botticelli's versatility, from this stage onwards, is only expressed in his choice of subjects, which as we have seen cover a wide range: from allegories and religious subjects to the illustration of literary themes. But the guiding principal through all these different subjects is the lyrical mood which is present in all Botticelli's paintings. The Madonna adoring the Child with three angels (*Madonna del Padiglione*) in the Pinacoteca Ambrosiana in Milan was painted in the 1490s. In this work Botticelli successfully blends the traditional aspects of Florentine painting (the solid construction of the elements creating the space: see the curtain held open by two angels) with a delicate landscape, plainly inspired by Leonardo's work. The features of the figures still show a subtle melancholy and each one seems deep in personal meditation. This division of emotions is unified by the religious aspect of Botticelli's own meditation.

Very different because of its bright, almost too brilliant colors, and because of the disproportionate sizes of the figures, half way between prostration and hope, is the painting called the *Mystic Nativity* in the National Gallery in London. Evil is conquered by brotherhood and by prayer; these are the thoughts of the elderly painter. This is his only dated work (the year 1501 is legible in the inscription in Greek at the top) and it contains, also in the inscription, a reference to the historical conditions of his country at the time — "during the dark moments of Italy". It is also his first work to refer to, even though only indirectly in the inscription, Savonarola (at least this is the opinion of many scholars). In this painting too, the presence of archaic elements, such as the olive branches tied to the scrolls or the reduced size of some of the figures, contrasts strongly with the wide-open space, with the poses of the characters and with the intensity of emotion which pervades the entire work. We may say that the painting is visionary in its conception and conservative in its figurative elements. The expressionism of Botticelli's later works derives also from this very contrast, which singles him out as an isolated figure in the artistic context of Florence at the beginning of the sixteenth century, characterized by the young Michelangelo and by the sharp division of artists into Classical or Mannerist.

Even more impressive, and, for this reason, appropriate as a conclusion to this partial analysis of Botticelli's painting, is the *Mystic Crucifixion* in the Fogg Art Museum in Cambridge, Massachusetts. The Christ figure on the cross dominates from above a city that looks very much like Florence. On the left is God the Father despatching groups of angels with shields with crosses on them, while on the right, in a black cloud, some devils are throwing burning torches. In the lower part is Mary Magdalen, desperately clutching the foot of the cross. Opposite her is an angel striking an animal that looks like a lion (perhaps it is a reference to the Marzocco lion, the emblem of Florence), while a second animal escapes from Mary Magdalen's gown. Here again the interpretations of scholars on the meaning of this allegory are manifold, but it seems certain that it was inspired by one of Savonarola's sermons. We could summarize the most likely interpretation by saying that Mary Magdalen represents the repenting city of Florence, which is protected against evil by divine intervention. The historical reference of all this is almost certainly the fact that, in 1502, Cesare Borgia called off his invasion of the territory of the Republic at the last minute and the city was spared. Thus, once again we see the political commitment of Botticelli, taking part as he did in the life of his city with his art and still capable of producing works of remarkable power. We must add here that the influence of Savonarola on Botticelli, so often denied by the scholars, is evident above all in the last years of his life in his choice of religious subjects which contain apocalyptic and prophetic elements and are, therefore, more easily expressed through allegories which are characteristic of the writings, the sermons, and the religious, civil and political activity of the Dominican from Ferrara.

Botticelli's dilemma, which although of an essentially personal nature must have influenced his artistic production and his pictorial style, is based on the contrast between two different worlds: the Humanist world with its chivalric and almost pagan content, experienced in the Medici circle, and the

95. Mystic Crucifixion
73 x 51 cm
Cambridge (Massachusetts), Fogg Art Museum

reforming and ascetic rigor of Savonarola, who used Christianity not only as a personal ethic, but also as a guide to a coherent civic and political commitment, contrasting 'Christ King of Florence' (which his followers wanted to carve over the door of Palazzo Vecchio) with the splendid but tyrannical and corrupt power of the Medici.

Botticelli lived intensely and coherently in both these cultural environments and from them he drew the inspiration for his art. His harshness, his imagination and the quality of his painting unite his works, regardless of which of the two cultural worlds inspired them. Even when he seems backward and closed in on himself — as in his last works — we cannot neglect his greatness, the greatness of a man who lived for sixty-five years and worked for the best part of half a century.

To conclude we shall discuss briefly Sandro's achievements in the field of drawing and the applied arts. We have already mentioned his interest in Dante and there are sources which state that he illustrated the *Divine Comedy* for Lorenzo di Pier-

96. Pallas
Florence, Uffizi, Collection of Prints and Drawings

97. Angel
Florence, Uffizi, Collection of Prints and Drawings

98. Birth of Christ
Florence, Uffizi, Collection of Prints and Drawings

francesco dei Medici between 1490 and 1496. These drawings are now dispersed, some in the Vatican Museums and some in the museums of Berlin. These drawings are comparable stylistically to his later works, because they are full of archaic elements and the figures in them have nothing at all realistic about them.

The doors of the Sala dei Gigli in Palazzo Vecchio seem to have been carved on Botticelli's design by Francione, a well-known Florentine carpenter, and by the sculptor and architect Giuliano da Maiano, probably at the time when these two artists were working in the building (1478). The two inlaid figures, which look very static, are *Dante* and *Petrarch*. Botticelli also designed the wood paneling for the study of Federigò da Montefeltro, the Duke of Urbino. This work dates from 1476 and consists of allegorical figures, typically Botticellian in their movements and poses, alternated with representations of objects. Botticelli was a true master of drawing, almost the emblem of fifteenth-century painting in Florence; his name stands out in the most fruitful and successful period of Florentine art, the late Quattrocento. It is difficult to separate his personality from the environment of his principal patrons, the Medici; this environment is usually considered serene, carefree (see, for example, Lorenzo the Magnificent's well-known carnival song 'Enjoy today; Nought ye know about tomorrow'), lucidly sceptical, culturally prolific, and economically rich. But in reality Botticelli's art reflects all the restlessness and worry of the society of his time and of the city he lived in. Perhaps the most 'Florentine' of all painters, Sandro Botticelli portrayed better than any other artist all the tension of an age of great cultural and political creativity, but also an age that witnessed overwhelming social and historical upheavals.

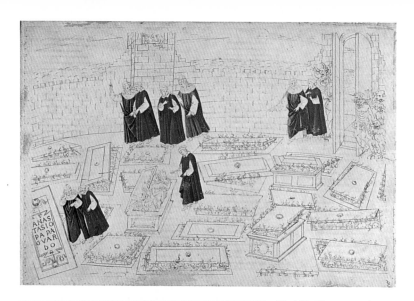

99, 100. Illustrations for the
Divine Comedy
Vatican, Vatican Library

LEONARDO

His life

1. Leonardo's house at Vinci

Leonardo was born in the village of Vinci, between the Tuscan cities of Empoli and Pistoia, on 15 April 1452. His father, Ser Piero d'Antonio was a notary. The future artist's mother was a woman from Anchiano named Caterina, who later married a peasant. Despite his illegitimacy, Leonardo was treated with affection in his father's house, where he was reared and educated. In 1468 his grandfather Antonio died, and the following year the paternal family moved to Florence. The boy's precocious artistic gifts led his father to send him to study with the most versatile and sought-after Florentine master of the time: the sculptor, painter, and goldsmith Andrea Verrocchio. Little is known about Leonardo's work under this master, and there are few examples of Verrocchio's painting. According to tradition (a tradition confirmed by scholarly analysis), Leonardo was responsible for the angel and the landscape in the *Baptism of Christ*, a panel now in the Uffizi, which certainly came from Verrocchio's shop. This is where Leonardo's artistic personality began to develop. From 1472 on, he was enrolled as a master in the Company of Painters, so we can assume his apprenticeship to Verrocchio had ended by that

year, though he remained in the master's shop. Leonardo was attracted to every sort of artistic discipline, driven by an unparalleled curiosity and by his ability to complement those disciplines with his scientific knowledge, the fruit of tireless investigation into natural phenomena, which he observed acutely.

In 1480 he was a member of that extraordinary academy, the garden of San Marco, under the patronage of Lorenzo the Magnificent. This was Leonardo's first venture into sculpture, an art which naturally attracted him because of the completeness of its very nature. In that same year he was commissioned to paint the *Adoration of the Magi* for the church of San Donato Scopeto, just outside Florence (the work is now in the Uffizi). But the Florentine environment had become too narrow and frustrating for him. Perhaps the fact that he was not one of the four masters invited to paint the walls of the Sistine Chapel drove him to seek a change of scene, or perhaps it was his natural restlessness which made him constantly try out new experiences, looking for new creative horizons.

In 1482, in any case, he presented himself to the

Duke of Milan, Lodovico Sforza, "Il Moro", with a letter in which he lists and describes his own capacities, including his talents as a civil engineer and designer of war machinery. His welcome in the Lombard city was favorable. He lodged with the De Predis brothers, painters, in the Porta Ticinese quarter, and in 1483 he was already engaged in decorating the great ancona (altarpiece) in the chapel of the Immacolata in the church of San Francesco Grande. Thus he painted the *Virgin of the Rocks* in the two versions now in Paris and London. During these years he was also occupied with the most vexatious and thankless assignment of his career: the equestrian monument to Francesco Sforza, for which he made countless sketches, drawings, models, constantly testing new ideas and techniques of casting. In 1489-90 he prepared the decoration of the Castello of the Sforzas for the approaching wedding of Gian Galeazzo Sforza and Isabella of Aragon. His activity gradually extended to one new area after another. In 1494 hydraulics became his concern, and he devoted himself to the reclamation of the Sforza lands in the Lombard plain. In 1495, however, the fresco of the *Last Supper* in Santa Maria delle Grazie became the almost exclusive object of his studies. The work was to be finished only in 1498. A year later Louis XII, king of France, invaded the Duchy of Milan. Leonardo abandoned the city and went to Mantua and Venice. In 1503 he was back in Florence, where he was commissioned to fresco the great Council Chamber in the Palazzo della Signoria, along with Michelangelo. Leonardo was assigned, as his subject, the *Battle of Anghiari*, while Michelangelo was to do the *Battle of Càscina*. Once again, Leonardo's eagerness to find new techniques for the execution of the painting prevented him from finishing the work. Probably in this same year he painted *La Gioconda* (Mona Lisa), which also remained unfinished.

Between June 1506 and September 1507 Leonardo returned once again to Milan. There, in 1512, the new Duke, Massimiliano Sforza, was installed. On 24 September of that year, Leonardo set out for Rome with his disciples; there he conducted mathematical and scientific studies of every kind. From there he traveled to several other cities, though always returning to Rome.

In May 1513 he accepted the invitation of the French king Francis I, who called him to Amboise. There Leonardo remained until his death. During his French years the artist created plans for festivities, but also continued with his hydrological projects, intended for several French rivers. On 23 April 1519 he made his will, remembering in it all those who were close to him. On 2 May of the same year he died, and was buried in the church of Saint Florentin at Amboise. During the religious wars of the sixteenth century his grave was violated and his remains scattered.

Verrocchio and Leonardo

Andrea del Verrocchio (born in 1435) had a renowned workshop in Florence, producing works in every artistic field: marble and bronze sculpture, painting, and examples of the goldsmith's art. Verrocchio's personality concludes the most active period of the Florentine Renaissance: far, by now, from the heroic manner of Masaccio and Donatello, he — and with him, other contemporary artists like the Pollaiolo brothers — concerned himself with a more naturalistic representation of the human form. Verrocchio's sculpture is well-known (the bronze *David* in the Bargello, the *Doubting Thomas* group on the facade of Orsanmichele, and the Colleoni monument in Venice are his most familiar works); but there is much uncertainty about his activity as a painter. The only panel surely conceived and executed in his shop is the *Baptism of Christ* in the Uffizi, which seems, when analyzed critically, an anthology of pictorial styles. The Christ and the Baptist possess the typical Florentine firm draftsmanship. The line, rich in movement, immediately suggests the master's sculptures. As we shall see, the angel on the left and the landscape, executed by Leonardo, are totally different. Andrea's shop, for that matter, welcomed several artists (including Botticelli and Perugino) who, having completed their training elsewhere, felt a need to confront their art with his. The shop's undeniable prestige and its reputation for attracting many patrons no doubt influenced Ser Piero's decision to send his son there to learn the art of painting. There Leonardo's meditations were to find the instruments most suitable to their figurative depiction. In fact, his first experience was gained in the space assigned him in the *Bap-*

2. *Andrea del Verrocchio and Leonardo*
Baptism of Christ
180 x 152 cm
Florence, Uffizi

3, 4. *Andrea del Verrocchio and Leonardo*
Baptism of Christ, details
Florence, Uffizi

5. *Drawing of a landscape*
Florence, Uffizi Prints and Drawings Rooms

tism. Andrea del Verrocchio died in Venice in 1488.

In his very first experience as a painter, the above-mentioned angel and the landscape background in Verrocchio's panel of the *Baptism of Christ*, Leonardo already reveals his technical maturity, his mastery of the means of expression (drawing and color, in this case), as well as his formal maturity. We can see how these two details are notably different from the rest of the painting. The stiff, almost metallic-looking palm on the left, the figure of Christ and the vigorous Baptist, have nothing in common with the adolescent angel whose outline is caressed and moulded by the light reflected also in the long waving hair. And they have nothing in common with the vast landscape which opens out just above the angels' heads. This view of nature is much more complex than the schematic landscapes to which fifteenth-century Florentine painting was accustomed: a winding river in a valley dotted with stylized cypresses and poplars. There, every form served to measure the space that was to be inhabited by man; here, there is no boundary, and you sense a broad nature waiting to be explored and discovered. We must therefore underline the total novelty of Leonardo's painting compared with his master's style or that of anyone else who may have had a hand in this painting. But this novelty is an achievement which owes its development to what the young artist found in Verrocchio's shop, although the pictorial conclusions — as can be seen — are completely personal and original: an advanced knowledge in the field of human anatomy, an absolute mastery of the depiction of movement, a great ability in modeling the material to the point of creating effects of vibrant chiaroscuro and a careful study of the portrayal of emotions. It is also true that all these elements bring us back more to Verrocchio's sculpture than to his painting, of which, in any case, we have very few examples. Still, these were no doubt the goals of Leonardo's studies with Verrocchio. During those years the younger man enriched his natural artistic bent with tecnical skills, receiving the means to reach at least a first stage in his artistic expression, which already appears quite distinct and more complex. In it, nothing of the master's style survives, but the development of Leonardo's art would be inconceivable without this patrimony of elements offered by Verrocchio's shop, with its wide range of activities. The relationship between master and pupil must be seen then in this perspective.

Florentine painting around 1480

For Florence, the years around 1480 were a time of relative political stability. When the final outbursts of hostility to the Medici were suppressed harshly in 1478, at the time of the Pazzi conspiracy, the personal regime of Lorenzo di Piero de' Medici was confirmed by popular support. There was also a total absence of political personalities who could arrest the slow but inevitable change from a republican form of government to a virtual dictatorship, though the magistrature and the traditional institutions were formally respected. Moreover, Lorenzo de' Medici was to become the "needle of the scale", in Machiavelli's expression, of the politics of all Italy, preserving the equilibrium among the powers that dominated the peninsula (Milan, Venice, the Papal States, Naples). Once the equilibrium was destroyed, then Italy was to fall immediately into the hands of foreign monarchies such as France and Spain which, having unified their own national territories under the crown, could think of expanding their power beyond their natural boundaries.

This period also saw an intense production in the city. True, Florence was no longer the only Italian city that could express the most progressive and, qualitatively, the highest art. Centers like Urbino and Mantua were developing, while Venice, with the Bellinis, was entering its finest period, the Cinquecento, and Rome, with the patron-Popes at the end of the century was to initiate those artistic enterprises that would make the city the absolute capital of Italian art in the following century. Florence, nevertheless, was still the place where artistic debate was at its liveliest. In 1466, the last survivor of the Renaissance's first artistic generation, Donatello, had died, and three years later, in 1469, the most interesting painter of the second generation, Fra Filippo Lippi, who had initiated a more illustrative and ornate form of painting, followed him to the grave. The active painters in the city then were Alessio Baldovinetti (1425-1499), Andrea del Verrocchio (1435-1488), Antonio (ca. 1432-1498) and Piero (1441-1496) del Pollaiolo, Domenico del

7. *Alessio Baldovinetti,* Annunciation
Florence, Uffizi

6. *Antonio del Pollaiolo*
Hercules and Antaeus
Florence, Uffizi

8. *Domenico Ghirlandaio,* Visitation
Florence, Santa Maria Novella

Ghirlandaio (1449-1494), to name only the most important.

Baldovinetti had made a timid attempt to introduce into Florence the rigorous manner of Piero della Francesca, though he retained only Piero's firm geometrical structure in the construction of human forms. Otherwise, Baldovinetti was a rather delicate painter, close to Fra Filippo Lippi in his taste for color and his felicitous decorative motives. The Pollaiolo brothers brought to Florentine painting new energy and power which they expressed in alert, athletic figures (such as the *Hercules and Antaeus* in the Uffizi and the *Dancing Youths* in the Villa La Gallina, near Florence). But even when they painted religious subjects (the *Altarpiece with three Saints* in San Miniato al Monte), they were able to give the subject a general impression of vitality. These same characteristics are found in their sculpture and their rare examples of goldsmith work (like the panel with the *Nativity* of the silver altar of San Giovanni Battista) which have remained to demonstrate their versatility as artists.

Domenico del Ghirlandaio was quite another personality. A gifted illustrator and narrator, and a skilled portrait-painter, he was also influenced by the naturalistic vein of the Flemish artists, represented in Florence by the *Adoration of the Shepherds* (also known as the *Portinari Triptych*, now in the Uffizi), by Hugo van der Goes; the painting probably arrived in Florence in 1478. In his fresco cycles (*Life of the Virgin and the Baptist* in Santa Maria Novella, *Stories of Saint Francis* in Santa Trinita), Ghirlandaio masterfully introduced the life of the leading Florentine families of the time and por-trayed for us the environment of the city. In his altarpieces, especially the *Nativity* in Santa Trinita, the Flemish influence is more evident in the limpid light of the background, the crystalline landscapes, and in the realistic depiction of the shepherds.

With these older masters, younger artists of the rising generation were asserting themselves: Alessandro Filipepi, known as Botticelli (born in 1455), Filippino Lippi (born in 1457), both active in the Pollaiolo brothers' shop, each of whom would later develop a highly personal style, rich in formal beauty, with a strain of melancholy in Botticelli's case and a gift for fantastic and complex invention in the case of Filippino. And finally, Leonardo himself.

This was the varied environment, with its articulated personalities and artistic expressions, that Leonardo found in Florence when he began his training as an artist in the school of Andrea del Verrocchio.

9. Sandro Botticelli
Annunciation
Florence, San Martino alla Scala

The Annunciation in the Uffizi

This painting has been in the Uffizi since 1867. It came from the church of San Bartolomeo a Monteoliveto, in the environs of Florence. Traditional criticism has assigned this panel to the young Leonardo da Vinci, still working, though with independence and confident mastery, in the shop of Verrocchio. No historian or biographer, including Vasari, mentions this work, but we should note that the attribution stems from a simple consideration of the quality of the painting, which could not be by Verrocchio or by any other pupil of his. In particular the broad landscape in the background, despite intruding elements which suggest human presence (the ships and the river harbor), so unusual in Leonardo, brings us back to Leonardo's meditations on nature, with the white peaks of very high mountains which stand out against the pale blue of the sky. Similarly, the beauty of the faces, from the very young and dazed Madonna to the noble profile of the angel, is convincingly Leonardo's. The composition is extremely simple: a group of dark trees, a carpet of grass and flowers with vibrant leaves, a stone parapet behind the Virgin, the outer walls and the entrance of a country villa. Verrocchio's style is perceptible in secondary details, though they are handled with a fullness Andrea never achieved in painting: the rich drapery, the lectern with marble reliefs of extraordinary refinement, derived from the bronze tomb of Giovanni and Piero de' Medici in San Lorenzo. Leonardo seems to be using his master's repertory in order to free himself gradually of it, moving towards works where his own genius can finally express itself with all the ideas and formal achievements of which he is capable. The general impression of this work, which still follows the traditional iconography of fifteenth-century Annunciations, is of an intensity found in no other Florentine painting of this period. Obviously, then, in making an attribution, scholars have insisted on the young Leonardo.

10. Annunciation
98 x 217 cm
Florence, Uffizi

11-12. Annunciation, details
Florence, Uffizi

13. *Annunciation, detail of the landscape*
Florence, Uffizi

14. *Drawing of a woman's head*
Florence, Uffizi Prints and Drawings
Rooms

15. *Annunciation*
14 x 59 cm
Paris, Louvre

16, 17. *Annunciation, details*
Paris, Louvre

174

The Annunciation in the Louvre

This was the central panel of a predella, which recent scholarship has linked with the altarpiece known as the *Madonna di Piazza* in the cathedral of Pistoia, painted by Lorenzo di Credi, a fellow-pupil with Leonardo in Verrocchio's shop (ca. 1478-1485). Critics have unanimously attributed this panel to Leonardo. Even within its limited dimensions, the painting's structure is complex. Note, for example, the spatial articulations represented by the stone parapet placed at a right angle, echoed in the wooden benches set beside and behind the Virgin. In this setting, indirectly constructed, the figures of the angel and the Virgin are introduced with great authority. The Virgin here is individualized with greater coherence than her counterpart in the Uffizi, and is enhanced by exquisite color contrast, such as that between the very dark blue of her dress and the pale blue of her cloak. The angel also indicates precious study of material and color: the forearm covered with ochre velvet, the delicately draped vermilion cloak. But the landscape is particularly original: the garden with its little low trees, so remote from all conventional depiction, and the background where, in the light blue sky, only faintly darker, subtle peaks of high mountains can be discerned.

Action and movement

The *Adoration* of Leonardo is an undoubtedly impressive painting also because the scene is unusually crowded and is made even more fantastic by the contrast between the figures in the light and the groups immersed in almost total darkness. The painting has as well the disturbing fascination of an unfinished masterpiece. Leonardo started painting it only after a tormented period of preparation, whose stages can be reconstructed through the surviving drawings. On the one hand, it is interesting to see how his initial idea of an *Adoration of the Shepherds*, drawn from the most commonplace traditional iconography, was soon rejected and extended to involve a whole throng of humanity in the sacred event. But at the same time, we cannot consider the Uffizi panel as a simple sum of sketches added one to the other. It is, instead, the fruit of the twenty-nine-year old artist's attention to the world around him and the formal concepts that study had

inspired. In fact, Leonardo had devoted himself to the investigation of human physiognomy: from the wrinkled faces of old people to the smooth profiles of adolescents. His observations of the real consistency of the human body and anatomy led him to draw the abandoned corpse of Piero Baroncelli, hanged in 1478 because of his connection with the Pazzi conspiracy against the Medici. Leonardo analyzed emotions and attitudes, in faces, in limbs, in the figures' poses, in the fall of drapery. And he also studied the movements and expressive capacities of animals. In plants, too, he was prompt to seize on every sense of life, every form. Finally, he carried out authentic scientific observations, stemming from his interest in humanity and in everything man tirelessly creates. But in this work the depiction of movement is supremely important; it is in fact one of the figurative components of Leonardo's apprenticeship with Verrocchio and is a part of the expres-

sive tendency of this phase of fifteenth-century Florentine painting. A basic artistic problem in the early Renaissance was the proper insertion of the human figure in space. When this problem had been solved and overcome, the new motive of artistic content — movement — was to concern a generation of painters, beginning with Andrea del Castagno, around the middle of the century. But while it represented for them only a further development in art's expressive capacities, for Leonardo it was an essential element in his own system, which made philosophical and pictorial speculation coincide. Movement is the foundation of life, and more, it is also an instrument for the expression of emotions. The figure "will not in itself be praiseworthy if it does not express, as fully as possible, the passion of its spirit with action". If this is the fundamental tenet of Leonardo's artistic expression (and the panel of the *Adoration* is its first true realization), then the consequences in the figurative field must be a profound investigation of the concept of movement, until every elementary particle of painting is directed towards achieving that *sfumato*, the subtlety, which "modeling the figures without lines, but only with lights and shadows, aims at making tangible the continuity of the world of appearances with the hidden world of forces", (Marinoni).

These, then, are the compositional elements of this extraordinary work, which appears, in its unfinished state, more immediately effective, freer, than any of the preparatory drawings. Around the Virgin and her Son we feel the emotions of a pensive humanity, doubting, distraught, awed, devout, imploring: a whole kaleidoscope of feelings and passions, virtually a complete array of symbols of man's inner activity, of his thirst for knowledge. No work of art, before this painting, had expressed such lofty conceptual content, depicted in such perfect form. Thus the *Adoration* becomes the expression of the human epic, and the first achievement of Leonardo in acquiring a truly universal dimension.

18. Drawing that shows Leonardo's interest in the representation of movement
London, British Museum

19. Drawing of the hanging of Piero Baroncelli
Bayonne, Musée Bonnat

20. Drawing of a rearing horse
Windsor, Royal Library

The Adoration

Leonardo was commissioned in 1481 to paint this work for the main altar of the church of San Donato Scopeto, just outside Florence, beyond the Porta a San Piero Gattolino (now called Porta Romana). But the artist never finished the painting and left it behind in Florence when he set out for Milan — as we have seen — in 1481. In a semicircle around the Virgin and Child is the crowd of those who are approaching the Holy Family to worship. There are people of every age, including some young people on horseback. The animals themselves — as was often to happen with Leonardo — seem to share the human emotions. In the background, with the ruins of a palace whose distinct stairs seem almost unreal, a procession of people, mounted and on foot, unfolds. At the extreme right there is an equestrian combat, whose meaning however, remains obscure. The two trees in the center, a palm and an ilex, act almost as the axes around which the whole scene unfolds in a spiral, as if inserted between the meditative figure of an old man on the left and that of a youth (pointing to the group of the Madonna and Child) at the extreme right.

Riderless horses also wander through the paint-

21. Adoration of the Magi
243 x 246 cm.
Florence, Uffizi

22. Perspective study for the
Adoration of the Magi
Florence, Uffizi Prints and
Drawings Rooms

23. Study for the Adoration of
the Magi
Paris, Louvre

24, 25. Adoration of the Magi,
details
Florence, Uffizi

179

ing, perhaps the symbol of a nature not yet subdued by man, while in the background rise the usual high peaks, here barely sketched, but no less solemn and looming than others in Leonardo's work.

26. *Adoration of the Magi, detail of the supposed self-portrait*
Florence, Uffizi

27. *St Jerome*
103 x 75 cm
Vatican, Pinacoteca

Saint Jerome

No contemporary source mentions the *Saint Jerome* in the Vatican Museum, and yet there has never been any doubt concerning the attribution of this panel. The stylistic evidence, linking it with the master's painting methods, is too obvious. Moreover, we have here the formal and structural resemblance (as well as the similarly unfinished state) to the Uffizi *Adoration*, even if the content is clearly different. In the latter we have a throng whose desire for knowledge drives it towards a mystery of universal significance; here we have a solitary hero, his face haggard from fasting and penitence, but his eyes filled with determination and will-power. Leonardo's faces never reflect weak or hesitant feelings: they are steeped in profound passions, revealed, however, not through distortions of the features, but through the intensity of the expression. The head of the Saint, formed through Leonardo's masterly anatomical knowledge, is still part of a Florentine tradition of draftsmanship which, through Antonio del Pollaiolo, extends to Andrea del Castagno and to Domenico Veneziano. Completely new, summing up the artist's anatomical experiments and the study of movement mentioned above, is the pose of the body, kneeling and bent forward, while the right arm is outstretched, grasping a stone, just before the penitent strikes his breast with it. The figure of the recumbent lion concludes the spiral that surrounds the pyramid represented by the figure of the kneeling Saint. The spiral begins in the mountain of the background, its form familiar by now, then winds around the rocky cave, Jerome's hermitage, to end in the curve of the animal's tail. The structural composition is thus typical of Leonardo. With it, he decidedly abandons the fifteenth-century type of composition, which grouped people and objects symmetrically; now he is moving towards a new concept of volumes and space, more atmospheric and less geometrical. Most critics place this work in Leonardo's first Florentine period, before his departure for Milan.

28. Drawing of the Madonna
suckling the Child and other
profiles
Windsor, Royal Library

Leonardo's women and children

The attraction Leonardo felt towards the beauty of young women and children is demonstrated by numerous drawings. They portray faces sometimes intent, sometimes smiling, attitudes of tender affection, gazes filled with shyness or silent contentment on one hand, and games, childish play, on the other, with delightful children as protagonists. In fact, it is hard to find in the master's work a single-minded interpretation of the female or the childish form, whereas most Quattrocento painters constructed the figure of the Virgin (emblematic of the mother-son relationship) according to unchanging formulas, trying as far as possible to express all feelings connected with that relationship in a kind of regal impassiveness thanks to which the Virgin can be only the Child's worshiper. Instead, Leonardo's typical way of facing human situations, namely through minute analysis of the emotional and physiological elements that form them, finds also in the subject of the "Madonna and Child" a further possibility of expression.

A different kind of emotional relationship is al-

29. Drawing of the Madonna offering a bowl of fruit to the Child
Paris, Louvre

ready being expressed in the so-called *Benois Madonna* in the Hermitage Museum, Leningrad. Here a very young Madonna, hardly more than a girl, is seen playing with her Son, showing him a flower. The girl is conscious of her action and smiles, while the child, who must still examine the object his mother has held out to him, seems grave, intent on observing it. These nuances of feeling show us how Leonardo succeeded in achieving, in painting, his private program of study of the human figure and of its physical components and its behavior. Naturally Leonardo's interest in the female figure cannot be limited to the subject dealt with here: there are also female portraits by Leonardo (which culminate, obviously, in the world-famous

Gioconda). One of them is the now firmly identified portrait of *Ginevra Benci* in the National Gallery in Washington, a work which can rightfully be considered the prototype of this genre of painting, even if it is stylistically still linked, in many ways, with late fifteenth-century Florentine painting and, especially, with the products of Verrocchio's shop. In any case, this is a work which also betrays Leonardo's efforts to insert the human figure into nature, an enterprise which — as we have seen — concerned him from his beginnings as an artist. Here we witness a first stage of this enterprise, where nature assumes the function of a background which puts the woman's figure in relief. She is not outstandingly beautiful, but her expression is intense, and her face

185

30. Drawing of the Madonna
and Child holding a cat
London, British Museum

31. Domenico Ghirlandaio
Birth of St John the Baptist,
detail
Florence, Santa Maria Novella

reveals a mixed feeling of pride and melancholy. The splendid evergreen bough that rises behind the figure has — if observed carefully — an autonomy of its own, both because of its relevance in the work's context and because of the loving care with which it was painted, although it is not possible to identify absolutely the species of tree. What is most striking is this female face whose penetrating gaze seems to ennoble the simple geometric form which traces its outline. We are spontaneously led to comparisons with the dignified but banal ladies in the domestic processions of Domenico Ghirlandaio's fresco cycles, painted almost at the same time as these early works of Leonardo. The comparison offers a further confirmation of the greater complexity and superior quality of the artistic program of the youth from Vinci. The so-called *Litta Madonna*, also now in the Hermitage in Leningrad, has been assigned by scholars to the Milan period. A drawing exists which is definitely related to this painting, but the painting nevertheless is most likely the work of a follower. In the painting the Virgin's attitude is more markedly affectionate; there is a tenderness and satisfaction in the contemplation of the Child,

who, intent on sucking his mother's milk, looks towards the imagined observer. This painting resumes the traditional theme of the "nursing Madonna" enriching it, however, with attentive observation of the Child. The somatic type of the infant Jesus is already the same as the one we will later see in the *Virgin of the Rocks* and in the *Saint Anne*: a blond, curly-haired baby, with very delicate complexion. In conclusion, we may observe that this beauty expressed in the soft forms of young Madonnas and the plump features of the Infants is, in Leonardo, something more than mere figurative representation. It is a speculation on the concept of maternity, seen in the emotional relationship with the child and entrusted to the instrument of painting, which in that very beauty finds its appropriate expression.

The Benois Madonna and Litta Madonna

The first of these works was originally painted on wood and was transferred to canvas when it entered the Hermitage. The painting was not discovered by scholars until it was shown along with other works from private collections in St. Petersburg in 1909; its provenance is unknown. Only its Russian history is documented: it was acquired by Tsar Nicholas II in 1914. The attribution to Leonardo was immediate and almost unanimous. The Virgin's fresh beauty and the Child's intense expression, as he looks at the flower his mother gives him, are noteworthy. These are perhaps the first figures conceived and realized by Leonardo in complete formal and stylistic independence of his master's shop, though still in his Florentine period. The work can be roughly dated somewhere between 1475 and 1480.

The *Litta Madonna*, on the other hand, belongs to the Milanese period; the Lombard elements in it are evident: a realistic care in the painting of the drapery and a general tone of domestic intimacy. This painting, which passed from the hands of the Visconti to the Litta family, was also purchased by a Tsar. The Emperor Alexander II, in 1865, added it to the Hermitage, where it was transferred to canvas. Recent scholarship tends to consider this a work by Leonardo completed by Boltraffio, one of his Milanese pupils.

32. Benois Madonna
48 x 31 cm
Leningrad, Hermitage

33. Litta Madonna
42 x 33 cm
Leningrad, Hermitage

189

34. Madonna of the Carnation
62 x 47 cm
Munich, Alte Pinakothek

The Madonna of the Carnation

Another work that would seem to evoke the sketches of a young Leonardo freed from Verrrocchio's tutelage, though nevertheless still affected by a passion and taste for the soft textures and dazzle of solid material (as practised in the workshop of the Florentine artist), is the Madonna sometimes referred to as the *Madonna of the Carnation* or "Madonna of the flowers". This painting is a free variant of the *Benois Madonna* in the Hermitage, being more complex in its composition and spatial arrangement, though perhaps somewhat high-flown and less spontaneous. How it arrived at the Alte Pinakothek in Munich, after its acquisition by a private German collector, is unknown to us. What is certain is that after a comprehensible, temporary attribution to Verrocchio or his shop, art critics subsequently almost universally assigned the painting to Leonardo, a judgement backed up by the most recent research. In fact, the richness of the drapery, the vastness of the mountain scenery with purple and gold hues tinging the foothills of peaks that fade into the sky, the vitality of the cut flowers in the crystal vase and the softness of the Child's flesh that foreshadows the tender putti of the *Virgin of the Rocks*, are elements that show a distancing from the more distinctive Verrocchiesque style and instead assume those formal and chromatic characteristics that would be the mature Leonardo's very own. Moreover, we should not overlook the striking similarities — in facial features and other details — with the *Benois Madonna* already mentioned (the gem fastening the Virgin's gown over her breast) and with the Uffizi *Annunciation*, works that in their figurative and expressive invention quite clearly reveal the stamp of Leonardo.

The Virgin of the Rocks in the Louvre

The first work that Leonardo executed in Milan is the so-called *Virgin of the Rocks*, which actually expresses the theme of the Immaculate Conception, the dogma that affirms Christ was conceived without original sin on Mary's part. This canvas was to decorate the ancona (a carved wooden altar with frames where paintings were inserted) in the chapel of the Immacolata in the church of San Francesco Grande in Milan. On 25 April 1483, the members of the Confraternity of the Conception assigned the work of the paintings (a Virgin and Child in the center and two Angel-Musicians for the sides), to Leonardo, for the most important part, and the brothers Ambrogio and Evangelista De Predis, for the side panels. Scholars now feel that the two canvases on this same subject, one in the Louvre and the other in London's National Gallery, are simply two versions of the same painting, with significant variants.

The Paris *Virgin of the Rocks*, entirely by Leonardo, is the one which first adorned the altar in San Francesco Grande. It may have been given by Leonardo himself to King Louis XII of France, in gratitude for the settlement of the suit between the painters and those who commissioned the works, in dispute over the question of payment. The later London painting replaced this one in the ancona. For the first time Leonardo could achieve in painting that intellectual program of fusion between human forms and nature which was slowly taking shape in his view of his art. Here there are no thrones or architectural structures to afford a spatial frame for the figures; instead there are the rocks of a grotto, reflected in limpid waters, decorated by leaves of various kinds from different plants while in the distance, as if emerging from a mist composed of very fine droplets and filtered by the golden sunlight, the peaks of those mountains we now know so well reappear. This same light reveals the gentle, mild features of the Madonna, the angel's smiling face, the plump, pink flesh of the two putti. For this work, too, Leonardo made numerous studies, and the figurative expression is slowly adapted to the program of depiction. In fact, the drawing of the face of the angel is, in the sketch, clearly feminine, with a fascination that has nothing ambiguous about it. In the painting, the sex is not defined, and the angel could easily be either a youth or a maiden.

35. *Virgin of the Rocks*
198 x 123 cm
Paris, Louvre

36. *Drawing of the face of the angle from the Virgin of the Rocks*
Turin, National Library

37, 38. *Drawings of plants and rocks, probable studies for the Virgin of the Rocks*
Windsor, Royal Library

39, 40. Virgin of the Rocks, details
Paris, Louvre

The Virgin of the Rocks in the London National Gallery

This version of the painting for the ancona in San Francesco has distinctly sixteenth-century characteristics: larger figures, made more plastic by a very decided chiaroscuro so unlike Leonardo that scholars were immediately led to consider the work a collaboration. The canvas is generally considered the one that replaced the first version of the Virgin of the Rocks on the altar of the Immaculate Conception, after that version had been given to Louis XII. This version was then, in 1785, purchased by the English collector Gavin Hamilton. It was joined, in England, in 1898, by the two musician-angels of the De Predis brothers, and the three paintings are now displayed together in London's National Gallery.

This version shows some details generally neglected by Leonardo in the other version: the haloes of the figures, the child Saint John's cross of reeds. Other elements which differ from the Paris picture are the pose of the angel, who no longer points his finger towards the little Paraclete, and his face, whose gaze no longer seeks out the spectator, but is directed inwards. The drapery, too, which in the Paris version was heavy and concealed the body, is lighter here, revealing the anatomical structure. Also the rocks seem painted in a more plastic fashion; the light does not glide over them, creating dewy areas of semi-darkness, but leaves strong contrasts of light and dark. The flesh of the children here is less tender, and though the shadows are insistent, the children's faces seem flatter and less sweet than those of the two sublime creatures in Paris. The intervention of followers on the painting already sketched by Leonardo has made the portrayal less vibrant, more banal, though it retains a compositional authority and an originality in its variants that make this work not a copy but an autonomous version, of high quality, of the unequalled masterpiece in the Louvre.

41, 42. Child from the Paris and London Virgin of the Rocks, details

43. Virgin of the Rocks
189.5 x 120 cm
London, National Gallery

Leonardo in Milan

Leonardo's first stay in Milan (1482-1499) in the period of his life most rich in activity, are the years that made his name and his personality well-known throughout Italy. During this time he undertook his largest number of important works, some completed, some left unfinished, some merely conceived or sketched. This is the moment when his art takes that firmly autonomous direction which, begun with the *Adoration of the Magi*, found in Milan its conformation, so that the style seen in his paintings was no longer based on "Florentine" or "Lombard" formulas, but was a Leonardesque style, later to have its own emulators, followers, and imitators.

As we have mentioned before, Leonardo seized the opportunity of Lorenzo the Magnificent's willingness to send artists to the various Italian states. He came to the Lombard capital, then perhaps Italy's most important city for its geographical position, wealth of industry, and political power. It also had a fertile populous territory, while Milan itself was a humanistic center filled with cultural ferment, even if it could not rival the refinement and creative ca-

pacity of the Florence of the Medici. In the famous letter to the Duke of Milan, Leonardo insisted on his abilities as an artist, and clearly hinted at an undertaking which must have been very dear to Sforza, namely the "construction of a bronze horse, which will be to the immortal glory and eternal honor of your father [Francesco I] and to the illustrious House of Sforza".

But when it came to the execution of this equestrian monument there was no lack of problems and hesitancy both on the part of the patron and of the master. Leonardo was troubled by the constant modifications of the original project, an ambitious group of dimensions never seen before (about 7.20 meters in height), with a rearing horse which presented difficulties of equilibrium and of casting. The Duke began gradually to harbor doubts concerning Leonardo's ability to execute the work, and in 1490 he wrote again to Lorenzo the Magnificent, asking for Florentine masters expert in casting bronze equestrian statues. Perhaps spurred on by this demonstration of his patron's lack of confidence

44. *Study for the Sforza monument*
Windsor, Royal Library

45. *Study for the Trivulzio monument*
Windsor, Royal Library

46. *Last Supper*
460 x 880 cm
Milan, Santa Maria delle Grazie

in him, Leonardo went back to work, and in 1491 he seemed to have made good progress, according to his own account. But then more doubts arose about the casting in bronze and the work's definitive appearance. We know that in 1498 a clay model was ready and the projects for the casting had already reached an advanced stage. In fact, the techniques worked out by Leonardo were later to be used by other artists. These techniques won him the reputation of being a precursor, an aspect of his work which modern writers have particularly accentuated. By a quirk of fate, Leonardo was unable to carry out this gigantic, tormented work according to his artistic meditations and his painfully acquired knowledge of the techniques of casting. In 1499 the Duchy of Milan was invaded by French troops under Louis XII. The Duke fled, and the model of the Sforza monument was consequently destroyed. Countless drawings of it remain: poses, attitudes, anatomies of horses, which show how Leonardo also dissected and studied these animals, with the spirit both of a scientist and an artist; there are also some sketches regarding casting techniques, with captions. A dejected annotation in one of Leonardo's notebooks, with the melancholy title *Epitaph*, perhaps concludes the artist's labors on this work: *If I have been unable to do, if I...* This unfinished sentence seems truly intended to underline the master's dazed disappointment at the failure to carry out another work of his.

We have already discussed the *Virgin of the Rocks* in its two versions, in London and Paris. We

199

various artistic techniques (it has been reproduced on tapestries, engraved, carved in wood). The literary references are meaningful, both for their quantity and quality. The fresco is mentioned by poets and historians, beginning with Matteo Bandello, almost a contemporary, in the dedication of the fifty-eighth Novella of the first part of his collection, and continuing through Goethe, who described it, after he had seen it in May, 1788. No other work, finally, has aroused greater public concern over its preservation and its restoration. It began to deteriorate rapidly soon after it was completed, and already by Vasari's time (1568) it could hardly be deciphered. The restorations were nearly all unfortunate, to tell the truth, except for the most recent ones, under the guidance of Mauro Pellicioli, which have actually made some recovery possible, such as the surface of the table and the figure of Judas. The earlier attempts contributed to worsening the appearance of the work, beginning in the eighteenth century and involving the various administrations which followed one another in the government of the city of Milan (first the Austrians, then the newly-born Kingdom of Italy, at the end of the last century). This itinerary of interventions is indicative of the fresco. In fact, it holds the fascination of a superb measure of content and form, perhaps never achieved again absolutely, except in some frescoes in Raphael's Rooms in the Vatican, where, for that matter, the illustrative effect is more dominant. The action in the Last Supper is choral: Christ's words pass, like a gust of impetuous wind, over the assembled disciples, who comment, in groups of three, on the Master's overwhelming revelation: "One of you shall betray me" (Matthew, XXVI, 21). It is as if the serenity of this room, classical in its architecture and its proportions, were suddenly destroyed, and among those present the knowledge is circulating of a tragedy that will soon be fulfilled, inevitably. Beyond the three openings in the back, a very clear, late-summer afternoon sky is the natural note Leonardo introduces into the depiction of an essentially human drama, fusing it, however, in supreme harmony with the surrounding atmosphere. Years of plans, countless preparatory drawings revealing differing compositional solutions are the prelude to the execution of this masterpiece, which was —

must add that the vicissitudes of this repeated panel were far from serene. There were endless disputes which set the patrons, the members of the Company of the Conception of San Francesco Grande, against Leonardo and the De Predis brothers, the artists of the works that were to decorate the altar of the chapel of the Immacolata in that same church. The Paris version is now in the Louvre precisely because King Louis XII personally intervened to settle the argument, and Leonardo probably gave him the painting out of gratitude for his arbitration. In any case, it is the first real painting Leonardo produced in Milan. However, far more tormented in its genesis and also the most significant work Leonardo ever painted — at least among those that have survived and are certainly his — is the painting that followed the Virgin of the Rocks, namely the Last Supper in Santa Maria delle Grazie. Probably no work of art has taken on the universal character that this fresco has, though it is now only a pale shadow of what it must have been when the master's hand had just completed it. It is of immense artistic and religious importance. Protestants and Catholics alike have accepted, without hesitation, the fact that it represents — and we know copies and imitations made for both religious areas — the central point of the Christian doctrine of salvation, the institution of the Eucharist during the Passover supper celebrated by Christ and his disciples together.

In fact, there are numerous versions and derivations of the fresco in every field of art and even in

again according to Bandello — characterized by alternating phases of execution: whole days of intense application, then a few minutes of rapid brush-strokes. This account may give an idea of the trepidation with which Leonardocarried out the most demanding work he had ever undertaken. His immense spiritual and technical engagement has left still visible marks in the painting, which, though veiled in the colors and the volumes of the figures, makes a profound impression even today and allows us to understand the grandeur and the originality of Leonardo's creation.

Compared with the *Last Supper*, the other works executed by Leonardo during his Milanese period take second place, though they represent a vast and various production also as far as subject and genre are concerned. Closely connected with Leonardo's life and activity as a courtier is the decoration of the so-called Sala delle Asse in the Castello Sforzesco. Some traces of the decoration were discovered during the 1893 restoration. It is an exceptional interlacing of branches of trees, with ropes, leaving only some patches of sky visible; they start at the beginning of the vault and form a kind of arbor with greenery, the coat-of-arms of Lodovico Sforza appearing in the center. The present state of the decoration is that given it during the late nineteenth-century renovation; but the idea, in its naturalistic vitality, can be assigned to Leonardo, while the execution of these ornamental paintings was surely the work of his disciples. His court activity also involved him in stage designing, in the organizing and staging of ceremonies (such as the receptions and festivities on the occasion of Gian Galeazzo Sforza's marriage to Isabella of Aragon in 1490). At the same time Leonardo had to attend to the execution of his reclamation project, demanded by Sforza for his landholdings near Vigevano, thus putting to the test his talents as a hydraulic engineer of which he himself boasted in his letter to Lodovico. Moreover, as we have seen, he was constantly occupied with the problems of casting the monument to Francesco Sforza and he also painted (if the attributions of the majority of Leonardo scholars and critics are correct) some portraits of personages who for one reason or another were connected with the Sforza court. We will discuss these at greater length below.

In short, Leonardo was continuously occupied, and his work served also to increase enormously his already exceptional reputation.

The last work executed by Leonardo before the King of France and his troops invaded the city and the artist left it (1499), is the cartoon for the *Madon-na and Child with Saint Anne*, now in the National Gallery, London. The cartoon is of exceptional importance because of the influence on Italian painting in the early sixteenth century of the pyramidal composition of the figures portrayed in it. But, in itself, the work is a unique example of formal beauty, compositional harmony, and profound conceptual significance. It is the logical conclusion of a complex investigation into the capacity of painting to reveal human feelings without upsetting the balance of forms which must be at the base of every experience. From the modulated, yet harmonic figures of the disciples, who start at the words of their Master in the *Last Supper*, to this compact group of the *Saint Anne*, where the faces seem to communicate to one another the feelings of the spirit (and, at least in our view, not reciprocally eluding one another, as some critics have thought), Leonardo's formal discourse is coherent and progressive.

In Milan, finally, he drew around him a group of followers and pupils (this is the final consideration we would like to make in this part of our discussion), such as Melzi, Marco d'Oggiono, Cesare da Sesto, Boltraffio, Salaino, and many others. He treated them with almost paternal generosity and affection, as we can see directly from his notebooks, indulgent even when their behavior could provoke severe reactions and punishments. (This was the case with Salaino, a youth of great beauty, but bizarre and full of all sorts of character defects). Intense work and affectionate ties are thus the chief characteristics of Leonardo's first Milanese period, perhaps the most important period — as we have tried to indicate — of his life as a scientist, artist, and man.

49. Last Supper, detail
Milan, Santa Maria delle Grazie

The Last Supper

The Duke Lodovico chose the Dominican church of Santa Maria delle Grazie both as his family chapel and burial-palace. In 1492 he had Bramante create a new choir in the form of a cube crowned by a dome and (perhaps in 1494) he commissioned Leonardo to paint the *Last Supper*. The painting was to occupy the north wall of the refectory, and Leonardo spent more than three years working on preparatory studies, sketches, and drawings. The Franciscan monk Luca Pacioli of Borgo Sansepolcro, mathematician and friend of the artist, in his dedication of the treatise *De divina proportione* to Lodovico, dated 8 February 1498, states that he saw the work completed. So Leonardo must have devoted himself to it from 1495 to 1498. The theme of the Cenacle, or Last Supper, is as old as Christian art itself, but it was only with conventual painting that it became the typical subject for the refectories of monasteries, where as a rule it was depicted in mural paintings of vast proportions. In the first preparatory drawings, Leonardo seems to want to accept the traditional scheme, with Judas — the traitor — seated opposite Christ. But, already at the beginning, "his conception of the theme was completely dominated by the idea of portraying the announcement of the betrayal as the central dramatic motive" (Heydenreich). In Leonardo's conception of the Last Supper, then, it is the human aspect of the drama being fulfilled which predominates, and not the sacred and mystical moment of the actual institution of the Eucharist, when Christ, taking the bread and the chalice, offers them to the disciples, saying: "Take, eat..." (Mark, XIV, 22-23). In the execution of the painting, Judas is seated on the

50. *Study for the Last Supper*
Venice, Academy

51. *Last Supper, detail*
Milan, Santa Maria delle Grazie

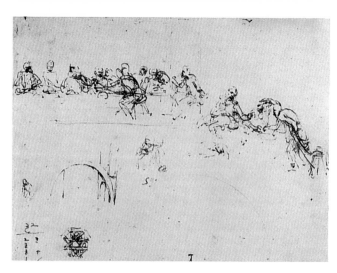

52. *Study for the Last Supper*
Windsor, Royal Library

53. *Study of horses' hind*
quarters
Windsor, Royal Library

54. *Study of the proportions of*
the human head
Venice, Academy

same side of the table as Christ and the other disciples. Only his attitude sharply distinguishes him from the others, as they echo the Master's words. As all, in fact, either lean towards Jesus or comment, aghast, on his revelation, Judas seems to detach himself purposely from the common drama, remaining isolated and ambiguous, with the burden of his betrayal. The unusual arrangement of the people is not the only novelty in Leonardo's fresco; also new is his identification, not entrusted to titles with the respective names, but rather to a complex of visual indications, which the gospel tradition and subsequent hagiography have handed down to posterity (particular function within the apostolic community, kinship, martyrology, attitudes towards the Master, and so on). And, naturally, the pictorial technique itself was entirely new, now surpassing fifteenth-century painting to express a far more complex sense of atmosphere, surroundings and color.

The masterpiece became immediately famous and popular with the public. Some sources report a significant tradition: the French King Francis I supposedly wanted to have the whole wall on which the *Last Supper* is painted sawn off and taken to France. Another historical fact is the painting's survival in 1943 when Allied bombs destroyed the ceiling of the refectory and almost the entire apse of Santa Maria delle Grazie. The painting's very poor state of preservation, which makes us regret the fact that we are unable to enjoy it completely, was attributed by certain historians (including Vasari) to the technique used by Leonardo. More recent restorations and a careful reading of the sources have proved instead that the painting's deterioration is due to the humidity which has always impregnated the wall and the entire refectory. But, beyond its present condition, Leonardo's idea and his achievement survive, giving this drama a truly universal scope and meaning.

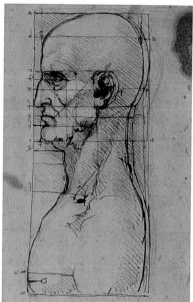

Anatomy, mechanics, caricature

"The ancients called man the lesser world, and truly this expression is well-founded, for as man is made up of earth, water, air, and fire, this body is a resemblance to the earth".

This sentence of Leonardo's may furnish the key to an interpretation of his concept of the world and of man, seen not only in strict interdependence, but actually similarly structured, and therefore capable of being studied with the same means. From the beginning of his career as an artist, he was an alert observer not only of landscapes but also of the traces of telluric upheavals which caused the earth's conformation (the view of the *Gonfolina Strait*, where the Arno's flow narrows before the river opens out in the lower valley, dates from 15 August 1473); and similarly, the artist observed man in his interior structure to which the exterior corresponds, physical aspect, physiognomy, expression of feelings, movement — all is minutely dissected, in order to discover the secret mechanism that governs man's vitality. The inner workings of the sensations of sight and hearing, the physiological instruments by which man can make his voice heard, the arrange-

ment of muscles enabling movement: these are the most important themes of Leonardo's anatomical research. The many anatomical drawings which he left behind, however, are not cold, didactic compositions; always present in them is that supreme quality which characterizes the master's works, so that even these scientific exercises have an independent artistic value, like every other creation of Leonardo's. We must bear in mind that the studies for the *Adoration of the Magi* and the *Last Supper* were made from naked figures, whose anatomy was carefully delineated. This method, which was to find followers from Cinquecento painting on, was actually begun by Leonardo. But man is not merely adorned with handsome features; in his life there is not only youth, marked by delicate complexion and perfect lineaments. Old age also exists, with its wrinkles and its deformities; ugliness exists, with its unpleasant and even repulsive features. Leonardo has therefore recorded the presence of deformity in man. We are told he visited the most ill-famed quarters of Milan, to draw the faces of those whose bodies and spirits had been in-

55. *Study of the proportions of the human body*
Venice, Academy

56. *Drawing of the assembly of a cannon*
Windsor, Royal Library

57. *Drawing of an assault chariot with scythes*
Turin, National Library

58. *Study of a man's head*
Venice, Academy

59. *Study of an old man's profile*
Firenze, Uffizi Prints and Drawings Rooms

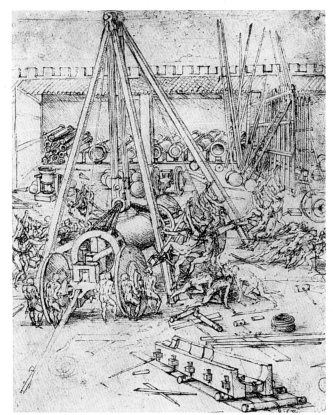

213

60. *Drawing of grotesque heads*
Windsor, Royal Library

61. *Study of caricatures*
Venice, Academy

delibly marked by poverty and vice. But we can also believe that this "underlining" in the negative sense, this distortion of man's features derives from the idea that both good and evil are part of humanity. They are not, however, considered in a moralistic sense, but simply represented as objective facts. For Leonardo, after all, the exercise of his art was also a philosophical speculation: "Painting then is philosophy... because it deals with the motion of bodies in the promptness of their actions, and philosophy is also a part of motion...".

Once the workings of human and natural organisms are known, they can be reproduced in machines which help man take his place in the world, encouraging his ambitions and his dreams of power. From the time of his study with Verrocchio, Leonardo was introduced to the learning of the "artes mechanicae, which had its natural seat in the shops of artists... an apprenticeship far more vast and eclectic [than mere artistic teaching] which was to produce an engineer or rather a technician-artist who could be called upon... to build a church, a palace, a fortress, war machines, bridges, dykes, and canals" (Marinoni). Thus we have Leonardo's letter to Lodovico Il Moro, where he lists his talents as a civil and military engineer (as well as his gifts as a musician and artist, naturally), a list compiled in order to whet the Duke's appetites in his warplans. So there are a whole series of sketches and studies for war machines, immense catapults, cannon with multiple barrels, grapeshot mortars, projectiles whose form suggests that of the lethal instruments of death of our own time. And, parallel to these, studies of civil engineering and mechanics: bridges, spinning machines, locks, watermills, compasses, springs, embankments, gears, even a vehicle amazingly like our modern bicycle. These remarks on Leonardo's studies of anatomy, physiognomy, and mechanics can help us understand the systematic foundation, the unity of the thought and activity of this great scientist, philosopher, and artist. In the past, critics tended to underline or exalt one or the other aspect of this complex personality, ignoring his constant coherence.

62. Study of the heads of an old man and a youth
Florence, Uffizi Prints and Drawings Rooms

The portraits

Among Leonardo's activities as a painter during his first stay in Milan we must include his portraits, which several sources mention clearly. The problem was one of identifying (not following the documents, which lack information and are very uncertain on the subject, but rather working from stylistic analysis) a certain number of portraits which could conform to Leonardo's figurative tendencies in this period. It must be said that the Lombard tradition of portraiture was quite distinct from the Florentine. The latter was celebratory and, in some instances, synthetic (even the so-called *Ginevra Benci*, for all its undeniably novel characteristics, also possesses these qualities), whereas Lombard portraiture was realistic, analytical, paying attention to style of dress, coiffure, and to accessory elements in general. Moreover the presence of Antonello da Messina in the Po Valley (he was in Venice in 1475) helped spread a certain kind of portraiture, with the figure against a dark ground and with a careful depiction of expressions and attitudes. In the works that scholars have indicated as possible paintings by Leonardo we can observe common characteristics, such as the background left in shadow, the figure seen at half-length or slightly more, in a three-quarters turn to enable the observer to distinguish the sitter more easily. The subjects of the portraits, however, remain unidentified, despite all the efforts of art historians and interpreters of the documents concerning Leonardo's activity. We can unquestionably place Leonardo's portraits in the circle of the Sforza court, where obviously what counted was the celebration of the individual, coinciding with that of the court itself. Clarity of forms, dignity of attitude, but at the same time an acute penetration of the character of the subject: in the portraits Leonardo immediately aligns his art with what we might call the avant-garde in this sort of painting, namely the portraiture of Antonello da Messina, definitively surpassing the celebratory formalism of the fifteenth century and heading decisively towards the figure of man depicted in the spiritual state that best defines him.

The subject of the so-called *Portrait of a Musician* in the Ambrosiana in Milan was at one time identified as Franchino Gaffurio, "maestro di cappella" of the Milanese cathedral; but the work actually appears simply as the portrait of a young man holding a length of paper with some musical annotation on it. The work can still suggest some geometrical volumes of Tuscan origin: the cap and the mass of curly hair which form two hemispheres at the sides of the face; but the incisiveness of the features and the chiaroscuro immediately suggest the Lombard atmosphere and a knowledge of Antonello's portraits. Heavily restored and repainted, the work was probably left unfinished, though at an advanced stage. This portrait — if it is by Leonardo — is the only one of the artist's with a male subject. It reveals a decisive personality, an intelligent and resolute gaze. No forced poses, therefore, aimed at a bombastic celebration of the sitter, but rather a depiction of moral strength through the intrinsic light of the face and the gaze. Antonello's lesson was learned and applied with a superior technique, showing that in Leonardo's sphere any artistic tendency could find affirmation and further development.

The second portrait of the Milanese group attributed to Leonardo is the *Lady with an Ermine*, now in the Czartoryski Gallery in Cracow, Poland. This is a remarkable portrayal of a slender maiden, with a faint smile and a penetrating gaze, holding in her arms a little white animal, gently pressing it with her agile, tapering hand. A transparent cap which passes beneath her chin softens the oval of the face, while a simple necklace of dark pearls, in two loops around her neck and extending in two strands over her bosom, barely suggested by the square-cut dress, is her only ornament. Her large, intent eyes are prominent, her nose is straight and fine, and her little mouth with thin lips is almost imperceptibly parted at the corners in a faint smile. Also remarkable is the handling of the fur of the animal, painted with a tiny paw upraised. The white color of this fur has caused the animal to be identified as an ermine in its winter coat, a symbol of purity. Despite some doubts about the identity of the subject, there is an hypothesis that she is Cecilia Gallerani, the favorite of Ludovico il Moro up to his wedding. The girl is recalled, in fact, as a friend of Leonardo's, who must, in fact, have painted her at the Sforza court, according to information from contemporary sources. Though the work has been so repainted that it is impossibile to attribute it definitively, the

63. Portrait of Isabella d'Este
63 x 46 cm
Paris, Louvre

state of preservation of the girl's face and of the ermine is fair, and can demonstrate the presence of a very notable technique and a skill of execution which can only belong to the environment of Leonardo, and to his immediate circle.

64. Portrait of a Musician
43 x 31 cm
Milan, Pinacoteca Ambrosiana

65. Lady with an Ermine
54 x 39 cm
Cracow, Czartoryski Museum

LA BELE FERONIERE
LEONARD D'AWINCI

Ginevra Benci

This panel, now in the National Gallery, Washington, portrays a young woman against a landscape with trees, illuminated by the glints of a stream. There are conflicting opinions as to the identity of the subject, and scholars similarly are not in agreement about the date of the work. Some feel that it belongs to the first Florentine period; others assign it to the Milanese years. In any case, the most generally accepted view is that the sitter is Ginevra Benci (a juniper — "ginepro" — branch, painted on the back of the panel, suggests her name), and that the work dates from the period when Leonardo was freeing himself from Verrocchio's tutelage — around 1475.

66. *Ginevra Benci*
42 x 37 cm
Washington, National Gallery

67. *Copy from Leonardo, Leda*
Rome, Galleria Borghese

68. *Study for the hair of Leda*
Windsor, Royal Library

The smile in Leonardo

Perhaps the greatest, most widespread interest in any of Leonardo's works is that which everywhere and at all times has been concentrated on the *Gioconda's* smile. Actually, other characters of Leonardo have the same smile — subtle and ironic, lips pressed together — as the protagonist of this famous canvas in Paris. The figures of the Virgin and Saint Anne in the cartoon and in the panel of the same title, for example, have it; and so does the *Leda*, which does not survive in the Master's version, though its derivative versions show an indisputable fidelity to Leonardo's model; and there is the mysterious, chiaroscuro *Baptist*. Leonardo's seal, you might say, has been imprinted on the face of each of these figures thanks to that smile which has noth-

ing ambiguous about it, but still leaves us a bit perplexed because of its allusive hint of irony. This sort of smile — from a figurative point of view — was not invented by Leonardo. It can be found in certain fifteenth-century Florentine sculptures, such as Antonio Rossellino's *Virgin* in the marble tondo of the Portuguese Cardinal's chapel in San Miniato al Monte, and much more widely in the works of Leonardo's master, Verrocchio. In these instances the smile has a specific function: to enliven, in a pictorial sense, the renewed sculpture of the Renaissance, whose founder Donatello had given it a severe and heroic form. But Leonardo, while surely inspired by that sculpture, takes his smile from there to give it quite a different function and meaning. In

it we may truly say that Leonardo's progress through the contents of painting is concluded. From the portrayal of childhood and maternal sentiment in the youthful *Madonnas*, to the moods and movement of the *Adoration*, to the dramatic and choral synthesis of the *Last Supper*, he reaches a reconsideration of the individual personality in the *portraits*. At this point Leonardo had to find the formal expression of man's attitude towards the world around him, towards that nature which, though investigated with such attention, still remains largely secret. This mixed feeling of confidence and uncertainty can only be expressed in the face: and expression in the face is the smile. Not a total smile, of irresistible joy or hilarity, for that would not express the doubts hidden in the human spirit; but rather a smile filled with irony and intelligence, aware of the boundaries of human knowledge; a smile, finally, where Leonardo's concept of the world is reflected in its entirety. And in this limited expression of human feeling the artist succeeds in synthesizing man's attitude towards what is around him: a universal expression, therefore, since it is largely valid even today.

The cartoon with Saint Anne

Drawn in charcoal with touches of paint, this cartoon is now in the National Gallery in London, moved there in 1966 from the Royal Academy, which had owned it at least since 1791. In 1763 the cartoon had been bought in Venice from the Sagredo family by the brother of the English ambassador resident there, Robert Udny. Critics seem to agree on the date of 1498 for the work, at the end of Leonardo's first period in Milan. The group is conceived and realized in a single block, where varying emotions are, however, concentrated, thus inspiring different interpretations of the work. The concatenation of emotions is reflected immediately in the attitudes of the figures, all of them possessing an inner movement, so that the whole group seems to rotate and to communicate, in this writhing, the intensity of the feelings it expresses. Saint Anne's energy, the Virgin's heartfelt sweetness, the Child's grave awareness and the devoted attention of the young Baptist find their synthesis in the compactness of the pyramidal composition. No painting was made from this cartoon. Bernardino Luini, adding Saint Joseph, painted a canvas from it, the *Holy Family*, now in the Pinacoteca Ambrosiana, Milan.

69. Cartoon with St Anne
159 x 101 cm
London, National Gallery

La Gioconda

Only the fame of the *Last Supper*, as we have seen, can be compared with that of this portrait, unconditionally celebrated for centuries. After painting it, Leonardo kept it for himself; then it passed directly to Francis I of France, and from him to the Louvre Museum, where it remains today. Scholars generally feel it was painted in Florence around 1503, but there is little agreement about the identity of the subject. Many critics accept the tradition, based on Vasari's report, that the sitter is *Monna Lisa*, wife of Francesco del Giocondo, a Florentine citizen. We must add, however, that this identification clashes with other, later observations of the painting. Since definitive documentation is lacking, in any case, a tradition with the authority of centuries behind it may be safely considered. The portrait's structure surpasses, in one bound, the Antonello scheme noted in earlier works in the genre. Here the subject is seen at half-length, seated, slightly turned, gazing towards the spectator. The background is no longer a darkness against which the figure stands out sharply; instead we have a landscape, "unreal and dream-like, and yet precise as a map... steeped in dampness and dissolved mists" (Ottino Della Chiesa). This is certainly the synthesis of Leonardo's landscape and topographical studies, carried out also for public works (the project for altering the course of the Arno with a canal, and the consequent flooding of the Valdichiana, led the artist to draw many maps of the region between the Tyrrhenian Sea and the Appenines). The fascination of this painting, apart from the familiar observations on the mystery of the smile and the charm of the young woman, is all too well-known and has given rise to hundreds of fantastic hypotheses. We can definitely state, however, that its true fascination lies in the perfect correspondence of expression between the person portrayed and the nature which serves as background, achieved by the "sfumato" technique. The unquestionable sense of irony in the young woman's face, which becomes a universal view of man's attitude towards nature, is thus fused with the execution of the landscape, synthesizing the grandeur of a world that man is in the process of discovering and interpreting. But much is still left unexpressed, in mystery. Leonardo therefore overcomes the eternal dilemma between the idea and its realization, because he places painting at the service of his conceptual meditations, and painting is at once an expressive and a visualizing medium. Moreover, moment by moment, he checks his pictorial technique against his concept of the world: "The image, before reaching the painter's hands, must undergo a long gestation in his spirit" (Marinoni). We can rightly say, in conclusion, that in the execution of *La Gioconda*, Leonardo succeeds in expressing fully this higher demand of his intellect and of his art. This harmony endows the work with its greatness and value.

70. *La Gioconda*
77 x 53 cm
Paris, Louvre

Saint Anne

On the subject of the Virgin and Child with Saint Anne Leonardo had already reflected in his Milanese period, when he prepared the cartoon with these figures, now in the National Gallery in London. But, as we said above, he never translated this cartoon into a painting. The painting we are considering here is neither a version nor a derivation of that earlier idea. Here the structure is autonomous, and also the conceptual significance differs considerably. Against the background of a circle of mountains emerging from mists, as if they were painfully taking shape from the chaos before the Creation, there rises the pyramidal group of Saint Anne, the Virgin, and the Infant Jesus, with a lamb, the symbol of his future sacrifice. The barely perceptible smiles of the faces are the only expression of feeling in the whole painting, which is actually an anthology of very beautiful parts (the mountains, the holy group, the tree on the right), not closely related to one another. We are far from the vibrant, loving colloquy of the London cartoon; still, in the tense movement of the Madonna, drawing the Child towards her, as he seems to want to elude her and play with the lamb, we find a typical Leonardo element, the depiction of movement closely involved in the structure of the group: a conceptual invention of extraordinary originality which did not fail to inspire later artists.

The work, unfinished, was almost certainly executed by Leonardo with the assistance of pupils during his stay in Florence in 1508, when he was commissioned to paint the panel for the main altar of the Santissima Annunziata. This painting, along with the notebooks and other works, went to Francesco Melzi when the master died. It was found by the French in 1629-30 at Casale Monferrato during the war for Mantua. It has been displayed in the Paris museum since 1810. Numerous copies of it are familiar, by pupils in Leonardo's circle and also by painters rather far from his school (even Flemish artists). The composition was recalled by the generation that followed Leonardo: we have only to think of the many *Madonnas* of Raphael and of the *Holy Family* (or *Doni Tondo*) of Michelangelo, which retain the figurative scheme of this *Saint Anne*, a further proof of the immediate interest and attention that each work of Leonardo's aroused as it appeared.

73. Study for the head of St Anne
Windsor, Royal Library

74. Virgin and Child with St Anne, detail
Paris, Louvre

Saint John the Baptist

From dark shadows this disturbing figure seems to advance painfully; the reed cross held to his chest and the animal skin which partially covers his body tell us that he is Saint John the Baptist, the Paraclete. The forefinger of his right hand is upraised, pointing to heaven, and this gesture is another element in the saint's iconography. He has come to preach penitence, to "prepare the way" for the coming of the Messiah. The face is a sharp oval, almost faun-like, framed by a cascade of curls underlined by glints of light; on the face there is an enigmatic, allusive smile, certainly unusual in the portrayal of the ascetic prophet who lived in the desert and nourished himself with locusts and wild honey. Mystery is the key word in describing this picture, surely one of Leonardo's last, to judge by its style and its expressive scope. The sources do not refer to it as a Baptist. Vasari speaks of an "angel" in the Medici collections, which he attributes to Leonardo, and the description coincides amazingly with the appearance of this Saint John. After a stay of about a hundred years in England, the panel has always been part of the collection of the rulers of France, so it cannot be the work described by Vasari. It may have been redone or transformed by the master himself or by pupils. Scholars have thus suggested that Leonardo may originally have conceived and begun an Annunciation angel, then developed it into this extraordinary figure, which undoubtedly arouses a feeling of uneasiness in the spectator rather than unconditioned admiration. And yet, in it we can discern the same spirit of problematical irony present in *La Gioconda*, expressed here, however, without the mediation of a landscape which can absorb it into a vaster system of relationships between man and nature. Therefore the *Saint John* seems more unpleasant and ambiguous to the eyes of those who observe it. In any event, the work belongs to Leonardo's production beyond a shadow of a doubt. And, as far as conception is concerned, it is the most modern of the master's works because in this figure he synthesizes all his conceptual investigation of the expression of feelings and human nature, and gives us an image charged with symbolism and allusions, purposely remaining on the boundary-line between mystery and reality. The fascination that contemporaries felt in this work is proved by the numerous copies and versions which are still preserved. Scholars place the painting in the last years of Leonardo's Roman period or the beginning of his French period (1514-1516).

75. St John the Baptist
69 x 57 cm
Paris, Louvre

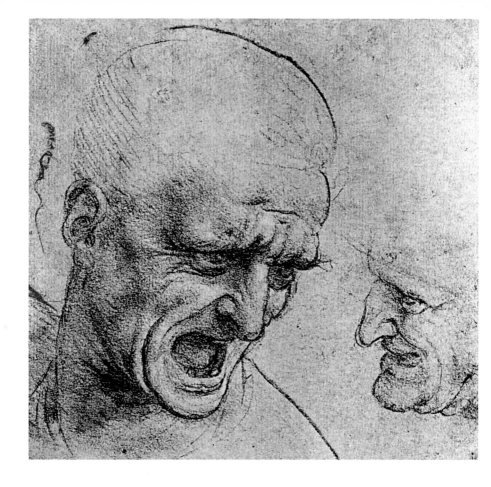

Violence and old age

Parallel to his production of paintings, Leonardo made a copious series of drawings, which fill the pages of his notebooks. Most of them — as we have indicated — illustrate all sorts of machinery, to be used in many branches of human activity, along with studies of a scientific nature, such as those connected with his research in mathematics, music, anatomy and botany. But there are also drawings that cannot be placed in a specific category; they are rather images that reflect Leonardo's intellectual investigations and, better than any other document, they serve to portray his personality. In these documents we discover the artist's mental quirks, his special meditations which found, with him, a literary as well as a figurative form. There are, for example, his so-called "prophecies", which solemnly adumbrate objects, animals and everyday actions. Similarly, there are drawings of allegories or representations of human figures like the *seated old man*, which lead us, with immediacy, to Leonardo's meditations on old age, and give us concretely a notion of what the artist was mentally developing,

76. *Drawing of heads, probably a study for the Battle of Anghiari*
Budapest, National Museum

77. *Copy from Leonardo*
Battle of Anghiari
Florence, Uffizi

realizing in practice the principle that — in his view — made painting coincide with philosophy, with the concept of the world in its physical and spiritual aspects. Towards the end of his life thoughts and figurative depictions of an apocalyptical character seem to predominate. This tendency of Leonardo's can be interpreted in various ways. Perhaps these are the normal reflections of a man well along in years, pondering death, but extending his thoughts to the broader theme of the end of the world and of mankind. Or perhaps he recalled, like an obsessive burden, his disappointment at works left unfinished, or lost through his constant search for new artistic techniques. An exemplary, significant instance among the works of Leonardo that were not completed is the *Battle of Anghiari*. It is significant, naturally, not only because of its fate, but also because it allowed the artist to deal with the theme of violence and human cruelty for the first time from the figurative point of view. Like the parallel *Battle of Càscina* assigned to Michelangelo, this work was commissioned by the Gonfaloniere of the Florentine Republic, Pier Soderini, in August 1504, to decorate one of the walls of what was then the Grand Council Chamber in the Palazzo della Signoria. Many of Leonardo's drawings are of clashes among mounted warriors and furious fighting among armed men. No doubt he conceived slowly his idea for the depiction of the battle in the fresco, whose central theme was the struggle for possession of the banner. Scrupulously recorded by documents, the painting was applied to the wall in 1505. But the technique with which it was executed required heat in order to dry it out. Fires were lighted in the hall, but the excessive size of the chamber did not allow a homogeneous effect, and as a result a part of the painted surface melted.

We can form an idea of the central part of the cartoon from the various copies that have been preserved. Among them there is one from a drawing of Rubens. It is a formidable conflict — fighting for the war-banner — among four horsemen and three foot-soldiers. For the first time in Leonardo, the expressions have been distorted to the limit of the hu-

man features' possibilities; rolling eyes, mouths opened wide in shouts meant to frighten the enemy or incite the shouter himself. The eyes of the horses also are charged with fury, and the hoofs are interwoven as the animals participate in the struggle, as if a sudden madness swept all away in its power, uniting man and beast in its irrational violence.

It seems almost impossible that the artist of *La Gioconda*, with its refined sense of measure expressed also in the subtle hint of irony, could have conceived such a terrifying scene. But we know that all of Leonardo's concepts move from a wider base, which is organized in a universal system. In it there is also room, then, for the category of violence and death. We refer to another work, whose poor state of preservation may have contributed to its loss: the *Leda*, which we know only through some preparatory drawings and derivative paintings of followers. It must be added to the number of Leonardo's works of art we no longer posses and — though it is not connected with the theme we are discussing — we mention it in the list of absences from the master's catalogue.

We know that thoughts of death and meditations

78, 79. *Drawings of cataclysms*
Windsor, Royal Library

80. *Drawing of a seated old man*
Windsor, Royal Library

81. *Map of Arezzo and the Valdichiana*
Windsor, Royal Library

82. *Study of trees*
Windsor, Royal Library

on catastrophes accompanied the artist in his late activity also from the drawings of cosmic disasters on pages 12378 and 12383 of the Leonardo collection in Windsor. In the first, a whirlwind of exceptional proportions seems to strike, at the same moment, an inhabited city and the rocky mountain that dominates it, as well as the sky itself. All are overwhelmed together, creating a kind of immense explosion. In the second drawing, after every trace of human habitation has disappeared, the sea and sky are racked by a tempest of prodigious force, which no element can resist. A kind of Last Judgment, the world's last day, with only the forces of nature,

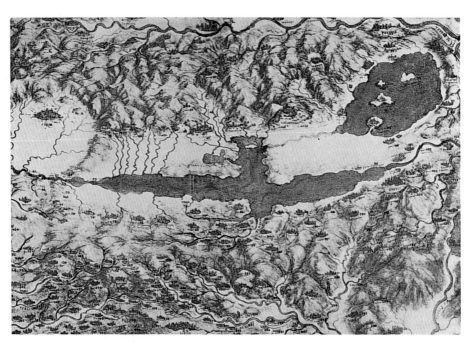

238

which manage to find an autonomous principle and a harmony even in this extreme destruction.

In coherence with the principle that the figurative image has the function of philosophical exposition, Leonardo then entrusted to the image the task of expressing his own concept of cosmic destruction: an equality of elements that fatally coincides with absolute harmony. It therefore begins and concludes the story of creation. Leonardo's system could not have a more logical conclusion. Then the eternal sleep could also enshroud the man whose sage's eyes and intellect, as he has left them for us in his *Self-portrait* — at once serene and severe — better than anyone else had investigated the mysteries of the world and its laws, man and his feelings; and in the most sublime way had known how to express and communicate them to others through his art.

83. Drawing with self-portrait
Turin, National Library

MICHELANGELO

Michelangelo Buonarroti

Michelangelo lived and worked for nearly a century: he was born in 1475, was apprenticed to Domenico Ghirlandaio in 1488 and worked continuously until six days before his death, in 1564. It was during these turbulent years that the medieval aspects of the Christian religion were swept away, especially by the violent surge of the Reformation; that the Polish astronomer Copernicus revealed to his contemporaries the true position of the earth in a heliocentric system; that men liberated themselves from the ways of thought of medieval Scholasticism to become spiritually free and independent individuals. No other artist managed, as Michelangelo did, to portray this change in his works, and no other man lived this change as intensely as he did. "But he who bears the palm from all, whether of the living or the dead; he who transcends and eclipses every other, is the divine Michelangelo Buonarroti, who takes the first place, not in one of these arts only, but in all the three. This master surpasses and excels not only all those artists who have well nigh surpassed nature herself, but even all the most famous masters of antiquity, who did, beyond all doubt, vanquish her most gloriously: he alone has triumphed over the later as over the earlier, and even over nature herself . . . ".

Giorgio Vasari, contemporary and friend of Michelangelo's, described him like this. Through his words of praise we can discern the major trends and objectives of the period we call Renaissance, and those of its later artistic form, Mannerism. Artists, philosophers and princes, each in his own field, began to contribute to the expression of a perfect terrestrial reality. They represented it as spiritually independent, standing in opposition to the supernatural or divine reality, upon which all medieval values had been based. These ideals of earthly perfection found their only precedent and model in the actions and works of the Classical masters. Thus, in all spheres of life, the Renaissance man tried to imitate the ancients, to accomplish once more the deeds of their heroes and to adopt their most typical qualities.

Michelangelo was born on the sixth of March, 1475 at Caprese, in Tuscany, the son of a civil servant of low rank. Part of his childhood was spent in Florence, part in the family country house outside the city. When he was six years old his mother died. For many years Michelangelo virtually boasted of the fact that his family had belonged for centuries to one of the uppermost classes of the city, according to their registration with the census. However, pursuing Platonic ideals, he never lived flamboyantly, never married and, unlike most of his contemporary fellow-artists, never tried to better his social position. For the best part of his life he cared above all for his father and his four brothers; it was only for a short period of time that, already in his sixties, he began to give importance to serious friendships, such as his relationship with Tommaso Cavalieri and Vittoria Colonna.

1. *Copy from the Tribute Money by Masaccio*
Munich, Graphische Sammlungen

2. *Copy from the "Sagra del Carmine" by Masaccio*
Vienna, Albertina

3. *Head of an Old Man*
Florence, Gabinetto dei Disegni e delle Stampe, Uffizi

4. *Madonna of the Stairs*
55.5 × 40 cms.
Florence, Casa Buonarroti

5. *Battle of the Centaurs*
84.5 × 90.5 cms.
Florence, Casa Buonarroti

6. *Crucifix*
135 × 135 cms.
Florence, Casa Buonarroti

Early period in Florence: 1475-1494

In 1488, when Michelangelo was 13 years old, his father apprenticed him to the *bottega* or workshop of the celebrated painter Domenico Ghirlandaio. But the following year Lorenzo de' Medici summoned him to his court and allowed him free access to his gardens, where the supervision of the precious collection of classical statues had been entrusted to the ageing Bertoldo di Giovanni, former pupil of Donatello. More or less teaching himself, the boy mastered the technical skills essential to his craft. He fashioned clay and practised drawing by copying earlier works, such as the Masaccio fresco of the *Tribute Money,* showing with what certainty of intuition he was able to choose those works which would help him develop his innate qualities.

In those years Lorenzo's circle was composed of the most famous poets, philosophers and artists of the time. One could believe that this environment had a strong influence on the boy, although it is difficult to assume that he ever seriously took part in this intellectual community. However, the two bas-reliefs created during this period persuade us of the contrary. The suggestion for the relief representing the *Battle of the Centaurus,* a subject taken from Greek mythology, probably came from Poliziano, who might have read and translated the corresponding literary passages to the young sculptor. The only essential element in this primordial combat is the naked human body, caught in moments of utmost strain or of perfect feminine beauty. Everywhere, round and swollen shapes rise up, moving out of the ground, one by one, to overcut each other and then only to sink back down into the depths again. Even the rocks and the clubs, the only weapons the fighters are given, are rounded. No geometric order and not even the force of gravi-

245

ty seem to rule over these figures and this action. Man alone with the strength of his body and the determination of his courage sets the terms of this chaotic struggle.

The representation of the *Madonna of the Stairs*, in its technique of the flattened relief, appears immeasurably different. On a smooth and flat surface of rock the Madonna sits serene yet monumental. She hardly seems to notice the Child curled up in her arms, taking her milk. Her intangible look, indifferent not only to the children on the stairs in the background but also to the onlooker, projects itself away onto something indefinable: it seems to gaze at a divine image. Here Michelangelo presents us with a "grand" human being, seen as an individual entity perfectly composed in its own right, while in the *Battle of the Centaurs* we had men in a deadly entanglement struggling for the posses-

sion of women. The sixteen year-old artist thus portrayed the two extremes of human experience and all this with a single means of representation: man and his body.

We learn from our sources that in 1494 Michelangelo presented the parish priest of Santo Spirito with a wooden crucifix: "in order to receive many favours from him, in order to be allowed a room to work in and bodies to study, for he could imagine nothing which would give him more pleasure."

Alas, we do not know this work: the crucifix reproduced here is perhaps the one which, amongst all the ones handed down to us, resembles it most.

First success in Bologna and Rome: 1494-1501

At the death of Lorenzo il Magnifico in 1492, Michelangelo returned to his father's home. It was in that same year that Savonarola began his violent sermons in the Dominican convent of San Marco in Florence. Contemporary sources tell us how attentively Michelangelo read the writings of this fanatically religious monk and what an impression they made on him; in a letter written in 1498 from Rome he himself expresses his worries over the per-

ils the monk might run into. These worries were justified, since Savonarola was burnt at the stake a short while later. Not long before the French king, Charles VIII, drove the Medici family out of Florence in 1494, Michelangelo took refuge in Venice and later in Bologna, the Medici having been his patrons. In Bologna he received a commission from the aristocrat Aldovrandi to complete the *Tomb of St. Dominic*, which had been begun two centuries

7. *Saint Petronio*
h. 64 cms.
Bologna, San
Domenico

8. *Saint Procolo*
h. 58.5 cms.
Bologna, San
Domenico

9. *Angel Holding a*
Candelabra
h. 51.5 cms.
Bologna, San
Domenico

previously by Nicola Pisano's workshop. There were three statues still missing, representing the patron saint of the city, *Saint Petronius, Saint Proculus,* and an *Angel Holding a Candelabra*. Michelangelo cannot have been very much allured by this commission; yet these small statues, the first free standing works of his that we have, in the distribution of movement, in their powerful poses, and in the assurance of their shapes, anticipate the genuine passion of his later works.

At the age of 21 the artist went to Rome for the first time. We still possess two of the works he created in this period; others must have been lost for

he spent five years there. The earlier one, a statue of *Bacchus,* was begun in 1497; it was commissioned by the banker Iacopo Galli for his garden and he wanted it fashioned after "the models of the ancients." According to a contemporary, it was a work "the form and aspect of which correspond, in every detail, to the intentions of the Ancients."

The body of this drunken and staggering god gives, at the same time, an impression both of youthfulness and of femininity. Vasari says that this strange blending of effects is the characteristic of the Greek god Dionysus. But in Michelangelo's experience, sensuality of such a divine nature has a drawback for man: in his left hand the god holds with indifference a lionskin, the symbol of death, and a bunch of grapes, the symbol of life, from which a Faun is feeding. Thus we are brought to realize, in a sudden way, what significance this miracle of pure sensuality has for man: living only for a short while he will find himself in the position of the faun, caught in the grasp of death, the lionskin.

In the *Pietà*, Michelangelo approached a subject which until then had been given form mostly north of the Alps, where the portrayal of pain had always been connected with the idea of redemption: it was called the *Vesperbild* and represented the seated Madonna holding Christ's body in her arms. But now the twenty-three year-old artist presents us with an image of the Madonna with Christ's body never attempted before. Her face is youthful, yet beyond time; her head leans only slightly over the lifeless body of her son lying in her lap. "The body of the Dead Christ exhibits the very perfection of research in every muscle, vein, and nerve. No corpse could more completely resemble the dead than does this. There is a most exquisite expression in the countenance. The veins and pulses, moreover, are indicated with so much exactitude, that one cannot but marvel how the hand of the artist should in a short time have produced such a divine work."

One must take these words of Vasari's about the

10. *Bacchus*
Detail of the faun
Florence, Museo Nazionale del Bargello

11. *Bacchus*
h. 203 cms.
Florence, Museo Nazionale del Bargello

"divine beauty" of the work in the most literal sense, in order to understand the meaning of this composition. Michelangelo convinces both himself and us of the divine quality and the significance of these figures by means of earthly beauty, perfect by human standards and therefore divine. We are here face to face not only with pain as a condition of redemption, but rather with absolute beauty as one of its consequences.

12. *Pietà*
h. 174 cms.
Vatican

13. *Pietà*
Detail of the Virgin
Vatican

14. *Madonna of Bruges*
h. 128 cms.
Bruges, Notre-Dame

15. *Doni Tondo*
diam. 120 cms.
Florence, Uffizi

At the service of the Florentine Republic: 1501-1505

On the 4th of August 1501, after many years of political chaos, Florence was declared a Republic, and a friend of Michelangelo's, Piero Soderini, was elected life gonfaloniere, a position of high governmental importance in Florence in those years. It is most likely that Michelangelo was never, in any other period of his life, so unconditionally in agreement with the political order of his native city as in the following four years. This caused him to express his political leanings in his works in such a way as he only rarely did in later years.

Twelve days after the Declaration of the Republic, he was commissioned to create the *David* by the Arte della Lana, the very rich Guild of Wool Merchants who were responsible for the upkeep and the decoration of the Cathedral. For this purpose,

he was given a block of marble which Agostino di Duccio had already attempted to fashion forty years previously, perhaps with the same subject in mind. Michelangelo breaks away from the traditional way of representing David. He does not present us with the winner, the giant's head at his feet and the powerful sword in his hand, but portrays the youth in the phase immediately preceding the battle: perhaps he has caught him just in the moment when he has heard that his people are hesitating, and he sees Goliath jeering and mocking them. The artist places him in the most perfect "contraposto", as in the most beautiful Greek representations of heroes. The right-hand side of the statue is smooth and composed, while the left side, from the outstretched foot all the way up to the disheveled hair,

16. *Pitti Tondo*
85.5 × 82 cms.
Florence, Museo Nazionale del
Bargello

17. *Taddei Tondo*
diam. 109 cms.
London, Royal Academy

18. *Pitti Tondo*
Detail of the Virgin
Florence, Museo Nazionale del
Bargello

is openly active and dynamic. The muscles and the tendons are developed only to the point where they can still be interpreted as the perfect instrument for a strong will, and not to the point of becoming individual self-governing forms. Once the statue was completed, a committee of the highest ranking citizens and artists decided that it must be placed in the main square of the town, in front of the Palazzo Vecchio, the Town Hall. It was the first time since antiquity that a large statue of a nude was to be exhibited in a public place. This was only allowed thanks to the action of two forces, which by a fortunate chance complemented each other: the force of an artist able to create, for a political community, the symbol of its highest political ideals, and, on the other hand, that of a community which understood the power of this symbol. "Strength" and "Wrath" were the two most important virtues, characteristic of the ancient patron of the city Hercules. Both these qualities, passionate strength and wrath, were embodied in the statue of David.

In 1504, after the completion of the *David*, the Republic commissioned Michelangelo with a new great task: he was to paint on the left wall of the large Council Hall a representation of *The Battle of Cascina*. In 1503 Leonardo had already been commissioned to paint a fresco of *The Battle of Anghiari* on the right wall and Michelangelo could not remain indifferent to the fame and skill of this great artist, 23 years his senior. So he decided at first to follow the example of Leonardo's drawings and to paint the scene of a battle of cavalry. But later he changed his mind and decided to portray the Florentine soldiers as they bathed in the Arno on the eve of battle: according to the story of a contemporary chronicler, it was not until they were warned by a more alert companion that they began to prepare themselves, in the nick of time, for what was to be a victorious battle.

Michelangelo's years in Florence brought him, in addition to these large and important tasks, also a series of private commissions, such as the *Madonna of Bruges* which, originally, may have been created for the Piccolomini Altar of the Cathedral in Siena. The old theme of the Mother and Child is seen here in a new grouping: Mary sits in an absolutely vertical position, peaceful and dignified, and her face shows the serious yet mild characteristics of Leonardo's women. The Child, on the other hand, is presented in a free and loose attitude, leaning against the Madonna's raised knee, almost like an ancient "putto" or little angel. He has got down from his mother's lap, thus acquiring remarkable independence. We no longer have the divine intimacy of Mother and Child: in fact, there is almost a slight contrast between the grave beauty of the

19, 20. David
h. 410 cms.
Florence, Galleria dell'Accademia

261

young woman and the youthful grace and mobility of the divine Child.

In the *Tondo Pitti* Michelangelo placed, next to the stern Madonna, a Child whose pose recalls that of ancient funeral genii. Thus the overall effect, despite the apparently playful attitude of the Child, is deeply serious, and the Madonna has an almost prophetic force, because of her size, which bursts out from the frame of the relief.

If one looks at the series of works so far discussed and understands the development of the artist, it becomes impossible to think of the *Tondo Doni* as the "exercise of a carpenter," as one critic proclaimed. Mary is on her knees in front of the richly clothed legs of St. Joseph and holds out to him, upon her right shoulder, the Child, whom Joseph has already grasped by the left hand. The way the Madonna looks up at the Child is both loving and worshipping. St. Joseph, who, in the works of other artists, is often an embarassed, secondary figure, here crowns the group with his powerful head. Could it perhaps be acceptable to interpret this Joseph as God the Father, the real Father of Jesus Christ and the one to Whom he must return?

Of all Michelangelo's representations of the Madonna, the *Tondo Taddei* is perhaps the most dynamic of them all. The Child, according to the model of an ancient sarcophagus representing a son of Medea in flight, is presented in an attitude of frightened escape when faced with a flapping bird which the childish St. John is showing him. This model blending of classical antiquity and nature, totally in agreement with the aesthetic theories of the time, gives this relief a grace in rendering the instantaneous event which is unusual for the artist.

The last commission which Michelangelo received during these happy four years spent in Florence, was a collection of the twelve Apostles for the niches of the Choir of the Cathedral, which he began in 1503. Although we have the drawing for another statue, *St. Matthew* was the only one he managed to complete before the contract was annulled when he moved to Rome.

21. *Saint Paul*
h. 127 cms.
Siena, Cathedral

22. *Saint Peter*
h. 124 cms.
Siena, Cathedral

23. *Saint Matthew*
h. 271 cms.
Florence, Galleria
dell'Accademia

*24. Study for the
Sistine Ceiling
London, British Museum*

*25. Sistine Chapel
Vatican*

Michelangelo and Pope Julius II: 1505-1513

When, by the will of Pope Julius della Rovere (1503-1513), Michelangelo went to Rome in March 1505, he realized, in the course of a year, how different in every way the atmosphere of the papal court was from that of his own native city. The Pope received him with a truly imperial commission: to build in the course of five years and for the sum of 10,000 ducats, a tomb for the Pope. Forty life-sized statues were to surround the tomb, which was to be 23 feet wide, 36 feet 3 inches deep and 26 feet 4 inches high; it was to be a free-standing tomb and to contain an oval funerary cell. Never, since classical times, had anything like this, in the West, been built for one man alone.

According to the iconographic plan, which we are able to reconstruct from written sources, this was to be an outline of the Christian world: the lower level was dedicated to man, the middle level to the prophets and saints graced with Divine Bliss, and the top level to the surpassing of both former levels in the Last Judgment. Only if we remember this can we understand the "Victories" and the "Slaves" intended for the lower level: the former were female figures with nude men in chains at their feet, the latter were nude men in chains. These are none other than the representations of virtues and the Liberal Arts, but, unlike the customary sixteenth-century portrayals, they are not presented as pure personifications of the highest ideals, but in the form in which men on earth experience them: without freedom and continually struggling against the powers opposing them. *Moses* and St. Paul (never executed) among others, were to have been placed in the middle level, surrounded by representations of examples of the active and contemplative lives. At the summit of the monument, following Giovanni Pisano's example of the tomb of an empress built 200 years previously, there was to have been a portrayal of two angels leading the Pope out of his tomb on the day of the Last Judgment.

Michelangelo immediately began his preparations for this task, but now he was to discover the imperious and capricious character of his patron: the Pope, in doubt of finding an appropriate place in which to erect his tomb, planned something even more grandiose: the restoration and remodelling of St. Peter's. While his mind was occupied with these new projects, he temporarily postponed the execution of the previous ones. Michelangelo tried in vain to obtain a Papal audience, until he was finally thrown out of the palace by a soldier; and on the 17th of April, the day before the first stone of St. Peter's was to be laid, he fled from Rome and, in distress, made his way towards Florence. Fear and bitterness filled his heart during the following two years, while, by order of Julius II, he had to stay in Bologna to complete a most unsatisfying commission. In 1508 he returned to Rome

without, however, being allowed to begin work on the tomb. Another bewildering task was waiting for him. He was to paint the Twelve Apostles and a few ornaments on the ceiling of the Sistine Chapel. He, who had always insisted that he was a sculptor, was thus to learn the art of fresco painting, and practise it on a vault decorated by fifteenth-century artists as a starry sky. However, as he began work on the project the affinity between the Pope and the artist made itself felt as in those earlier weeks when the tomb had first been planned. Julius II allowed himself to be carried away by Michelangelo's creative violence and the two inspired each other in turn with always grander designs for the decoration of the ceiling of the chapel; and the artist's imagination, years earlier stimulated at the idea of constructing the tomb, was finally, even though in a different artistic genre, given free rein. Michelangelo spent the time between then and the 31st of October 1512 painting more than 300 figures on the ceiling of the Sistine Chapel.

Between the lunettes and spandrels depicting Christ's ancestors are the *Prophets* and *Sybils*, who appear to be much larger than they really are. The violence and the power of these figures, however, is not due to their superhuman size, but mostly to

26. *Ceiling of the Sistine Chapel Vatican*

27. *Sistine Chapel The Prophet Zachariah Vatican*

28. Sistine Chapel
The Prophet Jonah
Vatican

29. Sistine Chapel
The Lybian Sibyl
Vatican

their isolation. Each of these figures, in its own way, seems totally enraptured in the spiritual act of contemplation, intuition and ecstasy; they seem the personification of that divine spirit which briefly at times uses them as agents in communicating to other men.

The artist began painting his scenes from the east side of the Chapel and in reverse order of the Bible. The second painting, which, together with the *Sacrifice and Derision of Noah,* belongs to the first phase of the work (before September 1509), represents the *Flood.* Michelangelo has caught the decisive moment in this painting: the last rising of the waters which drives men to the most desperate and extreme efforts. Every detail is dramatic in a simple yet highly effective way. Nevertheless, the themes of love and sacrifice are greatly superior to those of selfishness and of instinctive self-preservation. These human beings seem to yield amidst suffering and pain to a natural catastrophe, rather than to feel threatened and crushed by a punishment for their own evil.

Michelangelo's *Paradise* is not a dazzling garden. Adam and Eve are alone and nothing earthly can

30. Sistine Chapel
The Prophet Joel
Vatican

31. Sistine Chapel
The Creation of Adam, detail
Vatican

attract their attention. Only the Tree of Knowledge worries them, asking them to make a decision, which they are compelled to take together. The woman is no longer the guilty party, but both are guilty to the same extent and are moulded together in an insoluble unity, unable to resist the desire for knowledge.

As he goes on the artist limits himself more and more to fewer and larger figures. The means of representation become more elementary as the events go further back towards the origins of the world. The figure of God in the *Creation of Eve* occupies almost a third of this painting. All its power is gathered into His expression and into His raised hand ordering the woman to rise up from the man's side. In the *Creation of Adam,* God and man appear almost as equals. Adam lies on raised rocks and, lifting himself up slightly, without any show

32. Sistine Chapel
The Creation of Adam
Vatican

33. Sistine Chapel
The Creation of the Heavens, detail
Vatican

34. Sistine Chapel
The Creation of Eve
Vatican

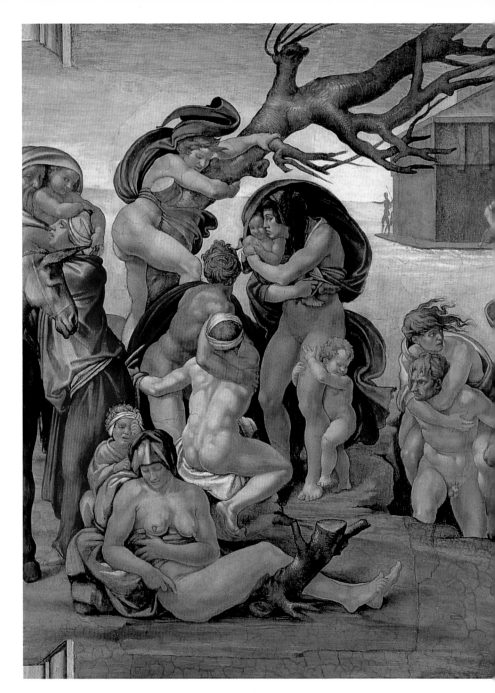

35. *Sistine Chapel*
The Flood
Vatican

36. *Sistine Chapel*
The Fall
Vatican

37. *Sistine Chapel*
Jesse-David-Solomon
lunette
Vatican

of effort he stretches out his arm towards God. He arrives floating in space, His powerful cloak flying about Him, accompanied by angels. When His pure, strong gaze meets the man's longing look, the spark of divinity passes from the pointed finger of His right hand to Adam. Michelangelo does not show us the event of man's creation, but the moment in which man receives his soul, the reward for his desire for divinity. At the right-hand side of the penultimate large scene, reproduced here, the *Creation of the Heavens,* a stormy image of God appears from the depths of space and with a powerful, creative gesture shows the way to the celestial bodies. There was only one more instance to paint: God creating earthly matter and light. One feels that the artist put into this scene all that was known in his time of the ancient myths and the philosophies concerning the creation of the world. With raised arms and spinning with a whirlwind effect, God, the pure spirit, the pure form, unites with primaeval matter to generate the first element.

Soon after the completion of the ceiling of the Sistine Chapel, in 1513, Pope Julius II died. In this same year Michelangelo and the Pope's heirs reached a new agreement concerning the tomb. It was decided that the tomb was to be smaller and placed against a wall. From a copy by Iacopo Rocchetti of a badly preserved drawing of Michelangelo's, we can see what the monument was to have looked like. Michelangelo began work at once on *Moses* and two of the "*Slaves*". His Moses has always been seen as an idealized portrait both of the Pope and of the artist. In fact one must interpret the combination of dignified passion for good and a simple yet powerful strength as the utmost ideal both of the Pope and the artist. The strong vitality and beauty of the *Dying Slave* and the *Rebelling Slave* are certainly enough to lift these statues far above the mark of pure bodily strength and its baseness. The road which Michelangelo had covered from the time when he was allowed to begin had been difficult and painful. Now he had at hand his personal experience for the representation of the Liberal Arts, figures in chains, which he shows us in their earthly semblance, almost like man fighting against destiny.

When Giovanni de' Medici, who had lived in the same house as Michelangelo from 1489 to 1492, was elected Pope in 1513, he too, as his predecessor, decided to take advantage of the artist's talent. In 1516, Michelangelo was so busy working for his new patron that he was forced to sign a new contract with Julius II's heirs for an even smaller tomb. The monument was thus reduced to the depth of a tabernacle, and single female figures were planned to replace the groups of Virtues and Vices. The façade of the lower level, meanwhile completed, was to stay as it was and it is greatly similar to the one finally set up in San Pietro in Vincoli; the upper level, on the other hand, was totally changed apparently as a result of what Michelangelo had learned while making the plans for the Church of San Lorenzo in Florence, which he had been working at since 1515. The construction acquired a new and powerful size: instead of a regular development, characteristic of the fifteenth century, we now have a contraposition of weights and supports, of lower and upper level. The tendency to annul static laws is a symptom of the imminent period of Mannerism, but complete monumentalization is a characteristic of Baroque.

According to his contract, the artist was now allowed to work on the tomb wherever he was. So it is probable that in 1519, in his Florentine studio, he was working at the four so-called "Boboli Slaves," which were to have been placed on the columns of the lower level, in the following order: *Atlas, The Young Slave, The Bearded Slave,* and *The Awakening Slave.* The statues are for the most part unfinished, because the Medici never allowed Michelangelo much time to work on things which had not been commissioned by them. Although these were not completed, each one of them shows once more, as the Louvre *Slaves,* how the artist had wanted to create symbols of man's struggle and his suffering.

In 1525 another plan was designed for the tomb of Julius II and, in 1532, yet another; and each time the size was reduced. It was now to be a simple mural tomb; *Moses* and the two Louvre *Slaves* were to be placed on the lower level, and a Madonna, a prophet and a Sibyl on the upper level. The Boboli *Slaves* were thus cancelled from the plan. It is possible that the statue of *Victory* was begun as early as 1519, but whether it was originally planned as part of the tomb is still uncertain. The strong manneristic features (exaggerated contortions and complex movements) link this figure more with the Boboli *Slaves* than with the later Roman sculptures.

38. Dying Slave
h. 229 cms.
Paris, Louvre

39. Rebelling Slave
h. 215 cms.
Paris, Louvre

40. *Young Slave*
h. 256 cms.
Florence, Galleria dell'Accademia

41. *Bearded Slave*
h. 263 cms.
Florence, Galleria dell'Accademia

◁
*Reconstruction of the first
project (1505) for the tomb of
Julius II*

▷
*Reconstruction of the second
project (1513) for the tomb of
Julius II*

278

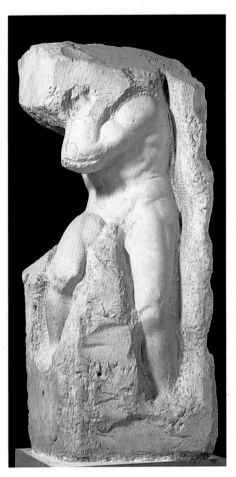

42. *Atlas Slave*
h. 277 cms.
Florence, Galleria dell'Accademia

43. *Awakening Slave*
h. 267 cms.
Florence, Galleria dell'Accademia

◁
Reconstruction of the third
project (1516) for the tomb of
Julius II

▷
Reconstruction of the fifth
project (1532) for the tomb of
Julius II

44. Moses
h. 235 cms.
Rome, San Pietro in
Vincoli

45. Moses, detail
Rome, San Pietro in
Vincoli

46. Project for the
façade of San Lorenzo
Florence, Casa
Buonarroti

47. Christ Carrying the
Cross, detail
h. 205 cms.
Rome, Santa Maria
sopra Minerva

At the service of the Medici Popes: 1513-1534

Even during the pontificate of the Medici Pope
Leo X (1513-1523), political developments gave
Michelangelo no peace. To begin with, the Pope,
whose family were enemies of the Della Rovere,
prevented the artist from continuing the work on
the tomb of Julius II. The design and the execution of the façade of *San Lorenzo* kept him more
or less occupied from 1515 onwards. In 1520, after useless wars, the Pope was forced to renounce
the façade and charged Michelangelo with the task
of building the *Medici Chapel* next to San Lorenzo and, in 1524, the *Laurentian Library*. But these
plans too were interrupted for many years, after
the Medici were driven out of Florence in 1526.
For the last time, Florence was once again declared
a Republic and Michelangelo, in the position of
Governor of the Fortifications, set to work study-

ing new plans of defense. However, treacherous
political schemes aided the return of the Medici and
his plans could never be put into effect.

When, in 1520 and 1521, Michelangelo received
the commission for the Medici Chapel, this task
might have held strictly personal interest for him.
For Leo X wanted to combine the tombs of his
younger brother Giuliano, Duke of Nemours, and
his nephew Lorenzo, Duke of Urbino, with those
of the "Magnifici", Lorenzo and his brother
Giuliano, who had been murdered in 1478; their
tombs were then in the Old Sacristy of San Lorenzo, built by Brunelleschi and decorated by Donatello. In his youth, Michelangelo had been their friend,
and Lorenzo Il Magnifico had been his most important patron.

But the renunciaton of the façade was so great

48. *Madonna and Child*
h. 226 cms.
Florence, New Sacristy of San Lorenzo

49. *Madonna and Child, detail*
Florence, New Sacristy c San Lorenzo

50. *Tomb of Lorenzo de' Medici*
Florence, New Sacristy of San Lorenzo

51. *Tomb of Lorenzo de' Medici*
Detail of Lorenzo
Florence, New Sacristy of San Lorenzo

52. *Tomb of Lorenzo de' Medici*
Detail of Twilight
Florence, New Sacristy of San Lorenzo

53. *Tomb of Lorenzo de' Medici*
Detail of Dawn
Florence, New Sacristy of San Lorenzo

54. Tomb of Giuliano de' Medici
Florence, New Sacristy of San Lorenzo

55. Tomb of Giuliano de' Medici
Detail of Giuliano
Florence, New Sacristy of San Lorenzo

56. Tomb of Giuliano de' Medici
Detail of Night
Florence, New Sacristy of San Lorenzo

57. Tomb of Giuliano de' Medici
Detail of Day
Florence, New Sacristy of San Lorenzo

a disappointment to Michelangelo, that he never really became engrossed in this new task, whatever potential personal importance these tombs might have held for him.

The plans for the Chapel which we still have, show us that his Medici patron allowed Michelangelo a far greater freedom in this task than he was allowed by Julius II in the decoration of the Sistine Chapel. The artist planned the principal group of the Chapel, dedicated to the Resurrection, for the entrance wall; the *Madonna*, as the Lux Aeterna, was to stand above the tomb of the "Magnifici," with the two patron saints of the Medici family, Cosma and Damiano, on either side. Two figures of nude men should have lain at their feet, as personifications of *Rivers*. A representation of Christ's Resurrection had been planned for the lunette crowning the whole of this group. The two candelabra at the altar on the opposite wall represent the pelican as a symbol of self-sacrifice and the Phoenix as a symbol of Resurrection. The tombs of the Dukes on the side walls are highlighted by the faces of the Dukes turned towards the Madonna. The heavy figures of *Night* and *Day, Dawn* and *Twilight* lie on the sarcophagi underneath them. The lunettes above the tombs were to contain

58. New Sacristy with the tomb of Giuliano and the Madonna and Child

59. Reclining Adolescent
h. 54 cms.
Leningrad, Hermitage

scenes from the *Old Testament*.

Not much of this vast plan was in fact carried out, yet it is enough to give us an idea of what Michelangelo's over-all conception must have been. Each of the Dukes' tombs is divided into two areas, and the border is well marked by a projecting cornice. In the lower part are the sarcophagi with the mortal remains of the Dukes, on which lie *Twilight* and *Dawn, Night* and *Day* as the symbol of the vanity of things. Above this temporal area, the nobility of the figures of the Dukes and the subtlety of the richly decorated architecture which surrounds them represent a higher sphere: the abode of the free and redeemed spirit.

The equal importance of the human figure and of architectural elements as means of expression show that Michelangelo had altered his conception of the world as he had expressed it in the ceiling of the Sistine Chapel. There, all the communica-

tion is in the figures: only man seems able to live and personify the highest spiritual experiences. But in the Medici Chapel, the whole "world" seems capable of the utmost beauty, even though it will never be the mortal world, to which we who enter the chapel belong, but it is a higher world, be it that of Christian Redemption or that of Platonic Ideals.

During his life Michelangelo had had the opportunity of knowing both these forms of the human spirit; the one in the Humanist circle of Lorenzo de' Medici, the other, albeit in an extreme form, through the religious teachings of Savonarola. The historical opposition of these forms had become a political topic in the struggle of Savonarola against the Medici; however, the blending of them does not seem to have afforded Michelangelo many difficulties, because his outlook was not so much intellectual, but rather artistic and emotional. In the figures of the *Madonna and Child* above the tomb

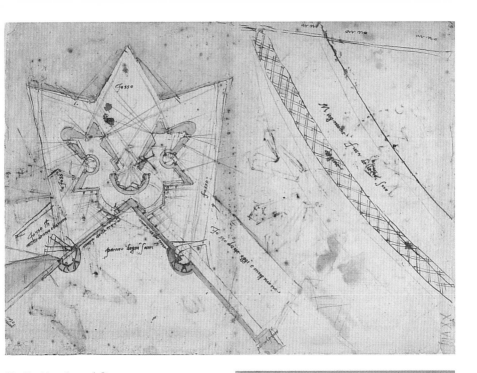

60, 61. *Hercules and Cacus*
h. 41 cms.
Florence, Casa Buonarroti

62. *Study for the fortifications of Porta del Prato*
Florence, Casa Buonarroti

63. *Study for the head of a woman*
Florence, Casa Buonarroti

64. *David/Apollo*
h. 146 cms.
Florence, Museo Nazionale del Bargello

65. *David/Apollo*, detail
Florence, Museo Nazionale del Bargello

66. Staircase of the Laurentian Library
Florence

of the "Magnifici", there is but little human contact, despite their physical closeness: the most glorious of women is moved by the Child in the same way as by the contemplation of the highest Platonic thought, and this seems to transpire from her face.

In 1521, when Michelangelo began this statue, he had only just completed *Christ Carrying the Cross* in the Church of Santa Maria Sopra Minerva; in this work, as in the 1499 *Pietà*, he did not portray pain as redemption in the medieval way, but perfect beauty as the expression of its consequence.

In 1530, the *David/Apollo* was commissioned by the hated Papal Governor of Florence, Baccio Valori. Here Michelangelo used an entirely different approach: pragmatic and political. This figure has had its double name for a long time, since it

DEO
PRAESIDIBVSQ.FAMILIAE DIVIS
CLEMENS VII.MEDICES
PONT.MAX.
LIBRIS OPT.STVDIO MAIORVM
ET SVO VNDIQ.CONQVISITIS
BIBLIOTHECAM
AD ORNAMENTVM PATRIAE AC
CIVIVM IS OB.VTILITATEM
D.D.

was not certain whether it was a representation of the Old Testament hero David or of the Greek God of Art, Apollo. But in the round rock under the youth's foot one can probably recognize the unfinished head of Goliath: so, once again Michelangelo has created a David. There is a blatant difference between this figure and the one which in 1504 rose to the position of the most powerful symbol of the Republic. In the place of Strength and Wrath, we have Melancholy, almost Regret. The victorious hero no longer celebrates his triumph; the blood that has been shed seems to have shown him the meaning of his actions and of its consequences. Michelangelo could not have admonished Baccio Valori in a deeper, more

67. The staircase of the Laurentian Library seen from above

302

68. Laurentian Library
Florence

meaningful and yet more respectful way.

A task quite new in the history of art was entrusted to Michelangelo when the Medici asked him to build the *Laurentian Library*. At first this commission was given little opportunity of development, for the year 1526 marked, for the time being at any rate, the end of the Medici rule. Only four years later was the artist able to continue his work. The columns, deeply set in the walls, with their anthropomorphically gigantic appearance, and the organic élan of the staircase show that, even as an architect, Michelangelo never began from abstract geometrical laws, but only from the human body.

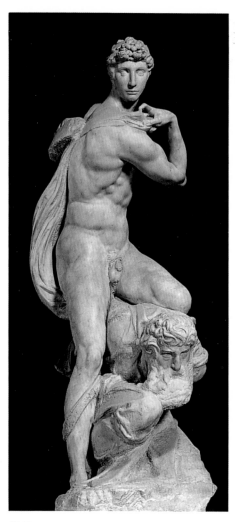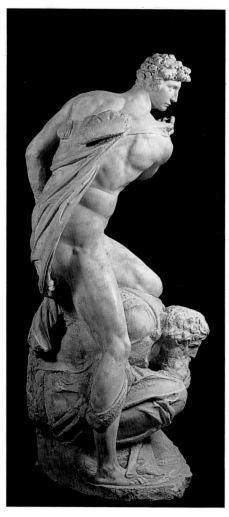

69,70. Victory
h. 261 cms.
Florence, Palazzo Vecchio

Transfer to Rome: 1534-1549

During a brief visit to Rome in 1532, Michelangelo met the young aristocrat Tommaso Cavalieri, whose beauty and nobility won his unconditional love, as is proved by many of his poems of that period. Cavalieri obtained from Michelangelo what the greatest men of the time asked for in vain. The artist prepared for him a series of drawings representing, among other things, *The Rape of Ganymede* and *The Fall of Phaeton;* the first draught of the latter, now in London, both in its composition and the idea of the fatal power with which destiny takes its course, clearly anticipates the fresco of the *Last Judgment.*

This fresco was commissioned by Pope Clement VII (1523-1534) shortly before his death. His successor, Paul III Farnese (1534-1549), forced Michelangelo to a rapid execution of this work, the largest single fresco of the century. The first impression we have when faced with the *Last Judgment* is that of a truly universal event, at the centre of which stands the powerful figure of Christ. His raised right hand compels the figures on the lefthand side, who are trying to ascend, to be plunged down towards Charon and Minos, the Judge of the Underworld; while his left hand is drawing up the chosen people on his right in an

72. Sistine Chapel
Last Judgment
Detail of the
Resurrection of the
Dead
Vatican

73. Sistine Chapel
Last Judgment
Vatican

74. Sistine Chapel
Last Judgment
Detail of Charon
Vatican

75. Sistine Chapel
Last Judgment
Detail of the Damned
Vatican

irresistible current of strength. Together with the planets and the sun, the saints surround the Judge, confined into vast spacial orbits around Him. For this work Michelangelo did not choose one set point from which it should be viewed. The proportions of the figures and the size of the groups are determined, as in the Middle Ages, by their single absolute importance and not by their relative significance. For this reason, each figure preserves its own individuality and both the single figures and the groups need their own background.

The figures who, in the depths of the scene, are rising from their graves could well be part of the prophet Ezechiel's vision. Naked skeletons are covered with new flesh, men dead for immemorable lengths of time help each other to rise from the earth. For the representation of the place of eternal damnation, Michelangelo was clearly inspired by the lines of the Divine Comedy:

Charon the demon, with eyes of glowing coal
Beckoning them, collects them all,
Smites with his oar whoever lingers.

According to Vasari, the artist gave Minos, the Judge of the Souls, the semblance of the Pope's Master of Ceremonies, Biagio da Cesena, who had often complained to the Pope about the nudity of the painted figures. We know that many other figures, as well, are portraits of Michelangelo's contemporaries. The artist's self-portrait appears twice: in the flayed skin which Saint Bartholomew is carrying in his left-hand, and in the figure in the lower left hand corner, who is looking encouragingly at those rising from their graves. The artist could not have left us clearer evidence of his feeling towards life and of his highest ideals.

In 1538, three years before the completion of the Last Judgment, Michelangelo had met Vittoria Colonna. She belonged to the circle of Juan Valdès, who was striving towards an internal reform of the Catholic Church. To put it very simply, one can say that the main conviction of this theological trend was the idea of the utmost need of faith, as opposed to good deeds or sacraments, because, in the last resort, it is only divine grace which is all-powerful. These almost protestant beliefs could not conquer, or in any way change, Michelangelo because too much of his work would have had to be denied. However, they must have to some extent disrupted his firm belief, as he had expressed it in his works, that by creating perfect physical beauty he had represented the essence of the supernatural and of the divine. It is true,

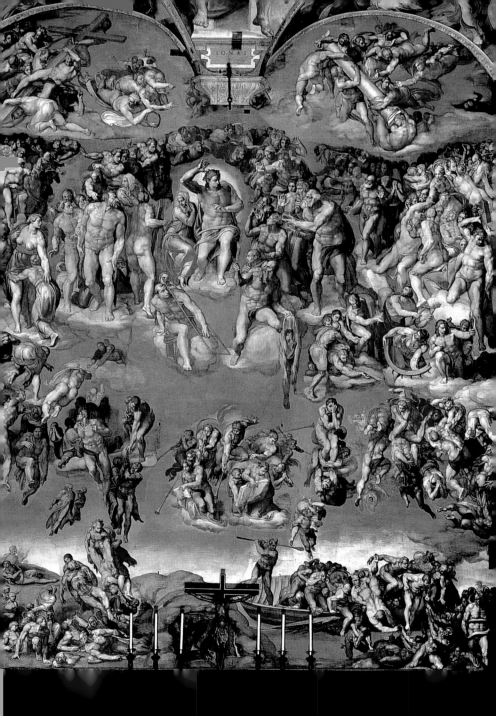

76. *Brutus*
h. 95 cms.
Florence, Museo Nazionale del Bargello

77. *Study for the Colonna Pietà*
Boston, Isabella Stewart Gardner Museum

however, that he felt the need for divine grace, and, from this point onwards, this had great bearing on his creative life. We find evidence of this in a drawing of the *Pietà*, made for Vittoria Colonna. When compared with the 1499 *Pietà*, we see clearly that the main objective is the thought of the Compassionate Christ and of the Redemption through Christ's Blood. The work turns openly towards the onlooker to admonish him, drawing his attention to the sacrifice of Golgotha.

Perhaps Michelangelo's last work of primarily political significance should be dated to the same year as the drawing for it: 1540. This was the bust of *Brutus*, which Michelangelo fashioned for Cardinal Niccolò Ridolfi, who, in 1530, had fled Florence for Rome like many other Florentines; although Michelangelo might well have been thinking of Lorenzino Medici, the well-known "Modern Brutus" who had killed Duke Alessandro de' Medici in 1537, this is clearly an idealized portrait of the patron. In the head, which shows strength of will in the way it is turned to the right, a cold tranquillity and great energy blend fascinatingly with hatred, wrath and bitter contempt.

The date for the completion of Julius II's tomb

(1532) had already passed when yet another contract for another altered plan, which had to be executed in the course of the following three years and in the agreed way, was signed in 1542. By this time converted to new beliefs, Michelangelo was allowed to do away with even the last two slaves. In their stead he created two new statues: *Rachel,* the symbol of contemplative life, and *Leah,* the symbol of active life. In this work we see that his original idea of the structure of the Christian world had, in 40 years, undergone a profound change; it had become a religious monument with Moses, the predecessor of Peter and all Popes in the middle, and supported on either side by the personifications of Faith (*Rachel*) and of Active Love (*Leah*).

Between 1537 and 1540, Antonio da Sangallo the Younger built the Pauline Chapel in the Vatican, as the Pope's private chapel. In 1541, Michelangelo was asked to decorate the central parts of the two longer walls with two frescoes. The first, *The Conversion of Saint Paul,* was begun in 1542; the second, the *Martyrdom of Saint Peter,* was painted between 1546 and 1550. Before this, no one had ever attempted to place these two themes next to each other. In fact, the

78. Model of a River
God
Florence, Casa
Buonarroti

79. Tomb of Julius II
Rome, San Pietro in
Vincoli

first edition of Vasari's *Lives* (1550) says that Michelangelo would paint, as a counterpart to the *Conversion*, the *Giving of the Keys*. According to the figurative traditions of the time, this subject would have been far more logical, but Michelangelo portrays what is by this time his plan of life: death

for the faith must follow conversion and be its confirmation. To Paul, who has fallen and has been forced to shut his eyes because of the brilliance of divine light, he gives his own face and makes Peter, nailed to the cross, in the supreme tension of the last moment of life, forcefully look at the spectator.

During these years the artist was given the most important architectural tasks of his career. In Rome he completed for the Pope the third storey, looking on to the courtyard, and the cornice, of the *Palazzo Farnese* and, still for Paul III, planned the remodelling of the Campidoglio, which was executed only years later. But his nomination to the post of Chief Architect of *Saint Peter's* was undoubtedly the most important task for Michelangelo, so important that it prevented him from returning to Florence before his death. Despite the doubts he had had, he took up Bramante's original plan of a central building, after the new construction had begun in 1505, but he simplified it in accordance with his own development since the beginning of the century. This one can outline in his works through the different plans for Julius II's tomb. Before 1564, the date of Michelangelo's death, only the drum of the dome with its gigantic and monumental row of double columns, so vital to the effect the building makes to the general view of the city, was completed.

80. Tomb of Julius II
Detail of Rachel
Rome, San Pietro in Vincoli

81. Tomb of Julius II
Detail of Leah
Rome, San Pietro in Vincoli

82. The dome of
St. Peter's
Vatican

83. Original wood
model for the dome of
St. Peter's
Vatican Museums

84. Section of the
wood model for the
dome of St. Peter's
Vatican Museums

85. Interior of the
dome of St. Peter's
Vatican

The late period: 1549-1564

After he had been converted, under the influence of Vittoria Colonna, death became a dominant theme in Michelangelo's poetry. Even his last sculptures — two or three Pietàs — deal with this theme, and some of them were probably planned to decorate his tomb. According to Vasari, the artist's wish was to be buried in Santa Maria Maggiore in Rome, at the feet of the *Pietà* on which he had worked between 1547 and 1553; this was before he smashed it in 1555, because one leg had broken off and because the block of marble was defective. This *Pietà*, which is now in the Cathedral of Flor-

ence, was begun the year of Vittoria Colonna's death. After having broken the statue, he let his servant take the pieces. Later the servant sold them and the new owner had it reconstructed following Michelangelo's models, so that the work has been preserved for us.

Michelangelo, in this *Pietà*, did not portray any precise historical moment; instead he erected a personal admonishment to himself, "One does not think how much blood it costs." He had once written this line, from the *Divine Comedy,* on the drawing for the *Pietà* which he did for Vittoria Colon-

86. *Conversion of Saint Paul*
Vatican, Pauline Chapel

87. *Crucifixion of Saint Peter*
Vatican, Pauline Chapel

na, and from the composition of this drawing he took this marble group. Nicodemus has taken the place of the Madonna and she, with Mary Magdalen now does what the angels did, supports the body. There is no longer only the Mother, but three people are now surrounding the Body, and Christ's "deadness" is expressed more effectively by the falling movement in which he is caught halfway. The figures are not isolated from the emaciated dead body: they are blended, in their fear, desperation and pain, into a single setting. The bodies are denied any independent power and there is nothing, like the Madonna's act of prayer in the drawing for Vittoria Colonna, to point to a higher meaning of this suffering, such as redemption.

About half a century separates this work from the *Pietà* in Saint Peter's: almost fifty years of ar-

88. *Pietà*
h. 226 cms.
*Florence, Opera del
Duomo*

89. *Palestrina Pietà*
h. 253 cms.
*Florence, Galleria
dell'Accademia*

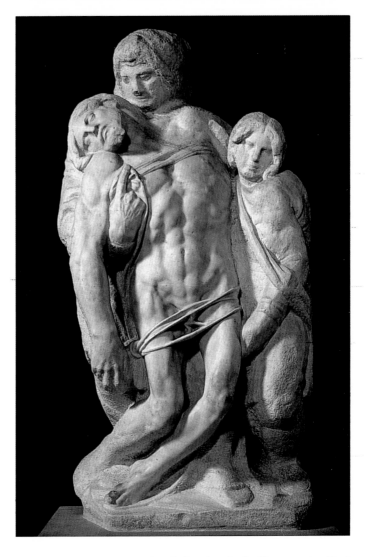

tistic evolution are here recognizable in their extreme poles. But this also marks the development
undergone by the whole of European culture: from
the Renaissance, from the revival of Antiquity and
the rediscovery of nature, to the splitting up of the
Christian Church, the return of faith after the Counter Reformation and the Manneristic art of an El
Greco. Only the figures of this Spanish artist, glowing signs of faith, can in some way be compared
to the work which Michelangelo fashioned up to

six days before his death. This was the *Pietà
Rondanini,* which, according to Vasari, he had already begun in 1555, before smashing the Florentine Pietà. He destroyed the first version of this too,
as can be seen in the second face of Christ in the
final version. This version, still unfinished at the artist's death, was probably begun not much later than
1555. The unity between Mother and Son is even
more intimate. It is almost impossible to tell whether
it is the Mother supporting the Son, or the Son sup-

90. *Rondanini Pietà*
h. 195 cms.
Milan, Castello
Sforzesco

91. *Crucifix*
41.2 × 27.9 cms.
London, British
Museum

92. *Plan for the church*
of San Giovanni dei
Fiorentini
Florence, Casa
Buonarroti

porting the Mother, overcome by despair. Both are in need of help, and both hold themselves up in the act of invocation and lament before the world and God.

The so-called *Pietà Palestrina* was attributed to Michelangelo for the first time in 1756 without any proven evidence. If it were his, it would have to be placed between the two Pietàs, but the heaviness of the figures and the square contours of the group make this attribution improbable.

During the last ten years Michelangelo mainly drew plans for new buildings and perhaps for further sculpture. After his reconciliation with Cosimo de' Medici, he designed new plans for *San Giovanni dei Fiorentini*. He had also been attracted to the Jesuit order by their zeal and eagerness and offered to help them without payment in constructing their church, *Il Gesù*. He planned for Pope Pius IV (1559-1565) new gates for the city of Rome, of which only the *Porta Pia* was, in fact, built. In 1563 he began to direct the transformation of the Baths of Diocletian into a Catholic church, Santa Maria degli Angeli. But the drawings he did for his own personal use show us better than any of these other works something of the artist's development during these years. The last of the six drawings of *Crucifixions* is probably to be dated to 1556. This shows us, once again, those same ideas which had tormented the artist during his work on the *Pietà Rondanini*: "Oh! Flesh, Blood and Wood, supreme pain, Through you must I suffer my agony." These lines, which the artist had written at the age of 57, seem to convey the dominant feeling in the Madonna and Saint John, gathered around the Cross. Fear and pain have drawn the Madonna to Christ's body, while St. John turns towards Him in supplication, with one arm around the Cross. In this female figure there is nothing of the Mother of God represented in his 1499 *Pietà*, nor does the Evangelist recall anything of the 1505 *St. Matthew*. Nowhere are the changes of this half century so clearly demonstrated as in the life and work of Michelangelo Buonarroti.

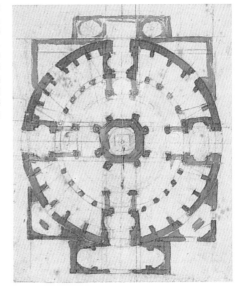

RAPHAEL

The Early Development

Raphael Sanzio was born in Urbino on 6 April 1483, a year after the death of Duke Frederick II. As Urbino's political leader and major artistic patron, Frederick had transformed the small hill town near the borders of Romagna, Tuscany and the Marches into a prosperous city which gathered cultural influences from the north and center of the Italian peninsula and which occupied an advanced position in the fields of art, literature and courtly custom in the last decades of the Quattrocento.

Urbino's good fortune grew with Frederick although it outlived him by very little, for Urbino was surrounded by powerful neighbors: Venice, Florence and the Papal States. The Duke had unified the Duchy of Montefeltro, which was legally under Papal power but which had actually split into many small feudal possessions. As the organizer of mercenary armies which he placed at the disposal of various Italian states, he increased his personal treasure and contributed greatly to the wealth of his city, which in this way came to know the most prosperous moment in its history.

This prosperity permitted numerous cultural and artistic initiatives, many of which are still visible today. Artists like Paolo Uccello — whose *Miracle of the Host* (1465-1469) is one of the freshest and liveliest narratives of the Quattrocento — and Piero della Francesca — who executed several masterpieces, among them the *Flagellation* (1455) and the *Portraits of Duke Frederick and Battista Sforza*, his wife (1465) — were attracted by the generosity of the leader-patron and by the initiatives and projects he proposed. Afterwards came those who showed themselves to be closest in thought and deed to the personality of the Duke: Justus of Ghent (who, in Urbino, combined the analytical characteristics of Flemish painting with the values of light and synthesis established by Piero della Francesca), Melozzo da Forlì, Filippo Brunelleschi, Luciano and Francesco Laurana, Francesco di Giorgio Martini (sculptor, painter and builder of fortifications) and Giorgio Schiavone.

This mixture of talent and activity gave rise to the construction of the massive and fanciful Ducal Palace and to the creation of a vaste and notable artistic circle.

Urbino was capable of mediating the most varied artistic tendencies, from the Venetian to the Florentine to the Umbrian. Its culturally and artistically fertile ground formed the substratum in which the composite and receptive art of Raphael is rooted.

Raphael was born, as we said, on 6 April 1483, to Giovanni Santi and Màgia Ciarla. His father, a painter, was well known in artistic circles in Urbino, even if he is better known in the history of art for his poetic eulogy of contemporary painting in the *Chronicle* of the deeds of Frederick II, written immediately, after the Duke's death. His works contain motifs from various sources, among them Piero,

Perugino (active in the Marches, in Fano and Senigallia, minor towns in the Duchy of Montefeltro) and Melozzo da Forlì.

Two artists were working in his father's workshop during Raphael's childhood. Evangelista da Pian di Meleto (whose artistic production has yet to be reconstructed) and Timoteo Viti da Urbino, who returned to his native Urbino from Bologna in 1495. The latter undoubtedly more deeply influenced the very young Raphael. The elements which this painter lacks — a sense of proportion and of composition — are visible in Raphael's early works, the first of which is, in Longhi's opinion, the *Banner* of Città di Castello (c. 1499). This work, which is in effect two paintings placed back to back, represents the *Crucifixion* on one side and the *Madonna of Mercy* on the other. The masterfully executed Madonna reflects the art of Piero della Francesca.

Around the beginning of the 16th century Raphael met Pietro Perugino, who influenced his painting perhaps more than any other painter. Perugino, who had been praised by Raphael's father in the *Chronicle*, reached his greatest fame in the last years of the Quattrocento. In addition, documents show that Raphael collaborated with Evangelista da Pian di Meleto on the altarpiece commissioned in 1510 for the Church of Sant'Agostino in Città di Castello. This piece, whose surviving parts are now dispersed in various Euro-

1. The School of Athens,
detail showing the portraits of Raphael and Sodoma
Vatican, Stanza della Segnatura

2. School of Perugino
Resurrection
Vatican, Pinacoteca

3. St Sebastian
43x34 cm
Bergamo, Accademia Carrara

chronologically by the *Resurrection* of 1501 in the Vatican Museum. This painting has also been cited as a work of collaboration by critics anxious to reconstruct the activity of the young Raphael during his association with Perugino. But today most critics agree that nothing in this panel — which is characteristic of the weak and mannered art that Perugino produced during this period — reveals Raphael's hand.

The contrary is true of the *St Sebastian* in the Carrara Academy in Bergamo. Here, graceful Peruginesque poses and the hazy transparency of color characteristic of Francesco Francia, are fused together in a way that clearly indicates Raphael's presence. His ability to compose clear and balanced forms becomes typical from this work on, as does the discreet and harmonious distillation of the formal elements of other painters in the clear, serene vision which seems characteristic of his artistic temperament.

The presence of Peruginesque motifs in Raphael's work is still quite evident in the *Crucifixion* of 1502-1503, now in the National Gallery in London. This painting originally formed the central part of an altarpiece commissioned for the Church of San Domenico in Città di Castello. It is the first work that Raphael signed. The signature, "Painted by Raphael of Urbino," documents his full artistic autonomy and indicates his background.

The composition derives from other panels on the same subject painted by Perugino; for example, the imposing Chigi Altarpiece for Sant'Agostino in Siena. But the rigorous correspondences of gesture that distinguish Raphael's figures from the sentimental and obvious poses of the master, clearly set the young pupil apart. The faces are treated with a subtler *chiaroscuro* and the volumes are, as a result, more slender than those of Perugino. Thus Raphael — even though he is unwilling and, perhaps, unable to break away from Perugino's influence — shows his true temperament in this painting. This temperament includes an extraordinary feeling for proportion and an acute visual sensibility. It is even more evident in the two predella compartments — one in the Cook Collection in Richmond and the other in the Lisbon Gallery — with *Stories from the Life of St Jerome.*

The works which conclude the young painter's Umbrian apprenticeship date to the years immediately after the London *Crucifixion.* They represent steps in a slow process which moves from the rejection of assimilated forms to a search for new figurative elements through which the artist can express his needs for clarity and formal balance.

In 1502-1503 Raphael also executed the *Coronation of the Virgin*, now in the Vatican Museum. This commission, originally intended for the Church of San Francesco a Monte in Perugia, was first awarded to Perugino, who entrusted it to his pupil. The altarpiece combines two scenes common in Quattrocento iconography: the Coronation (which occupies the upper part of the picture) and The Giving of the Girdle to St Thomas (in the lower part), an episode traditionally associated with the Assumption. The

pean and American museums, shows Peruginesque motifs, identifiable in the poses and features of the figures, though the grace of the compositions and the firmness of the figures surpass Perugino's capabilities.

As Venturi affirms, there must have been a "thorough familiarity with the master" behind "such a [profound] absorption of Peruginesque elements" in this early work by Raphael. Perhaps the only opportunity the young painter had to assist the master was provided by a fresco for the Collegio del Cambio in Perugia (1500). Here some critics, supported by tradition, claim to see the hand of the nineteen-year-old Raphael in the figure of *Fortitude*, which recalls certain aspects of Francesco Francia as transmitted by Timoteo Viti, his close follower.

Perugino's fresco for the Collegio del Cambio is followed

4. Crucifixion (Città di Castello Altarpiece)
279x166 cm
London, National Gallery

5. Coronation of the Virgin (Oddi Altarpiece)
267x163 cm
Vatican, Pinacoteca

two scenes remain separate from one another, and this clear division of the composition may indicate the painter's uncertainty of his compositional abilities. Nevertheless, the forms are already mature and certain innovations in perspective — such as the diagonal representation of the Madonna's tomb — constitute a departure from traditional Quattrocento compositional types. Extant drawings demonstrate the tremendous amount of thought which Raphael put into the panel's realization and some details, notably the highly individualized faces of the Apostles and the serene landscape in the background, are quite masterful. But the most meaningful passages are found in the predella scenes: the vast space which opens out beneath the colonnades of the *Annunciation*; the highly animated *Adoration of the Magi*; and the free quality of the atmosphere in the *Presentation in the Temple*, which foreshadows the extraordinary spatial intuition of some of the artist's future Vatican compositions.

Raphael was ready for new figurative experiments after these accomplishments. The search for further elements to

add to traditional modes of representation led him to Florence. Here a great demand for artists of all backgrounds continued to thrive, notwithstanding the terrible upheaval which the city suffered during this period.

Florence at the turn of the century was in the midst of a vast cultural and political crisis. Many of the artists who had developed the cultural values which characterized the city during the Quattrocento had either died or gone elsewhere and, as a result, these values were beginning to lose their splendor. This cultural crisis was complicated by political events, such as the invasion of Charles VIII of France and the consequent expulsion of Piero di Lorenzo de' Medici in 1494, and the dramatic experience of Savonarola which culminated in the public burning of the friar in 1498. Nevertheless, a great demand for artists of all sorts continued to exist. Many important works of art had survived the city's spiritual and political trauma and public participation in the artistic process was, as always, more lively in Florence than elsewhere.

One must not interpret Raphael's Florentine experience as a prolonged stay, for it was at most a series of brief visits which brought him into contact with some of the artists living there. The numerous works which Umbrian commissions continued to draw from him suggest that Raphael returned to Perugia frequently.

One such work is the celebrated *Marriage of the Virgin* now in the Brera Museum in Milan. This panel was commissioned by the Albizzini family of Città di Castello and was destined for the Church of San Francesco. Critics believe the painting to be inspired by two compositions by Perugino: the celebrated *Christ Delivering the Keys to St Peter* from the fresco cycle in the Sistine Chapel and a panel containing the *Marriage of the Virgin* now in the Museum of Caën. The structure of Raphael's painting, which includes figures in the foreground and a centralized building in the background, can certainly be compared to the two Perugino paintings. But Raphael's painting features a well developed circular composition, while that of Perugino is developed horizontally, in a way still characteristic of the Quattrocento. The structure of the figure group and of the large polygonal building clearly distinguish Raphael's painting from that of

his master. The space is more open in Raphael's composition, indicating a command of perspective which is superior to Perugino's. Some critics believe that Raphael's perspective construction reflects the architectonic research of Leonardo da Vinci and Donato Bramante. The work, signed and dated 1504, provides a good example of Raphael's style during this period.

Another Umbrian commission which seems to be bound up with Raphael's first visit to Florence and which presupposes, as we have noted, that the artist returned to Perugia, is the *Colonna Altarpiece* in the Metropolitan Museum, New York. The work is also called the *Madonna Enthroned with Saints Peter, Catherine of Alexandria, John, Cecilia (or Margaret) and Paul*. It was executed for the Sisters of St. Anthony of Perugia and is generally dated 1503-1505. Figurative elements which echo the style of Perugino and traces of Florentine painting from the first years of the Cinquecento, appear here in equal measure. The compositional structure of the angels in the lunette still reflects the Umbrian tradition, but a soft *chiaroscuro* which may derive from Leonardo is visible in the face of the central figure of God the Father. The vigorously conceived saints of the altarpiece itself recall the technique of Fra Bartolomeo della Porta, the Florentine painter and Dominican friar whose influence on Raphael's style is explained in greater detail below. This is particularly true for the figure of St Paul, constructed in the decisively monumental way which typifies the friar's style.

The three predella panels, containing representations of *The Way to Calvary*, the *Agony in the Garden* and the *Pietà*, surpass the figurative themes of the preceding century. In all three panels the atmospheric effects are freer than in previous works and the figures are more autonomous in the space they occupy. The sculptural quality of the *Way to Calvary* represents a definite departure from Quattrocento decorative tendencies. Raphael's encounter with contemporary Florentine art has begun to push the teachings of Perugino into the background and to prepare the way for the complete autonomy of expression which reveals itself in the following year.

Raphael in Florence

In 1505 Raphael was in Florence. The most notable artists active at the time were Leonardo Da Vinci, Michelangelo Buonarroti and the above-mentioned Dominican friar, Bartolomeo della Porta. Each of these artists had developed a different style of painting, but all were involved in a search for figurative elements which surpassed the Quattrocento models and for an expressive language in which color was more unified and space was freer.

Raphael became involved in this search, which goes be-

yond the lively curiosity of the first Florentine Renaissance and presupposes a new breadth of forms and a greater freedom of thought. Leonardesque "shading", which fused the representation of man and nature together in a single vision, replaced the Quattrocento notion of "functional line" (to use Berenson's term), the clearly defined contour which both delineated the figure and represented its movement. At the same time, a new, more monumental compositional type arose (though essentially new, it had already been

328

5-8. Predella of the
Oddi Altarpiece
representing the
Annunciation, the
Adoration of the Magi
and the Presentation
in the Temple
27x50 cm each panel
Vatican, Pinacoteca

foreshadowed in the works of some Quattrocento masters, for example, in the *San Barnaba Altarpiece* by Botticelli, 1486). It first appears in the art of Fra Bartolomeo who seems to be the artist to whom Raphael turned most of his attention at this time.

Raphael abandoned every trace of Peruginesque influence in Florence and returned to Umbria in the same year with new pictorial motifs which he was to express in two notable works, the *Colonna Altarpiece* (which we have already examined) and, a bit later, the *Ansidei Madonna*, also known as the *Enthroned Madonna with Saints John the Baptist and Nicholas of Bari*. This *Sacra Conversazione*, attributed to the years 1505-1506, shows the Virgin attentively reading a prayer book, with the Child in her lap. The two saints stand at her sides. The Baptist points to the Child (a traditional iconographic device) and St Nicholas is absorbed in a volume which he holds in his hand. The luminous landscape background and the high baldachin remotely recall the art of Piero della Francesca, but the figure types, still vaguely Peruginesque in their contours, are psychologically more complex and structurally more volumetric. The compositional scheme is reduced to a large arch whose central axis is represented by the baldachin. The result is a sense of monumentality and harmonic proportion which were to become constant in Raphael's art.

The figurative powers which Raphael developed in Florence led to "a more synthetic conception of form, a refinement of intellectual expression" (Venturi), which are visible in the *Knight's Dream* in the National Gallery, London, and the *Three Graces* of Chantilly. Critics believe that the two

9. Perugino
Christ Delivering the Keys to St Peter
Vatican, Sistine Chapel

10. The Marriage of the Virgin
170x121 cm
Milan, Brera Museum

panels may have formed a single diptych presented to So pione di Tommaso Borghese at his birth, in 1493. Th theme of the paintings may by drawn from the poem, *Pr nica*, by Silius Italicus, which was well known in antiquit and which humanistic culture restored to fame. In the fir panel, Scipio, the sleeping knight, must choose betwee Venus (pleasure) and Minerva (virtue); in the second, th Graces reward his choice of virtue with the Golden Apple of the Hesperides. The classical origin of this theme bring us back without doubt to the Florentine environment. Th composition, which is dominated by a sense of great har mony, is a figurative consequence of the literary theme.

These panels, which were originally attributed to the fir period of Raphael's activity, are now thought to have bee painted around 1504-1505. By comparing them to on another, we can begin to identify Florentine influences. A analytical rendering of detail distinguishes the first pane while an abstract quality characterizes the second. Th landscape background is deep and spatious and is reduce to broad fields of color. The figures of the three Grace

11. Madonna and Child (Connestabile Madonna)
dia. 17.9 cm
Leningrad, Hermitage

12. Madonna and Child (The Small Cowper Madonna)
58x43 cm
Washington, National Gallery of Art

which dominate the foreground are solidly constructed, but
they are also modelled by a delicate *chiaroscuro*.

The *Madonna del Granduca* (1504) in the Pitti Gallery in
Florence shows the pre-eminent influence of Leonardo. Its
simple composition is a prototype for the future Madonnas
of Raphael's last Florentine period. The figures of the Virgin
and Child emerge from a dark background (an element
evidently derived from Leonardo), bound together by a
sweet sentiment which derives largely from the gesture of
the Child who, while looking toward the spectator, presses
against his Mother. The painting belonged to the 17th century Florentine painter, Carlo Dolci, and then to Grand Duke
Ferdinand III of Lorraine from whom its name derives.

The *Small Cowper Madonna*, today in the National Gallery in Washington, is a more analytical variant of the homogeneous and resolute group of the *Madonna del Granduca*.
Here the painter expresses the influence of Leonardo in a
broad, soft landscape. This landscape contains a small
church with a cylindrical dome, which may be an allusion to
Bramante's architecture. According to Venturi, it recalls the
Church of San Bernardino in Urbino. The painting is generally dated 1503-1505.

The *St Michael* and *St George and the Dragon* in the
Louvre, and the *St George* of the National Gallery in Washington are bound together both by their subject — an
armed youth fighting a dragon — and by stylistic elements.
All three are assigned to the Florentine period and echo
those stimuli which Raphael received from the great masters who worked in Florence or whose paintings were visible
there. The influence of Leonardo — whose fighting warriors
from the *Battle of Anghiari* (1505) in the Palazzo della Signoria provided an extraordinary example of martial art
(the painting deteriorated very rapidly because of short-
comings in Leonardo's experimental technique and so is no
longer visible) — predominates in these works. But references to Flemish painting — particularly that of
Hieronymus Bosch (the glaring light and humanoid mon-
sters which populate the *St Michael* are characteristic of
Bosch) — suggest the environment of Urbino, where Northern influences were still quite vivid. Raphael's imagination,
which is particularly developed in the details of the *St
Michael*, is more balanced in the figure of the Archangel, the
focus of the entire composition. This sense of balance and
composure is developed further in the other two panels,
where the landscape, still of Umbrian derivation,
accentuates the serenity of the figures, notwithstanding the
dramatic character of the subject. Certain qualities of light,
like the reflections on the armor in the Washington *St
George*, foreshadow the compositions of the Vatican
"Stanze" (see the *Liberation of St Peter*). These small panels
are indicative of a moment in which the painter gathers the
stylistic fruits of what he has assimilated so far and, at the
same time, poses pictorial problems which will be developed in the future.

The *Portrait of a Young Man with an Apple* (1505) in the
Uffizi has been associated with these paintings. It is difficult

to perceive the hand of the artist in the face which, although beautifully drawn, lacks the physiognomic characteristics which typify Raphael's subjects. But the overall attention to the analytical effects of Flemish art leads us to attribute the work to Raphael, since his attention was turned to the production of this school precisely in these years. Furthermore, the compositional harmony which is a principal element of Raphael's art is visible in the compact forms of the solidly conceived portrait. The subject has been associated with Francesco Maria Della Rovere, and possibly correctly: the portrait reached Florence with the Della Rovere patrimony in 1631 on the marriage of Vittoria Della Rovere to the future Grand Duke Ferdinand II.

Another important aspect of Raphael's Florentine stay is the compositional evolution which his painting underwent. Perugino's compositions — like those of all Quattrocento masters — were based on linear rhythms. In Florence Raphael transformed his compositional type in a constructive-monumental sense. This transformation is recognizable mainly in the human figures, who are still harmonically enclosed in geometric schemes and accompanied by a clear daylight in the background.

An example of his ability to resolve natural elements in a synthetic vision which transcends particular situations is the portrait of a woman called *La Donna Gravida* in the Pitti Gallery, Florence. The subject is a pregnant woman, conscious of her approaching motherhood, who looks intensely toward the spectator, with her hand on her abdomen. The portrait is finely balanced. Solid forms are reduced to pure spherical volumes, overlaid with carefully chosen colors. The sense of color which this painting shows will be used again by Raphael in his portrait of Cardinal Fedra Inghirami.

The same conceptual content underlies the *Woman with a Unicorn* in the Borghese Gallery, Rome. This painting, which shows a young woman holding a small unicorn, was discovered during a restoration in 1930. Until then it had been covered by the image of a female saint with the iconographic attributes of St Catherine of Alexandria. Present day critics attribute the work to Raphael, referring it to 1505 and to the Florentine environment. It can, in fact, be inserted among the portraits of that period, for it represents an apex in the artist's stylistic development. The fullness of the well constructed figure is set apart from a vast landscape background, inspired by Leonardo but executed with the clarity typical of Raphael.

Leonardo's influence is particularly strong in the *Blessing Christ* (c. 1506) in the Tosio-Martinengo Museum in Brescia. Here Christ is shown emerging from the tomb. He is no longer an object of compassion, as in 14th and 15th century panels. Rather, he is depicted as the Resurrected Christ; he still bears the symbols of the Passion, the crown of thorns and the marks of the nails which bound his hands and feet to the Cross. Every element of the artist's experience with Perugino has by now been abandoned. The figure displays a smoothness of surface and a soft *chiaroscuro* modelling which clearly surpass the abilities of Raphael's master.

The controversial *Self-Portrait* in the Uffizi is very simil to the *Blessing Christ*, but its poor state of conservation h prevented critics from attributing it objectively ar definitively to Raphael. Nevertheless, many art historian consider it a work from the Florentine period. The soft ligh which pervades the portrait certainly recalls Leonardo, b the restless and problematic elements which Leonardo complex figurative research present are absent. The intens representation of the youth shows no sign of internal te sion. On the contrary, it communicates a serene observatic of reality through a pictorial rendering rich in synthetic c pacity.

The masterpieces of this period are undoubtedly the Po traits of Agnolo and Maddalena Doni in Palazzo Pitti. Th merchant Agnolo Doni married Maddalena Strozzi in 150 but Raphael's portraits (which remained in the family unt 1826, when they were acquired by Grand Duke Leopold of Lorraine) were probably executed in 1506, the period which the painter studied the art of Leonardo most closel The composition of the portraits resembles that of the Mor Lisa: the figures are presented in the same way in respect t the picture plane, and their hands, like those of the Mor Lisa, are placed on top of one another. But the low horizo of the landscape background, a "distant heir of Piero del Francesca" (Longhi), permits a careful assessment of th human figure by providing a uniform light which define surfaces and volumes. This relationship between landscap and figure presents a clear contrast to the striking setting of Leonardo, which communicate the threatening presenc of nature. But the most notable characteristic that di tinguishes these portraits from those of Leonardo is th overall sense of serenity which even the close attention t the materials of clothes and jewels (which draw one's atte tion to the couples' wealth) is unable to attenuate. Ever element — even those of secondary importance — work together to create a precise balance. These works, linke not only by the kinship of the subjects, but also by the evident stylistic homogeneity, mark the beginning o Raphael's artistic maturity.

Raphael's stylistic evolution also regards composition, a we have noted. He develops the pyramidal scheme of Leo nardo da Vinci and combines it with the monumental com positions of Fra Bartolomeo. His main interest is to maintai formal balance. The controlled use of light is one of the chi tools he uses to achieve this goal. At the same time, h welcomes new tools, among them the figurative motifs o Michelangelo.

Michelangelo's influence on Raphael is evident in th *Madonna of the Meadow*, one of the compositions featurin the Madonna, the infant Christ and young St John whic mark the central point of Raphael's activity in Florence. Th pyramidal structure of the figure group again recalls Leo nardo (whose cartoon for the *St Anne* was shown in 1506 i the Church of Santissima Annunziata). But Raphael exert his own balancing capacity on the Leonardesque volumetri

13. Madonna and Child (Madonna del Granduca)
84x55 cm
Florence, Galleria Palatina (Pitti Palace)

14. The Three Graces
17x17 cm
Chantilly, Musée Condé

15. The Knight's Dream
17x17 cm
London, National Gallery

conception, infusing it with the idyllic serenity which characterizes his paintings from this period. The work as a whole is structurally harmonic, from the figure group (dominated by the affectionate figure of the Virgin Mary who supports the Child and glances tenderly at the young St John) to the sweeping landscape (made luminous by the mirror-like lake which stretches from one side of the panel to the other). The twisting figures of the two children clearly reflect Michelangelo's figurative research. They are also visible in a nearly contemporary panel, called *La Belle Jardinière*. The *Madonna of the Meadow*, now in the Kunsthistorisches Museum in Vienna, passed from the Taddei family (for whom it was executed) into the Austrian collections in the 18th century. It is signed and dated 1506.

The *Madonna of the Goldfinch*, executed in 1507 for Lorenzo Nasi and now in the Uffizi, is another of Raphael's Florentine panels. It was severely damaged following the partial collapse of the Nasi house in 1547, as mentioned by Vasari. It was subsequently restored by Michele di Ridolfo del Ghirlandaio, the son of the artist who was deeply influenced by Raphael. The composition follows that of the *Madonna of the Meadow*, with the essential difference that the children in the *Madonna of the Goldfinch* are more firmly united with the central figure of the Virgin. The color is more lively than that of the *Madonna of the Meadow* and foreshadows the coloristic character of Raphael's Roman paintings. The landscape, and particularly the architectural forms it contains, reflects the influence of Flemish art, even though it is still structured in the Umbrian manner. This influence was as alive in Florence as it was in Urbino in the second half of the Quattrocento. It is perhaps most visible in

16. St Michael and the Dragon
31x27 cm
Paris, Louvre

17. St George and the Dragon
31x27 cm
Paris, Louvre

the sloping roofs and tall spires, unusual elements in a Mediterranean landscape. The influence of Michelangelo is again evident in the well structured figure of the infant Christ. It was to become even more evident in the works which followed.

The so-called *Belle Jardinière*, now in the Louvre, follows the *Madonna of the Goldfinch* chronologically. Its composition is a mirror image of that of the *Madonna of the Meadow*. The painting was commissioned by Fabrizio Sergardi, a Sienese nobleman, and was left uncompleted by the artist. Nevertheless, it is signed and dated 1507. According to tradition it was finished by Ridolfo del Ghirlandaio, although the recent restoration would seem to contradict this attribution. It was subsequently acquired by Francis I of France. The painting is known primarily for the harmonic and proportional balancing of the poses of the figures and for the high formal quality present in every element, particularly in the face of the Virgin, which served as a model of beauty for generations of artists.

18. St George and the Dragon; 28x22 cm; Washington, National Gallery of Art

*19. Portrait of a Young Man
with an Apple
47x35 cm
Florence, Uffizi*

Between Florence and Rome

Among the figurative components which Raphael drew from his Florentine experience (which, as we have seen, was interrupted by frequent trips to Umbria), those which derive from Michelangelo seem most prevalent in his last Florentine works. The work in which Michelangelo's importance to Raphael becomes most evident is the *Entombment*, now in the Borghese Gallery in Rome. The panel was painted in 1507 in Perugia for Atalanta Baglioni as a votive offering in memory of her son, Grifonetto, killed in a piazza in Perugia in the course of a family feud. The artist detaches himself both formally and iconographically from traditional representations of the scene. He does not depict the deposition itself, but the carrying of the dead Christ. The protagonists of the scene do not demonstrate their sorrow violently, but are reduced, through the Raphaelesque mode of feeling, to a sort of painful resignation. Critics have

20. The Woman with the Unicorn
65x51 cm
Rome, Galleria Borghese

21. The Blessing Christ
30x25 cm
Brescia, Pinacoteca Tosio Martinengo

22. Madonna Enthroned with Saints
John the Baptist and Nicholas of
Bari (Ansidei Altarpiece)
274x152 cm
London, National Gallery

pointed out a resemblance between Raphael's *Entombment* and classical bas-reliefs illustrating the carrying of Meleager, a hero of Greek mythology. The vision of space is less geometric than the Florentine vision, and it appears freer and closer to nature. The influence of Michelangelo is strong, however, and can be perceived without doubt in the limp arm of Christ as well as in the female figure at the extreme right. The latter mirrors the figure of the Virgin in the *Tondo Doni*, which Michelangelo executed between 1504 and 1506. The formal vigor and sense of open space which characterize Michelangelo's painting certainly must have had a profound effect on Raphael.

The three compositions of the predella (today in the Vatican Museum) are executed in a delicate monochrome. They represent Faith, Hope and Charity accompanied by small angels who bear objects symbolizing the virtues. The human figure completely dominates every composition and the sense of harmony is pervasive. Even in the secondary elements of his creations, Raphael does not spare his capacity to use line and pose to create an overall image of complete formal beauty.

Both the main panel and the predella were carried from Perugia to Rome by Pope Paul V. They were replaced by copies executed in 1608. The painting was subsequently included among the works taken by the French troops and was exhibited in Paris in the Napoleonic Museum from 1797 to 1815 when, following the restitutions ordered by the Congress of Vienna, it was returned to Rome.

The *Canigiani Holy Family* in Munich is attributed to the same period as the *Entombment* (1504-1506). The painting's name derives from the Florentine family who owned it before it passed into the Medici collection and then into Germany with the marriage of Anna Maria Lodovica de' Medici to the Palatine Elector. In this work Raphael synthesizes elements drawn from Leonardo and Michelangelo and compounds them with a decisively Northern landscape and delicate coloristic passages dominated by iridescent tones. The pyramid in which the figures are ideally enclosed is still drawn from models provided by Leonardo, but the relationships between the figures, developed through the glances they exchange and through the serene feelings they communicate, carry the composition onto a

SALVE·MATER·CHRISTI

23, 24. Portraits of Agnolo and Maddalena Doni
65x45.7 each
Florence, Galleria Palatina (Pitti Palace)

25. Self-Portrait
47.5x33 cm
Florence, Uffizi

calmly descriptive plane. The tone of the painting is thus quite different from the tense and restless art of Leonardo. His unsurpassed descriptive capacity permits Raphael to create an image full of human participation and limpid serenity.

The female portrait known as *The Mute Woman* represents a return to the influence of Leonardo. It certainly comes from the Florentine environment, for it was given in trust to the National Gallery of the Marches by the Uffizi, where it had been stored for several hundred years. It was attributed to Raphael only recently. Leonardo inspires mainly the pose of the figure (whose characteristically crossed hands constitute a very clear reference to the *Mona Lisa).* The neatness of the large areas of color which emerge in lighter tones from the near-black background, and the analytical treatment of the details of the woman's clothing are characteristic of Raphael. The dispersive effect of this attention to detail is fully compensated by the tones of color

— used here in a fairly limited range — which unify the composition as a whole.

The stylistic versatility which Raphael demonstrates in contemporary or nearly contemporary works executed for a homogeneous social environment is indicative of his extraordinary technical capacity. This versatility is expressed in a variety of compositional types, which can range from simple forms to more monumental and complex ones; and in conceptual expressions, which are sometimes calm and quiet and sometimes emphatic.

This range of figurative expressions appears in another work from the Florentine period, the *Madonna del Baldacchino*, in Palazzo Pitti. This painting was begun in 1507 for the Dei family and was intended for their chapel in the Church of Santo Spirito. The panel's monumental structure derives partially from the Venetian tradition and partially from Fra Bartolomeo. The Venetian influence is visible above all in the setting: the apse of a church which recalls the larger compositions of Giovanni Bellini. The influence of Fra Bartolomeo consists mainly in the monumentality and poses of the figures. The semi-circular arrangement of the saints around the Virgin and the unusually excited flying angels who hold open the curtain of the baldachin give the painting a sense of free atmospheric circulation. The figures, all posed differently, prepare a complex of expression which will find its natural outlet in the large descriptive compositions of the Vatican. The most recent restoration has shown that the altarpiece is entirely Raphael's work and that it was left incomplete.

Fra Bartolomeo's influence is particularly clear in the *Large Cowper Madonna* in the National Gallery in Washington. This panel, signed and dated 1508, was executed near the end of Raphael's stay in Florence. The composition is extremely simple and essential; the gesture of the Child who stretches his hand toward the Virgin while turning his attention toward the spectator, and the gesture with which the Virgin holds the hand to her breast, provide the only signs of life. The sentiment of anxious motherhood which enriched by greater awareness, will be fully expressed in the *Tempi Madonna*, now in the Alte Pinakothek of Munich appears here for the first time. The Virgin, who tenderly presses the Infant to her cheek, is the subject of the painting. But the two figures are conceived as a single group, and this fact dominates the scene's visual impact. The only natural elements are a small strip of landscape and the light blue sky in the background. The Madonna's swollen mantle is meant to indicate movement. The extreme synthesis of the color fields indicates Raphael's idealization of the subject. But the painter's need for formal beauty and the emotional reality of the subject matter are reconciled above all through the tender relationship between Mother and Child This panel, which critics place in the year 1508, is included among the works executed after Raphael's contact with Florentine art.

The *St Catherine of Alexandria* in the National Gallery London, is also assigned to this period. The martyr is shown

26. Portrait of a Woman (La Donna Gravida); 66.8x52.7 cm; Florence, Galleria Palatina (Pitti Palace)

27. *Madonna of the Meadow*
(Madonna del Belvedere)
113x88 cm
Vienna, Kunsthistorisches Museum

28. *Madonna of the Goldfinch*
(Madonna del Cardellino)
107x77 cm
Florence, Uffizi

almost full figure, turned toward the sky in an act of ecstasy which foreshadows the "devotional intonation of the large Roman altarpieces" (De Vecchi). The landscape is painted with particular care. Its light shading indicates a residual influence of Leonardo, although the jagged mountains which often characterize Leonardo's landscapes are absent. The delicate modelling of the saint, the slight torsion of her body as she leans on the wheel of her martyrdom (whose spikes have been reduced to rounded knobs in order to tone down the element of cruelty) fully express the balanced character of Raphael's art. The panel clearly shows the intense formal research which underlies Raphael's figurative creations. He is always careful not to excite emotions which he considers too intense and to mitigate tones and thematic elements in search of a perfect balance between design, color, pose and expression, and between the figurative and ornamental elements.

After having passed most of 1509 in Florence, Raphael prepared to leave for Rome. That he was present in Perugia for a brief period is certain. There he executed a fresco in

the Convent of San Severo which may be regarded as a predecessor of the compositions in the first frescoes of the Vatican Stanze. The painting, representing the *Holy Trinity and Saints*, consists of two parts and still shows the influence of Fra Bartolomeo, although the Umbrian environment causes Raphael to resume some elements of his experience with Perugino which he had seemed to have forgotten.

These works conclude Raphael's Florentine experience. They clearly demonstrate the stylistic knowledge and figurative means that he acquired through observing and frequenting the Tuscan masters.

Julius II Della Rovere was Pope when Raphael arrived in Rome. The group of humanists, literary figures and artists which had previously formed at the court of Urbino was reconstructed around his throne. There were close contacts between the Papal environment and that of Urbino, for the Della Rovere family dominated both Urbino and Rome. The Urbinate architect, Donato Bramante, who came to Rome from Lombardy, and whose *Tempietto* at San Pietro in Montorio was built along a central plan similar to that which

348

Raphael had painted in the *Marriage of the Virgin*, was particularly active. Furthermore, classical antiquity was the object of new studies and interests during the pontificate of Julius II. The discovery of an antique sculpture group, the *Laocoon*, in 1506, caused a great deal of excitement among artists and literary figures. The relocation of this and other statues from the Greek and Roman periods in the Belvedere Garden in the Vatican changed the stylistic tendencies of art in Rome. Even Raphael, who had just arrived in Rome, assimilated certain classical motifs which he believed responsive to his figurative research.

Julius II (pope from 1503 to 1513) was a complicated and dynamic personality. After having broken up the rival Borgia faction, he headed the so-called Holy League, whose goal was to drive the French out of the territories which bordered on the Papal States. This was accomplished with the aid of several Italian principalities. Julius' military undertakings were associated with an extraordinary wealth of initiatives in the re-organization of the state: he directed the re-ordering of the Papal finances (which Borgia expenditures had reduced to a deplorable state) and restored confidence in the money by minting new silver *giuli* whose nominal and real values were guaranteed to correspond. Much energy was also dedicated to city planning. New neighborhoods and streets were created (among them, the famous Via Giulia) and an ambitious project for the renewal of St. Peter's was begun. This creative fervor in the artistic field attracted the most famous artists of the time, from Antonio da Sangallo to Jacopo Sansovino, from Bramante to Pintoricchio, from Lotto to Michelangelo and from Signorelli to Raphael himself. Their presence contributed to the remaking of Rome. The political, social and demographic decadence which had afflicted the city in the Middle Ages were gradually and laboriously eliminated, and Rome became the most important cultural center in Italy.

Raphael in Rome: The Early Years

Raphael's first major undertaking in Rome was the decoration of the Stanza della Segnatura. He started work in June 1509, one year after Michelangelo had begun the vaults of the Sistine Chapel, another great pictorial cycle commissioned by Pope Julius. Both these works have a clear religious content, but their aims are different. The Sistine Chapel was intended for liturgical celebrations. Its ceiling is populated by figures who are independent of the environment and of nature and who are capable of recreating the complex and tormented expression of man's most deeply felt faith. The Stanza della Segnatura was a courtroom: its purpose was the administration of temporal power. Its decoration — harmonious settings populated by sacred and profane characters — reflected a Church by this time invested with worldly powers and occupied with their administration.

Julius II had commissioned the decoration of this room to the most well known painters active in Rome: the Sienese, Baldassare Peruzzi; the Vercellese (but naturalized Sienese), Antonio Bazzi, called "Sodoma"; the Lombard, Bramantino; and the Venetian, Lorenzo Lotto. But Raphael's program excited the Pope so much that — according to Vasari — the works already begun by the other artists were destroyed and the entire cycle was placed in Raphael's hands.

The illustrative program of the paintings of the Stanza della Segnatura, which combined antique thought with Christian humanistic re-interpretations, was certainly not conceived by Raphael. His abilities as an illustrator, however, immediately allowed him to give visual form to the complex doctrine which the subject matter implied. The accompanying diagram explains the content of the cycle:

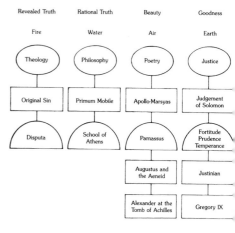

As a whole, the paintings can be considered a synthesis of motifs which illustrate "the agreement between ancient world and Christian spirituality" (Chastel), since they place the virtue of the religious tradition and the spiritual activities of man side by side in a cosmological environment (that is, an environment that refers to the elements which constitute the universe). To achieve this synthesis, Raphael chooses exemplary episodes from the Bible (the Original Sin and the Judgement of Solomon), from classical mythology (Apollo and Marsyas) and from the Aristotelian philosophical conception, reconsidered in the light of humanistic Platonism.

9. Madonna and Child with the
Young St John (La Belle Jardinière)
122x80 cm
Paris, Louvre

Humanistic-Platonic philosophy, which is basically the thought of Plato adapted to the Christian tradition by the philosophers of the early Renaissance, inspires the entire cycle. According to the most recent studies, the cycle represents the ideas of *Truth* (both the truth revealed by the Christian religion and the rational truth of classical philosophical speculation), *Virtue* (personified by ecclesiastic and civil law and symbolized by the Virtues) and *Beauty* (as it is expressed in poetry).

The realization of the frescoes for the Stanza della Segnatura involved numerous preparatory drawings. These drawings indicate the immense amount of creative energy which underlie the compositions. In fact, Raphael was immediately

recognized by the literary figures, thinkers and artists who populated Rome as a personality capable of interpreting the ideas of the intellectual speculation of his time in extraordinarily balanced figurative forms. In the vaults and wall panels, he adapts himself to the work already begun by others. His most original creations are in the large lunettes, where he fully integrates the suggested theme and its formal realization.

The first composition Raphael executed is the so-called *Disputa* or *Disputation of the Holy Sacrament*, the traditional name for what is really an *Adoration of the Sacrament*. The painting is built around the monstrance containing the consecrated Host, located on the altar. Figures re-

351

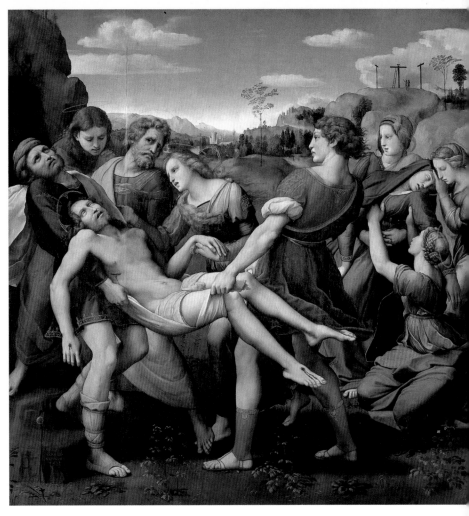

presenting the Triumphant Church and the Militant Church are arranged in two semicircles, one above the other, and venerate the Host. God the Father, bathed in celestial glory, blesses the crowd of biblical and ecclesiastical figures from the top of the composition. Immediately below, the resurrected Christ sits on a throne of clouds between the Virgin (bowed in adoration) and St John the Baptist (who, according to iconographic tradition, points to Christ). Prophets and saints of the Old and New Testament are seated around this central group on a semicircular bank of clouds similar to that which constitutes the throne of Christ. They form a composed and silent crowd and, although they are painted with large fields of color, the figures are highly individuated.

30, 31. The Entombment, with detail
184x176 cm
Rome, Galleria Borghese

32-34. Predella of the Borghese Entombment representir the Theological Virtues
16x44 cm each panel
Vatican, Pinacoteca

At the bottom of the picture space, inserted in a vast landscape dominated by the altar and the eucharistic sacrifice, are saints, popes, bishops, priests and the mass of the faithful. They represent the Church which has acted, and which continues to act, in the world, and which contemplates the glory of the Trinity with the eyes of the mind. Following a fifteenth century tradition, Raphael has placed portraits of famous personalities, both living and dead, among the people in the crowd. Bramante leans on the ballustrade at left; the young man standing near him has been identified as Francesco Maria Della Rovere; Pope Julius II, who personifies Gregory the Great, is seated near the altar. Dante is visible on the right, distinguished by a crown of laurel. The presence of Savonarola seems strange, but may be explained by the fact that Julius II revoked Pope Alexander VI's condemnation of Savonarola (Julius was an adversary of Alexander, who was a Borgia). The structure of the composition is characterized by extreme clarity and simplicity, which Raphael achieved through sketches, studies and drawings containing notable differences in pose. References to other artists are visible throughout the composition (the young Francesco Maria Della Rovere, for example, possesses a Leonardo-like physiognomy). But the layout, the gestures and the poses are original products of Raphael's research, which here reaches a degree of admirable balance and high expressive dignity.

Toward the end of 1509, Raphael began work on the wall opposite the *Disputa*. This second fresco, entitled the *School of Athens*, represents the truth acquired through reason. Raphael does not entrust his illustration to allegorical figures, as was customary in the 14th and 15th centuries. Rather, he groups the solemn figures of thinkers and philosophers together in a large, grandiose architectural framework. This framework is characterized by a high dome, a vault with lacunar ceiling and pilasters. It is probably inspired by late Roman architecture or — as most critics believe — by Bramante's project for the new St. Peter's which is itself a symbol of the synthesis of pagan and Christian philosophies. According to Chastel, it is "the only symbol capable of representing the work of the intelligence".

The figures who dominate the composition do not crowd the environment, nor are they suffocated by it. Rather, they underline the breadth and depth of the architectural structures. The protagonists — Plato, represented with a white beard (some people identify this solemn old man with Leonardo da Vinci) and Aristotle — are both characterized by a precise and meaningful pose. "The horizontal gesture of Aristotle symbolizes the organization of the world through Ethics and the vertical gesture of Plato represents the movement of cosmological thought which rises from the sensible world to its ideal principle" (Chastel). Raphael's descriptive capacity, in contrast to that visible in the allegories of earlier painters, is such that "the figures do not pay homage to, or group around the symbols of knowledge; they do not form a parade. They move, act, teach, discuss and become excited" (Venturi).

35, 36. *The Canigiani Holy Family, with detail*
132x107 cm
Munich, Alte Pinakothek

37. *Madonna del Baldacchino (after restoration)*
276x224 cm
Florence, Galleria Palatina (Pitti Palace)

38. *The Mute Woman*
68x48 cm
Urbino, Galleria Nazionale delle Marche

The painting celebrates classical thought, but it is also dedicated to the liberal arts, symbolized by the statues of Apollo and Minerva. Grammar, Arithmetic and Music are personified by figures located in the foreground, at left. Geometry and Astronomy are personified by the figures in the foreground, at right. Behind them stand characters representing Rhetoric and Dialectic. Some of the ancient philosophers bear the features of Raphael's contemporaries. Bramante is shown as Euclid (in the foreground, at right, leaning over a tablet and holding a compass). Leonardo is, as we said, probably shown as Plato. Francesco Maria Della Rovere appears once again near Bramante, dressed in white. Michelangelo, sitting on the stairs and leaning on a block of marble, is represented as Heraclitus. A close examination of the intonaco shows that Heraclitus was the last figure painted when the fresco was completed, in 1511. The allusion to Michelangelo is probably a gesture of homage to the artist, who had recently unveiled the frescoes of the Sistine Ceiling. Raphael — at the extreme right, with a dark hat — and his friend, Sodoma, are also present (they exemplify the glorification of the fine arts and they are posed on the same level as the liberal arts). The fresco achieved immediate success. Its beauty and its thematic unity were universally accepted. The enthusiasm with which it was received was not marred by reservations, as was the public reaction to the Sistine Ceiling.

39. Madonna and Child (The Large Cowper Madonna)
81x57 cm
Washington, National Gallery of Art

40. Madonna and Child (The Tempi Madonna)
77x53 cm
Munich, Alte Pinakothek

Raphael began the third composition for the Stanza della Segnatura at the end of 1509 or the beginning of 1510. It represents *Parnassus*, the dwelling place of Apollo and the Muses and the home of poetry, according to classical myth. Apollo plays a *lira da braccio* (an anachronism which, according to some, was meant to symbolize the perpetual value of the poetic message). He sits under a laurel grove with the nine Muses (who personify the nine types of art). Classical poets are represented in a harmonic ascending and descending movement from left to right. Some of them are portraits of contemporary or historical figures: Petrarch is recognizable in the group in the left foreground; so is Sappho, who holds a scroll bearing her name; Ennius is seated above them, listening to the song of the blind Homer (who appears as a protagonist, like Apollo), behind him stands Dante, who had also appeared in the *Disputa* as a theologist, evidently because of the doctrinal content of the

41. St Catherine of Alexandria; 71x53 cm; London, National Gallery

42. The Stanza della Segnatura in the Vatican Palaces

43. Disputation of the Holy Sacrament (La Disputa)
Vatican, Stanza della Segnatura

44. The School of Athens
Vatican, Stanza della Segnatura

Divine Comedy. Some see the portrait of Michelangelo in the bearded figure immediately to the right of the central group, although it is more readily identified with Tebaldeo or Castiglione, for the scene is, after all, a celebration of poetry. Compositional harmony and visual counterpoint characterize the fresco: the groups of figures are bound together by continuous lines and the single characters are represented in opposed but corresponding poses. Although the Parnassus lacks the high originality of the School of Athens, it demonstrates Raphael's illustrative ability. It is enriched by classical elements which must have held great appeal for a cultural class excited by the recent archaeological discoveries. Thus we must add Raphael's capacity to interpret contemporary taste to his genuine artistic skills.

The lunette containing the Cardinal Virtues (which rep-

resent "Good") is built around an allegorical theme. The volumetric modelling of the figures suggests the influence of Michelangelo. The relationship that binds the three figures together is clear and harmonic. Fortitude, dressed in armor, sits in the shade of an oak tree. Prudence is placed on the highest step of the base. She has two faces: one of a young woman who looks at her reflection in a mirror handed to her by a winged putto; the other, of an old man, the symbol of old age, of which prudence is the chief quality. Finally, Temperance is represented holding a pair of reins. The allegory was intended to include the figure of Justice as well. But Justice, being considered superior to the other virtues from a hierarchical point of view, is represented separately in one of the medallions of the vault. Three winged genii symbolize the theological virtues (Charity, gathering the fruits of the oak; Hope, in the center with a flaming torch; and Faith, at the extreme right, pointing toward the sky). Two additional putti complete the composition, "giving the whole scene a free and graceful movement" (De Vecchi).

After the completion of the Stanza della Segnatura, Raphael began the decoration of the adjacent room, afterwards called the Stanza di Eliodoro, after the subject of one of the works painted there. The cycle was painted between

September 1511 and June 1514. Julius II died during this period and his successor, Leo X (Giovanni de' Medici, son of Lorenzo the Magnificent) caused the last scenes to be completed.

In the meanwhile, Raphael had had contact with the art of Sebastiano del Piombo. Sebastiano had come to Rome in 1511 and had worked with Raphael in the villa of the wealthy Sienese banker, Agostino Chigi. The intense colors of the Venetian artist's paintings had attracted Raphael. The result of this contact can be seen in the richer range of color which Raphael used in these scenes.

The vaults of the ceiling represent episodes of divine intervention in the history of Israel (the Burning Bush, the Announcement of the Flood to Noah, Jacob's Dream, the Sacrifice of Isaac). The theme of the room is the presence of God in the history of the Church (including *Heliodorus' Expulsion from the Temple* [Maccabees, 3:24-27] and other episodes). It commemorates the conquest of Palestine by the Hellenistic kingdom of the Syrian Seleucides. The other episodes refer to the Middle Ages (for example, the *Mass at Bolsena* and *Attila's Meeting with Leo the Great*) or to the early years of the Christian Church (e.g., the *Liberation of St Peter*). Therefore the cycle is mainly descriptive. Raphael develops it with those characteristics of dignity and grandiosity which were by then his trademarks. He enhances his compositions by breaking up the symmetry and the en-

45-47. *The School of Athens,*
details representing Heraclitus with the features of
Michelangelo, Euclid with those of Donato Bramante, and
Pythagoras
Vatican, Stanza della Segnatura

48. *The Parnassus*
Vatican, Stanza della Segnatura

closed rhythm of the Stanza della Segnatura with more lively and colorful effects.

These trends appear first in the *Expulsion of Heliodorus.* The focal point of the scene is no longer at the center. Rather, it is shifted to the right. Here Heliodorus and his followers, profaning the Temple of Jerusalem, are driven out by an armed rider and by two running figures. In the center, the expanse of the wide nave, illuminated by the reflections of light in the vault, is a more effective space-determining motif than the large patches of blue sky which appeared through the coffered ceiling in the *School of Athens.* At the extreme left, Pope Julius II dominates the bystanders, and he reappears in subsequent scenes as well. Raphael's new compositional formula, so unexpected after the extremely controlled compositions of the Stanza della Segnatura, is visible in all its dynamic evidence from this fresco onward.

Another exceptional event is represented after the *Expulsion of Heliodorus.* It is the basis of the Catholic ceremony of the *Corpus Domini.*

In 1263 a priest from Bohemia, during a pilgrimage to Rome, saw blood dripping from the Chalice onto the Corporal cloth while celebrating Mass in Bolsena. This was interpreted as a supernatural answer to the priest's skepticism regarding the transubstantiation. The cloth, as proof of the miracle, was transferred to the neighboring city

N D M D X IIII

49, 50. *The Parnassus,*
details representing Dante Alighieri and the Muses
Vatican, Stanza della Segnatura

51. *The Cardinal Virtues*
Vatican, Stanza della Segnatura

52, 53. *The Expulsion of Heliodorus from the Temple,*
and detail of the high priest praying for divine aid
Vatican, Stanza di Eliodoro

54, 55. *The Mass of Bolsena, and detail of the throne-bearers of Pope Julius II*
Vatican, Stanza di Eliodoro

of Orvieto to be preserved in the Cathedral. The church was rebuilt (in its present form) to honor the occasion. Raphael represents the priest, the protagonist of the event, close to the center of the composition. As he raises the Host, two devotees lean over the semicircular screen which forms the background of the scene. This is a further attempt by Raphael to represent figures in a more dynamic way. Some critics believe he was inspired by Lorenzo Lotto, who was among the artists who had begun to paint the Stanza della Segnatura before his intervention. Pope Julius appears at the right of the scene, a symbol of ecclesiastical authority's presence during, and approval of, the miracle. The Pope's attendants stand one step below and behind him. The asymmetry of the composition regards time as well as space: the excitement of the figures at the left represents a reaction to the supernatural event, which they witness; the stillness of the Pope and his attendants indicates their *spiritual* presence, achieved through a meditative evocation of the event.

Raphael's assistants played a greater role in painting the Eliodoro cycle than in the Stanza della Segnatura. This is clearly a consequence of the growing number of commissions which the Romans granted to Raphael. The hand of Giulio Romano, one of his most faithful pupils, is visible in

56, 57. *The Liberation of St Peter, with detail*
Vatican, Stanza di Eliodoro

58. *The Meeting between Leo the Great and Attila*
Vatican, Stanza di Elidoro

59. *The Fire in the Borgo*
Vatican, Stanza dell'Incendio di Borgo

60, 61. *The Fire in the Borgo*, details
Vatican, Stanza dell'Incendio di Borgo

62. *Portrait of a Cardinal*
79x62 cm
Madrid, Prado

the episode showing the *Liberation of St Peter*. The composition of this fresco clearly reflects the order and unity of the *Mass of Bolsena*. But the story is broken down into three distinct episodes, taken from the *Acts of the Apostles*. The first shows the dismay of the guards; the second the appearance of the Angel of Freedom in the saint's cell; the third the bewildered Peter led by the hand of the divine messenger. The barred cell is on an upper level (like the altar in the *Mass*) and is reached by steps to the left and right. A group of agitated figures occupies the stairway at the left. Here, a soldier — whose armor reflects the light of the moon — asks his sleepy and bewildered comrades what is going on. At right, the angel leads the stunned and still-sleepy St Peter past another sleeping guard. Here, for the first time Raphael attempts a "night effect", using both the natural light of the moon and the autonomous light of the angel. This painting is the last fresco that can be attributed to Raphael with any certainty. The large cycles which follow (except for the *Sibyls* of Santa Maria della Pace) were entrusted mainly to assistants.

In the last episode of the Stanza di Eliodoro, Raphael returns to the symmetrical compositional type of the Stanza della Segnatura. The painting represents Pope Leo the Great who, with the assistance of God, prevented the Huns from attacking Rome. The figure of the Pope on horseback is a portrait of Leo X. It was originally intended to represent Julius II, but the Della Rovere Pope died before the completion of the cycle, and his portrait was substituted by that of his successor. The scene is divided into two parts: at left

than the other frescoes of the cycle. Many critics attribute this weakness to the extensive participation of Raphael's pupils, led by Giulio Romano.

The room of the *Fire in the Borgo* where, from 1514 to 1517, Raphael's workshop illustrated historical episodes in which the protagonists are the Popes who took the name of Leo, completes our examination of the Vatican cycles. This room contains episodes like the *Fire in the Borgo*, in which a miracle performed by Pope Leo IV caused a fire raging in Rome in 847 to be extinguished; the *Battle of Ostia*, in which the Saracens were lost in a storm at sea, presumably because of the presence of Leo IV, and the *Coronation of Charlemagne* by Pope Leo III on Christmas Day, 799. Here the illustration of themes drawn from the past mixes with the celebration of the political projects of the present Pope, in this case Leo X's reconciliation with France. The fourth subject, the *Oath of Leo III*, anticipates the numerous representations of popes and bishops in assizes which became common during the Counter Reformation in the late 16th century.

The *Fire in the Borgo* is the most complex of the four episodes. It is full of references to classical antiquity, to medieval architecture at the time of the affirmation of the Church, and to themes used by contemporary artists. It celebrates the intercession of Leo IV, by whose grace a fire which spread through the Borgo, a popular section of Rome near the Basilica of St Peter, was extinguished. The structure of the composition is complex: two colonnades of clear classical derivation define a square. The Pope, who again bears the features of Leo X, blesses the frightened crowd from a gallery located beyond the colonnades. The façade of old St Peter's appears behind him, in the background. The term 'scenographic' can appropriately be applied to this painting. Clearly, Raphael was concentrating on richer, more varied, but less harmonious compositional solutions than those of his previous paintings. The figure groups express great formal beauty, but they lack harmonious relationships and remain pure examples of episodical representation. The group in the left foreground, for example (made up of an old man on the shoulders of a young man, and a child), may be drawn from the episode of the *Aeneid* in which Aeneas escapes with his father, Anchises and his son, Ascanius. The woman with children in the center of the fresco and the water carrier at right, whose clothes blow in the wind, represent similar stereotypes. The nude descending from the wall at left recalls the heroic figures of Michelangelo. Notwithstanding these limitations, the scene is highly effective and demonstrates Raphael's skill as an illustrator, although, as the critics maintain, it was executed largely by his pupils.

63. The Prophet Isaiah
Rome, Church of Sant'Agostino

64. The Triumph of Galatea
Rome, La Farnesina

the Pope and his attendants, poised and solemn, offer a gesture of peace to the Huns. Above them, Saints Peter and Paul brandish a sword. At right, Attila and his attendants, also on horseback, are frightened to death at the view of the two saints, whose figures are counterbalanced by an armed foot soldier. In the background are Rome and Mount Mario, on which a fire is blazing.

This episode is clearly more fragmentary and dispersive

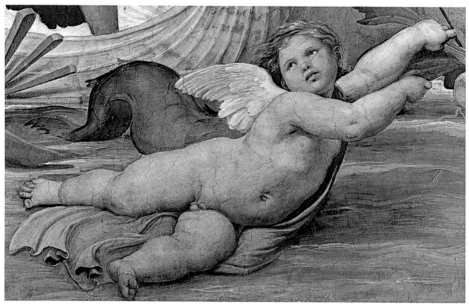

65, 66. The Triumph of Galatea, details
Rome, La Farnesina

67. Madonna and Child with the Young St John (Madonna del Duca d'Alba) dia. 98 cm Washington, National Gallery of Art

Raphael after the Vatican Stanze

The fame of his fresco cycles brought Raphael numerous other commissions in Rome. Some of these were executed at the same time as the monumental cycles of the Vatican Stanze.

One of the masterpieces of this period is the *Portrait of a Cardinal* today in the Prado in Madrid. This painting was once considered a work of the mature painter. But it has recently been dated 1510-1511 on the basis of its composition which resembles those of the *Portraits of Agnolo and Maddalena Doni* and the *Mute Woman*. The pose is identical: the figure is turned three-quarters out and the arm nearest the viewer defines the lower limit of the picture space.

Raphael returns to the representation of the Virgin and Child with St John in the *Madonna del Duca D'Alba*. The composition of this tondo is extremely simple. The pyramidal scheme is expanded in width. The cold and resonant colors contrast with the delicate greens and light-blues of the broad landscape background. Small, symmetrically arranged flowers provide centers of color against the ochre tones of the ground. The Virgin's eyes are symbolically fixed on the cross made of sticks which St John (who is the

precursor of Christ) and the infant Christ both hold. The vigorous modelling of her drapery may be inspired by Michelangelo. But, as Venturi notes, "the pure features, the radiant open eyes, translate the solemn... language of Michelangelo into the melodic language of Raphael". The work is roughly dated 1511.

The Sienese Banker, Agostini Chigi, played a very important role in the cultural and artistic activities which flourished around Julius II. His house was built on the outskirts of Rome in 1509-1510, and was designed as a model of luxury and elegance. He commissioned the most famous artists of the time, Baldassarre Peruzzi, Sebastiano Luciani (later called Sebastiano del Piombo) and Raphael himself to decorate it. All three painted frescoes based on classical mythology in Chigi's house (which was later acquired by the Farnese family and came to be known as "La Farnesina"). Raphael illustrated a theme from the Greek poet, Theocrates, on the walls of the Loggia (or porch), in a painting which combines the vitality of pagan narrative with his unusual compositional harmony. Galatea, the sea-nymph, rushes forward on a dolphin-drawn chariot. Her head is turned to one side and her glance is directed over

her shoulder toward the *amorini* or cupids who fly above her, bows drawn. A crowd of sea-nymphs and Tritons — fantastic creatures, half man and half fish — surround her. The powerful nudes possess the energy of Michelangelo, but the soft modelling of the winged cupids is peculiar to Raphael.

Agostino Chigi later commissioned other works to Raphael: the *Psyche*, also in the Farnesina; the *Sibyls* in the Church of Santa Maria della Pace; and the tondo in the Church of Santa Maria del Popolo.

A new fresco occupied Raphael during the period 1511-1512: the *Prophet Isaiah* painted for Johannes Goritz of Luxemburg, Head Chancellor of the Papal Court. That the work was commissioned by a foreigner is indicative of the extraordinary fame that Raphael had acquired. This powerful but composed prophet and the putti who surround him echo Michelangelo's figures in the *Sistine Ceiling*. Nonetheless, the putti, whose glances and poses are enlivened by a strong spiritual tension, are transformed by Raphael into tender and formally controlled children. Even the action of the wind that blows Isaiah's mantle is a life-giving device rather than an expression of dramatic feeling. The dedicatory inscription in Greek (which alludes to St Ann, patron of Goritz) and the Hebrew scroll which the

68. The Sistine Madonna
265x196 cm
Dresden, Gemäldegalerie

69, 70. The Madonna of Foligno, with detail
320x194 cm
Vatican, Pinacoteca

Prophet holds, reflect the learned environment in which the work was conceived.

The solemn forms of the Vatican Stanze, the Farnesina frescoes and the *Isaiah* appear again in two large panels representing the Madonna in Glory. The first was executed for Sigismondo de' Conti in 1511-1512 and is usually called the *Madonna of Foligno*. The second, dated 1513-1514, is called the *Sistine Madonna*.

Raphael's pictorial research had been enriched by his solutions regarding the use of light in the *Expulsion of Heliodorus* and the *Liberation of St Peter*. These pictorial devices reappear in the *Madonna of Foligno*, now in the Vatican Museum. The Madonna and Child, borne by a cloud of angels and framed by an orange disk, dominate the group of saints below them, among whom is the donor. This group

378

includes — from left to right — *St John the Baptist, St Francis, Sigismondo de' Conti* and *St Jerome*. A small angel at the center of the composition holds a small plaque which was originally intended to carry the dedicatory inscription. The painting was commissioned to commemorate a miracle in which the donor's house in Foligno was struck by lightning or — according to another version — was struck by a projectile during the seige of Foligno, although it was not damaged. The stormy atmosphere of the landscape background and the flash of lightning (or explosion) which strikes the Chigi Palace (visible at left) illustrate the legend. The strong characterization of the figures, the volumetric fullness of the putti and the refined *chiaroscuro* distinguish the panel (which was taken as loot by Napoleon's army in 1799 and returned in 1815) as a work of the mature artist.

The canvas with the Virgin, Child and Saints Sixtus and Barbara, usually called the *Sistine Madonna* (now in the Dresden Museum), is characterized by an imaginary space created by the figures themselves. The figures stand on a bed of clouds, framed by heavy curtains which open to either side. The painting was probably intended to decorate the tomb of Pope Julius II, for the holy Pope Sixtus was the patron saint of the Della Rovere family and St Barbara and the two winged *genii* (visible at the bottom of the picture space) symbolize the funeral ceremony. The canvas was located in the Convent of St Sixtus in Piacenza and was later donated by the monks to Augustus III, King of Saxony. It was carried to Moscow after the Second World War, and

was later returned to Dresden. The Virgin actually appears to descend from a heavenly space, through the picture plane, out into the real space in which the painting is hung. The gesture of St Sixtus and the glance of St Barbara seem to be directed toward the faithful, whom we imagine beyond the ballustrade at the bottom of the painting. The Papal tiara, which rests on top of this ballustrade, acts as a bridge between the real and pictorial space.

The Pope who had commissioned the pictorial cycles and the works that had so contributed to the artist's fame, is depicted — according to historical sources, in the master's hand — in a portrait "so animated and true to life that it was frightening to behold, as though it were actually alive" (Vasari). The original painting was intended for the Church of Santa Maria del Popolo in Rome, but never arrived there. The Uffizi canvas is a copy which arrived in the Medici collections in Florence from Urbino with the Della Rovere inheritance. Attributed by critics to 1512, it shows the Pope seated with the tiara on his head, dressed in a white surplice and a purple mantle. Here the simple but effective tonal contrast, first used in the *Portrait of a Cardinal*, reappears. The Pope, though old, still seems very vigorous and the Della Rovere energy is clearly visible in the hand that grasps the right arm of the chair with strength and pride. The two acorn-shaped knobs on the back of the chair recall the Pope's coat of arms. The intimacy of the image, although weakened by the executor of the copy, indicates that Raphael has progressed from the narrative compositions of

71. *Portrait of Julius II*
108.5x80 cm
Florence, Uffizi

72. *Portrait of Fedra Inghirami*
89.5x62.3 cm
Florence, Galleria Palatina (Pitti Palace)

73. *Portrait of Baldassarre Castiglione*
82x67 cm
Paris, Louvre

74. *Portrait of Cardinal Bibbiena*
85x66.3 cm
Florence, Galleria Palatina (Pitti Palace)

the Vatican Stanze to the full dominance of individual subjectivity.

Meanwhile, Raphael had passed from the highly synthetic and expressive compositions of the first years of the decade to representations which were more and more complex and even more dispersive. Most of these were also finished by his pupils, for, as we mentioned above, this was the busiest moment in Raphael's career.

The *Madonna dell'Impannata* in the Pitti Gallery in Florence was also painted with the help of assistants. According to some critics, the assistants executed the entire painting.

But others see the master's hand at least in the major figures (some say in the Christ child, some in St Elizabeth, some in both figures). The composition is innovative in respect to the usual iconography of the holy family. It shows St Catherine, St Elizabeth, Christ, the Virgin and St John gathered together in a group. A large tent is visible in the background and a window covered by linen (the *impannata*, or cloth covering of a window, which gives the painting its name) can be seen at the extreme right. Like many other works by Raphael, this painting was carried off by the French in 1799 and was not returned until after the Congress of Vienna, in 1815.

In 1514 Raphael executed another small but significant fresco cycle for Agostino Chigi. The frescoes represent the *Prophets and Sibyls*. They are located in the chapel at the left of the apse of the Church of Santa Maria della Pace in Rome. The figures occupy a trabeated loggia, on two levels. The structure of the loggia reflects the architecture of the chapel: its arches coincide with those of the window and entrance. The *Prophets* (Habakkuk, Jonah, David and Daniel, according to the most widely accepted interpretation) are generally attributed to a collaborator (perhaps Timoteo Viti) who must have based them on an original drawing by Raphael, for they are highly coherent. The *Sibyls* (Cumaean, Persian, Phrygian and Tiburtine) are attributed to Raphael. Like the Virtues in the Stanza della Segnatura, each of the figures is accompanied by an angel who indicates the divine spirit present in their prophecies.

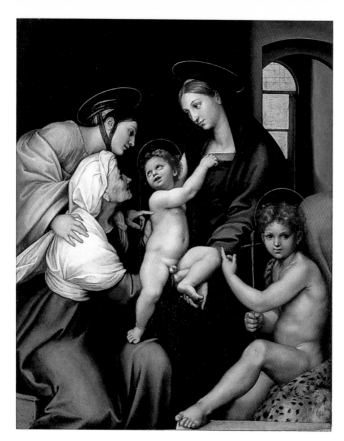

75. Madonna dell'Impannata 160x126 cm Florence, Galleria Palatina (Pitti Palace)

76, 77. Sybils and Angels, and detail showing the Tiburtine Sybil Rome, Church of Santa Maria della Pace

Between the Sibyls at the top of the arch is a small angel holding a lighted torch, the symbol of prophecy, which enlightens the darkness of the future.

Raphael probably accompanied Leo X when he went to Bologna to meet the King of France, Francis I, in 1515. He may have passed through Florence, where Leo was welcomed with great enthusiasm by his fellow citizens. Leonardo da Vinci — who later accepted the French King's invitation to Paris — and Michelangelo — to whom Leo X commissioned the New Sacresty of San Lorenzo — also followed the Pope.

A letter which Raphael sent to the painter, Francesco Francia, provides proof of this journey. According to a legend, Francesco Francia died after seeing the *St Cecilia* which Raphael painted for the Church of San Giovanni in Monte in Bologna. The story is almost credible, for the Bolognese artistic environment still revolved around the style of Perugino. The painting, which is now in the Museum of Bologna, was placed in San Giovanni in Monte in 1515. It was painted some time before, however. The figures re-

present St Paul, St John the Evangelist, St Cecilia, St Augustine and St Mary Magdalene. The four saints who surround the protagonist form a niche which is strengthened by the poses and gestures of the figures (the glances of the Evangelist and St Augustine cross, St Paul's is lowered and the Magdalene turns hers toward the spectator). Only St Cecilia raises her face toward the sky, where a chorus of angels appears through a hole in the clouds. The monumentality of the figures, typical of Raphael's activity during this period, dominates the other figurative elements. The still life of musical instruments on the ground has been attributed to Raphael's pupil Giovanni da Udine, according to a tradition begun by Vasari.

The *Madonna della Sedia*, in the Pitti Gallery in Florence, was probably painted during the period immediately after the completion of the Stanza di Eliodoro. The qualities of color and light which this tondo possesses result in great compositional harmony. A circular motif dominates the painting, in perfect agreement with the form of the support. The Virgin is by no means conceived in aristocratic terms.

78. St Cecilia
238x150 cm
Bologna, Pinacoteca Nazionale

79. Madonna and Child with the Young
St John (Madonna della Sedia)
dia. 71 cm
Florence, Galleria Palatina (Pitti Palace)

Her clothes are modest, and even the maternal sentiment expressed in the painting is not altered by the knowledge of its sacred nature. Rather, it is expressed in an instinctive gesture of affectionate protection of the Child. The rich and polished back of the chair which gives the work its name (*sedia* means chair) thus stands in clear contrast to the figure. The young St John fills the space left free by Virgin and Child and balances the composition, though remaining outside the tender relationship which links mother and Child.

Many critics associate the composition of the *Madonna della Sedia* with that of the *Madonna della Tenda* (so called because of the curtain which forms the background) in the Alte Pinakothek of Munich. Here again the Madonna is shown in a three-quarters view with the Child and the young St John. But a relationship exists among the figures which is absent in the *Madonna della Sedia*. The Virgin smiles at her Child, whose attention is turned toward St John. The face of the latter bears an expression of loving devotion. By comparing Raphael's mature works to one another, one detects a process of continuous growth, of stylistic evolution. The elements used are always new, as is the pictorial style. But the master's extraordinary capacity to harmonize the composition and the formal beauty of the figures, made more evident by the expression of serene emotion, are unifying motifs.

There are two extant versions of Raphael's *Portrait of Cardinal Inghirami*: one in Boston and the other in Palazzo

Pitti. Each has been considered the original at one time or another, but the dispute is useless, since both are highly coherent and the differences between them are slight: the physical structure of the Cardinal is more massive in the Boston portrait and leaner in the Pitti one. The red of the Cardinal's clothing dominates both. Inghirami's crossed eyes, a physical defect which the artist does not leave out, acquire a discreet tone which almost dissolves in the inspired pose of the figure. Without idealizing, but also without falling into unpleasant naturalism, Raphael maintains a harmonic equilibrium between realism and dignified celebration, a primary characteristic of portrait painting.

The *Portrait of Baldassarre Castiglione* (now in the Louvre), a literary figure active at the court of Urbino in the early years of the 15th century and author of the *Courtesan*, the book which summed up the tastes and culture of the Renaissance, may or may not have been painted by Raphael. According to a letter of 1516 from Pietro Bembo to Cardinal Bibbiena, "The Portrait of M. Baldassar Castiglione... [and that of Duke Guidobaldo di Montefeltro] would seem to be by the hand of one of Raphael's pupils". But the high quality and masterful combination of pictorial elements which distinguish the painting (note the affection inherent in the intelligent and calm face of Castiglione) lead one to believe that the master participated in some way in its execution. Certainly the shaded tonalities of the clothing and the unusually light background indicate the hand of a skillful and experienced painter.

*80. Madonna and Child with the Young St John
(Madonna della Tenda)
68x55 cm
Munich, Alte Pinakothek*

Also in 1516, Agostino Chigi commissioned the decoration of his chapel in Santa Maria del Popolo to Raphael. Raphael designed the architecture of the chapel and planned Agostino's tomb. He prepared the cartoons for the mosaic of the dome, fusing together classical motives (the Planets, represented as pagan gods) and Christian ones (the figure of God the Father who sets the heavens in motion with an authoritative gesture). But his activity in this year included other works as well. He was widely recognized at the humanistic court of Leo X, who made him the architect of St Peter's on 1 August 1514, and this increased his work load. He was placed in charge of the marble which came to St Peter's from excavations and from antique monuments. He gathered statues, medals and antique objects for Alfonso I d'Este. Finally, he tried his hand as a sculptor. The largest task he undertook in the course of the year was the preparation of the cartoons for the tapestries for the Sistine Chapel depicting the *Stories of Saints Peter and Paul*. The completed tapestries were acquired by Charles I, King of England, and are now in the Victoria and Albert Museum in London.

The *Donna Velata* in Palazzo Pitti is another portrait dated 1516. Tradition identifies the subject with "la Fornarina", the woman whom the painter loved in his last years and whose face reappeared in both his paintings and those of his followers. The painting shows greater attention to color and to the rendering of skin and clothes in respect to previous female portraits. The regular oval of the young woman's face stands out against the dark background and her eyes hold an intense and penetrating look. The silk of her sleeves contrasts with her ivory-like skin, and is closely associated with the thin pleating of the dress, held up by a corset with golden embroidery. As in the portrait of Castiglione, the figure radiates a sense of great dignity and restraint. But greys and light-blues dominated the portrait of Castiglione: here the warm tonalities of white and gold take over. Raphael is preparing the wider color range and the more complex composition which will be expressed in the *Portrait of Leo X*.

During this period Raphael was much sought after by priests and cardinals who competed in the decoration of their mansions in Rome. Cardinal Bernardo Dovizi da Bibbiena, a cultured playwright, and (like Leo X) a passionate scholar of classical antiquity, undoubtedly had more contact with Raphael than any of his colleagues. Raphael painted a portrait of the Cardinal which clearly expressed his shrewd and malicious spirit and his taste for beautiful things and fine luving. The attribution of the portrait (now in the Pitti Gallery) is not certain, but the composition and the characteristic use of white and red suggest Raphael's hand. However, the rendering seems more rigid than in the paintings certainly painted by Raphael. Some critics therefore attribute it to a pupil of Raphael, or suspect that it may be a copy of an original which might have been lost. The Cardinal was so close to the artist that he offered his niece Marietta, in marriage.

In the same year as the *Portrait of Cardinal Bibbiena* (1516), Raphael and his followers were commissioned to decorate the bathroom of the Cardinal's Vatican apartments, the so-called *Stufetta*. The ornamental motives employed in the *Stufetta* paintings derive from those of the *Domus Aurea*, the villa of the Emperor Nero situated between the Palatine and the Velian hills. The *Domus Aurea* had recently been rediscovered. By 1516 it had become an object of great enthusiasm for contemporary artists. The names of Giovanni da Udine, Domenichino and other lesser known painters are still visible, scratched in the walls of the monument. Raphael painted the *Story of Venus* on the walls of the *Stufetta*, perhaps at the suggestion of the Cardinal. He represented the episodes of the story in the same techniques used in the *Domus Aurea*: stucco and fresco. The decoration of the borders started a new ornamental style, called "grottesque", which derives from the decoration of the "grotto" of Nero's villa. The new style was widely used throughout the Cinquecento and after. It replaced the "candelabro" motif of the Quattrocento, generally made up of plants, animals and stylized putti growing out of a vase or amphora. Raphael thus left his mark in the field of decorative tastes as well as in that of pictorial style.

81. Portrait of a Woman (La Donna Velata)
82x60,5 cm
Florence, Galleria Palatina (Pitti Palace)

82. The Vision of Ezekiel
40x30 cm
Florence, Galleria Palatina (Pitti Palace)

83. The Loggia of Psyche
Rome, La Farnesina

84. The 'Stufetta' of Cardinal Bibbiena in the Vatican Palaces

85. The Second Loggia, called 'Raphael's Loggia', in the Vatican Palaces

86-88. The 'Loggetta' in the Vatican Palaces, with its frescoes by the school of Raphael, and details of the grotesque decoration

In the following year, 1517, Agostino Chigi commissioned Raphael to decorate the ground floor loggia of the villa in which the artist had painted the *Galatea* five years before. Like the *Galatea* and the *Stufetta*, this cycle reflects the cultured atmosphere which flourished in Rome under Julius II and Leo X. The frescoes represent the *Story of Psyche*, a myth derived from the *Golden Ass* of Apuleius (2nd century A. D.). Although the preparatory drawings and the general conception of the stories are by Raphael, the bulk of the painting was carried out by his pupils, notably

89-92. School of Raphael
Details of the fresco
decoration of the Second
Loggia showing: the
Separation of Land and
Water; the Creation of the
Animals; Isaac and Rebecca
Spied upon by Abimelech;
Jacob's Dream

93. Portrait of a Woman
(La Fornarina)
85x60 cm
Rome, Galleria Nazionale

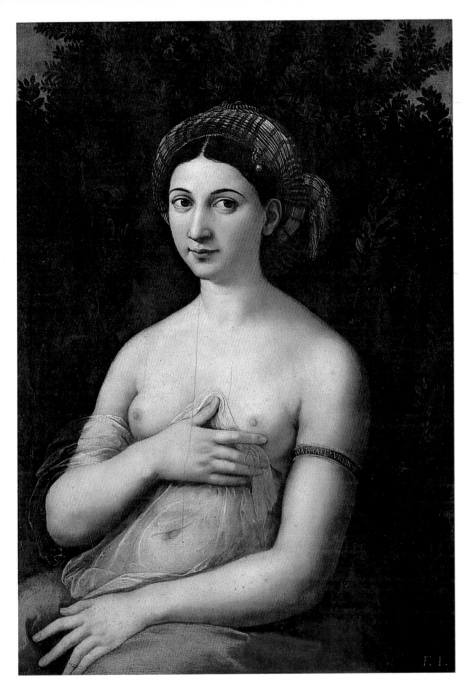

94, 95. Cartoons for the tapestries of the Sistine Chapel
London, Victoria and Albert Museum

96. Portrait of Leo X with two Cardinals
155.5x119.5 cm
Florence, Uffizi

Giovanni da Udine (who painted the rich plant festoons of the frame) with the collaboration of Giulio Romano, Raffaellino del Colle and Gianfrancesco Penni. The two major scenes were painted in the vault. They are The Marriage of Cupid and Psyche and the Council of the Gods, conceived in terms of tapestries and embroideries.

Some elements deriving from Michelangelo are present in Raphael's works from the period after 1517. The Vision of Ezekiel is a typical example. The Vision shows the same balanced composition present throughout Raphael's works. The origin of the subject is the Bible (Ezekiel, 1:4-12). But instead of describing the four Kerubim (inspired by Babylonian iconography) as the Prophet did, Raphael represents a classical divinity with the traditional symbols of the Evangelists. This interpretation is confirmed by those critics who, like Antonio Natali, can see in the painting the apocalyptic vision of St John at Patmos. A centrally placed tree dominates the low, broad landscape and the sky is turbulent and stormy. The divine group hovers amid the clouds, surrounded by an aura of bright light. The angel, eagle, lion and ox which symbolize the Evangelists, together with two cherubs, spiral around the vigorous central figure. The painting, now in the Pitti Gallery in Florence, is believed to have been painted in 1518. Like many other paintings by Raphael, it was removed to Paris by Napoleon's army and returned to Tuscany in 1815.

Raphael was very active during the last two years of his life. Francis I, King of France, commissioned two paintings from him in 1518: the first representing St Michael and the second, the Holy Family. Critics have attributed both to Raphael's workshop, underlining the chiaroscuro effects and the leaden tones which mark them. Raphael himself was engaged with his project for the decoration of the Vatican Loggias, which was completed in 1519.

But his greatest masterpiece, possibly the only work he executed without help during these last years, is the Portrait of Pope Leo X and Cardinals Luigi de' Rossi and Giulio de' Medici (later to become Pope Clement VII), both relatives of the Pope. This group portrait (which created a sensation, notwithstanding the existence of precedents) is focused on the central figure of the Pope. The two Cardinals, Luigi de' Rossi on Leo's right (whose sharp features, modelled by strong chiaroscuro effects, suggest the hand of Giulio Romano) and Giulio de' Medici on his left, act as a royal escort. An illuminated prayer book lies open on the table in front of Pope Leo. On the same table rests a finely carved bell. Both objects undoubtedly reveal the exquisite tastes of the Pope who was, as we have seen, an active patron of the arts. The uniform tone of color, expressed in various red nuances; the quiet atmosphere, alluding to the power of the Pope and the splendor of his court; and the compositional harmony, make this portrait one of the most admired and significant works of Raphael. These paintings symbolically close the painter's career. He had enjoyed the patronage of two Popes and his presence in Rome had made the city the most important artistic center in Italy.

His map of ancient Rome was dedicated to this task and to recovering evidence of Rome's former greatness. He worked on it throughout 1519, and aroused great enthusiasm. A letter of praise by Castiglione, written in Latin after the death of the artist, summarizes this enthusiasm.

Much of Raphael's energy during these last years was directed toward public activity, or at least toward commissioners who were influential in city life and life within the Papal States (he designed a villa, known as the Villa Madonna, for Cardinal Giulio de' Medici). Furthermore, many critics attribute to him a series of compositions of the Holy Family and of Saints which were then executed by his followers. The famous portrait of a young woman, called La Fornarina, must also be viewed in this perspective, although it is signed, in Latin, "Raphael from Urbino". The signature is engraved on the thin ribbon that the girl wears just under her left shoulder. Tradition identifies her with Margherita Luti, a Sienese woman whom Raphael loved, the daughter of a baker from the Roman district of Santa Dorotea. The stiffness of her features and the heavy chiaroscuro effect make La Fornarina an almost certain workshop piece, for Raphael's own work from this period is far more delicate.

According to Vasari, Raphael's pupils — among them Giulio Romano, Gianfrancesco Penni, Vincenzo Tamagni, Perin del Vaga and Polidoro da Caravaggio — executed a cycle of thirteen Bible Stories in the vaults of the Logge adjoining the buildings that Bramante had built in the Vatican for Julius II. The Gallery was planned by Raphael, who also designed a decorative cycle of grotesques and stucco-reliefs. The latter were executed according to the ancient technique studied during the excavation of the Domus Aurea. The Bible Stories occupied Raphael's workshop from 1518 to 1519. They are reknown both for their pictorial value and for the influence they had on later decorative cycles.

The Biblical episodes were painted in the ceiling vaults, within differently shaped frames. Together they form a swarm of figures, isolated and in groups, arranged in an extraordinary variety of compositions and poses. Michelangelo's Doni Tondo introduced mannerism as a principle of figure design; the Vatican Logge introduced descriptive mannerism, a style of painting divorced from the precepts and principles of the early Renaissance. This style gave rise to lively and refined images packed with allusions, symbols and allegories, and often inspired by literary texts. It soon became an international movement. It was used with, or instead of, the classicizing tendency from which it originated, throughout the 16th century.

Raphael's pupils later reaffirmed their interest in classical antiquity and its interpretation in the decoration of the Loggetta, a small porch adjacent to the above-mentioned Stufetta, or bath room, of Cardinal Bibbiena. The decorative program consisted of grotesque figures and of scenes from the Apollo myth. Only two of the three original paintings have been preserved. The scholar, Regid de Campos, reconstructed the third scene, whose theme was almost certainly the Flaying of Marsyas. The other two scenes represent Olympus praying to Apollo, and Apollo and Marsyas. Architectural structures, animals, winged cherubs and false niches containing reproductions of statues (which Regid de Campos has identified as the *Seasons*) — similar to those which appear in Roman wall paintings — accompany the three scenes. This refined decorative complex was the logical completion of the *Logge* and the last reflection of the classical tendencies of art at the court of Leo X. Raphael was overwhelmed by commissions by this time. He dedicated himself to the design and planning of the works which were entrusted to him, and left the material execution to his pupils. The latter participated (together with Sebastiano del Piombo, who painted in a Michelangelo-like style) in the decoration of the fourth room of the Vatican Palace, the Stanza di Costantino. Here Raphael's influence is weaker than in the other rooms. The figures are extremely agitated. They violate that norm which Raphael observed even in his more dynamic creations, for instance, the frescoes for the Stanza di Eliodoro.

Raphael's health deteriorated rapidly, undermined by his relentless activity and by the excesses of his private life. Bad health prevented him from finishing the *Transfiguration*, now in the Vatican Museum. Vasari, not without prejudice, compares the unrestrained life of Raphael to the austere and heroic one of Michelangelo, of whom he was a passionate admirer and around whose art he had structured his *Lives of the Artists*. Cardinal Giulio de' Medici commissioned the *Transfiguration* in 1517 to Raphael for the French Cathedral of Narbonne. However, it remained in San Pietro in Montorio after 1523. Taken to Paris 1797, it was brought back in its present location in 1815.

The composition of the *Transfiguration* is divided into two distinct parts: the Miracle of the Possessed Boy on a lower level, in the foreground; and the Transfiguration of Christ on Mount Tabor, in the background. The transfigured Christ floats in an aura of light and clouds above the hill, accompanied by Moses and Elijah. Below, on the ground, are his disciples. Some are dazzled by the light of glory, others are in prayer. The gestures of the crowd beholding at the miracle link the two parts together: the raised hands of the crowd converge toward the figure of Christ. In this very grand composition Raphael has summed up all the elements present in the best of contemporary painting, including references to classical antiquity, Leonardo da Vinci (without doubt based on his recall of impressions garnered during his stay in Florence), and — not without a certain narcissism — himself. This work sets the stage (just as surely as Michelangelo's *Doni Tondo*) for Mannerism. The numerous drawings (both by Raphael and pupils) for the characters in the painting, together with the number of variants of the first draft which were revealed by restoration work in 1977,

97. The Transfiguration (before restoration)
405x278 cm
Vatican, Pinacoteca

98-100. The Transfiguration, with details (after restoration)

show just exactly how carefully meditated a composition it is. The restoration also dispelled any doubts as to the authenticity of the attribution to Raphael; the retouching and corrections are proof that the painting (although unfinished) is actually entirely in his hand.

The *Transfiguration* is the last bequest of an artist whose brief life was rich in inspiration, where doubt or tension had no place. Raphael's life was spent in thoughts of great harmony and balance. This is one of the reasons why Raphael appears as the best interpreter of the art of his time and has been admired and studied in every century.

On 6 April 1520, precisely 37 years after he was born, Raphael died in Rome, the city that he had helped make the most important center of art and culture that had ever existed.

TITIAN

1. *Birth of Adonis, detail*
Padua, Museo Civico

The Early Years

Tiziano Vecellio was born at Pieve di Cadore into a family of ancient roots and distinguished traditions. No document records the precise date of his birth which has long been the subject of much critical debate: the problem is not insignificant since it involves the piecing together of the chronology of Titian's early works. A document in the register of deaths of the parish of San Canciano in Venice, where the painter ended his days on the 27 August 1576, states that he "died at the age of a hundred and three" ("morto de anni cento e tre") thus leading a body of critics to deduce that he was born in 1473. This theory that Titian was over a hundred years old at his death seems to find confirmation in a letter of 1 August 1571 to Philip II in which the painter laments the fact that he was then ninety five years old.

This reconstruction is at odds with the written testimony of some of his contemporaries. In the second edition of the *Lives of the Artists*, published in 1568. Vasari maintains that Titian was 76 years old at the time of their meeting in Venice in 1566. Dolce, writing in 1557, states that when Titian was working on the frescoes of the Fondaco dei Tedeschi between 1508 and 1509 "he was only just twenty". So, on the basis of these accounts,

Titian was born sometime between 1488 and 1490.

The third theory is based on the presumed dating of an early work, the votive altarpiece, now in Antwerp, depicting *Pope Alexander VI Presenting Jacopo Pesaro to Saint Peter*. This was painted to celebrate the defeat of the Turks at Santa Maura on 30 August 1502: the victorious papal fleet was led by Jacopo Pesaro while his cousin Benedetto commanded the allied Venetian fleet. Some critics believe the altarpiece should be dated close to the event with which it is so explicitly linked; this means fixing Titian's birth date in the first half of the 1480's since he must have been at least twenty when he painted the altarpiece.

Out of the three hypotheses the second one still seems the most likely. In fact, leaving aside the information supplied by Titian's contemporaries, which certainly came from the painter himself, it should be pointed out that if Titian really was born in 1473 his earliest works would have been produced unusually late in his life — when he was over thirty years old. On the other hand the proposed dating of 1503-1506 for the Antwerp altarpiece is by no means certain. In fact it should be given a later dating, placing it just before the altarpiece now in the sacristy of the church of the Salute and datable to 1510, with which it has notable stylistic similarities.

The contemporary sources agree that Titian was a particularly precocious artist. Little more than a child when he arrived in Venice, he and his brother Francesco entered the workshop of Sebastiano Zuccato, father of the San Marco mosaicists Valerio and Francesco. Titian then passed into the workshop of Gentile and Giovanni Bellini, the leading artists of the day. Here he met the rising stars of Venetian painting, Sebastiano del Piombo and Giorgione. It was above all with the latter that Titian had the most contact. So much so that in 1508 and 1509 both young painters worked, although probably not simultaneously, on the decoration of the facade of the recently constructed Fondaco dei Tedeschi. Giorgione was given the main facade on the Grand Canal while the younger Titian got the side giving onto the street — the 'calle del Buso'.

Very little has survived of this imposing decorative scheme which was celebrated with enthusiasm by contemporaries. The ruined figure of a *Nude* by Giorgione and five fragments by Titian's hand are preserved in the Galleria Franchetti of the Ca' d'Oro in Venice. By comparing for example Titian's so-called *Judith* or *Justice* with the Giorgione *Nude* it is easy to pinpoint the essential differences which divide the two artists at this stage. Titian is dynamic and severely vigorous in his depiction of the powerful female figure caught in the act of trampling on a bleeding head; the drawing is incisive and the colour realistic. Giorgione, on the other hand, immerses himself in a stylized elegance, adopting a self-consciously artificial colour scheme

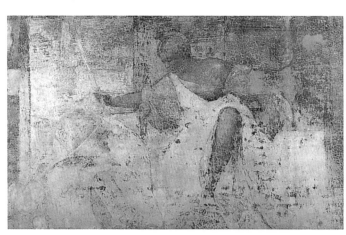

2. *Judith (1508/1509)*
212x345 cm
Venice, Ca' d'Oro

3. *The Legend of Polydorus (c. 1508)*
35x162 cm
Padua, Museo Civico

4. *Birth of Adonis (c. 1508)*
35x162 cm
Padua, Museo Civico

5. *Orpheus and Eurydice (c. 1508)*
39x53 cm
Bergamo, Accademia Carrara

— that "tinta sanguigna e fiammeggiante" ("blood-red and blazing hue") commented on by Anton Maria Zanetti in 1760. Generally speaking Titian's Fondaco frescoes are more nordic than classical in spirit; possibly the intent was to exalt the civic and military virtues of the Venetians in the face of any possible enemy and in particular against the German army of the Emperor. Indeed, the end of 1508 and the beginning of 1509 was a particularly difficult period for Venice, with storm clouds gathering on the horizon as a result of the terrible danger constituted by the League of Cambrai. It is evident in this and in other early paintings of Titian that he was interested in the works of the numerous northern artists then in Venice. Prominent among these was, of course, the figure of Albrecht Dürer who was present in the Venetian area for the first time in 1494-95 and then again in 1505-06 when he was invited by the German merchants of the Fondaco to paint the *Madonna of the Rose Garlands* for the vicarial church of San Bartolomeo. There is no doubt that the very young Titian was part of that band of local painters who (as Dürer himself recounted in a letter to his friend Pirckheimer in 1506) tormented Dürer during his days in Venice,

pursuing him right up to the door of his studio in their efforts to divest him of drawings and ideas. Titian's interest in the northern world is also documented by Vasari, who recalls how as a young man the painter had extended his hospitality to a number of German artists so that he could learn from them the secrets of landscape painting, and that the young Titian also used to study animals "from life". Vasari mentions this in reference to Titian's painting of the *Flight into Egypt* commissioned by Andrea Loredan; this is identifiable with the canvas now in St Petersburg. But many other paintings dating from the very earliest years of Titian's activity reflect this deep interest in the realistic depiction of the natural world; for example the 'cassone' (wedding-chest) panels from the Padua Museum, the *Landscape with Endymion* of the Barnes Collection in Merion and the *Orpheus and Eurydice* in Bergamo. The portraits from this period are also strongly realistic. Of remarkably fine quality are two portraits in the National Gallery, London; the *Portrait of a Man* (early critics erroneously identified it as a portrait of Ariosto; it is perhaps a likeness of Titian's earliest patron — a member of the noble Barbarigo family) and a portrait of a woman

6. *Portrait of a Man (1508/1510)*
81x66 cm
London, National Gallery

7. *Portrait of a Woman called 'La Schiavona'*
(1508/1510)
117x97 cm
London, National Gallery

known as *La Schiavona*. With unrestrained skill Titian poses these personalities in such a way as to make the most of a novel compositional idea; the figures stand out in bold relief against the plain background and the colour emphasises the unusual lighting, revealing the mood of the sitters as well as capturing their physical presence.

"He saw and understood the idea of painting perfectly"

In these portraits Titian paints in a new, straightforward style which challenges the sentimentality of Giorgione. This departure from the latter's style is, however, less evident in Titian's religious paintings. Among his youthful works a good example is the altarpiece for the church of Santo Spirito in Isola (now in the sacristy of the church of the Salute) painted to celebrate the end of the tragic plague which had struck the city in 1510. Here the four saints who are traditionally invoked for protection from the plague — Saints Cosmas and Damian to the left, Roch and Sebastian to the right — are placed in pairs on each side of the altar where Saint Mark, patron saint of Venice, is seated. A new stylistic direction is evident in the way Titian paints the four standing saints. They have a classical nobility of form and a hieratic air which points to the influence of Bellini. On the other hand, the saints on the left — certainly portraits — are given a very realistic sense of individuality which

is in strong contrast to the almost Giorgionesque reserve of the figures to the right. The Santo Spirito altarpiece seems to assume a significant position in Titian's artistic development; it comes at that moment when, following the death of the thirty-three year old Giorgione in the autumn of 1510, Titian reflects on his example. This reflection results in works of the very highest quality of style and poetical feeling: the *Interrupted Concert* (Pitti Palace) the *Fête Champêtre* (Louvre), the London *Noli Me Tangere* and the *Three Ages of Man* in Edinburgh. It is not surprising that these works have been the subject of scholarly debate concerning their attribution to either one of the two artists.

The Pitti *Concert* is centred on three figures who emerge strongly from the dark background: a singer, a harpsichord player and a Dominican friar who holds a viola da gamba. The less imposing figure of the singer is placed a little further back in the composition, while that of the musician (who looks over his shoulder without interrupting his playing) and the friar dominate the painting with their expressive poses and vigorous three-dimensionality — qualities common to Titian's portraits such as the so-called *Ariosto* in London.

The Louvre *Fête Champêtre* is even more reminiscent of Giorgione's style. Here the pastoral subject matter imposes a certain restaint on the emergence of those stylistic and psychological qualities which characterize the early work of Titian. It now seems indisputable that this painting is by Titian's hand, although it is so replete with Giorgionesque elements (the interplay of light and colour and the complex composition, for example) that any doubts in the past as to its attribution were more than justifiable. On the other hand, the typically Titianesque qualities of the canvas lie in the tense handling of colour and drawing, the vitality of the scene, the resonance of the colour which seems to be almost saturated with light and the studied sensuality of the figures, with the two magnificent female nudes who are much more provocative and physical than, for example, Giorgione's Dresden *Venus*.

In the Edinburgh *Three Ages of Man* the young

8, 9. St Mark Enthroned with Saints (1510)
230x149 cm
Venice, Church of Santa Maria della Salute

410

10. *The Interrupted Concert (1511/1512)*
86.5x123.5 cm
Florence, Galleria Palatina, Pitti Palace

11. *Fête Champêtre (1511/1512)*
105x136.5 cm
Paris, Louvre

12. *The Three Ages of Man (1511/1512)*
90x151 cm
Edinburgh, National Gallery of Scotland (on loan from the Duke of Sutherland Collection)

Titian again reaches the heights of poetic feeling. It has been rightly noted that: "the teaching of the old masters is transported beyond any idealized concept of beauty'or intimist dream, in favour of a feeling of *joie de vivre*. This is created through the way in which the generous forms, painted in large areas of colour, and the splendour of the sumptuous hues are offset by the recession into space through alternating areas of luminosity and atmospheric half-shadows". It is precisely in Titian's use of full-bodied colour, made more incisive by the light which gives lustre to the brilliance of the tones, that Titian is so unmistakably different from Giorgione, even when he is imitating Giorgionesque themes.

These three paintings are linked not only stylistically but also thematically; they illustrate the concept of musical harmony as a reflection of cosmic harmony. In the *Noli Me Tangere* Titian abandons the esoteric themes of the learned humanist circles to return to religious subjects, although Giorgionesque elements are still very evident. For example the group of houses overlooked by old city walls to the right of the painting derives unchanged from the background of Giorgione's Dresden *Venus*.

The frescoes carried out by Titian in 1511 for the Scuola del Santo in Padua also bear the imprint of Giorgione's influence. In addition to the finished frescoes — the *Miracle of the Newborn Child* on the north west wall, the *Healing of the Wrathful Son* and the *Miracle of the Jealous Husband* both on the north east wall — Titian planned a fourth scene, although he only got as far as the remarkable under-drawing, discovered in 1969. The subject of this fresco is unclear; it perhaps illustrates one of those numerous miracles performed posthumously by Saint Anthony. The finished frescoes show Titian painting in a straightforward, expressive style typical of the didactic tradition of Fran-

413

ciscan narrative painting, which favoured depiction of the miracles of Saint Anthony in a clear and un-complicated manner which would be easily under-stood by the masses. Yet there is a grandiosity in Titian's narrative powers which enables him to project the tragic message of the stories and the dra-matic intensity of the emotions of the participants.

It is frequently acknowledged that the succession of terrible events which marked the end of the first decade of the century weighed heavily on the poet-ic quality of Titian's work in this period. The cul-mination came in 1509 at Agnadello, where the Venetian Republic suffered a heavy military set-back at the hands of the troops of the League of

13. Noli Me Tangere (1511/1512)
109x91 cm
London, National Gallery

14. The Miracle of the Newborn Child
320x315 cm
Padua, Scuola del Santo

15. The Healing of the Wrathful Son
(1511)
327x220 cm
Padua, Scuola del Santo

16. The Miracle of the Jealous Husband
(1511)
327x123
Padua, Scuola del Santo

*17. Sacra Conversazione
(1512/1514)
138x185 cm
Mamiano (Parma)
Magnani Rocca Collection*

Cambrai and the safety of Venice herself was threatened when the Imperial forces established a bridgehead on the threshold of the lagoon. Nevertheless Titian demonstrates his ability to react decisively to this painful nightmare by developing a new humanism of heroic character in his art. From it emerges his faith in man and in his dominion over the world. This is forcefully expressed in Titian's numerous portraits where the psychological introspection of the personalities is complemented by their wonderfully plastic quality. This can also be seen in the many *Sacra Conversazione* paintings from this period, such as the grandiose altarpiece, datable between 1512 and 1514, in the Magnani Rocca Collection at Mamiano. The donor, who is perhaps a certain Domenico Balbi, is portrayed with extraordinary psychological insight. Of particular interest are the monumental figures of the Virgin Mary and Saint Catherine, who dominate the foreground in sure possession of the space they occupy, presenting themselves confidently to the viewer. Another masterpiece from these years displays the same style although the subject matter is quite different: the *Sacred and Profane Love* in the Borghese Gallery, Rome which was painted in 1514 on the occasion of the marriage of the ducal chancellor Nicolò Aurelio to Laura Bagarotto-Aurelio's coat of arms appears in the bas-relief which decorates the sarcophagus-shaped fountain, on which are seated the twin Venus figures symbolizing celestial Love (the nude figure) and earthly Love (the clothed one); the complex allegorical subject matter reflects the sophisticated tastes of the cultured patron. The painting must also be considered as something of a milestone in Titian's career as an artist. The reference to the antique past in the allegorical bas-relief decorating the sarcophagus can be seen as a piece of self-conscious classicism which serves to underline the meaning of the subject matter. But the superb vitality of the artist bursts forth in the two female figures who are symbolically counterpoised, but at the same time so in harmony with each other that they express that *joie de vivre*, that delight in the senses and in the events of human life that was to become characteristic of the Venetian Renaissance.

In this period Titian often uses the female image to supply his wealthy patrons with paintings which subtly allude to earthly love. This is the case with the *Flora* in the Uffizi Gallery; this is not a portrait but an allegorical figure of *Flora Meretrix*, protagonist of the most popular and licentious ancient Roman festivals.

18. Sacred and Profane Love (1514)
118x279 cm
Rome, Borghese Gallery

"The people began to be astonished by the new 'maniera'"

Titian's fame was now at its peak: in 1513 he had been invited by Pope Leo X, through the mediation of Cardinal Bembo, to move to the papal court, but he had turned down this tempting proposition in order to offer his services to the Venetian Republic, declaring his desire to succeed the elderly Giovanni Bellini in the 'Senseria' or Agency of the Fondaco dei Tedeschi. In practice the artist who held this office was tacitly recognized as the official painter of the Venetian state. In the meantime he confidently offered to demonstrate his exceptional skills by painting, in the Grand Council Chamber of the Doge's palace, the *Battle of Cadore* "which is most difficult and until this moment no man has wanted to burden himself with such an undertaking". The office of the 'Senseria' was not assigned to him until 1517, following the death of Giovanni Bellini, and work on the canvas of the *Battle* was so long drawn out that it was not completed until 1538. By then Titian was long established as the most important artist in Venice.

At the same time Titian began to make himself known to 'foreign' courts. In 1516, for example, he made contact with Alfonso I d'Este, Duke of Ferrara for whom he was to work for a decade on pictures destined for the Alabaster Chamber. Between 1516 and 1518 he executed the *Worship of Venus* now in the Prado, then, between 1523 and 1524, the *Bacchanal of the Andrians*, also in the Prado and, finally, the *Bacchus and Ariadne* now in London. In these Dionysian themes (which should also include the Edinburgh *Venus Anadyomene*) Titian combines a richness of colouristic expression with a great formal elegance. These are the elements which characterize this whole so-called "classic" phase in Titian's development and which is dominated by the supreme masterpiece of the Frari *Assumption of the Virgin*.

Titian worked on this huge altarpiece for more than two years from 1516 to 1518. It has to be seen as another milestone in Titian's career establishing him as a more universal artist who drew inspira-

19. Flora (c. 1515)
80x63 cm
Florence, Uffizi

20. The Worship of
Venus (1516/1518)
172x175 cm
Madrid, Prado

tion from outside the confines of Venice. Indeed the powerful figures of the Apostles reflect the influence of Michelangelo, whereas the painting demonstrates clear iconographical similarities with the works of Raphael. Above all, what emerges most strongly in the *Assumption* is Titian's desire to break definitively with the traditions of Venetian painting in order to arrive at a synthesis of dramatic force and dynamic tension which will become from this moment on the most obvious characteristic of his work.

Particularly representative of this phase are the *Tribute Money* in Dresden, painted for Alfonso d'Este and the *Madonna of the Cherries* in Vienna, where the somewhat old-fashioned composition, derived from models such as Dürer's *Madonna of the Siskin* (1506), is enlivened by the rich luminosity of the colour and by the majestic three-dimensionality of the forms.

21. Bacchanal of the Andrians (1523/1524)
175x193 cm
Madrid, Prado

22. Bacchus and Ariadne (1523/1524)
175x190 cm
London, National Gallery

In 1520 Titian put his signature to the altarpiece for the church of San Francesco at Ancona (now in the Civic Museum), commissioned by Luigi Gozzi, depicting the *Madonna in Glory with the Christ Child and Saints Francis and Aluise with the Donor*. While the influence of Raphael's *Madonna of Foligno* is evident in the composition, the vitality of the figures is entirely Titianesque. These same characteristics emerge even more strongly in another religious masterpiece from this period, the *Polyptych* of the Resurrection in the church of Santi Nazaro e Celso in Brescia. It was painted between 1520 and 1522 for Altobello Averoldi, papal legate to Venice. New Mannerist tendencies are apparent here, possibly transmitted to Titian through the work of Pordenone, and these elements subtly contribute to the dramatic intensity of the work. In both those works the landscape backgrounds are of the very highest quality, with recognizable views of Venice and Brescia.

The first half of the 1520's saw the production of a great many portraits, some of which are truly great works of art. Among these is the presumed portrait of *Vincenzo Mosti* in the Pitti Palace, remarkable for its harmonious colour scheme and for the freedom of the brushstrokes which enliven the details of the clothes and the face. The sitter's features are highlighted and accentuated through a device typical of Titian's portraiture, a touch of light colour at the neck — in this case the iridescent white of the refined shirt collar. Another masterpiece is the superb *Man with a Glove* in the Louvre; here the severe self-confidence exhibited in so many of Titian's portraits for once gives way to an appealingly melancholy figure. In the portrait of *Federigo Gonzaga* in the Prado, Titian indulges in the chromatic interplay of the variegated blue of the duke's doublet with the white of the faithful dog, portrayed together with his master.

As if to consolidate Titian's artistic supremacy in Venice, the 1520's saw the production of two masterpieces for the major monastic churches of

the city — Santa Maria Gloriosa dei Frari and Santi Giovanni e Paolo — where the great personalities of the Republic were buried. The *Pesaro Altarpiece*, placed above the altar of the Immaculate Conception in the Frari church, was commissioned in 1519 but Titian took seven years to complete it. The traditional scheme of the *Sacra Conversazione* with the Madonna and Child, saints and donors, is completely transformed and the altarpiece becomes an excuse for a magnificent group portrait of members of the Pesaro family. They are depicted with unparalleled realism in a bright, sunny light which transforms the clothes and the standards into a fanfare of colour.

The *Martyrdom of St Peter Martyr* must have been as revolutionary as the *Pesaro Altarpiece*. Delivered on 27 April 1530 to the friars of the church of Santi Giovanni e Paolo, it was unfortunately destroyed by the fire which devastated the Chapel of the Rosary — where, by a tragic twist of fate, the altarpiece had been moved for restoration — on 16 August 1867. All that remains are enthusiastic contemporary accounts of the work (Vasari described it as: "by far the most finished,

23. Venus Anadyomene (1519/1525)
76x57.3 cm
Edinburgh, National Gallery of Scotland (on loan from the Duke of Sutherland Collection)

24, 25. Assumption of the Virgin (1516/1518)
690x360 cm
Venice, Santa Maria Gloriosa dei Frari

26. *Madonna in Glory with the Christ Child and Saints Francis and Alvise with the Donor (1520)*
312x215 cm
Ancona, Museo Civico

27. *Madonna of the Cherries (1517/1518)*
81x99.5 cm
Vienna, Kunsthistorisches Museum

28. *The Tribute Money (1516/1518)*
75x56 cm
Dresden, Gemäldegalerie

29. *Polyptych of the Resurrection*
detail of Saints Nazaro and Celso with the donor
Altobello Averoldi

30. *Polyptych of the Resurrection*
detail of St Sebastian

31. Polyptych of the Resurrection (1522)
Brescia, Church of Santi Nazaro e Celso

the most celebrated, the greatest and the best conceived and executed of all the pictures painted so
far by Titian") and a few copies such as the one
now on the altar, thought to be by Loth. From these
it is possible to imagine the extraordinary dynamism
of Titian's composition, with the action set on the
edge of a great dark wood which provides a gloomy
backdrop to the scene of slaughter. It is perhaps
possible to discern some compositional similarities
between the *Saint Peter* altarpiece and the deeply
moving painting of the Louvre *Entombment of
Christ*, datable towards the end of the 1530's. Here
too, all the intensely dramatic figures are placed

32, 33. *Polyptych of the Resurrection*
details of the Angel of the Annunciation and of the
Virgin Annunciate

34. *St Christopher* (1523)
300x179 cm
Venice, Doges' Palace

well to the foreground, juxtaposed against the wooded background. Points of similarity are also evident in the London *Madonna and Child with the Young Saint John the Baptist and Saint Catherine*, painted in 1530 possibly for the Duke of Mantua, and the *Adoration of the Shepherds*, a charming night scene painted between 1532 and 1533 for Francesco Maria della Rovere.

By now Titian's working life was marked by frantic activity. In 1523 he had made contact with Federico Gonzaga in Venice and in 1529 Titian repaid the visit by going to Mantua; the new Doge, Andrea Gritti, claimed from Titian, in his capacity as official painter of the Republic, the portraits his position obliged him to paint, the projected *Battle of Cadore* and a "votive painting". The latter was not delivered until October 1531 and was to be destroyed in a fire of 1574. In the meantime another important turning point in Titian's career took place in Parma in 1529; here, through the good offices of Federico Gonzaga, he met his future patron —

the Emperor Charles V. At their second meeting, which took place at Bologna in 1533, Charles V enobled Titian with the title of Count Palatine and made him a Knight of the Golden Spur; it was also on that occasion that Titian painted the portrait of the ruler now in the Prado.

In Venice Titian had become friends with Pietro Aretino and Jacopo Sansovino (who had both arrived in the city in 1527 following the Sack of Rome) thus forming the triad that was to dominate Venetian cultural life for many years. Titian's new position as Imperial painter brought with it an enormous quantity of privileges and, above all, a renown unattainable for any other artist. Therefore it is no surprise that in 1532 Titian is featured in Ariosto's *Orlando furioso* alongside the very greatest of modern artists, Raphael and Michelangelo, and

35. Portrait of Federico Gonzaga ((1523/1526)
125x99 cm
Madrid, Prado

36. Man with a Glove (1520/1525)
100x89 cm
Paris, Louvre

37. Portrait of Vincenzo Mosti (1520/1525)
85x66 cm
Florence, Galleria Palatina, Pitti Palace

38. *Entombment of Christ (1525/1530)*
148x212 cm
Paris, Louvre

39. *Adoration of the Shepherds (1532/1533)*
95x115 cm
Florence, Galleria Palatina, Pitti Palace

40. *Pesaro Altarpiece (1519/1526)*
478x266.5 cm
Venice, Santa Maria Gloriosa dei Frari

that all the Italian princely courts vied with each other to obtain works by his hand. For Francesco Maria della Rovere, Duke of Urbino (whose majestic portrait Titian painted together with that of his wife Eleonora Gonzaga) he produced at the beginning of the 1530's that triumph of sensual beauty — the *Mary Magdalene* now in the Pitti Palace and the mysterious *Bella* also in the Pitti. In 1538 Titian painted for the duke's heir, Guidobaldo, the so-called *Venus of Urbino* perhaps the most seductive of Titian's images of women. If the pose of this Venus brings to mind that of Giorgione's Dresden *Venus* (which the young Titian had completed after Giorgione's death) the intent of the painting is quite different. Titian's Venus has nothing to do with Giorgione's idealised image of female beau-

41, 42. *Madonna and Child
with the Young Saint John
the Baptist and Saint
Catherine (1530)*
101x142 cm
London, National Gallery

43. *Portrait of Ippolito dei
Medici (1532/1534)*
139x107 cm
*Florence, Galleria Palatina,
Pitti Palace*

44. *Portrait of Charles V (1533)*
192x111 cm
Madrid, Prado

45. *Portrait of Francesco
Maria della Rovere (1538)*
114x100 cm
Florence, Uffizi

46. *Portrait of Eleonora
Gonzaga della Rovere (1538)*
112x102 cm
Florence, Uffizi

47. *Mary Magdalene (c. 1533)*
84x69.2 cm
Florence, Galleria Palatina, Pitti Palace

48, 50. *Venus of Urbino (1538)*
119x165 cm
Florence, Uffizi

49. *La Bella (1536)*
89x75.5 cm
Florence, Galleria Palatina, Pitti Palace

ty; she is presented to us quite simply as the goddess of carnal love — a courtesan in her boudoir.

The year 1538 was another decisive one for Titian. Resisting the blandishments of the Spanish emissaries who were intent on luring him to Madrid, he decided once again to remain in Venice, where he finally completed the *Battle of Cadore* which he had begun back in 1513. This huge canvas was also destroyed in the fire of 20 December 1577 and all that remains are a few preparatory drawings and a copy in the Uffizi Gallery. From these and from the written testimony of those who saw the work *in situ*, it is clear that Titian had in mind the battle frescoes planned by Leonardo and Michelangelo for the Palazzo Vecchio in Florence. He brought to his canvas a scene of passionate commotion and heroic turmoil emphasised by the energetic dynamism of the figures. The lost *Annunciation* of 1537 (carried out for the Murano convent of Santa Maria degli Angeli but rejected by them) must have displayed similar characteristics; it is known today only through an engraving by Caraglio.

Titian and Mannerism

In 1539 Titian completed the *Presentation of the Virgin at the Temple* for the 'Scuola Grande' of Santa Maria della Carità, now the Accademia Gallery of Venice. The painting is remarkable for its glowing colours and for the careful depiction of naturalistic detail. The architectural vistas, inspired by stage-sets for the theatre, play a fundamental rôle in the work. It is evident from this use of perspective and from other stylistic clues that Titian was receptive to the influence of Tuscan-Roman painting filtered through the work of Porta and Salviati who arrived in Venice in 1539 and, later, through Vasari himself who came to Venice for the first time in 1541 to stage Aretino's play *Talanta*.

Titian's relationship with these artists in particular and Mannerist painting in general has been explored in various ways. For instance, in comparison with Pordenone (the painter considered to be the promotor of the Mannerist style in the Venetian area) Titian was more independent in adopting the imported Michelangelesque foreshortenings and it is worth remembering that he had used such devices before in his Frari *Assumption*. However, Titian's Mannerist leanings seem to be more a con-

51-53. *Presentation*
of the Virgin at
the Temple (1539)
345x775 cm
Venice, Academy
Gallery

cession to fashion than the result of a conversion to the style. After all, Salviati, Porta and Vasari had been called to Venice by members of the aristocratic intellectual elite who had close political ties with the papal court. It is Giulio Romano who probably exerted the greatest influence on Titian who had direct experience of his Mantuan works. In fact, Titian's repertoire of muscular nudes derives from Giulio Romano rather than from Tuscan artists present in Venice. The same is true of the spiralling movement of figures, the counterpoised poses and the strong intersecting diagonals in works such as the Louvre *Crowning with Thorns* (1540), the Accademia *St John the Baptist* of the same year and the ceiling paintings of 1542-1544 for Santo Spirito in Isola, now in the sacristy of the church of Santa Maria della Salute. In these canvases, as well as in works with secular or mythological subjects such

54. *St John the Baptist (1540)*
201x134 cm
Venice, Academy Gallery

55. *Sacrifice of Isaac (1542/1544)*
328x284.5 cm
Venice, Church of Santa Maria della Salute

as *Alfonso D'Avalos Addressing his Troops* (1540-1541) and the so-called *Pardo Venus*, we see Titian's Mannerism at its height. Often verging on the brutal and bombastic, it is a style which saturates his work with intense drama. Yet it is worth noting how the three-dimensional clarity of Titian's figures, the bold effects of foreshortening and the strong contrasts of light and shade manage to achieve a perfect synthesis with the

56. Alfonso di
Avalos Addressing his
Troops (1541)
223x165 cm
Madrid, Prado

continual dominance of colour in his work.

A series of magnificent portraits belong to the period of Titian's so-called "Mannerist crisis". These include the Washington portrait of *Cardinal Pietro Bembo* datable to 1539-1540 and that of *Ranuccio Farnese*, probably executed in Venice in 1542, when the twelve-year old grandson of the Pope was nominated Prior of San Giovanni dei Furlani, the property of the Knights of Malta. This series of portraits include the Naples *Portrait of Paul III Farnese* and the Pitti *Portrait of a Nobleman*, the latter known as the *Young Englishman* because of the sitter's intensely blue eyes. The Washington *Portrait of Doge Gritti*, painted some years after his

death in 1538, and the portrait of Titian's friend *Pietro Aretino* (Pitti) also belong to these years. In these works Titian lays bare, with a forcefulness which borders on the cynical, not only the physical features of his sitters, but also their psychological state. And so we are presented with the heroic moral tension of the warrior Doge, the overbearing arrogance of the Tuscan poet, the deeply-felt piety of the pope and the rigorous austerity of the "Young Englishman", all expressed in a stunning symphony of colour.

From 1539 onwards Titian established strong ties with the all-powerful Farnese family, which included Pope Paul III. As we have seen, Titian had ex-

440

57. *Pardo Venus (1540)*
196x385 cm
Paris, Louvre

58. *Danaë (1544)*
117x69 cm
Naples, Capodimonte National Gallery

ecuted portraits of the young Ranuccio Farnese and of the Pope himself. In 1545 Titian at last agreed to go Rome, accepting the invitation of the Pope's nephew, Cardinal Alessandro Farnese, who had promised the painter benefices for his son Pomponio, who was a priest. He departed from Venice in September of that year and after a brief stay in the Marches, as guest of the Duke of Urbino, he reached Rome on 9 October. It seems likely that at this point in his career Titian would have felt himself almost obliged to experience at first hand the origins of the Mannerist style, which was rooted in the works of Raphael and Michelangelo. Nevertheless one has the impression that Titian had overcome his "Mannerist crisis" of the early 1540's even before setting out for Rome. Indeed, he carried with him the remarkable Naples *Danaë*, painted for Ottavio Farnese, which he had completed shortly before his departure. This work constitutes the clearest evidence of a decisive stylistic change of direction in Titian's painting at this time. The powerful physicality of the *St John the Baptist* or the athletic protagonists which throng the biblical narratives for

59. Portrait of Pietro Bembo (1539/1540) 94.5x76.5 cm Washington, National Gallery of Art

60. Portrait of a Gentleman known as "The Young Englishman" (1544/1545) 111x96.8 cm Florence, Galleria Palatina, Pitti Palace

61. Portrait of Pope Paul III (1545/1546)
106x85 cm
Naples, Capodimonte National Gallery

62. *Portrait of Doge Andrea Gritti (1544/1545)*
133.6x103.2 cm
Washington, National Gallery of Art

63. *Portrait of Pietro Aretino (1545)*
96.7x77.6 cm
Florence, Galleria Palatina, Pitti Palace

Santo Spirito in Isola give way to a sensuous naturalism which reveals a renewed interest in the unconstrained use of rich colour, especially in the landscape.

It is clear that a work such as the *Danaë* could never have been fully appreciated in the artistic climate of contemporary Rome. Indeed, Vasari recounts how the great Michelangelo went to pay his respects to Titian in his rooms and, having seen the *Danaë*, praised its "colouring and style". On leaving the painter's house, however, Michelangelo could not resist adding that "it was a shame that in Venice they did not learn to draw well from the beginning and that those painters did not pursue their studies with more method".

It was highly unlikely that Titian's sojourn in Rome would herald any significant change in his work, given the great divide which separated his painting — on the conceptual as well as stylistic lev-

el — from the style dominant in the papal city. He did, however, stay on in Rome for several months, partly because he was still hoping (in vain as it turned out) for the benefices promised to his son Pomponio. Titian painted three portraits for the Farnese family, the most important of which is the one of *Pope Paul III with his Nephews Alessandro and Ottavio*, now at Capodimonte. This is a masterpiece of psychological insight in which the resonance of the colours plays its part by creating a feeling of distress.

The Roman interlude is only thinly documented in Titian's surviving correspondence. We have only one letter — to Emperor Charles V — in which the painter mentions his interest in the monuments of antiquity: "I am learning — he wrote — from these marvellous ancient stones". His stay in Rome came to an end in the early months of 1546; on 19 March he received honorary citizenship at a ceremony at

the Capitol and left for Florence shortly afterwards — the first stage of his rapid return journey to Venice.

On his return Titian was faced with a number of works left incomplete at his sudden departure for Rome. Among these was the resplendent *Votive Portrait of the Vendramin Family*, now in London; begun in 1543, it was only now brought to completion. In this work Titian takes up once more that scheme of composition experimented with twenty years earlier in the Pesaro altarpiece for the Frari church. Here, depicted with great realism and calm monumentality, the elderly Gabriele Vendramin,

surrounded by his sons and grandsons, kneels before the altar which bears the sacred reliquary of the True Cross — property of the confraternity of Saint John the Evangelist. As in the earlier work, it is Titian's use of bright colour — vibrant notes of intense hues — which dominates the painting.

At the same time Titian was working on the central canvas for the ceiling of the meeting-hall in the 'Scuola Grande' of Saint John the Evangelist, leaving his assistants to finish the decoration. He also completed, with workshop assistance, the altarpiece for the church of Serravalle, begun in 1542.

*64, 66. Votive
Portrait of the
Vendramin Family
(1547)
206x301 cm
National Gallery,
London*

*65. Pope Paul III
with his Nephews
Alessandro and
Ottavio (1546)
214x174 cm
Naples, Capodimonte
National Gallery*

Charles V and Philip II

At the beginning of 1548 Titian left Venice once more, this time for Augsburg where he met Charles V, fresh from his great victory over the Protestant League at Mühlberg. Titian was accompanied by his son Orazio and Lambert Sustris, a young Dutch painter who had only recently joined his workshop. At Augsburg (where he remained until October 1548) he was kept frantically busy painting, chiefly, portraits of the Emperor and important members of his court. Of the Emperor's portraits the Prado *Charles V on Horseback* stands out. Here Titian displays the warrior virtues of this proud old monarch in clear contrast to the melancholy and slightly pained image of the same Emperor in the Munich *Charles V Seated*, where he seems weighed down by the cares of state and religion.

Apart from the portraits, Titian also worked on the first version of the Prado *Venus with Organist and Small Dog*, one of his most successful compositions and destined to be repeated often by Titian and his workshop. At Augsburg he also received a commission from Queen Mary of Hungary to paint four ceiling canvases for her summer residence at the castle of Binche in Flanders. These

67. Portrait of Charles V on Horseback (1548)
332x279 cm
Madrid, Prado

448

morality-paintings were to depict the famous legendary torments of the 'Damned': those of Tityus, Sisyphus, Tantalus and Ixion. On his return to Venice Titian painted the *Tityus and Sisyphus* which were complete by June 1549. It is possible that he never executed the remaining two canvases. The most obvious characteristics of the two paintings despatched to Flanders and now in Madrid is the evidence of a return to the expressive vocabulary of Mannerism, which derives ultimately from Michelangelo. Moreover, here Titian painted 'lightning flash' effects of light and used a thicker 'impasto' of colour which makes these canvases quite different from the somewhat monochromatic flatness of the earlier ceiling paintings for Santo Spirito in Isola.

The altarpiece for the church of San Giovanni Elemosinario in Venice belongs to this stylistic phase, although the date of the work has long been a matter of debate. However, the fiery colours, offset by the white gleam of the saint's robe, leads one to place this complex painting (in which there are still echoes of Pordenone's approach to composition) close to the Prado 'Damned'.

At the beginning of November 1550 Titian, who was then more than sixty years old, undertook a second journey to Augsburg to meet the Emperor. Charles V had called a meeting of the Diet at Augsburg and had used the occasion to announce his intention to abdicate in the near future, leaving the Imperial crown to his brother Ferdinand and that of Spain to his son, Prince Philip, who from that moment became the most important of Titian's patrons. Immediately Titian painted a full length portrait of Philip, now in the Prado. This is a remarkable exercise in court portraiture. with the deathly pale figure of the prince, confined within his splendid armour, who emerges imperiously from the shadows in a glow of light; in the same way a shaft of light picks out the great plumed helmet placed on the red velvet covering of the table behind the prince. The portrait can be considered as a sort of heraldic image, a symbol of the military and political power of the prince, but at the same time Titian gives us a psychological insight into this introverted personality, who would turn out to be indecisive in affairs of state and torn between a fanatic religious faith and a tortured, repressed sexuality.

Titian returned to Venice in August of 1551. From this time on he considerably reduced his work for local patrons, making way for painters of the younger generation, Tintoretto, Paolo Veronese and Jacopo Bassano, while he himself concentrat-

68. *Portrait of Charles V Seated (1548)*
205x122 cm
Munich, Bayerische Staatsgemäldesammlungen

ed on the numerous commissions from the Hapsburgs and their *entourage*. Titian's connection with Philip II (who ascended the throne in 1556) and the Spanish court was not financially rewarding, as is made clear in the many letters Titian wrote to the king in his frequently unsuccessful efforts to obtain money promised him. On the other hand the relationship was extremely positive from the artistic point of view, in that he was left at liberty to experiment with the inventiveness, interpretation and execution of the works asked of him.

He continued to paint portraits of dignitaries connected with the Imperial court. These include the bishop prince of Trent, *Cristoforo Madruzzo*, now in São Paulo and the *Captain with Cupid and a Dog*, now in Kassel. The importance of these per-

450

69, 70. *Venus with Organist and Cupid (1548)*
148x217 cm
Madrid, Prado

71. *Sisyphus (1549)*
237x216 cm
Madrid, Prado

sonalities is made explicit by the fact that they are depicted full-length, which previously had been the case only with Titian's portraits of Charles V and Philip II. At the same time Titian was working on the *Trinity in Glory*, now in the Prado. This huge canvas was commissioned by Charles V during his stay at Augsburg and Titian had taken almost four years to complete it. The complex iconography (centred on the glorification of the Spanish court which is identified here with the heavenly court) has lent itself to various interpretations, from a *Paradise* to a *Last Judgement*. In the right margin of the painting appears Titian's foreshortened self-portrait. He places it below the figures of Charles V, his wife Isabella, Prince Philip and other notables, as if the painter wished to testify that he was accepted as part of their world.

Again for the Hapsburgs, Titian executed between 1553 and 1554 two "mythological fables" of clearly erotic intent — the *Venus and Adonis* and the *Danaë*, both now in the Prado. The latter is really a variation on the canvas painted ten years earlier for the Farnese family. With greater fidelity to Ovid's text, the Cupid has now been replaced by the elderly nurse who attempts to use her apron to gather the shower of gold into which Jupiter had

72. *St John the Alms-Giver (1548/1549)*
264x148 cm
Venice, Church of San Giovanni Elemosinario

73. *Portrait of Philip II in Armour (1551)*
193x111 cm
Madrid, Prado

74. *Captain with Cupid and a Dog (1551)*
223x151 cm
Kassel, Gemäldegalerie

transformed himself in order to possess the young woman. The *Venus and Adonis*, on the other hand, became the prototype for a whole series of replicas of this subject. In both paintings the scene of the union of the lovers is bathed in the warm light of sunset, where the diffuse softness of the colours holds sway. The female nudes reveal the continuing inspiration of Michelangelo's sculpture, such as the *Dawn* and *Night* from the Medici tombs in Florence. But what is entirely personal to Titian is the quality of the colour, which fragments into patches of dazzling luminosity — a perfect complement to the ecstatic sensuous abandon of the figures.

Of the same high poetic quality is the Washington *Venus at her Toilet*, which can probably be dated to 1554-1555; the figure of the goddess derives from the celebrated Roman statue of Venus owned by the Medici family.

In the late 1550's Titian executed three altarpieces of great importance. In 1557 he completed the *Annunciation* for the church of San Domenico Maggiore in Naples, in 1558 the *Crucified Christ with the Virgin Mary, Saint Dominic and Saint John* for the church of San Domenico at Ancona and, in 1559, the *Martyrdom of St Lawrence* for the Venetian Crociferi church (subsequently the Jesuit church) which had been commissioned by Lorenzo Massolo back in 1548. The three paintings are stylistically similar although the Venetian altarpiece stands out for its very fine quality. In each of them Titian handles nocturnal scenes with a completely new technique of painting. In fact, he achieves

75. *The Trinity in Glory (1554)*
346x240 cm
Madrid, Prado

76. *Annunciation (1557)*
232x190 cm
Naples, Capodimonte National Gallery

those effects of strong light coming from within the dark backgrounds of the paintings by applying blobs of luminous pigment (white leads, lacquer reds, bright yellows, blood-red crimsons) onto a thickly layered, smokey background. This technique, which Titian was to use for the rest of his life, is beautifully described in a seventeenth century text by Marco Boschini, who based his account on the testimony of Palma the Younger, a pupil of Titian in his youth: "He began his paintings with such an

unbroken layer of colours that this served (so to speak) as a bed or base for the images which he would then create on them. I have seen massive strokes of colour with streaks of pure red-ochre for the half-tones; at other times he used a splash of white-lead with a brush already stained with reds, black and yellow, to outline light areas, and with a few touches a figure of rare promise would appear. After laying these foundations he would turn the paintings to the wall, sometimes leaving them for months without looking at them. When he decided to work on them again he subjected them to a rigorous examination as if they were his mortal enemies, seeing if anything particularly struck him, or if he could discover anything that did not conform with his careful conception of the works. Like a benevolent surgeon tending a patient, ascertaining whether it was necessary to bleed a swelling or reduce an excess of flesh, he brought them

77. Danaë (1553/1554)
129x180 cm
Madrid, Prado

78. Venus at her Toilet (1554/1555)
124.5x105.5 cm
Washington, National Gallery of Art

to the perfection of nature and of art and having done this he would leave the canvas to dry and turn to another painting to do the same thing. And every so often he would flesh out the figures, going over them many times, until they lacked only the breath of life, and never completing a figure in a single stage... but for the final touches he would blend the transitions from highlights to half-tones with his fingers, merging one tint with another, or with a smear of his finger he would apply a dark accent in some corner to strengthen it, or with a dab of red, like drops of blood, he would enliven the surface, and so he continued to transform and perfect his life-filled figures, And Palma swore to me that in the final stages of the work Titian painted more with his fingers than with his brush."

And so Titian disintegrates that process of building up figures through drawing and a sculptural sense of the three-dimensional. The definition of detail and the homogeneous use of colour which had characterized his painting for so long, now gives way to a method based solely on colour, applied with broad brushstrokes and completed by working the pigments with the fingertips just like a sculptor modelling in clay.

This stylistic phase, which has been defined as "magical impressionism", was not fully appreciated by Titian's contemporaries. Some of them attributed this rapid and abbreviated way of painting to the physical decline of the old painter and in particular to his failing sight. Never was such an ungenerous judgement levelled at an artist. Consider, for example, a work such as his Prado *Entombment*, sent to Philip II in 1559: a profoundly moving masterpiece of great psychological intensity

79. Venus and Adonis (1553/1554)
186x207 cm
Madrid, Prado

which became something of a prototype for the religious paintings pervaded by a bitter pathos that Titian was to produce in the last years of his life.

Of similar style are two celebrated mythological paintings painted for Philip II and now in Edinburgh: *Diana and Callisto* and *Diana and Actaeon*. Here, too, the tragic stories (the huntsman Actaeon accidently discovers the grotto where Diana and her nymphs are bathing and because of this he is transformed into a stag and torn to pieces by his hounds; Callisto was one of Diana's nymphs and as such had to be as chaste as the goddess; made pregnant by Jupiter and found out by Diana, she is driven away) push Titian towards a dramatic emphasis in which vibrant colours play their part with their rich hues and strong contrasts. The following years were particularly busy ones for Titian; he painted other mythological pictures for Philip II, in-

cluding the splendid *Rape of Europa* in Boston. Painted between 1559 and 1562, it also reveals a profound sense of tortured despair, as does the London *Death of Actaeon*. Here the dramatic scene of the young hunter attacked and ripped apart by the pack of dogs takes place in a landscape of livid colours heavy with premonition. To these years belongs the Wallace Collection *Perseus and Andromeda* (1562-1563) with its sublime depiction of the monster rising at night from the billowing moonlit waves.

The year 1562 almost certainly saw the production of two exceptionally fine works: the Berlin *Self-Portrait* and the *Annunciation* for the Venetian church of San Salvador. The former presents us with the image of the painter (then over seventy) emerging majestically from the shadowy background like some ghostly apparition. Titian is dressed in a voluminous white shirt topped by a fur-edged robe; nothing in the painting alludes specifically to his craft but the great gold chain he wears is a proud reminder of the honour bestowed on him in 1533 when Charles V made him a Knight of the Golden Spur. This was long assumed to be an unfinished work because of the fragmented brushstrokes and the lack of firm outlines so typical of the late works of Titian. But there is nothing casual in the seeming incompleteness of this and other contemporary works. It was a conscious artistic de-

80. Crucified Christ with the Virgin Mary and Saints Dominic and John (1558) 375x197 cm Ancona, Church of San Domenico

81. Martyrdom of St Lawrence (1559) 493x277 cm Venice, Jesuit Church

82. Entombment (1559) 137x175 cm Madrid, Prado

83. *Diana and Actaeon (1559)*
190.3x207 cm
Edinburgh, National Gallery of Scotland (on loan from the Duke of Sutherland Collection)

84. *Diana and Callisto (1559)*
187x205 cm
Edinburgh, National Gallery of Scotland (on loan from the Duke of Sutherland Collection)

85. *Rape of Europa (1559/1562)*
185x205 cm
Boston, Isabella Stewart Gardner Museum

cision on the part of Titian, who finds direct emotional communication through these luminous effects, and through that very "unfinished" quality of the painting, which becomes a vehicle for the expression of what may be seen as the unquiet, questing soul of the elderly painter. Once more Titian's superb technical expertise becomes a tool for the expression of profound feeling; and it is precisely this quality which has been appreciated by modern critics, resulting in a reassessment of the final phase of Titian's artistic career. Vasari was certainly wrong in equating incompleteness with imperfection when he wrote about the incandescent *Annunciation* for the church of San Salvador, commissioned in 1559 by the wealthy merchant Antonio Cornovì della Vecchia and probably completed in 1562. This painting must be considered as one of the greatest of Titian's final works, replete with

the ingredients typical of his late style: the restrained sensuality of the glowing angel whose hair and great open wings seem made of molten gold in the flashing light; the broken brushstrokes which do not seek to define form; the dark chasm of the background which opens up into a vision of fiery heaven with its pyrotechnic display of cherubs encircling the dove of the Holy Spirit.

86. Death of Actaeon (1562)
179x189 cm
London, National Gallery

87. Annunciation (1559/1562)
403x235 cm
Venice, Church of San Salvador

The Final Years

The elderly Titian's final years are marked by the anguish of personal tragedy. The year 1556 saw the death of his close friend of thirty years, Pietro Aretino. In 1558 Charles V died in the solitude of the monastery of St Yuste; sentiments of gratitude and respect had long bound Titian to his old patron. A year later his brother Francesco died — a trusted and unobstrusive collaborator on countless painting projects. The effect these losses had on Titian is clear in some of his letters to Philip II but his paintings remain the most eloquent testimony of his distress in these years. Take, for example, the Prado *Entombment* of 1565 (similar in its composition to the version sent to Philip II in 1559) where the disjointed gestures of the onlookers communicate their strident grief at the death of the Saviour. Even potentially joyous mythological sub-

jects such as *Venus Blindfolding Cupid*, painted around 1565 and now in Rome, is pervaded with a degree of tension which is clearly evident in the sad and pensive expressions and in the intense colours of the fiery sky.

In the same period Titian handled his various versions of the *Penitent Mary Magdalene* with a similar dramatic intensity. This is particularly evident in a comparison of the St Petersburg canvas — considered the prototype for the series — with the early Pitti *Mary Magdalene* painted for the Duke of Urbino in 1533. In December of 1567 Titian sent to Spain his second *Martyrdom of Saint Lawrence*, destined for the high altar of the monastic church of St Lawrence at the Escorial. Here too, he repeats the composition used earlier for the altarpiece of the same subject for the church of the Crociferi, completed in 1559, but handles it in a more tortured way, giving free rein to the expressiveness of his late style. In this period, which saw Titian focussing his attention on religious themes, he still found the energy to paint portraits. Between 1567 and 1568 he produced two of his greatest masterpieces in this field: the Prado *Self-Portrait* and the *Portrait of Jacopo Strada* in Vienna.

In the new *Self-Portrait* Titian departs completely from the scheme of the earlier one in Berlin. He depicts himself in profile, dressed in black and holding a paintbrush in clear allusion to his craft. Around his neck is the gold chain which reminds us that he held the rank of Knight of the Golden Spur. But, above all, the impression of inner strength and self-assurance exuded by the Berlin self-portrait has disappeared. In just a few years there has been a marked physical decline and, more significantly, the portrait suggests an erosion of the aging painter's self-confidence.

The portrait of the well-known antiquarian *Jacopo Strada* is of the very highest quality. It is painted in energetic dabs of brown and ochre yellow, offset by the black velvet jerkin with a silver fox fur flung around the shoulders. The careful depiction of the details which allude to the profession of the sitter (the statuette, the coins, the cartouche and the books) do not distract from the characterization of Strada, who is looking enquiringly at someone outside the painting.

Connected to these paintings is the London *Allegory of Time Governed by Prudence*, where portraits of Titian, his son Orazio and his grandson

88. Martyrdom of St Lawrence (1567)
175x172 cm
Escorial, Monastery of St Lawrence

464

89. Venus Blindfolding Cupid
(c. 1565)
118x185 cm
Rome, Borghese Gallery

90. Penitent Mary Magdalene
(c. 1565)
118x97 cm
St. Petersburg, Hermitage

91. *Self-Portrait (1567/1568)*
86x69 cm
Madrid, Prado

Marco are each coupled with an animal head: respectively a wolf, a lion and a dog, symbolizing the past, present and future. In the upper part of the painting there is an inscription which is the key to the complex allegorical meaning of the work: "EX PRAETERITO PRAESENS PRUDENTER AGIT, NI FUTURUM ACTIONE DETURPET" ("From the (experience of the) past, the present acts prudently, lest it spoil future action").

Approaching the eighth decade of the century the chronology of Titian's works becomes less clear chiefly because of their stylistic similarity. There are numerous devotional paintings, including the deeply felt *Madonna and Child* in London and the small *Altarpiece*, probably executed by 1566 for the Vecellio family chapel in the archidiaconal church of Pieve di Cadore. The series of paintings dedicated to the passion of Christ are outstanding. These include: the Munich *Crowning with Thorns*,

the Saint Louis *Mocking of Christ*, the St Petersburg *Ecce Homo* and the two versions of *Christ Carrying the Cross* in St Petersburg and in Madrid. In these works, pervaded with immense dramatic power, the brushstrokes gradually dissolve into rapidly applied dabs of pigment. The aim is no longer to reproduce nature but to directly convey the raw emotion of the painter, who is participating fully in the tragic subject of his picture. This explains, in the Munich painting, the depiction of the tortured body of Christ, drenched in blood and sweat, and the sinister sulphurous flashes

466

92. Portrait of Jacopo Strada (1567/1568)
125x95 cm
Vienna, Kunsthistorisches Museum

93. *Allegory of Time Governed by Prudence*
(1565/1570)
75,6x68,7 cm
London, National Gallery

94. *Madonna and Child (1565/1570)*
75x63 cm
London, National Gallery

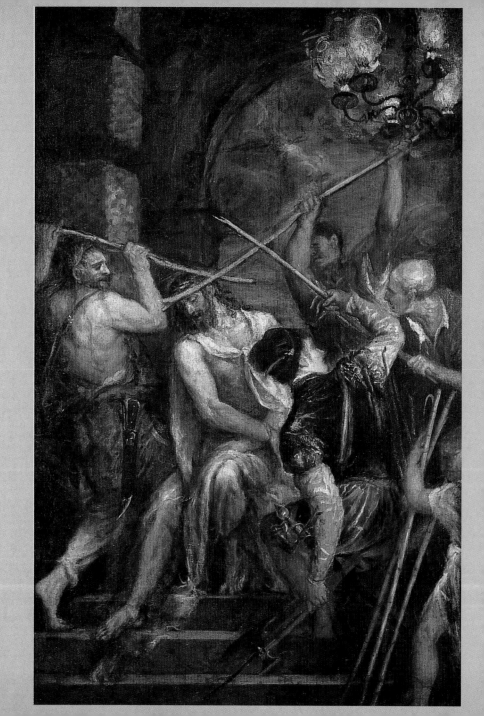

95. *Crowning with Thorns*
(1570/1575)
280x182 cm
Munich, Alte Pinakothek

96. *Mocking of Christ*
(1570/1575)
109x92 cm
Saint Louis, The Saint Louis
Art Museum

97. *Christ Carrying the Cross*
(1570/1575)
98x116 cm
Madrid, Prado

98. *Tarquin and Lucretia (1571)*
189.9x145.4 cm
Cambridge, Fitzwilliam Museum

99, 100. *Doge Antonio Grimani*
Kneeling before the Faith
(1575/1576)
373x496 cm
Venice, Doges' Palace

101. *Spain Succouring Religion*
(c. 1575)
168x168 cm
Madrid, Prado

473

102. Saint Sebastian (c. 1575)
212x116 cm
St Petersburg, Hermitage

of light which appear in the small Saint Louis canvas.

Titian's connection with Philip II continued right up to the painter's final days. Amongst the last pictures sent to Spain was the important *Tarquin and Lucretia*, now in Cambridge. It displays remarkable invention in the breath-taking speed with which the action takes place, emphasised by the rivulets of streaming light in the foreground of the painting. It is probable that the canvas of the same sub-

ject in Vienna represents Titian's first thoughts for this painting and it is here, more than in any other picture, that it is easy to imagine Titian giving the final touches to his work by rubbing in the pigments with his fingertips in the way recounted by Palma the Younger.

Titian's very last works were produced between 1575 and 1577. Two were official commissions: one, for the Doge's palace, depicting *Doge Antonio Grimani Kneeling before the Faith in the Presence of Saint Mark*, clearly carried out with the help of assistants and the second, which is entirely autograph, sent to Philip II. depicting *Spain Succouring Religion* and commemorating the participation of the Spanish fleet at the Battle of Lepanto. The remaining works of Titian's *oeuvre* belong to the final months and days of his life. For the most part they were in his studio at his death and were then sold off to various Venetian collectors by his son Pomponio. Amongst these were the hellish *Saint Sebastian* in St Petersburg, a masterpiece of painterly skill which reaches heights of virtuosity in the exceptional landscape background; the disturbing *Youth with Dogs* in Rotterdam, whose mysterious subject matter critics have failed to decipher; and the evocative *Shepherd and Nymph* in Vienna, streaked with glowing light.

An awareness of impending death weighs heavily on two paintings Titian was working on in the summer of 1576, when Venice was devastated by a terrible plague which was to kill his favourite son Orazio. The iconography of the *Flaying of Marsyas* in Kroměříž derives from a Giulio Romano fresco of the same subject in the Sala delle Metamorfosi of the Palazzo Te in Mantua, but Titian accentuates the terrifying savagery of the mythological scene through the churning background of ruddy-browns, and the gloomy colours fitfully lit by sudden flashes of light. The "hidden" meaning of the painting has been variously interpreted; however the presence of Titian himself, in the guise of King Midas, has favoured a reading of the painting as the painter's meditation on his own life and on his illusion that he could "transform material into precious painted images, an illusion extinguished by his final realization that artistic accomplishments are as nothing in the face of the misfortunes of history".

This was exactly the case with his *Pietà*, in the Venice Accademia, which Titian painted for the Chapel of Christ in the Frari church on the understanding that he would be buried there. But when the old painter died on the 27 August 1576 the painting was still incomplete; it passed into the hands of Palma the Younger who merely added

103. *Youth with Dogs*
(c. 1575/1576)
99.5x117 cm
Rotterdam, Museum Boymans
van Beuningen

104. *Shepherd and Nymph*
(1575/1576)
150x187 cm
Vienna, Kunsthistorisches
Museum

some glazing and the minimum of retouching. In this grandiose canvas, which is centred on the themes of death, the eucharistic sacrifice and resurrection, we can read the artistic testament of Titian. As in the other paintings from this period, the *Pietà* is imbued with a feeling of intense drama, a repressed anguish which is given vent in the tragic figure of Mary Magdalene screaming her despair and in details such as the horrendous lions' heads (which serve as bases for the statues), symbolic of the terrifying mysteries of the hereafter. And over the whole canvas the brush and fingers of the old

105. The Flaying of Marsyas (1575/1576)
212x207 cm
Kroměříž, State Museum

106. Pietà (1576)
353x348 cm
Venice, Academy Gallery

artist have skimmed tremulously, bestowing touches of light to the figures silhouetted against the silvery architectural backdrop.

CARAVAGGIO

Certain figures in the history of civilization give a special impetus to the course of events. They stimulate technological or cultural advances that otherwise would have taken much longer to achieve. With regard to the Western artistic tradition, for instance, Giotto and Masaccio come to mind (just to limit our discussion to painting). After them, Caravaggio alone, perhaps, can be considered part of this very special elite, possibly together with Paul Cézanne. Caravaggio, as we shall see, was such a forcefully innovative painter that his mark remained deeply impressed on the entire course of Western painting.

When Caravaggio began to work independently, at the beginning of the 1590s, the prevailing artistic style, in Italy as elsewhere, was late mannerism. This term is generally applied to most sixteenth-century art, which was concerned with developing and varying the styles of the great masters of the first quarter of the century (Raphael, who died in 1520; and Michelangelo, who painted the Sistine Ceiling between 1508 and 1512) according to a formula that, although it was initially innovative and anticonformist (Pontormo, Rosso Fiorentino), later became tired and sterile, generating a conventional approach to painting that promised little in the way of important developments. After 1575 a few leading painters began to react against late mannerism. In Florence Santi di Tito and Lodovico Cardi, called Cigoli, sought a simpler, more direct way to express feelings and emotions. In Bologna the Accademia of the Carracci championed the necessity of reestablishing a direct relationship with the great masters of the beginning of the century, especially Raphael, in order to propagate a classical style — a style that would have more than just incidental value and that would adapt painting to noble and lofty ideas. These Emilian artists (Annibale Carracci, Domenichino, Guido Reni, Giovanni Lanfranco, and Guercino) all worked in Rome, where their artistic principles were widely accepted.

Caravaggio's painting style also arose as a reaction to mannerism. It offered a new and promising path for the future that led in the direction of naturalism, as Caravaggio declared and as his biographers and contemporary theorists clearly recognized. Thus the specific solution he found, and not only his general role as an innovator, relates him to Giotto and Masaccio, two artists who had discovered a way out of a stylistic impasse through the direct study of objective reality. This of course does not mean that Caravaggio was out of step with his times, independent of other stylistic tendencies,

or disdainful of the study of the art of earlier masters. Unlike his contemporaries, who saw only the innovative aspect of his art (and in some cases even judged it negatively), we perceive in Caravaggio's paintings the influence of such artists as Raphael and Michelangelo. But we are surprised by the intelligence with which he used what he drew from the great art of the past, in accordance with his own very personal principles.

Caravaggio's naturalistic outlook had important, if incomplete, precedents that are closely related to the region where he was born and trained as an artist. Michelangelo Merisi (this was Caravaggio's real name) was born, to Fermo Merisi and Lucia Aratori, in 1570 or 1571. Whether his precise birthplace was Caravaggio, or Milan, as recent research suggests, is uncertain. The town of Caravaggio is not far from Treviglio, in an area of Lombardy that is closer to Bergamo than to Milan. Michelangelo's father died a young man. What he did for a living is unknown, but it seems he was an architect, or at least a master builder, and that his family was fairly well to do. In 1584 the young Merisi entered the workshop of the mediocre Milanese mannerist painter Simone Peterzano. Judging from his contract, he stayed there for four years; a document of 1589 shows that he was again at Caravaggio. When he moved to Rome, in all likelihood in the second half of 1592, he was already more than twenty years old, and he probably was not at the very beginning of his career.

So, Caravaggio was trained in Lombardy where he had as a model that peculiar realism characteristic of Lombard art, the essence of which has been recognized and defined by modern scholars. Even late Gothic art in Lombardy, from the end of the fourteenth century to the middle of the fifteenth, is distinguished by a particular attention to the results of direct observation of nature. This attitude was assimilated and developed by the great Renaissance master, Vincenzo Foppa of Brescia, of whose work it became a central feature. In the sixteenth century artists such as Girolamo Savoldo, Girolamo da Romano (called Romanino), Alessandro Moretto, Giovan Battista Moroni, and particularly the Venetian Lorenzo Lotto during his many years at Bergamo, showed a pronounced curiosity toward nature (not a dispassionate interest, but a participatory and sympathetic one, in the etymological sense). The relation between objects and natural and artificial light, and the ability of color to construct and define, are elements that Caravaggio assimilated from the local tradition (it is no coincidence that the artists mentioned above worked in

Bergamo and Brescia, half way between Milan and Venice), although he would dramatically develop them far beyond their foreseeable limits.

Caravaggio's first biographers (Giulio Mancini, Giovanni Baglione, and Giovan Pietro Bellori) say that he went to Rome when he was about twenty (in reality he was just a little older, as we have seen). They tell of a difficult initial period in which the artist had little to live on, and of his "service" with Cavalier d'Arpino, a famous late mannerist painter, for whom the young Caravaggio painted chiefly "flowers and fruit." Apparently the master immediately recognized the young painter's skill in this field, a skill that is also apparent in certain early works containing particularly handsome still-lifes. Recently scholars have even attributed to Caravaggio some highly innovative still-lifes (among the very first examples of this genre, which would later enjoy enormous success) formerly ascribed to his master. On the basis of an inventory made in 1607, when numerous paintings in Cavalier d'Arpino's workshop were confiscated (some of which have now been found, it seems), Federico Zeri has attributed to Caravaggio two still-lifes (one of vegetables, the other of game) now in the Galleria Borghese. His proposal has yet to be closely examined by critics, but his argument is certainly convincing.

On the basis of what we know from Caravaggio's biographies and from the documents, it is possible to place with certainty the artist's first independent works before 1595. Two of these paintings are in the Galleria Borghese in Rome; they were given to the Borghese family by Pope Paul V after being seized from Cavalier d'Arpino. The first, the so-called Sick Bacchus, is certainly a self-portrait, although the hypothesis, according to which Caravaggio painted it in the hospital after being kicked by a horse, has now been abandoned. We know that the artist was too poor to hire models, and so painted his own image in the mirror. In this first version of the theme the observer finds the immediacy of the image quite striking, especially if he or she is acquainted with the cultural climate of the period in which the picture was painted. The youth dressed as Bacchus is seen as through a window that opens on an image of reality objectively portrayed, without being interpreted or improved by the painter. The figure stands out in a directly perceptible manner made possible, in part, by a modern "point of view" that make us think, four centuries later, of a photograph. Of course the painting also contains meanings that are not immediately identifiable, or that demand an erudite interpretation; and this obliges us to recall what we said before, that Caravaggio's naturalism does not by any means imply that his art arises without deep cultural matrices.

The highly skilled rendering of the fruit and ivy that we find in the Sick Bacchus is merely an introduction to the spectacular basket held by the youth in the other Borghese painting from this early period. Here Caravaggio's capacity for the surface textures of the fruit and leaves appears straight-away as the most advanced of the art of his age. It is quite understandable that the

1. *Still-Life with Flowers and Fruit*
cm. 105x184
Rome, Galleria Borghese

2. *Sick Bacchus*
cm. 66x52
Rome, Galleria Borghese

young Lombard's skill made a keen impression in Cavalier d'Arpino's workshop, and that it soon asserted itself in the city's learned circles. The youth with the fruit basket looks out at the observer with a velvety gaze, his lips parted in an inviting manner. It is an ambiguous expression that has led some scholars to hypotheses of dubious validity; but it is true in any event that the slant of the head and the direct gaze, which recall the Venetian portraits of Giorgione, introduce us here to a much more immediate and disturbing relation between the viewer and the object of the painting.

The same immediacy pervades the Youth Bitten by a Green Lizard in the Longhi Collection in Florence. Several copies were made of this picture, as of almost all Caravaggio's paintings, and this attests to the extraordinary success his works met with. The action is frozen in a fraction of a second, as in a snapshot. The virtuoso rendering of the fruit and flowers is accompanied (and we know that this was particularly appreciated by the artist's contemporaries) by that of the carafe of water in which the roses stand. A similar composition existed in another youth with a vase of roses. Unfortunately the

3. Youth with Flower Basket
cm. 70x63
Rome, Galleria Borghese

4. Youth Bitten by a Green Lizard
cm. 65.8x39.5
Florence, Longhi Collection

original has been lost; the best copy is in Atlanta, Georgia.

Caravaggio built his reputation on these early paintings, as we have said. The first collector of his works was the learned and influential Cardinal Francesco Maria Del Monte. An inventory of his collection, made after his death in 1626, includes eight paintings by Caravaggio, five of which can be dated to the early part of the artist's career, or at least before the end of the century. Thus we know that the young painter succeeded very soon in establishing a market for his highly novel

art. Moreover, that his early paintings were so greatly appreciated by one of the outstanding cultural figures of his milieu suggests that they contained, in addition to their ostensible meaning, allusions to deeper meanings that the collectors or the cultivated public of the artist's time recognized at a glance, and that are being rediscovered by modern iconologists. In the famous Basket of Fruit in the Ambrosiana in Milan (where the entire collection of Cardinal Federico Borromeo, to whom this painting formerly belonged, is preserved) the artist draws a deliberate contrast between healthy and sick fruit, between green and brown leaves. The work appears to make reference to the cyclical character of nature and to the coexistence in life of contrary principles. As a matter of fact, these themes come across so forcefully that this painting, which has been called the first still-life of the seventeenth century (and one should add, of the modern age), can be seen more as a melancholy existential meditation on nature than as a proud affirmation of her positive qualities.

The association of a single figure with a still-life recurs in the Bacchus in the Uffizi. This painting is also a self-portrait. Mention has been made of the dangerously tilted goblet that seems about to spill its contents, and the rippled surface of the wine — devices that give the image a sense of precariousness — as well as of the face skillfully reflected in the pitcher. But the important thing to notice here is the absolute newness of the invention, where one does not see a classically idealized Bacchus, but the image of a young man, almost a boy, whose features are hardly refined, and who is dressed — or perhaps it would be better to say disguised — as Bacchus, in a manner which today would be considered provocative. Caravaggio deliberately chose a model that could not be associated with the grotesque Bacchus or with the handsome young Bacchus of antiquity. Instead of Bacchus the god, he represents a common person brought in off the street and disguised as Bacchus. It appears as though, after posing for the painter, the model were about to stand up, throw off the drape, drink down the wine, and head off for the tavern.

A gang of friends animates the Concert in the Metropolitan Museum in New York, from which all trace of irony, or parody, is missing. The two figures

5. *Basket of Fruit*
cm. 46x64.5
Milan, Pinacoteca Ambrosiana

6. *Bacchus*
cm. 95x85
Florence, Galleria degli Uffizi

seen frontally are undoubtably portraits, and this fact dis-
orients those who would like to make a conventional
reading of the scene and concentrate on the noble, classical character of the composition, organized around the
traditional opposition between the figure of the lute
player and the corresponding figure whom we see from
behind. The face between these two is Caravaggio's; the

7. *Concert*
cm. 92x118.5
New York, Metropolitan Museum of Art

8. *Lute Player*
cm. 94x119
Leningrad, Hermitage

9. *St. Francis in Ecstasy*
cm. 92.5x128.4
Hartford (Connecticut), Wadsworth Atheneum

figure on the left is taken from an earlier composition, the Youth Peeling a Pear, which we know only from two copies. The broad play of drapery recalls the Lombard influences mentioned above, particularly the experiments of Girolamo Savoldo of Bergamo in rendering cloth and clothing.

Another painting with a single figure, the Lute Player in the Hermitage in Leningrad, takes up the theme of music. In this extraordinary work the young Caravaggio's trademarks — the carafe with flowers and the fruit — mingle with sheets of music and the instrument in the foreground. The figure of the youth seems, as Giovanni Baglione (1642) notes, "real and alive." Here, beyond the traditional interpretation, one feels the repercussion of an immediately real presence.

During these early years in Rome, around 1595, Caravaggio dealt for the first time in his career with religious subjects and genre scenes. The former belonged to the most widespread tradition. The latter were quite new; thanks to him, they would enjoy immense success in seventeenth-century Europe.

The Stigmatization of St. Francis in the Wadsworth Atheneum in Hartford, Connecticut, belongs to the first category. The painting was once in Trieste, and its subsequent passage through various collections is well

10. *Martha and Mary Magdalen*
cm. 97.8x132.7
Detroit, Institute of Arts

11. *The Fortune Teller*
cm. 99x131
Paris, Louvre

12. *The Fortune Teller*
cm. 115x150
Rome, Musei Capitolini

documented. Scholars agree in considering it one of the artist's first works. It has a perfectly Lombard air: The broad lines of the composition recall mannerist motifs like those of Peterzano, whereas the intimacy of the nocturnal setting brings to mind Savoldo and Lotto. But Caravaggio's characteristic approach to reality is already at work, and his brushstroke shows a magic that could be obtained only by a thorough analysis of Venetian painting. This he probably studied after his first years with Peterzano and before leaving his birthplace for Rome. The references to the art of Giorgione and to that of the young Titian (in addition to a meditation on Titian's later works, which Caravaggio would use only in subsequent paintings), were restricted for years by certain schools of art criticism in the attempt, at the time well founded, to emphasize the artist's substantial pertinence to the Lombard tradition. However even the better Lombard art owes much to Giorgione and Titian, and scholars have recently begun to take a more balanced view of the influence of Venetian painting on Caravaggio. His infallible ability to overcome the traditional dilemma of color and *disegno* by individuating optical reality as it really appears to the observer, is based on a conception of color as a structural element

491

that is deeply indebted to Venetian art; and it would indeed be surprising if such an open-minded artist had not studied the Venetian masters of the early sixteenth century.

Caravaggio's portrayal of St. Francis receiving the stigmata in ecstatic rapture was revolutionary; as was his treatment of another, iconographically very unusual theme. He showed Martha reproaching Mary Magdalen for her vanity, a subject that we know through a series of copies. One of these, now at the Institute of Arts in Detroit, has recently been recognized, probably correctly, as the original. As has already been pointed out, the religious theme is treated in a substantially profane manner. It is a pretext for making passages of highly intense painting and for constructing an image that, seen in the context of the usual dichotomy of Caravaggio's early years, is more of a genre scene than a religious one. The painting does not illustrate a precise subject, but merely alludes to it, moving toward another field of interest.

A genre scene may be defined as a conventional subject of a profane nature drawn from everyday life, but immediately removed from direct observation (which belongs to the initiators alone) to take its place in the current of conventional reproduction (which belongs to the more or less tight ranks of imitators). These paintings for private enjoyment fared very well with their public, and it is exciting to trace the origins of a form of figurative expression that later enjoyed such success. Two themes from Caravaggio's early years can be placed in the category of genre paintings. One, I Bari, represents a card game. It is known through several copies and through an original formerly in the Sciarra Collection in Rome, now unfortunately lost. It was a subject that Caravaggio must have been quite familiar with through personal experience, as we shall see.

The other theme, preserved in two paintings, both of which are probably originals, painted at a distance of several years, shows a Gypsy reading the palm of a youth while skillfully removing the ring from his finger. The first example is in the Louvre; the second (which tecnical analysis recently confirmed as an autograph copy) is in the Pinacoteca Capitolina in Rome. Contemporary sources tell us much about this composition. Indeed, Bellori (1672), a writer who was highly critical of Caravaggio (as we shall see better below), tells a particularly significant story: "Having been shown the most famous statues of Phidias and Glycon so that he could study them, his only response was to extend his hand toward a crowd of men, pointing out that nature had given him enough masters. And to lend authority to his words he called a gypsy that happened to be passing by in the street, and bringing her to his rooms, portrayed her in the act of forseeing the future, as these women of Egyptian descent are known to do. He made a young man with one gloved hand on his sword, the other, bare, held

out to her, and she takes it and reads it; and in these two half-figures Michele translated the truth so purely, that it confirmed what he said."

This painting can thus be considered a precise illustration of Caravaggio's aesthetic creed. His attitude of dissociation with the past must have been difficult for his contemporary artists and connoisseurs to understand, and especially to share in. He maintained that the subject matter of painting should not be drawn from ancient or modern history, that is must not be celebrative or commemorative, laden with a moral lesson, or set up as an example. Furthermore, he believed that the study of famous old masters must not inspire the artist and form his technical training. Caravaggio's masters are not the mythical names of a more or less distant past, but men in general. His lesson is not drawn from history, but from life. According to his conception, the painter must be a careful observer of what lies around him, and not a student of preexisting technical and cultural traditions. Statements of this kind must have sounded thoroughly heretical in the context of late mannerism. As it turned out the artist's attitude did not meet with indifference, but with enthusiastic acceptance by a few sympathizers, and with opposition by most of the artist's audience, which, as always, tended to be conservative. Caravaggio's outlook became increasingly overpowering, however. It eventually influenced every artistic trend in Europe. Even his religious paintings became essential to the aesthetic and cultural climate of the cities they were located in (Rome, Naples, Messina and Syracuse). But we know from the sources, or we can guess, how heated the discussions that accompanied these works must have been.

Bellori, just before the passage we quoted, writes that Merisi "knew no master other than the model." Francesco Scannelli (1657) defines him "the first head of the naturalists." The Fleming Karel van Mander, writing at a very early date (1604), mentions "Michelangelo Caravaggio who does wonderful things in Rome," and says that he " is one who does not care much for the works of any master... he says... that all things are trifles, childishness, nonsense, whoever painted them, if they are not taken from life, and nothing can be good or better than following nature... and copying her in painting." In the transcript of a legal action brought against him by Baglione, Caravaggio tells the judge that a "skillful" painter is one who "knows how to paint and imitate natural things well." Finally, a letter written by the eminent patron of the arts, Marchese Vincenzo Giustiniani, confirms Caravaggio's indifference toward the traditional artistic hierarchies that see history painting as the highest genre. In reference to the difficulty of the various ways of painting, Giustiniani tells that "Caravaggio said that it took as much workmanship to make a good painting of flowers as of figures." This claim reveals Caravaggio's full revolutionary importance. In its origin-

13. Mary Magdalen
cm. 106x97
Rome, Galleria Doria Pamphili

14. *Narcissus*
cm. 110x92
Rome, Galleria Nazionale di Arte Antica

15. *St. Catherine of Alexandria*
cm. 173x133
Lugano, Thyssen-Bornemizsa Collection

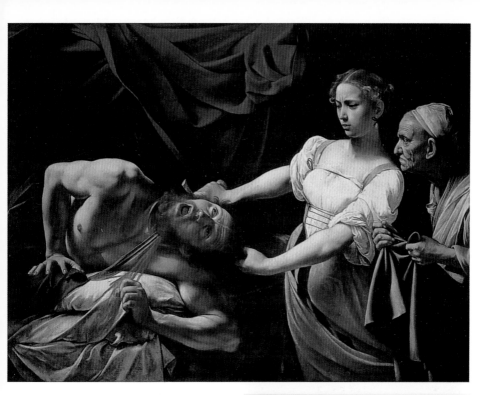

16. *Rest During the Flight into Egypt*
cm. 130x160
Rome, Galleria Doria Pamphili

17. *Rest During the Flight into Egypt, detail*
of Joseph and the angel.
Rome, Galleria Doria Pamphili

18. *Judith*
cm. 144x195
Rome, Galleria Nazionale di Arte Antica

19. *Judith, detail of the servant.*
Rome, Galleria Nazionale di Arte Antica

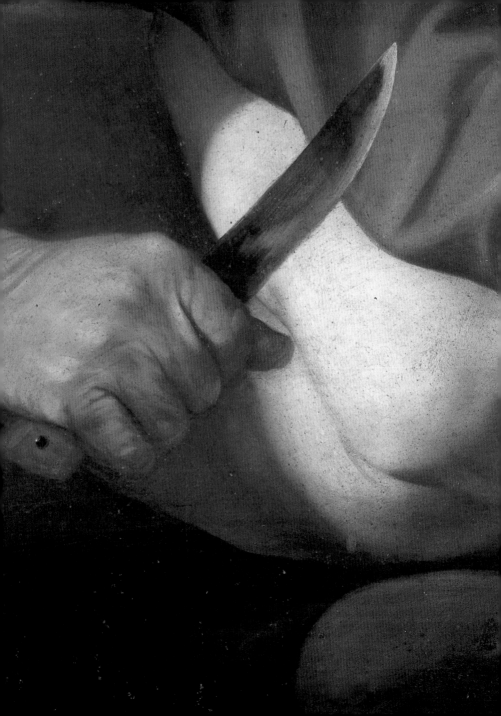

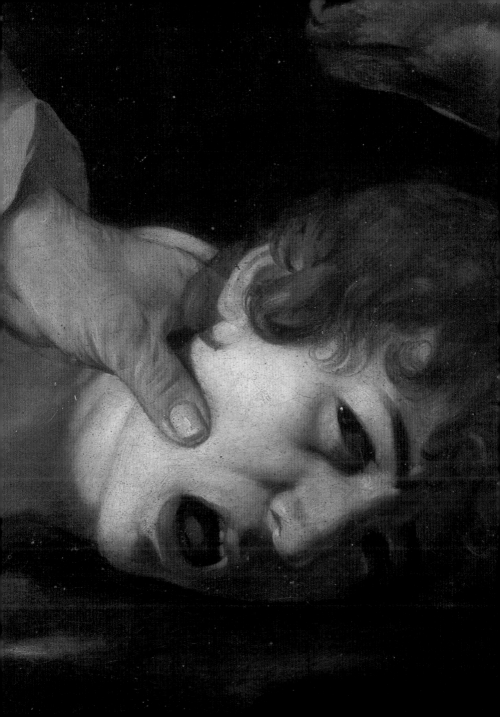

al context, it chiefly regards the question of technique; but it is not arbitrary to link Giustiniani's comment to Caravaggio's aesthetic principles as a genuine opening both in the direction of the still-life and in that of the genre scene.

This brings us to the last years of the sixteenth century. Caravaggio was gradually gaining acceptance among a select audience; his economic and social position was improving. At this time he made some of his most fascinating creations. Bellori magically describes the Magdalen in the Galleria Doria Phamphili in Rome, seen earlier in the Pamphili home by Scannelli (1657), as follows: "he painted a girl on a chair with her hand in her lap, drying her hair; he painted her in an interior, and by adding an ointment jar and jewelry, he imagined her as the Magdalen." Bellori emphasizes how the painting is not planned from the beginning as an exemplary description of the biblical figure, but how the identification is almost made afterward, at the moment the artist adds the ointment jar and jewelry. The painting does not represent Mary Magdalen; it represents a girl who is "imagined" as Mary Magdalen. And this interpre-

tation sticks, even when we recognize that the figurative sources of the painting include the sixteenth-century images of "Melancholia," including the famous engraving by Dürer. Again it must be pointed out that Caravaggio's attitude toward reality did not preclude familiarity with earlier figurative sources nor their use in his art. Besides, everyone felt — and feels — the discreet charm of this intimate image, whose domestic setting so clearly anticipates the central theme of seventeenth-century Dutch painting, that in looking for a close affinity for Caravaggio's painting we are obliged to turn to Vermeer.

A similar concentration on the expressive core of the composition, undiminished by superfluous elements, is apparent in the Narcissus in the Galleria Nazionale di Arte Antica in Palazzo Barberini in Rome. The attribution of this painting to Caravaggio has been discussed at length, and it is still questioned by some scholars. In this case there are no contemporary sources we can refer to (an inventory of the time mentions a Narcissus by Caravaggio, but there is nothing to prove that this is the painting referred to), and the attribution rests entirely on stylistic bases. It seems, though, that here as else-

20. Abraham and Isaac
cm. 104x135
Florence, Galleria degli Uffizi

21. Head of Medusa
cm. 60x55
Florence, Galleria degli Uffizi

where the intuition of Roberto Longhi (who was the first to attribute the painting to Caravaggio) is correct, because of the very special mixture of sixteenth-century Lombard tradition and modern use of light, the way in which the material of the clothing is rendered, and the painting's inventive genius (although, because the numerous copies of Caravaggio's originals are often very good, the sole criterion of quality is not sufficient grounds for an attribution to the master).

The splendid St. Catherine of Alexandria formerly belonged to Cardinal Del Monte, one of the artist's patrons. It is now in the Von Thyssen Collection, which is located in Lugano, although the painting is not always in that city. Here we see a single female figure, as in the Doria Magdalen, in an interior devoid of architectural allusions. But the image appears with a different boldness and an immediacy that combine the nobility of the subject (St. Catherine was a king's daughter) with the almost plebeian pride of the model (no doubt a Roman woman of the people, possibly the same one who posed for a portrait formerly in Berlin and destroyed during the war). The breadth of conception and realization, and the perfect mastery of a very difficult composition (the

figure and objects completely fill the painting, in a subtle play of diagonals) are striking. Caravaggio here chose a "grand" noble approach that heralds the great religious compositions he would soon do for San Luigi dei Francesi. The extraordinary virtuosity in the painting of the large, decorated cloth is absorbed as an integral part of the composition. This is something his followers would not often succeed in doing, for they frequently dealt with the single components of the painting individually, with adverse effects on the unity of the whole.

At roughly this same time, the artist made three paintings, of Old and New Testament scenes, showing actions carried out by several figures. In this way he experimented with complicating his compositions, gaining valuable practice for the great religious paintings mentioned in passing, above. These compositions with biblical subjects were intended for the private devotion of noble families, rather than for the decoration of public religious buildings. Just how much genuine devotion they inspired in their owners and in the guests who frequented their homes or private chapels, is unknown.

In the Rest During the Flight into Egypt in the Galleria Doria Pamphili in Rome, the dominant feeling is

22. *Portrait of Maffeo Barberini*
cm. 121x95
Florence, private collection

23. *St. John the Baptist*
cm. 132x97
Rome, Musei Capitolini

24. *Calling of St. Matthew*
cm. 322x340
Rome, San Luigi dei Francesi

one of extreme gentleness. It is a miracle of peace and quiet. Beneath an oak tree, after removing the large sack with their few personal objects and the water flask from the back of the mule, Joseph holds for the angel the score of the music that helped put to sleep the Christ Child and, it seems, his mother, too. In the quiet light, less violently defined than in the artist's other works, is set what with a classical term we may call an idyll, a small elegiac scene. The naturalistic rendering of the landscape, at the upper right, and of the plants, in the foreground, where artistic and scientific knowledge are combined, recalls the works of Leonardo da Vinci (who worked for many years in Lombardy). The angel is

painted with great delicacy; its classical but subtly animated pose betrays the study of earlier models, and recalls in particular certain works of Andrea del Sarto, as in the Chiostro dello Scalzo in Florence (in all likelihood visited by Caravaggio on his way to Rome, but in any event widely known through drawings and prints).

The atmosphere of the other two paintings is entirely different. The Judith, recently acquired by the Galleria Nazionale d'Arte Antica in Rome, is surprisingly brutal. As early as the eighteenth century the writers Charles De Brosses and Joseph Lalande, who saw the work in the Palazzo Zambeccari in Bologna, were surprised by its extreme realism. But the painting had it

most tremendous effect on an English traveller, Lady Anne Miller, who saw it in 1770. She writes: "This picture is too well done; it struck me directly, that it must have been taken from life. The idea threw me into a trembling, and made me very sick; producing the same effects upon me, that perhaps I might have experienced from the presence of [a] real execution: the separation of the neck, the force she uses, the spouting of the blood from the divided arteries, and her contenance [*sic*], whilst she turns away her face from the dreadful work she is about, and which nevertheless expresses a fierceness and a sort of courage little befitting a woman, joined with the writhing convulsions of the body of Holofernes make it a picture quite improper for the inspection of those who have any degree of feeling: it is by Michael Angelo da Caravagio [*sic*]." So, the painting made

its point. As for the presence of a real execution, there was certainly no lack at the time of cases for study. The genuine aggressiveness toward the viewer that Caravaggio sometimes shows, here reaches its peak, establishing a precedent that would be repeated by such artists as Jean de Boulogne, called Valentin, and Artemisia Gentileschi. Every element is carried to extremes: the horror of the head of Holofernes; the red of the tent, blood, and blade; the astonished expression of the servant, and even the sculptural severity of Judith, the true biblical heroine. I doubt that the painting is still as repulsive today as it was for eighteenth-century observers. Now it evokes a sense of extreme admiration, almost attraction, not because it sets in motion responses and secret sadisms; but because it is so full of skill, imagination, and manual quality — in short, of artistic power — that

25. *Calling of St. Matthew, detail of Christ and St. Peter.*
Rome, San Luigi dei Francesi

26. *X-ray of the detail with Christ and St. Peter, showing the two different versions of Christ's arm and head. The drapery belonged to the figure of Christ.*

we are fascinated.

At the last possible moment, as we know from the biblical passage, Abraham's knife was diverted from his son's throat. The Abraham and Isaac in the Uffizi, cited in the Barberini Inventory as early as 1608, is of uncertain date. Some critics place it at the beginning of Caravaggio's Roman sojourn, others as late as 1603. We prefer to include it at this point, toward the close of the century, considering it similar in theme, technique, and style to the Flight into Egypt and the Judith. Bellori (1672) offers an admirably synthetic description of the picture: "The sacrifice of Abraham, who holds the iron near the throat of his son who cries out and falls". The painting, organized around the diagonal that descends from upper left to lower right, represents an episode traditionally interpreted with reference to Christ, because of the obvious parallel between the son of Abraham and the Son of God, both innocent victims. Some scholars see a church with a baptistery in the background, a further allusion to the Redeemer. Notice, however, how little there is in common between Christ's attitude and that of Isaac, who "cries out" and does not seem at all willing, as he appears to be in many earlier representations, to be sacrificed. Notice also the landscape: its atmospheric quality and the way distant objects gradually fade into their surroundings constitute Caravaggio's clearest admission of his debt to Venetian painting and to Giorgione.

The "aesthetic of exclamation" by which the artist renders feelings with dramatic violence, as in the figures of Judith and Isaac, reaches its highest expression in the famous Head of Medusa given to the Medici by Cardinal

27. Calling of
St. Matthew, detail with
St. Matthew (figure on
the right).
Rome, San Luigi dei
Francesi

28. Calling of
St. Matthew, detail with
the two central figures.
Rome, San Luigi dei
Francesi

Del Monte and now in the Uffizi. This is a round shield (although it was obviously never used as such) that the artist's patron evidently desired to keep as a strange and unusual object.

There is a celebrated iconographical precedent for this painting (even though it is not extant) by Leonardo da Vinci. But it is unusual, and Caravaggio's treatment of the theme remains impressed in our memory by virtue of its inventiveness and absolute originality. The "serpent-covered" head (as it is called in a Medici inventory of 1631) is painted on a convex surface, an expedient already used by sixteenth-century mannerists to emphasize the metamorphism of the image (its property of subtly changing in relation to the way the light strikes it), or even to render reality in a deformed way. The con-

vexity of the support helps project the head into real space, the space occupied by the viewer. Giovan Battista Marino, a poet who maintained that the goal of verse is wonderment, wrote (in 1513-14) of this painting, which he saw in the Gallery of the Grand-Duke of Tuscany: "That proud and ferocious Gorgon / horribly magnificent / in serpentine volumes / of frightening hair," and even earlier, in 1603, another poet, Gaspare Murtola, told of the "poisonous hair / armed with a thousand snakes."

The St. John the Baptist presents us with a much more restful image. This painting exists in two versions, both of which are probably by Caravaggio (who frequently copied his own paintings, as we have seen with the Buona Ventura in the Louvre and the Pinacoteca

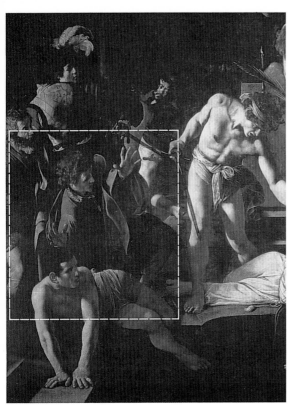

29. Martyrdom of St. Matthew
cm. 323x343
Rome, San Luigi dei Francesi

30. Martyrdom of St. Matthew, detail
with the group of figures on the left.
Rome, San Luigi dei Francesi

31. X-ray of the lower left part of the
Martyrdom, showing three figures from
the first version, later eliminated.

Capitolina). Both versions are in Rome, one in the Musei Capitolini, the other in the Galleria Doria Pamphili. The image is a masterpiece of virtuosity whose appeal lies in its soft, caressing light and velvety rendering of cloth, flesh, and plants. The figure is identifiable as St. John only by virtue of the symbols of Christ displayed in the painting: the ram (sacrificial victim), and the grape-leaves (from whose red juice, akin to the blood of Christ, springs life); otherwise the iconographical subject (the simple, immediately apparent image) appears as a nude youth with an ironic, if not allusive, expression. Its cultivated content and its destination for an aristocratic patron (Mattei) are underscored by the artist's explicit use of a great figurative source of the past: Michelangelo's Ignudi from the Sistine Ceiling. But whereas Michelangelo created abstract and ideal figures with cold lights and a merely theoretical plasticism, Caravaggio models his figure on the careful observation of nature, achieving an image of perfect realism. It releases a sort of charge of attraction, drawing in the viewer, in much the same way that the Amor Victorious in Berlin would

do a few years later: through the single figure turned toward the observer.

The artist's works that we have looked at so far were all intended for private patrons, even though many of them were religious paintings. Caravaggio's achievements were not so widely acclaimed, in the beginning, that they could be set above the altars of Roman churches, before the eyes of a general public accustomed to images of a very different kind. Nevertheless, when he was called on to furnish large religious paintings for important churches in the city, he realized them without compromise, without making the slightest attempt to simplify or soften the virulence of his message. His first church commission arose just at the turn of the century. Never has another coincidence of this kind been so justifiably pregnant with meaning.

In 1565 the French monsignor Matteo Contarelli acquired a chapel in San Luigi dei Francesi, but when he died twenty years later it had not yet been decorated. The executor of his will, Virgilio Crescenzi, and later his

32. X-ray of the right part of the Martyrdom. At the top center is one of the figures still present in the painting. The classical figure in the foreground is part of the first version.

33. Martyrdom of St. Matthew, detail of the right part of the painting. Rome, San Luigi dei Francesi

son, Giacomo, undertook the task. The decorative scheme called for a statue of St. Matthew and the Angel, commissioned first to Gerolamo Muziano, and then to the Flemish sculptor Cobaert, for the high altar; and for a fresco cycle for the walls and ceiling by Cavalier d'Arpino. The latter decorated the vault in 1591-93, but the walls were left bare (this may reflect at least in part the Crescenzis' intentions to speculate on the interest on the Contarelli estate). At any rate, on 13 June 1599 a contract was stipulated before a notary by which Caravaggio undertook to execute two paintings for the lateral walls, for which he was paid the following year (1600), after the paintings had been set in place. Later, on 7 February 1602, after Cobaert's statue had been judged unsatisfactory, an altarpiece was entrusted to

Caravaggio in a separate contract that called for delivery of the work by 23 May, the Feast of the Pentecost. This painting, as we shall see, was rejected; the artist made another one (which was accepted) in a surprisingly brief time, receiving payment for this second work on 22 September.

The recent discovery of a series of documents that has made it possible to reconstruct the complete course of events with great accuracy, has confirmed or denied several hypotheses set forth by scholars over the past fifty years regarding the dating of the paintings for San Luigi dei Francesi. The first version of the altarpiece depicting St. Matthew and the Angel (the one that was rejected and later destroyed, unfortunately), in particular, had been given an early date which the sources showed

34. St. Matthew and the Angel
cm. 296.5x189
Rome, San Luigi dei Francesi

35. St. Matthew and the Angel
cm. 232x183
Formerly at Berlin, Kaiser Friedrich
Museum, destroyed.

to be inadmissable. The discovery also casts new light on the paintings for Santa Maria del Popolo (especially the first version of the Conversion of St. Paul), which were made right after the first two paintings for San Luigi. This development should serve as a warning to those scholars who feel they know how to distinguish, with great subtlety, the smallest inflection of style, so as to obtain unquestionable relative or absolute datings, even to within a few months (despite the fact that they are dealing with events of four centuries ago). The path of an artist's career is not always straight. It is full of changes of mind, and above all, of experiments that lead in different directions but that are conducted simultaneously. Two different orders of artistic inquiry do not necessarily represent different periods in an artist's ca-

reer. If the artist is open to experimentation and tends to reject normally accredited conventions, more than one line of action may appeal to him at any given time.

An examination of the two paintings of the side walls of San Luigi dei Francesi, which Matteo Contarelli wished to show the Calling and Martyrdom of his namesake, provide us with an extraordinary panorama of Caravaggio's art. We have seen that many of his compositions thus far contain a limited number of figures: normally from one to three. The subject is expressed as a rule with little interest in the depth of the painting. Even when the figures are placed before a landscape, they stand out prominently in the foreground, so that the landscape appears as little more than a backdrop. There are seven figures in the Calling of St. Matthew, and thirteen in the Martyrdom. They diminish in size in relation to the painting's surface, leaving room for the background. In the Martyrdom, we also see an arrangement in echelons that is unprecedented in Caravaggio's art. It is even more surprising because it is achieved with very little allusion to the architecture of the setting, deriving its force from the arrangement of the figures in space.

Caravaggio did not arrive at the final version right away, and it is important to remember that even compositions that appear to have been born in an instant are the fruit of a long preparatory study. X-ray analysis has proven absolutely indispensable in revealing to our later vision forms and figures that the artist, after sketching them on the canvas, believed would remain concealed from all eyes, including his own, beneath the final version. Thus, in an early version of the Calling of St. Matthew, the figure of Christ stood alone and was not covered, as in the final version, by that of St. Peter. The latter's presence involved the accentuation, in the final version, of his role as mediator (he would be the first pope) between man and God. Indeed, we see a sort of division of Christ into two parts, as though two persons have germinated and branched off from the same trunk. This already emphasized Christ's human and divine nature. Peter laboriously and almost stiffly repeats the gesture of Christ, which in comparison is handled with the greatest eloquence. In addition, we immediately notice the painting's total independence from the designs of earlier religious painting. From this we may conclude that the artist is not interested in instructing, admonishing, or stirring his audience to religious feeling, as the Counter Reformation expected art to do. He felt it was not his task. He seems to say, this is what happened. Christ and Peter suddenly came in and made it clear that they wanted to talk to Matthew, while the two youths, taken by surprise, prepared to face an intrusion whose nature they were unsure of; and indeed two other figures, unaware of what was going on, continued counting the money. Matthew brought his hand to his chest, as though to ask if it were he that they wanted. An instant before, the scene had been different; an instant later, it would no longer be the same. If a scene is to be instructive, it must be prepared, planned, and arranged. If it is devoid of this kind of orientation toward a specific end, then the artist is virtually free to shape it as he likes and to change it from one moment to the next, not preparing it, but taking note of it.

Here, for the first time, the viewer no longer synthetically embraces all the painting's content. A more complicated scene is played out before his eyes. This calls for a diachronous reading more than a synchronous one. The eye must follow the event, running along the entire network of relations set up by the figures' gestures and gazes. Caravaggio would make extensive use of these internal references, obliging his viewers to run through the entire genetic process of the painting, to follow the artist along the path that he proposes or actually imposes on the observer. Thus guided by the artist, the viewer cannot escape his intentions. The painter is therefore able to charge the picture with meanings knowing that his audience will have to pause and reflect on them; hence the claim to an absolutely global consideration of the work, and the particular eloquence of Caravaggio's paintings from this moment onward — an eloquence that does not proceed by classical, universal truths as in the Carracci and their current, but by contingent details whose exemplary value the artist succeeds in identifying and pointing out to the observer. This is why these paintings cannot leave one indifferent and why the viewer who begins to look at the painting cannot stop even if he wants to, until he reaches the end.

In the Martyrdom of St. Matthew the composition is expanded to cover a complexity of subject that is unprecedented in Caravaggio's work, and that frankly we could not have expected on the basis only of his earlier paintings. It is quite true that all he lacked was the chance given by a specific commission: otherwise the artist was ready to contend with the greater complexity of ideas mentioned above. The Martyrdom is not only one of the most memorable creations of Western art; it is also remarkable for its innovative power, its wealth of explicit and implicit meaning, and its ingenious composition. X-ray analysis has shown that the first conception of the scene had three classical figures in the foreground: one in the middle seen from behind, which took up the motif of the angel in the Rest During the Flight into Egypt, and two others inspired by antique sculpture filtered through the late works of Raphael, an artist whose influence can also be seen clearly in the final version. Caravaggio arrived at the definitive painting, which is very different, with astonishing rapidity, reworking, discarding, or changing his first ideas. That such an exacting work was done directly on the canvas, without the usual recourse to drawings on paper, is truly unusual; but then there is not a single drawing that can be attributed to Caravaggio with certainty. This is another feature that distinguishes him from his fellow artists.

Caravaggio leaves the setting of the event unclear. The three seminude figures in the foreground, of which the two on the right contemplate the Martyrdom (the action is not contemporaneous, but relived, as we are thus given to understand) create a chronological and spatial detachment. They belong to an indefinite space. They seem to sink, before the step of the altar on which the crime is committed, into a sort of pool, the Pool of Bethesda of the Holy Scriptures from which one re-emerges regenerated. The six figures on the left show different states of mind. They are grouped together in couples. The first two, reminiscent of the figures of Gior-

36. Conversion of St. Paul
cm. 237x189
Rome, Odescalchi Balbi Collection

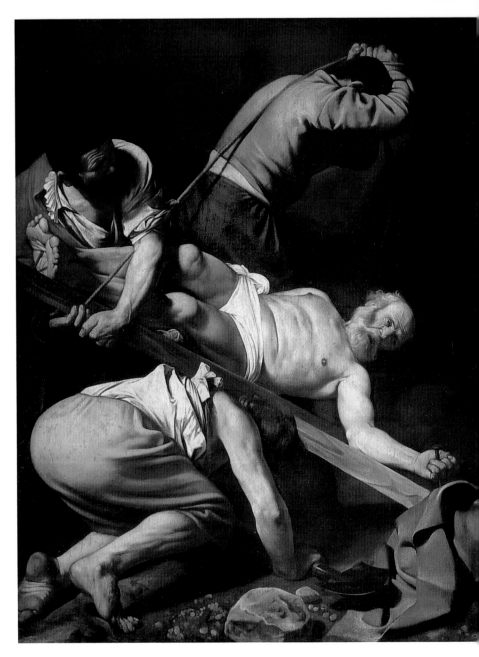

37. *Crucifixion of St. Peter*
cm. 232x201. Rome, Santa Maria del Popolo

38. Conversion on the Way to Damascus
cm. 230x175. Rome, Santa Maria del Popolo

*39. Crucifixion of
St. Peter, detail of
the figure at the
upper left.
Rome, Santa Maria del
Popolo*

*40. Supper in Emmaus
cm. 139x195
London, National Gallery*

gione and Savoldo, express immense surprise and wonder — the emotions with which the one in the green gown opens his arms, offering his hands, especially his left hand, to a highly refined play of light. Two others, elegantly dressed, show their intention to call each other out of the action, in which they do not wish to become involved. One wears the usual feathered cap. The third couple moves away despite their emotional involvement, as though against their will. The figure seen frontally is Caravaggio himself, who seems to want to impress the scene well in his mind, in order to paint it later. The splendid figure of the assassin carries out a precise action that not everyone notices: he grabs the saint's outstretched arm, to keep him from receiving the palm of martyrdom from the angel who reaches dangerously downward (in a pose taken from a figure in Michelangelo's Last Judgment). The youth on the right is an explicit expression of Caravaggio's characteristic and well-known "aesthetic of exclamation." He contrasts strongly with the contemplative attitude of the figures on the right, which is the same attitude in which the classical painters represented the shepherds in the "Et in Arcadia Ego", dreamy and idyllic images that have nothing of the fierceness of this scene. The traces of setting are reduced to an absolute minimum. X-rays show that an earlier version contained classical architectural elements, which the artist removed.

Cobaert's statue for the altar of the chapel was (fortunately) rejected, and Caravaggio, as we have said, was engaged to paint a St. Matthew and the Angel. The first version of this painting was likewise refused by the patrons. The artist's desperation was appeased by Marchese Vincenzo Giustiniani's offer to acquire it, and a second, acceptable version was produced. It still stands over the altar today. The first painting, which ended up in Berlin, was unfortunately destroyed during the Second World War. It was another masterpiece. It contained, in the angel who with gentle indulgence guided the saint's uncertain hand as he wrote, one of the most charming figures ever painted by the artist. The first painting was criticized for Matthew's lack of decorum; the figure, which hardly appeared as a saint, was seated cross-legged, his feet turned outward toward the viewer. In the final version, likewise a splendid feat of imagination but certainly less fascinating than the first, the angel much more correctly counts on his fingers, in the traditional Scholastic fashion, the arguments than the saint should take note of and develop. A whirlwind of drapery envelops the angel. The saint balances on his bench, in precarious equilibrium, like a modern school-

boy; but this time the unorthodox elements do not seem to have raised particular objections.

Caravaggio's other great ecclesiastical enterprise of these years falls between the two canvases for the side walls and the altarpiece. On 24 September 1600, immediately after finishing the wall paintings for San Luigi dei Francesi, Caravaggio received the commission for two paintings, a Crucifixion of St. Peter and a Conversion of St. Paul, from Monsignor Tiberio Cerasi, for the latter's newly acquired chapel in Santa Maria del Popolo. For the altar Monsignor Cerasi had ordered an Assumption from Annibale Carracci, certainly excited by the idea of effecting such a close comparison between the greatest (and for the time being, the only) representatives in Rome of the classical and naturalistic currents. The contract explicitly mentions two cypress panels (Caravaggio certainly did not like to work in fresco, as was more usual for commissions of this kind, because he was not able to make the corrections that, as we have seen, were so important to him). The extant paintings with the subjects indicated in the contract are on canvas; and as there is another version of the Conversion of Saul in the Balbi Odescalchi Collection in Rome, painted on a cypress panel, and a Crucifixion of Peter in Leningrad, attributed to various artists, it is logical to assume that there was at one time an original by Caravaggio. The evidence seems to back up Baglione's assertion that, again, Caravaggio's first versions did not meet with the client's approval, and were acquired by others (in this case, Cardinal Sannesio) and replaced by more acceptable paintings.

The Balbi Odescalchi Conversion, after overcoming the reservations of the past regarding its attribution, has had to deal with many more concerning its date, because many scholars consider it too early to be the first version of the painting for Santa Maria del Popolo. But the considerations made above concerning the contemporaneous intersection in Caravaggio of different and even contrasting motifs and ideas, are even more valid here; and the nonstylistic evidence (subject, size, technique) is too powerful to allow for different interpretations. Certainly, the style of the painting is not nearly so exact as that of the paintings for San Luigi; and above all, the tangled and crowded composition is full of mannerist features, particularly in the figure of Saul, whose debt to Michelangelo is nevertheless superficial. But the painting contains, in the angel and in Christ, two of the best-known models for Caravaggio's figures of those years, as is readily seen; and the Lombard treatment of

*41. Supper in Emmaus, detail.
London, National Gallery*

42. Supper in Emmaus, detail.
London, National Gallery

the landscape is a constant throughout Caravaggio's career, with the exception of his very last years.

The two later paintings for Santa Maria del Popolo compelled the artist to contend with vertical composi-tions, unlike those of San Luigi. Here again the scale of the figures is increased in relation to the surface. The ac-tion, instead of stretching out in a narrative, is concen-trated solely on setting up the very central core of the

43. Doubting of
St. Thomas
cm. 107x146
Potsdam, Neues Palais

44. Christ in the Garden
cm. 154x222
Formerly at Berlin, Kaiser
Friedrich Museum,
destroyed.

45. Capture of Christ
cm. 134x172.5
Odessa, State Museum of
Eastern and Western Art

scene. All elements that are not absolutely necessary are left out of the Crucifixion: The saint and the three executioners appear without a landscape. Caravaggio does not give up the specific definition of the gestures, to which a perfect necessity is attributed, best exemplified by the executioner who bends down, his spade still in his hand, to lift up the cross on his back. Here the artist, no doubt in deference to the severity of the setting, renounced his aesthetic of horror. The blood does not gush forth as from a fountain, but forms tiny rivulets. The expression on the saint's face is introspective, sorrowfully accepting, devoid of all expressionistic satisfaction. Even the colors are muted.

The same internal atmosphere pervades the Conversion on the Way to Damascus, one of the artist's finest achievements. The rendering of Saul (how different from the complacent movement of the first version!) shuns a demonstration of mere skill; his out-flung arms (whose circular rhythm is fused with the profile of the animal) express calm acceptance of the will of God, relating this figure psychologically with the greatest traditional depositary of this sentiment, the Virgin of the Annunciation. The horse does not neigh madly, but seems to return to its stall at the end of the day, tired and peaceful. The absolute rarefaction of expressive means to which Caravaggio resorts here is a new development after the extremistic superficialities of his first decade. Those who admired his skill then, find here that Caravaggio could be not only a marvellous phenomenon of cultural fashion, but one of the few very great artists who change the course of world art.

The same expressive principles are to be found in another group of paintings that appear to have been done around the same time as the Contarelli and Cerasi cycles. The Supper in Emmaus in the National Gallery in London, formerly in the collection of Ciriaco Mattei, brings the flowing gestures of the figures together in a mood of noble containment. It is the moment of the disciple's recognition of Christ. The latter is young and beardless, his left hand transfixed by the light. The still-life is rendered with the artist's characteristic naturalism, but in duller tones. Even the decorative element of the rug or tablecloth on the table lacks that masterful effect of texture and color visible elsewhere in the earlier works.

Three other paintings of episodes drawn from the life of Christ attest to the artist's interest in unprecedented treatments of themes already dealt with at length by

46. David
cm. 116x91
Madrid, Prado

47. St. John the Baptist
cm. 102.5x83
Basel, Öffentliche Kunstsammlung

traditional iconography. A Christ in the Garden from the Giustiniani Collection, destroyed in Berlin during the war, is known to us today through extant photographs. This was a wonderful composition that caught the instant in which Christ awakes the sleeping apostles. The construction of the scene descends toward the lower right corner. St. Peter in particular is shown in a classical position (which has been called Carracci-like), with the containment that characterizes this moment in the artist's career. The palace in Potsdam known as Sanssouci houses a Doubting of St. Thomas surely by Caravaggio (and also originally from the Giustiniani Collection). This is another of his major masterpieces. The tightly closed composition concentrates the viewer's attention, like that of the apostles, on the physical act of proving the identity of Christ, which is studied with objective naturalism, without a touch of the complacent realism that the theme would have allowed. Here we have one of the surest precedents for the art of Velasquez (this is not a general reference: the Spanish artist may have seen this painting during his two visits to Rome); indeed the composition is so modern that a straight line may be drawn from paintings like this one, to Manet.

The Capture of Christ in the Museum of Eastern and Western Art in Odessa, though still of uncertain attribution, is very probably the original known through a series of copies. In evaluating the composition we must bear in mind that the left side has been mutilated; but the tight rhythm, with which the curve that descends slightly toward the left also describes a normal rotation of the paintings, is among Caravaggio's greatest creations. The artist's followers, and especially the Frenchman Valentin, would have liked this theme very much.

Other themes of Caravaggio's reexamine the single-figure painting in a new light. A probable original in the Prado in Madrid addresses the subject of David and Goliath, which the artist repeatedly dealt with later in his career, with a perfect linearity of means and intelligence of iconographic invention. As in the early Renaissance, David is shown as the adolescent who triumphs not by his strength, but by his power of character and his faith. The oblique pose of the figure (David stands partly parallel to the picture plane) is constructed with admirable skill.

Another painting that may belong to this moment of Caravaggio's career is the much-debated St. John in Basel, who seems to draw the bouquet of flowers in his right hand away from the lamb to keep him from nibbling on it. The Amour Victorious in Berlin, clearly attributable to the artist, has always been considered one of his greatest masterpieces. Caravaggio painted it for Marchese Giustiniani, in competition with Baglione (a rival artist who at one point actually sued Caravaggio, even if he was later to become his biographer). Caravaggio's painting, which, as we know from the sources,

Giustiniani preferred over all the other paintings in his collections, is described with singular felicity in the inventory of 1638: "A painting with a laughing Cupid, in the act of mocking the world." In effect the figure sets up a direct, special, and privileged relationship with the viewer, with an immediate appeal that is truly extraordinary. One is bewildered by this painting, by the absolute freedom that the subject obviously enjoys, detaching himself from mere mortals who must obey the laws of nature. The figure is indeed "in the act of mocking the world," with a complete impunity, a self-assurance that produce a mixture of astonishment and envy. As early as 1603 Murtola wrote: "Don't look don't look / in this canvas Love / will set fire to your heart." The painting probably shows Earthly Love (Baglione had painted Divine Love) triumphant over the Virtues and Sciences, symbolized by the musical instruments, pen and book, compass and square, scepter, laurel, and armor at his feet.

The next phase of Caravaggio's career was distinguished by intense creativity. Single figures alternate with small groups in paintings for private collectors and a few splendid altarpieces, two of which are still among his most admired works. But these are also years in which his increasing fame as an artist collided headlong with the highly censurable episodes to which a quarrelsome and trouble-making character compelled him. This was the extremist aspect of a potentially positive character, akin to his passionate nonconformism. Unfortunately his lack of self-control, coupled with his desire to crush all opponents almost physically, resulted in bloody and even fatal conflicts which, in addition to placing his life in jeopardy, obliged him to flee from Rome and to wander around for years before meeting with his solitary death on the Tuscan coast. The same excessive and irrepressible desire to make himself known that led him, as soon as he had a little money, to parade around town expensively dressed and accompanied by a page who held his sword, caused him to suspect offences and enemies where in all likelihood there were neither. In any event the acts of blood and violence with which he was associated became increasingly numerous after 1600. They also became more and more

48. *Amor Victorious*
cm. 154x110
Berlin, Staatliche Museen

49. *Deposition*
cm. 300x203
Vatican, Pinacoteca

50. *Madonna dei Pellegrini*
cm. 260x150
Rome, Sant'Agostino

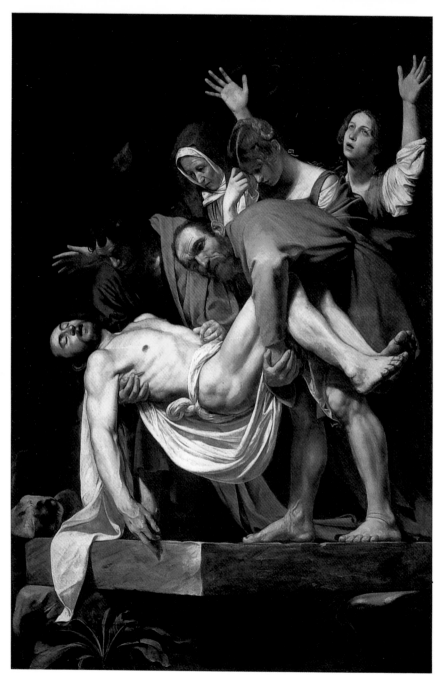

51. *Madonna dei Palafrenieri*
cm. 292x211
Rome, Galleria Borghese

52. *St. John the Baptist*
cm. 172.5x104.5
Kansas City, Nelson Gallery

serious, culminating in murder in 1606. On 19 November 1600, he was sued for assaulting a certain Girolamo Stampa with a club and sword. On 7 February 1601 he reconciled himself with a sergeant at arms of Castel Sant'Angelo whom he had wounded with his sword. The year 1603 witnessed the lengthy episode of the suit for defamation brought against him by Baglione, of which there are numerous reports, and which got Merisi a brief prison term. On 24 and 25 April 1604 a waiter in a tavern denounced him for having thrown a tray of artichokes in his face (when Caravaggio had asked which were cooked in butter and which in oil, and had been told to stick his nose in them and he'd figure it out by himself, he reacted as mentioned), and possibly for hav-

ing threatened him with his sword. In October and November 1604 he was brought in twice by the police for having insulted them with cries of "up my ass," apparently without provocation. On 28 May 1605 a dagger and sword were confiscated from him. On 20 July he was back in prison for slander against a certain Laura and her daughter. On 29 July the notary Pasqualone reported him for the blows on the head received from Caravaggio's sword over a certain Lena, the painter's girlfriend. On 1 November he was denounced for throwing stones through his former landlady's windows. On 24 October, when questioned after being injured, he replied in typical mafia style: "I cut myself [on the throat and on the left ear!] with my own sword. I fell down on

the street, I don't remember where, and there wasn't anybody around". He wound up with a 500-scudo fine and confinement to his own home. This unbelievable crescendo led to the quarrel of 31 May 1606, which broke out on the sidelines of a tennis court and involved Caravaggio and seven others. Caravaggio killed Ranuccio Tommasoni of Terni, and, himself injured, was compelled to take refuge in the fiefs of his friends, the Colonna. Some writers have taken great pleasure in Caravaggio's "criminality," particularly in the positivist period. It seemed all too easy to link the artist's tenebrous aesthetics, the use of dark tones as a general policy (Bellori writes, "he always used a black background," and says of Caravaggio himself, "he was of a dark countenance"), with a similarly colored soul. Certainly, of our three great innovators of painting, Caravaggio makes an abysmally bad impression, as opposed to Giotto, who may be taken as an "average" figure (Giotto was well immersed in his century, intent on building himself a name and fortune), and to Masaccio, as "positive" (Masaccio is the fair and unselfish person par excellence).

Nevertheless Caravaggio produced the supremely "classical" Vatican Deposition during these troubled years. Executed between 1602 and 1604 for the so-called Chiesa Nuova, Santa Maria in Vallicella in Rome,

this was one of the more widely admired and closely studied paintings of its age, as the free copies by Rubens, Fragonard, Géricault, and Cézanne, its extreme popularization through immense series of prints, and the numerous contemporary copies attest. The interpretation of the event is, as in the second St. Paul for Santa Maria del Popolo, restrained and limited in its effects; even Mary Cleophas, with her arms outstretched, expresses a gesture of universal execration that leads the viewer to pious meditation, rather than to a piercing cry as in his earlier aesthetics. A precise equilibrium governs the composition. The physical weight of the body becomes the moral weight of the world's grief. The figure on the right, Nicodemus, turns toward the observer to establish a psychological bond that is also a specific reference: the scene is viewed as from the tomb; the impression is almost as if the figures are about to surrender the body of Christ, if not to the observer, at least to someone standing in the same place. The identification is therefore complete, the involvement inescapable. The way the painting affected nineteenth-century artists is understandable. It combines a structural classicism that is timeless (Cézanne) with an extremely strong sense of drama (Géricault).

There are two other altarpieces that do not aspire to

53. *St. John the Baptist*
cm. 99x134
Rome, Galleria Nazionale di Arte Antica

54. *St. Jerome*
cm. 112x157
Rome, Galleria Borghese

55. *St. Jerome*
cm. 110x81
Montserrat, Monastery

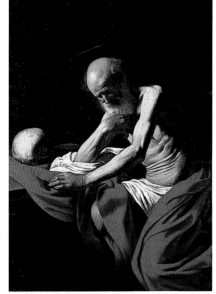

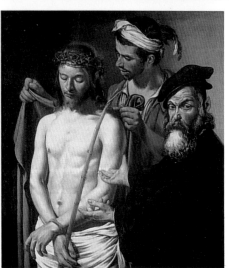

56. *Supper in Emmaus*
cm. 141x175
Milan, Pinacoteca di Brera

57. *Ecce Homo*
cm. 128x103
Genoa, Palazzo Rosso

58. *Supper in Emmaus, detail.*
Milan, Pinacoteca di Brera

59. *Death of the Virgin*
cm. 369x245
Paris, Louvre

60. *Death of the Virgin, detail.*
Paris, Louvre

61. *The Seven Acts of Mercy*
cm. 390x260
Naples, Church of Pio Monte della Misericordia

62. *Madonna del Rosario*
cm. 364x249
Vienna, Kunsthistorisches Museum

the majesty of the Vatican Deposition. The Madonna di Loreto, or Madonna dei Pellegrini, which may still be seen on the altar for which it was painted, in Sant'Agostino in Rome, was criticized, according to Baglione (1642), for the indelicacy of the pilgrims' muddy feet and ragged bonnets. But it has been rightly observed that the criticisms that were levied in academic circles must have regarded instead the absolute iconographic novelty of the painting, which consisted in making no reference to the Sacred House of Loreto, but in showing the pilgrimage itself — and as usual, devoid of hagiographic references. The portrayal of the Madonna as a woman who appears at the door to show the pilgrims the blessing Child, the goal of their journey, is achieved less through the barely noticeable halos, than through the true majesty of her splendid person (for whom the model was that Lena on whose behalf Caravaggio fought with the notary Pasqualone, the girl's disillusioned suitor). Portrayed in a precocious nineteenth-century manner that foreshadows Courbet, the woman appears in the statuary pose of classical art, as further proof of

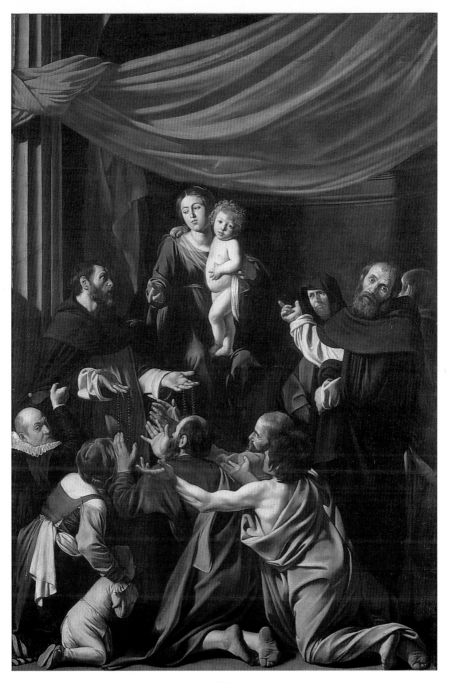

537

Caravaggio's ability to see ordinary events as history.

The so-called Madonna dei Palafrenieri was painted for an altar in St. Peter's, but was removed after only two days. Today it is in the Galleria Borghese. In this allegory of the Immaculate Conception, the Madonna and Child crush the serpent in the presence of St. Anne, patron saint of the Palafrenieri. St. Anne's pose (her head is tilted and her hands are joined) takes up the conventional iconography of one of the witnesses of the Crucifixion (the Virgin and St. John), as though to introduce the purpose of the Conception, Redemption. At the same time St. Anne, over whom the light plays forcefully, drawing her out of the shadows just far enough, is painted in the same style that would predomin-

ate in Caravaggio's last years. Once again the artist alludes skillfully, almost tacitly, to a room of which he gives no description. The parts that the artist has chosen to model in the light emerge from the darkness. Certainly we cannot help remembering Bellori's observation that Caravaggio's paintings could not be viewed to advantage in dark chapels.

These two paintings bring us to the years 1505-06. In this period Caravaggio did not put aside his private commissions; indeed, they became ever more numerous (he was actually well enough off to turn down a commission from the duke of Modena). At this point in his career, as earlier, this kind of commission called for paintings containing one or more figures. Two figures of

saints appear in more than one version. The artist dealt
with St. John the Baptist in two splendid compositions,
one in the Kansas City gallery, the other in the Galleria
Nazionale di Arte Antica in Rome. The former is laid
out vertically, the latter horizontally. Both lend themselves to a modernistic reading aimed at pointing out a
certain air between contempt and arrogance. In effect
what we are dealing with here are splendid exercises in
modeling the body through the play of light and shadow. In the version now in America, the figure is set before a dense curtain of plants; in that in Rome, there is
only the trunk of a cypress tree, on the left. Both are admirable feats of painting, and it is understandable that
collectors competed with each other for the artist's
works. Caravaggio in turn knew how to make apparently uninteresting religious themes into paintings desir-
able even for his aristocratic patrons.

The St. Jerome is another of these. In both the horizontal version in the Galleria Borghese, and the vertical
one in the Spanish monastery of Montserrat (the latter
painting was in a private collection in Rome until the beginning of our century), Caravaggio redeems the apparently dry theme by his brilliant handling of the color of

65. Christ at the Column
cm. 134.5x174.5
Rouen, Musée des Beaux-Arts

66. Salome with the Head of the Baptist
cm. 90.5x107
London, National Gallery

67. David with the Head of Goliath
cm. 90.5x116.5
Vienna, Kunsthistorisches Museum

68. Portrait of Alof de
Wignacourt
cm. 195x134
Paris, Louvre

69. Portrait of Alof de
Wignacourt
cm. 144x95
Florence, Palazzo Pitti

the mantle, which seems to flow briskly through the painting. Finally, a St. Francis in Meditation removed from the church of Carpineto Romano to Palazzo Venezia in Rome (which appears to be better than another version in the Chiesa dei Cappuccini, also in Rome) proposes again an intimate, self-absorbed figure. Caravaggio's attention to the texture of the drapery reaches extraordinary heights of refinement, recalling the intense works of Velasquez. A copy in the Pinacote-

ca in Cremona shows another way in which Caravaggio approached the same subject.

Among the compositions with more than one figure, a Supper in Emmaus painted for Marchese Patrizi and documented by Bellori, today in the Pinacoteca di Brera in Milan, appears to have been painted some years after the other version, in London. The atmosphere in which the figures are immersed is barely perceptible, as is the psychological feeling; and the painting style, which by now has become that of Caravaggio's last years (relatively speaking: the artist was thirty-five), is frayed and tenuous, devoid of the boldness that characterizes the London painting. This is a singular qualitative achievement. It corresponds to a substantial and definitive ripening of the painter's artistic thought. It is exactly because of this quality that I cannot imagine that the Christ with Pilate in the Pinacoteca at Palazzo Rosso in Genoa is by Caravaggio's hand. It is distinguished by a hard and schematic sign that seems to do little credit to a painter who, at more or less the same time, was making paintings like the Brera Supper.

Just before leaving Rome as a result of the murder of Tommasoni (he had already had to go briefly to Genoa because of the Pasqualone affair) Caravaggio executed his most complex painting thus far (with the possible exception of the Martyrdom of St. Matthew). The Death of the Virgin for Santa Maria della Scala in Trastevere was, like many of Caravaggio's paintings, rejected by the religious community of the church for which it was intended. But in this case, in addition to the testimonies of the artist's contemporaries, it is quite clear why the painting must have provoked the patrons' outrage. Fortunately the work was acquired by the duke of Mantua, to whose attention it had been brought by his vigilant emissary, Rubens. From Mantua the painting reached the collection of Charles I of England, and following later vicissitudes, ended up in the Louvre.

In this immense canvas, the apostles speak in groups or contemplate their sorrow in silence. Mary, "swollen, her legs uncovered" (Baglione), lies as though suspended on the coffin. It has rightly been observed that this painting, rejected on the grounds that it lacked religious emotions, is the most deeply religious painting of the entire seventeenth century. It has also been pointed out that the artist has not made a representation of death, but has shown a real death. Thus the painting offends the sensibility not only of its own time, but of all times, because of what it suggests about the obscure, fearful meaning of the end of life. The legends that accuse Caravaggio of having used a woman drowned in the Tiber as his model, appear posterior. But the painting expresses a sense of tragically imminent death, and communicates a deep anguish even to those who know nothing of the external circumstances. The large, red drape is one of the chromatic devices to which the artist turned, as we know, to enliven a surface too heavily laden with dull colors. But it is also used to close the background and to concentrate attention on the central figure of the Virgin, whose short axis, from her hands to her face, is the real expressive center of the painting. It is no coincidence that the baroque painter par excellence, Rubens, immediately understood a painting so different from his own principles. His great intelligence led him straightaway to admire and respect Caravaggio's unquestionable dramatic force.

Real-life drama and drama relived came together in the artist's flight from Rome, which took place at this time. On one of the Colonna estates, probably at Zagarolo, he executed a half-figure painting of the Madonna in Ecstasy known through numerous copies, the original of which is in all likelihood a painting in a private collection in Rome, recently brought to light by Marini (1974). The Saint Francis in Cremona may also be from this period, if it is by Caravaggio.

From the fiefs of the Colonna family Caravaggio took refuge in Naples, in 1606. There he began to work again with his usual, astounding speed. Early in January 1607 he was paid for the immense altarpiece commissioned to him by the Pio Monte di Misericordia (where it may still be seen today). The painting shows the Seven Acts of Mercy. It is as complicated in its organization as the Death of the Virgin. Caravaggio actually had to add a series of figures (two angels and the Madonna and Child, the latter painted later) in the upper part of the painting, which make the composition of the picture the most complex, perhaps, in any of his works. Caravaggio did not paint exemplary episodes intended to stir the viewer to religious piety through the illustrative emphasis of gestures and feelings. Rather, he entrusted the educational effectiveness of his works to the evidence of things in themselves, in the conviction that nothing should be added above and beyond what is already contained in the intrinsic eloquence of the various poses. On the right appear the burial of the dead and the epi-

sode of the so-called Carità Romana (Cimon's daughter giving her father suck in prison), which contains at once the two charitable acts of visiting prisoners and feeding the hungry. Dressing the naked appears in the foreground, symbolized by St. Martin and the beggar. Next to this scene, the host and St. James of Compostela allude to the offering of hospitality to pilgrims. Relieving the thirsty is represented by Samson drinking from the ox jaw. The youth on the ground behind the beggar of St. Martin may also represent the merciful gesture of caring for the sick. We readily apprehend the artist's power of synthesis, which concentrates a conceptual content that is potentially quite dispersive, in the model behavior of a few figures. The large painting was widely copied and studied by seventeenth-century Neapolitan painters, who drew ideas and formal devices from it. Caravaggio's presence in Naples, limited to a few months divided between two stays, was of decisive importance to the development of the Neapolitan school of painting. From Giovan Battista Caracciolo, called Battistello, to the Spaniard Juseppe de Ribera and Mattia Preti, painters working in Naples received a fundamental impulse from Caravaggio. The major exhibition of seventeenth-century Neapolitan painting that originated in London toward the close of 1982 and traveled to Washington and other cities, testifies to this influence.

Caravaggio painted another great ecclesiastical work immediately after the Seven Acts of Mercy. This is the so-called Madonna del Rosario, which after various turns of fortune (at the end of the seventeenth century it reached Anversa through the successive attentions of Frans Pourbus, Louis Finson, and Rubens) is now in Vienna's Kunsthistorisches Museum. Three different levels of participation are visible in the picture's pyramidal structure. At the bottom is the host of the faithful, the people of humble birth. Among these is the patron of the painting, turned toward the viewer. On the middle level appear the Dominicans (the painting was undoubtably made for a Dominican church, possibly even San Domenico in Naples), mediators between the faithful and the Virgin. The latter is shown at the top with the Christ Child. The painting further demonstrates the artist's ability to transfer the themes and techniques of his usual manner to a grand and noble painting. One who knew the Caravaggio of the first ten years might well have asked how and if it would have been possible to reconcile the novelty and nonconformist attitude implicit in his style with the unavoidable rules of large church altarpieces. Here the familiar pyramidal scheme, used by Leonardo and Raphael in their easel paintings, is extended to unprecedented dimensions, although it is balanced by the addition of the Dominican group on the

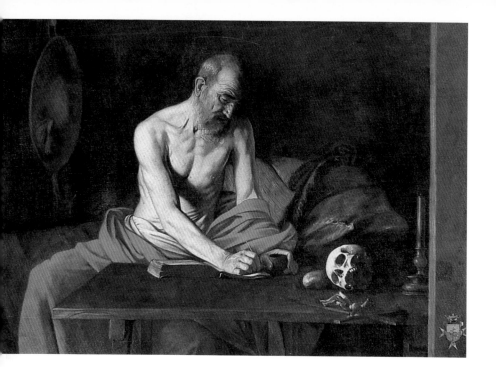

70. Sleeping Cupid
cm. 71x105
Florence, Palazzo Pitti

71. St. Jerome
cm. 117x157
La Valletta, St. John Museum

right. Between the latter and the central pyramid is a diagonal up-grade that ends in the drape, which is more schematically rendered than in the artist's other works. The viewer is left with a feeling of admiration for the nobility of this extraordinary work, which is eloquent without being emphatic or rhetorical.

It is still a matter of opinion among scholars whether the Flagellation of Christ (located in San Domenico in Naples until a few years ago, when it was transferred for safer keeping to the Pinacoteca di Capodimonte) was also painted during Caravaggio's first stay in Naples, or if it was made during the few months that he spent in the city just before his death. We prefer to keep it in this realm of ideas, but not without pointing out that the doubts as to the date are entirely justified, as Caravaggio's style is essentially uniform during the later part of his career. The shadows are denser, the contours are frayed, the colors are softened, and the light takes on an increasingly important role in modeling, defining, and building up forms. The only reality that exists is the one we see, not the one we expect, guess at, or imagine. This extraordinary painting lost half of its meaning when it was removed (for apparently irrefutable reasons) from the church and placed in the museum. It stood out on the distant altar of its chapel as soon as the visitor entered the church, magically capturing his eye with magnetic force. Stylistically, the painting returns (through its patent reference to a famous prototype by Sebastiano del Piombo in San Pietro in Montorio, in Rome) to manneristic conventions. It owes much to Michelangelo in the twisting of Christ's body, in his contorted step, and in the positions of his tormentors, which seem to make reference to Michelangelo's late work in the Pauline Chapel in the Vatican.

Another important painting, already mentioned by Bellori (according to whom it was taken to Spain by the viceroy, Benavente), has come to light fairly recently and has been acquired by the Cleveland Museum. This is a Crucifixion of St. Andrew, in which four variously characterized onlookers witness an unusual event narrated in the Golden Legend of Jacopo da Varazze. It seems that an order was given to take the dying saint down off the cross after two days of agony; but his will to die as his Savior had died struck the ruffian charged with the task and paralyzed him in the act. The painting is executed in a fast and summary manner. Changes of mind are not lacking (as the restoration of the painting showed), but this is usual for Caravaggio. In the head of the old woman Caravaggio indulges in a grotesque allusion of a kind that would be developed by his followers to the point of exaggeration.

Another work probably done by the artist at this time is a Christ at the Column in the Museum of Rouen, which Longhi recognized as autograph. This is a splendid composition, full of life and movement, carried out in grand style (the copies are all more contracted, unable to reproduce the ease of the original). The outstanding rendering of the anatomy of Christ's torso is the fruit of a truly admirable observation and understanding of nature.

The three figures of the Salome in the National Gallery of London are larger in scale. This painting was also recognized by Longhi, who was undoubtedly the greatest modern connoisseur of Caravaggio. Much more than in the artist's other canvases, attention is concentrated on the psychological differentiation of the faces. Caravaggio would take up the same composition in a later painting.

Finally, mention should be made of a fine painting in the Kunsthistorisches Museum in Vienna, representing David with the Head of Goliath. Although the attribution to Caravaggio is still uncertain, the painting is very probably an original from the artist's first period in Naples, carried out in a style that Battistello would have liked particularly.

From Naples, for no apparent reason except his own personal choice and a nomadic inclination that reflects a deeply restless character, Caravaggio went to Malta. Here the Grand Master of the Order named him "Cavaliere di Grazia" on 14 July 1608. The artist's stay in Malta could have been an oasis of calm, a moment of rest, a reflective pause. Instead it marked the point of no

return after which Caravaggio's misshapen life raced toward an all too appropriate end. Just three months after receiving his knighthood, on 6 October, documents show that Caravaggio escaped (in the most classical way, by climbing down the walls on a rope) from the prison and then from the island of Malta. Why he was imprisoned is not known. There is reason to believe he had an argument with a higher-ranking knight, a "Cavaliere della Giustizia." It must have been serious, if Caravaggio chose to escape. The order expelled him "tamquam membrum putridum et foetidum," and relentlessly persecuted him.

In Malta the artist made at least five paintings that are still extant today. Two are portraits of the Grand Master of the Order, Alof de Wignacourt: one full-figure, showing the master in armor and accompanied by a page, now in the Louvre; and the other, more of a sketch than a finished painting, individuated a few years ago by Mina Gregori in the Florentine collections of Palazzo Pitti. The former is an uneven painting that leaves a lot of questions unanswered; but the opinion that Caravaggio executed only some of the "noble" parts, such as the grand master's head, seems correct. The latter is a fine painting, but it must be seen through its incompleteness and its poor state of conservation.

Another of the Maltese paintings, a Sleeping Cupid, is in the Galleria Palatina in Florence. It came to the Medici Collections at a very early date: In 1620 it had already been copied in a fresco by Giovanni da Sangiovanni. An inscription on the back not only helps in attributing the painting to Caravaggio, but tells that it was done in Malta in 1608. This is an anguished, irreverent reworking of a theme that had enjoyed great success and had been painted in many different ways since classical antiquity. What counts is that Caravaggio transformed an idyllic motif into a darkly dramatic one, eliminating all trace of pleasure and bathing the putto in restless sleep and deep shadow. This abandonment takes on a sick quality, giving the image an extraordinary psychological modernity.

Another excellent work is the St. Jerome in the Museum of La Valletta in Malta. The saint, it has been shown, is a portrait of Grand Master de Wignacourt. The half-figure, executed with the ascetic precision that characterizes Caravaggio's late nudes, stands out against the dark shadow of the background. The still-life of few objects — the stone for beating his breast, the candlestick, the crucifix, and the skull, which make up an unusual "memento mortis" — is equally severe and restrained. A St. John Drinking, in a private collection in Malta, may also be by his hand. But without a close examination it is difficult to hazard an attribution.

The most important painting that Caravaggio made in Malta is the Beheading of the Baptist, which is still in the Oratorio di San Giovanni (now St. John Museum) in La Valletta. This is one of Caravaggio's most extraor-

72. *Beheading of the Baptist*
cm. 361x520
La Valletta, St. John Museum

73. *Beheading of the Baptist, detail of the artist's*
signature.
La Valletta, St. John Museum

dinary creations. For many it is his greatest masterpiece, as meaningless as such a choice may be. It is character- ized by a magical balance of all the parts. It is no acci- dent that the artist brings back into the painting a pre- cise reference to the setting, placing behind the figures, as a backdrop, the severe, sixteenth-century architec- ture of the prison building, at the window of which, in a stroke of genius, two figures silently witness the scene (the commentators are thus drawn into the painting, and no longer projected, as in the Martyrdom of St. Matthew, toward the outside). This is a final compen- dium of Caravaggio's art. Well-known figures return (the old woman, the youth, the nude ruffian, the beard- ed nobleman), as do Lombard elements. The technical means adhere to the deliberate, programmatic limita- tion to which Caravaggio adapts them; but amid these

soft tones, these dark colors, is an impressive sense of drawing that the artist does not give up, and that is visi- ble even through the synoptic glints of light of his late works. This eminently classical balance, which projects the event beyond contingency, unleashes a harsh drama that is even more effective to the extent that, having gi- ven up the "aesthetic of exclamation" forever, Caravag- gio limits every external, excessive sign of emotional emphasis. The painter signed in the Baptist's blood: "*f* [perhaps to be understood as *fecit*, rather than *frater*] michela...": This is the seal he placed on what may well be his greatest masterpiece.

Caravaggio fled from Malta to Sicily, and the ex- traordinary reputation that accompanied him imme- diately brought him a series of ecclesiastical commis- sions. Four of these paintings are still extant. They were executed with the same dizzying speed, as though the painter felt a disturbing impatience that compelled him to complete a task as quickly as he could, as soon as he had solved the artistic problems it posed. Like other artists in their later works — Titian, Michelangelo, and Rembrandt, for instance — he attained a rarefaction of form, a severity in the use of decorative artifices, that ruthlessly seem to correspond to a sort of inner moral dialogue, more than to a commission addressed to the public. But Caravaggio's case is unique, because he had begun to paint in this way before he was forty — an age that he would never reach. One cannot help thinking that it foreshadowed his demise.

The first of the Sicilian paintings to be completed was the Burial of St. Lucy. It was recently restored at the Istituto Centrale per il Restauro in Rome (all the Sicilian paintings have come down to us in a poor state of preservation). An immense empty space hovers above the crowd of onlookers, in one of the most potentially hazardous, but successful designs in the history of painting. The figures are rendered in a cursory manner, with glints of light. The viewer is struck by the enormity of the figures in the foreground with respect to the others. Such variations of size are unusual in the artist's works.

In the Resurrection of Lazarus, painted at the end of 1608 or the beginning of 1609 for a Genoese merchant named Lazzari (and today in the Museo Nazionale in Messina), Caravaggio makes vague references to an antique sarcophagus with the death of Patroclus. However he abandons all trace of classicism in the livid body, caught at the instant it begins to return to life, stirring the onlookers to a series of wonderfully varied expressions and poses. The ancient gesture of predilection that we encountered in the Calling of Matthew and (limited to the wrist and hand) in the angel of the Abraham and Isaac in the Uffizi, returns in the painting in Messina in the pose of Christ who indicates the beautiful group of the two sisters who lovingly bend over Lazarus restored to life. Here, too, we find a large empty area in the upper portion of the canvas, not unlike that which existed in the Adoration of the Shepherds (where the top of the stable is summarily traced out), before it was cut down to its present size, to fit the space available in the church of Santa Maria degli Angeli (the painting is now in the Museum of Messina).

Here again Caravaggio appears as a powerful innovator, owing not to an eccentric abstract intention, but to a personal, unprecedented meditation on themes that would appear not to have anything to disclose. The Adoration, which contains in the group of shepherds one of the more beautiful examples of paintings of the century, is by no means idyllic and peaceful. The joy for the birth of the Savior is overshadowed by the melancholy for the destiny of suffering and death that awaits him. A deep sadness pervades the entire composition, a sense of imminent death.

A similar painting represents the Nativity with St. Lawrence and St. Francis, unfortunately stolen in October 1969 from the church of San Lorenzo in Palermo, where it had been since it was made. There is no question that the composition is less successful than in other cases: the contained and pensive atmosphere, however again shows that at this stage Caravaggio associated the idea of the advent of Christ not with the joy of Redemption but with a future that was at best uncertain.

In Sicily Caravaggio did at least one other work, a Christ Bearing the Cross that has disappeared altogether. But soon afterward, in the same year (1609) he returned to the continent and set out for Rome, the city to which he felt most closely tied, but where he would never again set foot. In October 1609 he was wounded ("they say he was disfigured"), probably by emissaries of the Knights of Malta, who had not forgotten him, in a tavern near the harbor of Naples. In the months before and after the event he painted, in Naples, his last works. The final phase of his career has been reconstructed only recently, and many of the particular assertions regarding this period, made in the last few years, have yet to be confirmed. We wish to take account of them here, because taken as a whole these attributions faithfully reflect a period whose very identification (scholars have only lately begun to speak of a second Neapolitan period) is no simple matter.

None of the paintings from this period is documented, but there are likely hypotheses. Bellori (1672) tells us that Caravaggio had executed a Salome to send to the Grand Master of Malta to appease him. And it is natural to identifiy this work with the painting in the Casita of the Prince in the Escorial in Madrid, which essentially follows the Roman version, today in London. The only, slight change is in the pose of the executioner. And yet the two works are very obviously different. The later version rises out of an abyss of shadow. The executioner thoughtfully observes the result of his work, instead of lifting up the Baptist's head with certainty.

Another comparison can be made between the

74. Burial of St. Lucy, detail.
cm. 408x300
Syracuse, Santa Lucia

75. Resurrection of Lazarus, detail.
cm. 380x275
Messina, Museo Nazionale

76. Adoration of the Shepherds
cm. 314x211
Messina, Museo Nazionale

77. Nativity with St. Francis and St. Lawrence
cm. 268x197
Formerly at Palermo, San Lorenzo

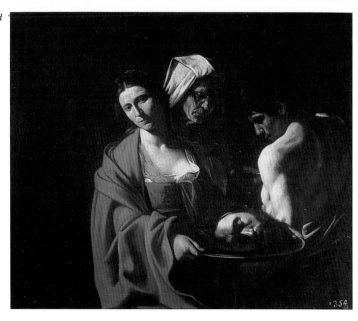

78. Salome with the Head
of the Baptist
cm. 116x140
Madrid, Escorial

Young St. John in the Galleria Borghese in Rome and the paintings of the same subject in Kansas City and in Palazzo Barberini in Rome, which we have already mentioned. The Borghese St. John is also the most soberly thoughtful. The body is delicate and the expression is dreamy, so much so as to suggest a considerable distance in time from the other two.

The David with the Head of Goliath, also in the Galleria Borghese in Rome, is considered by some scholars to be the artist's last work. Much has been written about the overpowering invasion of real space that results from David's gesture, the meager painting style, the artist's identification with the head of Goliath (undoubtedly a self-portrait). The expression on David's face is devoid of boldness, the clothing he wears is light, little more than a veil, by no means a pretext for painting folds cleverly given relief. The youth's head is also a kind of idealized self-portrait that gazes with sadness on the giant's severed head.

The three paintings we have discussed so far are attributed to Caravaggio by general consensus. Other attributions are more "open". In the case of the Martyrdom of St. Ursula now in the Banca Commerciale in Naples, documents that were discovered and published five years after the attribution had been made by Mina Gregori on purely stylistic bases, confirmed Caravaggio as the author of this painting. It was executed for Marcantonio Doria of Genoa in May 1610, just two months before the artist's death. The painting was shown in the

exhibition in London and other cities, mentioned above, and on this occasion it was possible to evaluate its absolute originality. For the first time Caravaggio painted not only an action as it was taking place, but its results as well, giving the painting an allusive aspect (rather than an immediately real one) that corresponds to the "baroque" propensities that have been acknowledged in his late works. It is clear that in the close space of the painting the King of the Huns would not have been able to shoot the arrow that has struck St. Ursula, right next to him. Until now Caravaggio had never painted an event on a level that was not that of direct reality, without reproducing it as it actually would have appeared.

Also included in the exhibition was a Denial of St. Peter from an unnamed private collection, known to the specialists for some years and considered by many to be a very late, autograph Caravaggio. The attribution appears justified by the quality of the stylistic features (the painting's relation to a similar subject cited by Bellori in Naples has yet to be determined). Here we see only the three figures, from the waist up. In the total absence of references to objects, the meaning is conveyed entirely by the obvious evidence of the poses. The direct specification of the light source is so precise that it completely excludes the entire profile of the ruffian's face from our field of view, in a solution of unprecedented boldness. The rendering becomes extremely synoptic: the face of the woman servant is little more than a pure volume. Peter's wrinkled forehead is a series of tightly con-

79. *Young St. John*
cm. 159x124
Rome, Galleria Borghese

80. *Denial of St. Peter*
cm. 94x125
New York, Shickman Gallery

81. *The Tooth-Drawer*
cm. 101x150
Florence, Galleria degli Uffizi

densed brushstrokes (with reference to the Martyrdom of St. Ursula, a Neapolitan correspondent of the Doria family wrote them that Caravaggio laid his paint on the canvas thickly, as a rule).

The Crowning with Thorns, which recently came into the collections of the Cassa di Risparmio of Prato is extraordinarily modern in style. The scene is viewed as through a telephoto lens, with the figures pressed against each other. The attribution, proposed by Mina Gregori, is undoubtedly appropriate to the end of Caravaggio's career. Another attribution by this scholar is the so-called Tooth-Drawer (*Cavadenti*) belonging to the Gallerie Fiorentine and deposited at Montecitorio (where it was restored in an incompetent and harmful way, making it more difficult to study). It is easy to understand why such a proposal, which presents a ple-

beian and vulgar aspect of Caravaggio that we encounter in his life but not in his works, met with much opposition. It must be pointed out, however, that even in the painting's unsatisfactory state of preservation an original quality of execution transpires that corresponds to the epitomized achievements of the late Caravaggio. It is also to be thought that there must have been a prototype, as so many of the works of Caravaggio's followers deal with this type of genre scene. The presence of the prototype in Naples would help explain some of the returns to this theme, including the late and striking works of the eighteenth-century Neapolitan painter, Gaspare Traversi.

Caravaggio also painted church paintings during his last period in Naples: in particular, a Resurrection of Christ in the Certosa di San Marino, which unfortunate-

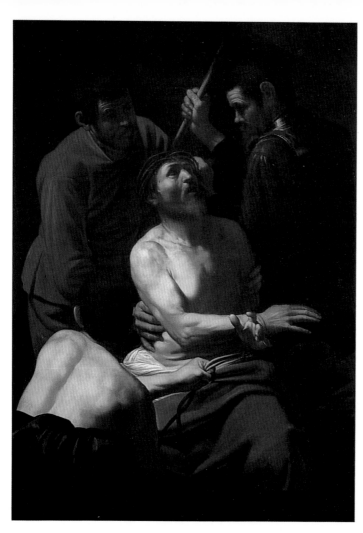

82. *Crowning with Thorns*
cm. 178x125
Prato, Cassa di
Risparmio

83. *Annunciation*
cm. 285x205
Nancy, Musée des
Beaux-Arts

ly has been lost but which, judging from the descriptions, contained the usual iconographic innovations. There is reason to believe that the artist's last altarpiece is the Annunciation that reached the high altar of the cathedral of Nancy in Lorraine just after the church was founded (1609). Today it is in the museum of that city. Whether the painting was made in Sicily or during the second period in Naples is not known. Its style would seem to exclude earlier datings, for it is clearly a very late work. It has been pointed out that the angel comes into the painting from real space, cancelling the separation between the picture and the viewer in a way typical

of the baroque aesthetic (as we also saw in the Borghese David). Here, too, the angel's face is practically invisible. Nor does the Virgin look at him: She is completely self-absorbed, her pose is devoid of joyous acceptance. She seems instead crushed by the expectation of an unbearable future. The spiritual testament that Caravaggio left us with this large, two-figural painting, where once again the Virgin is not distinguished by deifying attributes, is an infinite existential sadness, which seems to contain no hope of redemption.

Few artists have had as great an influence, directly or indirectly, as Caravaggio. When he died on 18 July

1610, overcome by fever on the Tyrrhenian coast at Porto Ercole (while waiting for a pardon that would have permitted him to return to Rome), he was already very famous, and younger artists were painting pictures in his "maniera." Some of his followers picked up only a few elements of his style, quickly changing them into conventions, and by so doing becoming as unlike Cara-vaggio as they could. Others were more deeply affected, and did not draw merely upon the artist's technique (the use of light and shadow) or thematic propensities (paint-ing still-lifes, or the common people), but tapped the un-derlying spirit of continuous inquiry as well. Scholars, following the path marked out by Roberto Longhi, have engaged in the immense task of classifying, distinguish-ing, or recognizing influences; and heated discussions between those who wish to enlarge the sphere of Cara-vaggio's followers and those who prefer to restrict it, have not been uncommon. Whereas for some critics (Bellori, for instance, or the advocates of classicism) Caravaggio was a constant source of trouble (and traces of this attitude, which sees Caravaggio as a corruptive influence, survived until very recently), certain great artists saw him as a brilliant source of inspiration. We have mentioned Rubens in this connection; but it must be pointed out that, contrary to the restrictive theories that have been advanced, especially outside Italy, without Caravaggio the three great painters of the seventeenth century — Velasquez, Rembrandt, and Vermeer — would not have been the same. Velasquez saw the artist's works first hand, in Rome. Rembrandt and Vermeer saw what Caravaggio's Dutch followers brought back to Holland. The great multitude of foreign artists who turned to Caravaggio for inspiration from a very early date spread the characteristics of his style throughout France, the Low Countries, and the Iberian Peninsula. And in Italy, Caravaggio influenced all great painting of the seventeenth and eighteenth centuries, either positively or negatively, and we presuppose his importance even when we fail to mention it. Here we have followed only his own path of creative development. Along this path we have highlighted the most fascinating stages. From the boldness of the early works, through the splendid maturity of the central ones, up to the solitary monologue of the late paintings, we have acknowledged the regenerating creativity that animated a life otherwise characterized by a lucid desire for self-destruction.

New attributions and additions

When this short book appeared in the book review section of the prestigious journal 'The Burlington Magazine' it was described as "well informed and well illustrated". For a book aimed at the general reader one could not have hoped for a better appraisal. As space permits only the briefest of updates of this monograph, which was first published some years ago, I propose to leave unaltered both my interpretation of Caravaggio's work and the stylistic analysis of his paintings. I will, therefore, limit myself to two areas: brief indications of my reconsideration of some paintings and of specific problems; and the addition of at least some of those recently discovered paintings whose attribution to Caravaggio has met with sufficient critical acceptance.

It was a mistake not to include in the first edition of the book the only mural painting by Caravaggio. This is the ceiling painted in oils for the small "alchemy room" of Cardinal del Monte (Zandri, 1969) situated in what is now a corridor of the Villa Boncompagni Ludovisi. Mentioned by Bellori and datable between 1597 and 1600, this is a work of exceptional importance. Of slightly earlier date (c. 1595-6) is the painting I Bari, or the Cardsharps, which had once belonged to the Sciarra branch of the Barberini family and which was still untraced at the time of the first edition (see p. 14). Happily, it has now found its way to the Kimbell Art Museum, Fort Worth — a truly epoch-making rediscovery.

Caravaggio had painted for Cardinal del Monte an earlier version of the Lute Player, now at Leningrad and formerly in the Giustiniani Collection. This first version is now owned by Wildenstein's of New York who have given it on loan to the Metropolitan Museum, New York. Denis Mahon has published both the Cardsharps (1988) and the Lute Player (1990) with the addition of excellent technical appendices by Keith Christiansen.

There is now a reproduction of the Martyrdom of

84. *Jupiter, Neptune and Pluto*
Rome, Casino Boncompagni Ludovisi

85. *The Cardsharps*
cm. 94x131
Fort Worth, Kimbell Art Museum

St. Ursula, of the Banca Commerciale Italiana, Naples, which was not possible to illustrate in the first edition (see p. 73). In addition, a chronological error needs correction: the Crowning with Thorns in Prato is datable to around 1603 (recently discovered documentary evidence seems to confirm the attribution to Caravaggio). Once more, the restricted length of this volume does not allow for any consideration of some much debated works such as the Vienna Crowning with Thorns and the St. Francis paintings in Carpineto Romano, in the Church of the Capuchins, Rome and in Cremona. Another St. Francis, in the Barbara Johnson Collection,

has been published by Bologna. Mina Gregori has attributed to Caravaggio a Sacrifice of Isaac from the same collection; judgement should be reserved on these works until they have received further careful examination. Also, it is not possible to discuss here those numerous Still-lifes attributed to the young Caravaggio.

One aspect of Caravaggio's output which we know considerably more about today is his production of autograph duplicates (but I am not entirely convinced that the London version of the Youth Bitten by a Lizard is by his hand; therefore I refer here only to the Longhi Collection painting). In any case, it is clear that Caravaggio produced an impressive number of paintings during his short life and that the great majority of them have survived — a truly rare phenomenon.

Finally, Testori has published (1984) what is perhaps the only surviving drawing by Caravaggio: a study of a head for the Adoration of the Shepherds, stolen in 1969 from the Oratory of San Lorenzo, Palermo and which, sadly, has still not come to light.

5

7

86. Lute Player
cm. 100x126.5
New York, private collection

87. Martyrdom of St. Ursula
cm. 154x178
Naples, Banca Commerciale Italiana

CANALETTO and the Vedutisti

1. *Gentile Bellini*
The Procession in Piazza S. Marco
Venice, Gallerie dell'Accademia

The Origins

It is a deep-rooted tradition among writers of history that Venice went through a deep crisis in the eighteenth century, a crisis that was both the harbinger and cause of the conclusion, in the May of 1797, of the thousand-year existence of the Serenissima, as the Republic of Venice was known. On closer examination, however, this crisis turns out to have been restricted largely to the Republic's institutions, evident in the ruling oligarchy's inability to renew its own structure and adapt it to changing political, social, and economic requirements. In other areas, though, the lagoon city was experiencing one of its periods of greatest splendor, underlined by exceptional fervor in the field of art and culture. The face of the city itself was undergoing profound changes: numerous new churches were built, from that of San Stae to that of Santa Maria della Consolazione or della Fava, from the Gesuiti to the Gesuati, from the Pietà to San Simeone Piccolo and the neoclassical Maddalena del Temanza. New public buildings were going up, including the Teatro della Fenice. Many private residences were built from scratch (Palazzo Grassi, Ca' Corner della Regina, Palazzo Duodo, and Ca' Venier dei Leoni, just to mention the most important), while others were enlarged (Ca' Labia), restored, and modified to suit the taste of the time (Palazzo Balbi Valmarana Smith, Ca' Dolfin Manin), or completed (Ca' Rezzonico). Several great Schools completely renovated their old seats (La Carità, I Carmini, San Giovanni Evangelista).

Painters played a preeminent role in this frenzy of con-struction, as they were called on to decorate the new buildings with canvases and frescoes: from the matchless Tiepolo to Sebastiano Ricci, and from Crosato to Piazzetta and Diziani. Yet Venetian artists did not just specialize in the large-scale decorations with a historical, religious, or mythological theme required by this type of patronage, but in all the other genres as well. In portraiture, with the delightful pastels of Rosalba Carriera, to be counted among the highest achievements of rococo, and with the courtly images of Alessandro Longhi; in landscape, a field dominated by the classical works of Marco Ricci and the Arcadian style of Giuseppe Zais and Francesco Zuccarelli; in the genre scene, with the small but penetrating canvases of Pietro Longhi; and finally in the landscape and views of the city itself.

It is curious to note that this last genre of painting was less highly regarded in local artistic circles than the others, with the result that the most celebrated artist working in that field, Antonio Canal known as Canaletto, was not admitted to the Academy of Painting and Sculpture until several years after its institution, in 1763. And yet this genre is an extremely important one, not only because of the quality of the works that it produced, but also and above all because it has spread the unique image of the lagoon city through the world, making a decisive contribution to the birth of the *myth* of Venice.

The custom of filling their canvases with images of Venice was certainly not a monopoly of eighteenth-

century painters, but had deep roots in the local figurative culture. In fact it is possible that the first decoration of the Doge's Palace, dating from the fourteenth century and subsequently destroyed, included a number of representations that contained precise references to places in Venice, for instance in the scenes telling the story of the reconciliation between Pope Alexander III and Emperor Frederick Barbarossa, which took place in Venice through the mediation of Doge Sebastiano Ziani. While this is no more than a hypothesis, it is certain that Venice is triumphantly present in the series of *teleri*, or large canvases, painted in the last decade of the fifteenth century by Gentile Bellini and his assistants for the hall of the Albergo della Scuola Grande di San Giovanni Evangelista, now in the Gallerie dell'Accademia. In his depiction of the miraculous events brought about by the reliquary of the Cross kept in the School, Gentile chose the most realistic approach, setting them

in the places where the miracles were actually supposed to have occurred. Thus the merchant Jacopo de Solis calls for help for his sick son during the procession through St Mark's Square, and the miraculous healing of a madman by the Patriarch of Grado, Francesco Querini, takes place in a loggia of the palace that the latter owned on the bank of the Vin, near Rialto.

The images of the city furnished by Bellini and Carpaccio — the authors of these paintings — are clear, distinguished by a realism of almost Northern European stamp, to such an extent that it is possible to recognize features of Venetian topography that have since been modified: the old layout of the area of St Mark's, with the hospice of the Orseolo on the right, where the Procuratie Nuove now stand; or, in Gentile's painting, the iconography of the original mosaics on the front of St Mark's, only one of which has survived; the wooden drawbridge that linked the area of the Rialto market

2. Gentile Bellini
The Procession in Piazza S. Marco, detail
Venice, Gallerie dell'Accademia

3. Vittore Carpaccio
The Miracle of the Relic of the Holy Cross
Venice, Gallerie dell'Accademia

with San Bartolomeo prior to the construction of the stone bridge we know today; or the extremely rare image of the Fondaco dei Persiani, with the whole of its outer walls faced with inlaid marble — looking almost like a refined Oriental carpet — that can be glimpsed on the right, between the piers of the bridge, in Carpaccio's *teler*.

It has often been said that these works cannot be considered *vedute* in the modern sense of the term, in that the city merely provides the backdrop to an event that is taking place, and is not in itself the protagonist of the paintings. Yet it seems obvious that, even though the paintings in question have a narrative intent, it is really late fifteenth-century Venice that plays the leading role, in the splendor of its architecture and the opulence of its everyday reality, and that this reality is the true protagonist of the paintings. In short, if we were to exclude the large canvases painted by Gentile and his pupils for the Scuola di San Giovanni Evangelista from the genre of the *veduta*, then the same would have to be done with many of the eighteenth-century works that are unanimously regarded as examples of *vedutismo*: from the numerous entries of ambassadors painted by Carlevarijs and Canaletto to the regattas, the departures and arrivals of the Bucentaur, and the dogal festivals, to cite only the most famous.

Vice versa, it can be said that Bellini's *teleri*, with their

4. Bonifacio de' Pitati
*The Eternal and Piazza
S. Marco, detail*
Venice, Gallerie
dell'Accademia

5. Titian
*Ancona Madonna,
detail*
Ancona, Museo Civico

6. Sebastiano del
Piombo
Death of Adonis, detail
Florence, Galleria degli
Uffizi

566

accurate depiction of the city's appearance, were actually the root of eighteenth-century *vedutismo*, for they contain all the elements that were to be found in the works of the artists active two centuries later.

The same predilection for representation of the city crops up, undoubtedly with the intention of eulogizing and celebrating the glories of Venice, in numerous other pictures painted during the Renaissance. In the canvas now in Oxford's Ashmolean Museum, for instance, Giorgione placed his *Madonna reading* next to a window overlooking the basin of St Mark, where it is possible to identify the Doge's Palace and the tower of the campanile, still lacking the spire that was not constructed until 1513. Carpaccio set the same scene alongside the Lion of St Mark, the symbol of the city, that he painted for the Doge's Palace. Even Titian, in the *Ancona Madonna*, has left us an unforgettable back-lit vision of the area of St Mark's seen from the basin. Sebastiano del Piombo painted the death of Adonis — in the canvas now in the Uffizi — on the edges of a wood that he places on the island of San Giorgio, realistically setting in front of it, on the other side of the basin of St Mark, the wharf with the Doge's Palace on the right and the campanile and buildings of the Mint on the left. Finally, in a canvas intended to decorate the offices of a magistrature in the Palazzo dei Camerlenghi, Bonifacio de' Pitati offers us a highly animated picture of St Mark's Square. Painted from a bird's eye view, as had been the fashion ever since the publication of Jacopo de Barbari's excellent woodcut, it looks toward the basin, while the Eternal hovers overhead, accompanied by the dove of the Holy Spirit. Many other views of Venice can also be found in the paintings in the Doge's

7. *Joseph Heintz the Younger*
The Bull Hunt in
Campo S. Polo
Venice, Museo Correr

Palace, such as the canvases of the Maggior Consiglio or Titian's fresco of *Saint Christopher*.

The example set by these *veduta*-like inserts was not immediately followed up. The fact is that, while the view gradually took on a great deal of importance in the Low Countries and Northern Europe in general, especially in the seventeenth century, Venetian painters of the same period had other interests, which did not include the accurate representation of places.

It was a painter from the north, Joseph Heintz the Younger (ca. 1600 - ca. 1678), a native of Augsburg and trained at the Bohemian court, who revived interest in this specific genre around the middle of the seventeenth century. Heintz — who also painted a large number of historical or religious pictures — produced a long series of works devoted to typical Venetian festivals in 1646 (the date written on one of the canvases now in the Museo Correr in Venice): from the *Bull Hunt in Campo San Polo* to the *Procession to il Redentore*, and from the *Entry into San Pietro di Castello* of the new patriarch to the *Outing by Boat to Murano*. In these paintings the typically Northern European predilection for the accurate reproduction of reality is combined with a lively use of color and effects that already foreshadows the work of certain eighteenth-century *veduta* painters, such as Carlevarijs and Richter.

Luca Carlevarijs

Luca Carlevarijs from Friuli (Udine 1663 - Venice 1730) — whom the sources describe as "knowing a great deal about Architecture" and who was also a student of the science of perspective, as is clearly apparent from the preparatory drawings for his engravings — is rightly considered the father of eighteenth-century Venetian *vedutismo*. His approach to the genre took place by degrees: in fact his early work was in the field of landscape painting, with numerous pictures linked stylistically to the models of such Northern European artists as Cavalier Tempesta, alias Pieter Mulier, Hans de Jode, and Johann Anton Eismann, with whom he came into contact during his visit to Rome as a young man, according to the authoritative testimony of Moschini (1806), as well as in Venice, where many Northern European artists (including Tempesta and Eismann) were present at the end of the seventeenth century.

Carlevarijs's move from landscape to the *veduta* is marked by the collection of 104 engravings entitled *Fabriche, e Vedute di Venetia*, printed in 1703, though it was in fact the fruit of long preparation that must have occupied the artist for several years, and by the execution of a series of canvases depicting solemn entries of foreign ambassadors, on their way to present their credentials to the government of the Serenissima. Such entrances provided an occasion for regattas, parades on the water, and festivals, and in this sense Carlevarijs's canvases were perfectly in keeping with the tradition referred to above, which had its roots in the works produced by the Bellini workshop.

On the other hand the link with Gaspar van Wittel, who is often cited in the literature as the forerunner of eighteenth-century Venetian *vedutismo*, seems to be much less close. Van Wittel came to Rome as a very young man around 1647 and devoted himself to the painting of views, depicting the ancient and modern architecture of the papal city with a cold and calculating eye, in net contrast to the local tradition of landscape painting, whose greatest exponent was Salvator Rosa. In this sense, the example he set was to have a particularly strong influence on the birth of the eighteenth-century school of Roman *veduta* painters, which grew up around the painter Gian Paolo Panini from Piacenza.

In the last decade of the seventeenth century, Van Wittel made numerous journeys to Northern Italy, visiting Venice between the end of 1694 and 1695. It seems certain that he painted no views of the city during his stay, which was fairly short (in fact the ones we know of all bear dates later than 1697), but limited himself to making drawings from life. It was only later, in his studio in Rome, that he used these to produce paintings on canvas. In any case the Venetian *vedute* of Van Wittel — of which about twenty are currently known to exist — are distinguished by their accuracy in the depiction of details, their topographical precision, the crystalline quality of their color, and the exactness of their proportions: all characteristics that are clearly visible in the *Piazzetta* in Rome's Galleria Doria Pamphilj or the *View of the Bacino di S. Marco* in the Prado, dating from 1697, but only to a lesser extent in the works

8. Luca Carlevarijs
Seascape
147.5x179 cm
Private Collection

9. Gaspar van Wittel
The Island of San
Michele: looking toward
Murano
36x47 cm
London, private
collection

10, 11. Luca Carlevarijs
The Sea Customs
House with San Giorgio
Maggiore
50x96 cm
Venice, private
collection

of Carlevarijs. What we see in the pictures of the artist from Friuli, in fact, is an evident concession to the picturesqueness typical of the Venetian tradition, and while the rendering of the architecture is fairly precise, it is still shrouded in a rose-colored mist which blurs and softens the details, especially in the background. Often, moreover, the relationship between the works of architecture and the boats and figures that fill the *vedute* is imprecise. Such characteristics are already evident in the oldest paintings representing the entrances of ambassadors to the Doge's Palace, of which the masterpieces appear to be the one recording *Lord Manchester's Embassy to Venice*, on September 22, 1707 (Birmingham, City Museum), and the canvases devoted to the visit by Frederick IV of Denmark (1709), as well as in the earliest *vedute* of Venice, like that of the *Sea Customs House with San Giorgio Maggiore* in a Venetian private collection and the pair of pictures in Potsdam, depicting the *Wharf: looking toward the Doge's Palace* and *Piazza S. Marco with Jugglers*.

Throughout his career Carlevarijs alternated works of landscape — often in the special variety of the *capriccio*, i.e. the fantasy landscape, characterized by the presence of ancient buildings and ruins — with his better known paintings of *vedute* of Venice, though he also tried his hand at the *veduta* of Rome, with the splendid *St Peter's Square* based on a model by van Wittel, in a private collection, or of the Veneto countryside, with the limpid pictures of *Villa Baglioni at Massanzago*, which has recently turned up on the antiquarian market in Venice, or the *Visit to the Villa* in a private

collection in London, for which there is a very fine preparatory drawing in the Museo Correr in Venice.

Particularly excellent results emerged from the prestigious commission he received from Alvise Pisani, perhaps around the beginning of the second decade of the eighteenth century, for several canvases commemorating the crucial moments in the career of that nobleman, who was elected doge in 1735. The best of these is undoubtedly the one recently acquired by the Bayerische Staatsgemäldesammlungen in Munich, depicting the *Arrival of the Venetian Ambassadors Niccolò Erizzo and Alvise Pisani in London*, of great narrative vivacity.

Carlevarijs's style did not change much over the course of time and even his last works — the painter died in 1730, after suffering from progressive paralysis for two years — reveal the same refined skill in staging *vedute* of St Mark's, thronged with numerous and varied figures. In fact it is these figures, drawn from life in black pencil in the numerous sheets of his sketchbook, many of them now in Venice's Museo Correr or the Victoria and Albert Museum in London, that bring to life the paintings, with their gaudy colors and frenetic activity. Works like the *View of the Wharf from the Bacino di S. Marco* in Montecarlo or the *Piazzetta and Library* in the Ashmolean Museum in Oxford, both painted during the last decade of Luca's life, can justly be considered some of the most interesting achievements of eighteenth-century Venetian *vedutismo*.

The figure of Carlevarijs has not so far received the critical appreciation that he deserves. Nevertheless, he

12, 13. Gaspar van Wittel
The Piazzetta: from the Bacino di
S. Marco
27x42 cm
Rome, Galleria Doria Pamphilj

14. Luca Carlevarijs
The Wharf: looking toward the
Doge's Palace
73.4x117.4 cm
Potsdam, Schloss Sans-Souci

15. Luca Carlevarijs
Piazza S. Marco with Jugglers
73.2x117.2 cm
Potsdam, Schloss Sans-Souci

has at least been given the credit, no small thing in it-self, for having made a decisive contribution to the renewal of Venetian art, shifting it away from the baroque and turning the attention of local artists toward the landscape and the *veduta*.

Along with Heintz and Carlevarijs, it is worth considering another artist whose work is very little known but of considerable quality, the Alessandro Piazza who painted two series of pictures, the first in the Worchester Art Museum and the second in Venice's Museo Correr, dating from the turn of the century and characterized by rich and dense brushwork and interesting color effects.

Another painter whose style is very similar to Carlevarijs's, with the result that his works are often confused with those of the artist from Friuli, is the Swedish painter Johann (Giovanni) Richter. Born in Stockholm around 1665, he came to Venice in 1710 and stayed there until his death in 1745. Richter was also fond of painting scenes of the area around St Mark's that was so dear to Carlevarijs. Far more original, however, were

his pictures of the lagoon, in which he proposed views that were unprecedented in the Venetian world. In these works (see in particular the *Island of San Giorgio Maggiore* in Stockholm's Nationalmuseum and the *View of the Giudecca Canal* in a private collection in Milan), Richter chose a distant point of view and liked to set boats, often enlivened by the presence of elegantly dressed young women, in the foreground, in a belt of shade that was intended to lend depth to the background. The principal works of architecture were almost never depicted from the front, but at an angle, and were painstakingly represented down to the smallest detail. Frequently — and this is the case with the *veduta* in Milan and various others — the use of the "camera obscura" caused the painter to noticeably reduce the space that actually existed between buildings, resulting in curious "corridor" effects that had nothing to do with reality.

In this Richter — and before him, though in a less obvious manner, the artist who can be considered his master, Carlevarijs — should be seen as the forerun-

573

16. Luca Carlevarijs
The Arrival of the Venetian Ambassadors Niccolò Erizzo and Aluise Pisani in London
135.9x252 cm
Munich, Bayerische Staatsgemäldesammlungen

17. Luca Carlevarijs
View of the Wharf from the Bacino di S. Marco
85.7x163.8 cm
Montecarlo, private collection

18. Luca Carlevarijs
The Piazzetta and the Library
46x39 cm
Oxford, Ashmolean Museum

ner of the Venetian conception of the *veduta*: not as a faithful reproduction of reality, but almost as an assemblage of architectural elements. In fact, in the canvases of Canaletto, Bellotto, Marieschi, and Francesco Guardi, it is not "truthfulness" that we should be looking for, the perfect reproduction of reality as it appeared to their eyes: in a word the *photographic view*. For this we have to go instead to the work of the cartographers, such as the invaluable survey carried out by Lodovico Ughi on the basis of scientific measurements and printed in 1729. The painters — and in this sense the example of Richter is a particularly important one — saw Venice "with their own eyes," and this was how they depicted the city, through the filter of their own sensibility and culture and without feeling obliged to reproduce reality exactly.

There was another Northern European painter who dedicated himself, though only sporadically, to the *veduta* of Venice in the early decades of the eighteenth century: Antonio Stom (1688-1734), who painted a series of ornamental panels originally located over the doors of Palazzo Priuli at Piove di Sacco and then in a private collection in Bologna. They depict Venetian festivals (*The Regatta, The Festival of the Sensa; Fight on the Bridge of Fists; The Bull Hunt; The Place of Assembly; The Meeting*) and a few *vedute* in which he blends the style of Joseph Heintz the Younger with Carlevarijs's taste for small figures. The *View of Piazza S. Marco* from a window of the Procuratie Vecchie is particularly interesting, not only for its unusual point of view but also for the cool palette of colors, of grayish tone, laid down in thick brush strokes, and the lively

rendering of the figures in the foreground, of far higher quality than the static and vague ones sketched in the background. Yet it also reveals Tonino's limited grasp of perspective, especially obvious in the incorrect angle given to the facade of the Doge's Palace on the Piazzetta and the unconvincing detail of the island of San Giorgio Maggiore in the background.

The work of Bernardo Canal (Venice 1664-1744), father of the much more famous Antonio, known as Canaletto, is also very similar to the style of Carlevarijs. Bernardo achieved his greatest successes in the field of theatrical scene painting, in which he was assisted by his sons Antonio and Cristoforo, but he did not disdain the painting of *vedute*. There are few works that we can be certain are his, no more than a group of five canvases datable to 1734, one of them signed, in a private collection, and another two, signed and dated 1737, that have recently appeared on the antiquarian market, based on two of the engravings that Visentini had made from paintings by Canaletto. Recently a few other *vedute* have been grouped with these by critics, on the basis of stylistic similarities.

The fact that the few works certainly by Bernardo all date from the fourth decade of the eighteenth century suggests that he started painting *vedute* when already an old man, probably spurred on by the success of his son. And yet his works do not take the pictures of Antonio as a model, but those of the now dead — and surpassed — Carlevarijs, from whom they derive their rosy atmosphere, lively small figures, and even the characteristic way of arranging the clouds in the sky in order to confer depth of perspective on the scene.

19, 20. Johann Richter
View of the Giudecca
Canal
60x80 cm
Milan, private collection

21. Antonio Stom
*View of Piazza S. Marco from
the Procuratie Vecchie*
106x123 cm
Private collection

22. Bernardo Canal
*The Grand Canal with the Church
of La Carità*
70x120 cm
*Bassano del Grappa, private
collection*

23. Bernardo Canal
*The Grand Canal with the
Fabbriche Nuove at Rialto*
70x120 cm
*Bassano del Grappa, private
collection*

Canaletto

As has already been said, Canaletto — Zuanne Antonio Canal, born in the Venetian parish of San Lio on October 28, 1697 — commenced his artistic career as a painter of scenes for the theater. The oldest of these, produced from 1716 onward, were made for the Venetian theaters of Sant'Angelo and San Cassiano. In 1719 Bernardo and Antonio were in Rome, where they had gone to work on the sets of Alessandro Scarlatti's *Tito Sempronio Gracco* and *Turno Aricinio*, staged at the Teatro Capranica during the Carnival of 1720. It was in Rome, if we are to believe the account of Anton Maria Zanetti (1771), that the young Canaletto started to move in a new direction and, having "left the theater, weary of the intrusiveness of dramatic poets, gave himself up totally to painting *vedute* from life." "This was," adds Zanetti, "around the year 1719, in which he solemnly repudiated, as he put it, the theater." The extremely reliable testimony of the eighteenth-century historian has been interpreted in various ways, and some have pictured the young and ignorant artist suddenly discovering, through his encounter with the works of such Roman *veduta* painters as Codazzi, Panini, or Van Wittel, the new world of the *veduta* and, one is tempted to say, romantically immersing himself in it.

It is likely, however, that things took a different course and that Canaletto's move from scene painting to the *veduta* occurred in a more or less natural way. While it is possible, in fact, that at the start of his career Bernardo worked in the baroque style of the Bibiena family tradition, it is also true that a new type of scene painting emerged in the early years of the eighteenth century, in Venice as well as in Turin and Rome: a style that could be described as "pictorial" in contrast to that of the Bibiena, based on "perspective." In practice this meant no more fantastic and absurd baroque sets, no more exaggerated forms and strange fantasies with endless vistas of colonnades, monumental heap of architecture, and a profusion of decorative elements, but scenes that were largely confined to the backdrop, with themes linked to the painting of ruins and landscapes.

Most of the credit for introducing this new style to Venice must be given to Marco Ricci. The painter had dedicated part of his career to stage scenery, with some

24, 25. Canaletto
Grand Canal: looking East from the Campo S. Vio
140.5x204.5 cm
Madrid, Thyssen Bornemisza Collection

26. Canaletto
Grand Canal: looking Northeast from Palazzo Balbi
toward the Rialto Bridge
144x207 cm
Venice, Ca' Rezzonico

27, 28. Canaletto
Rio dei Mendicanti
143x200 cm
Venice, Ca' Rezzonico

success if it is true that the main purpose behind his first visit to England, made in the company of Giannantonio Pellegrini between 1708 and 1712, was to participate in the staging of Italian operas at the King's Theatre in the Haymarket. Subsequently, in 1716, Ricci resumed this activity in Venice and, two years later, took over the job of painting scenes at the Teatro Sant'Angelo from the Canal family.

We know little of Marco's activity in this field. However the fifty odd stage designs now in the Royal Library at Windsor Castle — dating from his last stay in Venice and coming from the collection of the British consul Smith — provide us with an excellent picture of how he used the same figurative and thematic repertory in his set designs as he did in his paintings: large squares with arcades, vistas of colonnades and courts, prisons, huge parks, and spacious frescoed rooms, glimpsed through a series of arches decorated with historical scenes. So it seems reasonable to assume that the young scene painter Canaletto would have been interested in the innovations brought about by his more established colleague and that his sets — of which unfortunately nothing has survived — were in some ways similar to Marco's. Support for this hypothesis comes from an examination of Canaletto's earliest pictures, the *Capricci* in private collections in Venice, Milan and Switzerland and in the Wadsworth Atheneum in Hartford.

29. Canaletto
Piazza S. Marco
140.5x204.5 cm
Madrid, Thyssen Bornemisza Collection

In fact the scenic layout and dense, glowing tones of color that appear in these paintings are a clear testimony to the effect that Ricci's work had on the young artist. The influence of the painter from Belluno is also apparent in Canaletto's very first *vedute* of Venice, the four large canvases that were owned by the prince of Liechtenstein in Vienna at the end of the eighteenth century and are now split equally between the Thyssen collection in Madrid and the Venetian Museo del Settecento in Ca' Rezzonico. It is highly likely, in my view, that the four *vedute* were not painted at the same time, but in groups of two at different moments, several years apart. In fact in the *Gran Canal: looking East from the Campo S. Vio* in the Thyssen collection we can see the scaffolding that was mounted on the dome of the church of La Salute in September 1719 in order for consolidation work to be carried out, while the *Piazza S. Marco: looking East along the Central Line* in the same collection shows the area at a time when the new paving designed by Andrea Tirali was being

30. Canaletto
The Piazzetta: looking toward the Clock Tower
172x135 cm
Windsor Castle, Royal Collections

laid, in the state in which, according to the records, it must have been in 1724.

Above all, however, the four paintings are not perfectly homogeneous from the stylistic point of view, and it seems to me that it is possible to use them to trace the development of the early phase of Canaletto's style. In the *Grand Canal: looking Northeast from Palazzo Balbi toward the Rialto Bridge* in Ca' Rezzonico, the brownish tones typical of Ricci's paintings are clearly visible. The figures are small and fairly imprecise, but caught in extremely lively positions. In addition, Canaletto makes use here of an *escamotage* that probably derives from the tradition of set design, using two different sources of light in the foreground so that the shadows of both Palazzo Balbi, on the left bank, and those of the houses of the Mocenigo, on the right bank, are cast onto the waters of the Grand Canal. The *veduta* of the *Rio dei Mendicanti* in the same Venetian museum, on the other hand, is far more luminous and brighter in its coloring. The figures are noticeably larger in proportion to the buildings and each of them is depicted with precision and in rich detail.

It appears, therefore, that in the brief space of two or three years that separates the execution of these two pairs of paintings, Canaletto's style underwent a distinct modification, moving in the direction of a better relationship with reality. On the other hand, it seems possible to discern in the *Rio dei Mendicanti* and the contemporary *Piazza S. Marco* the first glimmerings of

31. Canaletto
Piazza S. Marco with the Basilica
76x114.5 cm
Cambridge (Massachusetts), Fogg Art Museum

the research that was to lead the painter, over the course of the second half of the seventeen twenties, to that "conquest of light" that was to characterize his subsequent production. And, significantly, this took place at the same time as that other great protagonist of Venetian painting in the eighteenth century, Giambattista Tiepolo was developing his own style. From roughly the time when he executed the frescoes in Palazzo Sandi (1725), Tiepolo progressively abandoned the gloomy tones of the tradition of Piazzetta and Bencovich and started to produce paintings of ever greater luminosity, this time taking the works of the 16th-century Paolo Veronese as his model.

Canaletto's success in Venice must have been immediate, as his pictures soon began to supplant those of the established Carlevarijs on the shopping lists of collectors. Moschini (1806) states that Luca died of a broken heart when he saw that he had been surpassed by this new star of Venetian *veduta* painting. And while this is not in fact true, the comment does offer a convincing confirmation of the rapid rise of the young artist.

The reasons for his popularity with his contemporaries become apparent if we read the letters that were ex-

32. Canaletto
Grand Canal: looking toward the Church of La
Salute from the Campo S. Vio
46x77.5 cm
Windsor Castle, Royal Collections

changed in 1725-6 between the painter Alessandro Marchesini, a native of Verona but resident in Venice, and the merchant and collector Stefano Conti of Lucca. The latter had asked Marchesini — who combined his work as a painter of historical and religious pictures with the role of an intermediary between his colleagues and collectors — to procure for him two *vedute* of Venice, to go with the three by Carlevarijs that he already owned. In response to this request; Marchesini informed him that "Ser Lucca… is old now" and that his place had been taken by "Sig.r Ant. Canale, who universally astounds everyone in this town that sees his works, which are of the character of Carlevari but in them one sees Light inside the Sun." Thus Marchesini was pointing out the thematic continuity of Canaletto's paintings with those of Carlevarijs, but at the same time showing that he understood Antonio's desire to give the maximum of luminosity to his *vedute*. That Marchesini's enthusiasm made an impression on the collector is proved by the fact that Conti purchased from Canaletto — notwithstanding the difficulties that arose from the painter's already numerous commitments and the high price of the works — not two but four *vedute*.

The canvases acquired by Conti are now in the collection of the Hosmer heirs in Montreal. The preparatory drawing for one of them, depicting the *Rialto Bridge*, the first to have been painted, still exists and is in the Ashmolean Museum in Oxford. This drawing made from life (it was not for nothing that Marchesini had written to Conti that Canaletto "always goes to the place, and fashions everything from life") is of great interest, as it shows the attention that the painter paid to the representation of light, underlined by the word "sun" written in ink in the part of the *veduta* where the incidence of light was strongest and most dazzling. This brightness was transferred faithfully from the drawing to the painting, further proof of Canaletto's interest in the realistic rendering of natural light.

However the paintings for Stefano Conti, characterized by their free and dense brushwork, had not yet achieved the peaks of luminosity that were to connote Canaletto's *vedute* in the late twenties. Rather they show a marked contrast of chiaroscuro between shaded and sunlit areas, a legacy of the influence of Ricci which is a feature of Antonio's early works.

The next and, one is inclined to say, definitive step came immediately after he had finished the work for Conti, when Canaletto came into contact with the Irishman Owen McSwiney, a failed theatrical impresario who had been forced to leave England. At first McSwiney convinced Canaletto to collaborate — together with Pittoni, Cimaroli, and Piazzetta — on the execution of

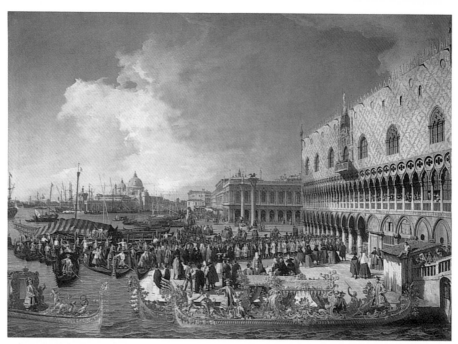

33, 35. Canaletto
The Reception of the Ambassador in the Doge's
Palace; 184x265 cm
Milan, Crespi Collection

34. Canaletto
The Bucintoro Returning to the Molo on Ascension
Day; 182x259 cm
Milan, Crespi Collection

two *Allegorical Tombs* that were to be part of a series of imaginary monuments dedicated to illustrious figures in the history of late seventeenth-century Britain, entrusted to the most celebrated artists of the Bolognese and Venetian schools. At the same time, however, he persuaded him to produce two small *vedute* on copper for the Duke of Richmond, who had also been the client for the *Tombs*.

In these small works, sent to England in 1727, Canaletto abandoned the dramatic style and strong chiaroscuro of his juvenile phase and embarked on an intense luminosity that placed the emphasis on the details of the *veduta* and of the works of architecture of which it was made up. The extent to which McSwiney's advice influenced this new shift is hard to tell, but one gets the impression that the go-between's desire to obtain works more in keeping with the taste of British buyers, and therefore more precise in their topography and accurate in their pictorial representation, was perfectly in harmony with the painter's own desires, and merely accelerated a process that was already under way. Moreover, it was in just these years that Newton's scientific theories on light and its breakdown into separate colors on the one hand, and on the absolute nature of space on the other, started to become familiar in Venice. And the hypothesis of those who claim that the young painter may have come into contact with and appreciat-

36. Canaletto
The Arrival of the French Ambassador in the
Doge's Palace
181x259 cm
St. Petersburg, Ermitage

ed the revolutionary discoveries that were coming out of England appears highly credible.

In the meanwhile, the collaboration between Canaletto and McSwiney was coming to an end. In 1730 the impresario was already complaining to the Duke of Richmond that the painter was late in delivering two more paintings on copper ordered by the illustrious client. This negligence on the part of Canaletto may have been the consequence of his new relationship with the intermediary who was going to launch his career in a definitive manner, Joseph Smith. Banker, merchant, and a man of considerable culture and broad interests, Smith was a collector of the highest caliber. In addition he provided a point of reference, in part through his role as British consul in Venice (a post that he held uninterruptedly from 1744 until his death), for the English aristocracy that came to the city on the Grand Tour or for reasons of business.

Smith and Canaletto quickly formed a close relationship, and it was through the former that the painter obtained the majority of his profitable commissions from

37. Canaletto
The Bucintoro Returning to the Molo on Ascension
Day
187x259 cm
Moscow, Pushkin Museum

British clients. Canaletto also painted numerous pictures for Smith himself: when the consul sold his own art collection to George III of England in 1762, fifty paintings by the Venetian master arrived at Windsor, together with over a hundred and fifty drawings.

The first canvases he painted for Smith were six fairly large views of St Mark's Square and the surrounding area. On the basis of details of topography, these can be dated to between 1726 and 1728, that is to say around the same time as the execution of the two paintings on copper for the Duke of Richmond. In comparison with these, the canvases now in Windsor are closer to his juvenile style in their brownish tones and dense brushwork, together with a fleeting interest in figures of a large size. The works that followed immediately afterwards, though, were completely different. Canaletto started to paint a Venice flooded with sunlight: an animated, luminous city, whose details were depicted with great care. This change is evident not only in the twelve of Smith's canvases now in Windsor that can be dated to 1730 or before, but also in the vedute of Piaz-

za S. Marco with the Clock Tower in Kansas City, the Entrance to the Grand Canal in Houston, and the Piazza S. Marco with the Basilica in Cambridge.

In any case Canaletto's vedute cannot be described as "photographic": the painter used several different points of view in a single work, adjusting reality to suit his own needs and his own poetics. Marchesini's comment ("he paints on the spot and not from imagination at home as does Ser Lucca") was not only unfair to Carlevarijs, for the claim was untrue, but misleading if it gives us the idea that Antonio used to take his canvases, easel, paints, and all the rest to the chosen location and paint there what he saw. What the artist did in fact was make sketches on the spot — with the aid of the camera obscura — and then paint his pictures from these in the studio.

An exceptional example of this modus operandi is provided by the so-called Quaderno Cagnola in the Galleries of the Academy of Venice, which contains numerous pencil sketches made "on the spot" and later inked over. These sketches, which bear a series of written notes that were sometimes used to identify the site for later inclusion in the painting ("Campo S.M.a shapely first part / on the left looking toward the church"), and at others provided information about colors or particular situations ("dirty"), were then put together on the canvas to compose the veduta. Obvi-

ously the individual points of view were retained and did not always coincide. This procedure is part of the reason for certain distortions of perspective and unnatural enlargements that become apparent on careful examination of Canaletto's *vedute*. At the same time it has to be remembered that these views are the product of the creative genius of an artist who was not necessarily interested in the perfect reproduction of reality. As a result there were times when he altered — one is tempted to say "capriciously" — certain aspects of what he saw.

So Canaletto's *vedute* constitute a fairly curious case: the combination of a number of exact reproductions — the ones in the *Quaderno Cagnola* that is — produces pictures that do not wholly correspond to reality. This explains why there has been such a fierce debate among critics over the presumed "realism" of Canaletto, considered by some almost as a forerunner of photography — it has been said that his *vedute* are distinguished by "an absolute sense of reality" — while others, more correctly, hold that what Canaletto was actually doing was to "seek the impression of reality."

As has already been mentioned, the works that he painted for Smith up to 1730 form a homogeneous

38, 39. Canaletto
The Stonemason's Yard
124x163 cm
London, National Gallery

group of twelve views of the Grand Canal. They were hung in Smith's own residence at Santi Apostoli, which looked onto the Grand Canal: this was the house known as Palazzo Balbi-Mangilli-Valmarana, which the future consul was to have rebuilt in a classical style by Antonio Visentini between 1740 and 1751.

The canvases came to represent a sort of collection of samples for potential buyers who stayed in Smith's home. Indeed, in order to make the paintings known to the largest possible number of connoisseurs, Smith had Visentini make engravings from the *vedute*, together with two more pictures by Canaletto depicting *A Regatta on the Grand Canal* and *The Bucintoro at the Molo on Ascension Day*, painted in 1734. The collection of reproductions of the fourteen *vedute* was published in 1735 under the title *Prospectus Magni Canalis Venetiarum*. The venture proved so successful that Smith decided to publish another edition, seven

592

40, 41. Canaletto
The Fonteghetto della Farina
66x112 cm
Venice, private collection

years later, with the addition of a further twenty-four of Visentini's engravings from Canaletto's paintings, and the publicity must have been effective, since Canaletto made several replicas of the paintings for different buyers.

At the same time as this series for Smith, Canaletto painted some canvases for the Imperial ambassador to the Republic of Venice, Count Bolagnos, who wanted a record of the ceremony of the presentation of his credentials to the doge, which took place on May 29, 1729. Consequently the two paintings, now in private collections, must have been painted after this date. The first of them depicts the *Reception of the Ambassador in the Doge's Palace* and is based on similar subjects painted by Carlevarijs. It most closely resembles the *Reception of the Count of Colloredo* now in Dresden (1726), from which Canaletto took the scenic layout, but differs from it in the clarity of light and brightness of color. The second represents *The Bucintoro Returning to the Molo on Ascension Day* and must be considered one of Canaletto's highest achievements. The painting is limpid and drenched with light, and the brushwork is fluid and precise in its description of the tiniest details of the boats and the lively small figures that make up the gaily colored procession waiting to follow the doge's ship to San Nicolò del Lido.

It is a matter of debate whether these paintings constitute Canaletto's first venture into the specific field of the representation of public ceremonies, or had been preceded by pictures of similar subjects painted to commemorate the reception of the French ambassador Jacques-Vincent Lanquet, Count of Gergy, on Novem-

ber 4, 1726. In fact the two canvases that have been identified as depicting this event, now in the Hermitage in St Petersburg and the Pushkin Museum in Moscow, can certainly be dated, on the basis of objective comparisons, to the same period as the *vedute* commissioned from Count Bolagnos. Hence we must conclude that they are updated replicas, certainly painted by Canaletto himself given their high quality, of the canvases executed in 1726 for the Count of Gergy — mentioned as already finished in the Marchesini-Conti correspondence — and subsequently lost.

A number of other superb masterpieces can be dated to the years between the end of the third and the beginning of the fourth decade of the century. They include *The Stonemason's Yard* in the National Gallery in London, formerly the property of Sir George Beaumont, which depicts stonemasons at work in the Campo di San Vidal in dazzling sunlight and, on the other side of the Grand Canal, over which the bridge had not yet been built, the buildings of the Scuola and the church of Santa Maria della Carità, still flanked by the slender campanile that collapsed in 1741. The *Fonteghetto della Farina* (Flour Warehouse) in a private collection in Venice dates from the same time and was probably painted for the Venetian man of letters and bibliophile Giovan Battista Recanati. It depicts, in an image of ex-

42. Canaletto
The Grand Canal between Palazzo Bembo and Palazzo Vendramin Calergi; 47x80 cm
Woburn Abbey, private collection

43. Canaletto
Campo Santa Maria
Formosa
47x80 cm
Woburn Abbey, private
collection

44. Canaletto
View of the Entrance
to the Arsenal
47x78 cm
Woburn Abbey, private
collection

traordinary luminosity, the building that was to become — in 1750 — the first seat of the Academy of Painting and Sculpture (and which now houses the Harbor Office of Venice). The picture is of considerable topographic interest, since it shows a site that underwent profound alterations in the early nineteenth century, when the elegant Coffee House designed by Lorenzo Santi was built and the bridge that used to lead over the Rio della Luna and through the arches under the Fonteghetto to Calle Vallaresso was dismantled, isolating the area of St Mark's from that of San Moisè. It was not until later that the narrow street along the canal was created, served

by a new bridge set further to the left with respect to the Fonteghetto.

In the thirties Canaletto received many more commissions from Great Britain: these included twenty-two *vedute* for the Duke of Bedford, now in Woburn Abbey, four for William Holbech at Farnborough Hall, dispersed in 1930, six for Francis Scott, the second Duke of Buccleuch, reproducing subjects already painted in the canvases for Smith, and seventeen for the Earl of Carlisle at Castle Howard, some of which were sold after the Second World War. The *vedute* painted for the Duke of Bedford, datable to no later than 1735,

598

45. Canaletto
Campo San Rocco
47x80 cm
Woburn Abbey, private collection

reproduce the most famous sights of Venice, from St Mark's Square to the Grand Canal, though a few of these are devoted to less well-known locations. Among the latter should be counted the limpid *View of the Entrance to the Arsenal* which shows, to the right of the canal leading to the shipyard, the 16th-century Oratory of the Madonna, demolished by the French in 1809; that of *Campo Santa Maria Formosa*, with Codussi's church forming the pivot of a scenic *veduta* that unnaturally enlarges the actual space; and the one depicting *Campo San Rocco*, where the 16th-century facade of the Scuola made famous by Tintoretto's cycle of paintings performs the same function as Codussi's church in the previous *veduta*.

It is not certain whether the paintings that were sent to Castle Howard in the early eighteenth century were commissioned by the third Earl of Carlisle, Charles Howard, who employed such Venetian artists as Jacopo Amigoni, Giannantonio Pellegrini, and Marco Ricci on the decoration of his stately home, or his son, the fourth Earl. The numerous works that once hung in the residence of the Earls of Carlisle included some of the artist's greatest masterpieces, and in particular the extraordinary *Bacino di S. Marco: looking East*, which has been in the collection of the Museum of Fine Arts in Boston

since 1939. This panoramic *veduta*, painted simultaneously from several raised points of view in the vicinity of the promontory of the Customs, extends from the eastern end of Giudecca, on the right, to the Granaries of Terranova on the left. The unusually wide *veduta* is flooded with brilliant light. The waters of the basin are streaked by dozens of boats of every kind, thronged with numerous figures. The long line of buildings is depicted in detail, with great care, and the presence of the new campanile of the church of Sant'Antonin allows us to date the picture to 1738 with some confidence.

Other paintings that were originally in Castle Howard include the *vedute* of the *Basilica and Doge's Palace* and the *Entrance to the Grand Canal from the Bacino di S. Marco*, further splendid examples of Canaletto's mature style that are now in the National Gallery in Washington.

Another important group of Canaletto's works dating from the fourth decade is that of the twenty-one *vedute* acquired in Venice in the middle of the nineteenth century by the last Duke of Buckingham and Chandos. On the latter's death these were bequeathed to the Harvey collection at Langley Park and were dispersed in the fifties. Nine of them were engraved by Visentini and appear in the 1742 edition of the *Prospectus*: this suggests that they too may have been part of the Smith collection.

Many of the canvases that used to belong to Buckingham have come back to Italy and ten of them are in a private collection in Milan. They include several ex-

46. Canaletto
The Bacino di S. Marco: looking East
125x204 cm
Boston, Museum of Fine Arts

601

47, 48. Canaletto
*View of Campo Santi
Apostoli*
45x77.5 cm
Milan, private collection

49, 50. Canaletto
*View of San Giuseppe
di Castello*
47.5x77.5 cm
Milan, private collection

51. Canaletto
Piazza S. Marco: looking
toward San Geminiano
68.5x93.5 cm
Rome, Galleria Nazionale

52. Canaletto
The Rialto Bridge: from the
South
68.5x92 cm
Rome, Galleria Nazionale

53, 54. Canaletto
The Doge visiting the Church
and Scuola di S.Rocco
147x199 cm
London, National Gallery

55. Canaletto
The Molo and the Riva
degli Schiavoni: from
the Bacino di S. Marco
46.5x63 cm
Toledo (Ohio), Museum
of Art

56. Canaletto
The Molo with the
Library and the
Entrance to the Grand
Canal
110.5x185.5 cm
Rome, private collection

57. Canaletto
Grand Canal: from
Palazzo Balbi
45x73 cm
Florence, Galleria degli
Uffizi

58. Canaletto
View of the Doge's
Palace
51x83 cm
Florence, Galleria degli
Uffizi

ceptional masterpieces, such as the *View of Campo Santi Apostoli* dominated by the tall seventeenth-century campanile that already has the elegant belfry built at the beginning of the eighteenth century to a design by Andrea Tirali, and that of *San Giuseppe di Castello*, showing the buildings — including the ancient church dedicated to St Nicholas — that stood on the site where Giannantonio Selva laid out the Napoleonic Gardens in the early nineteenth century.

Other pictures that are very similar in style to the group once owned by Buckingham are the four limpid *vedute* in the Galleria Nazionale at Palazzo Corsini in Rome, representing the *Piazzetta looking toward the Basin*, *Piazza S. Marco looking toward San Geminiano*, the *Grand Canal: looking toward Ca' Foscari from the Rialto Bridge*, and the *Rialto Bridge: from the South*: all subjects that he had already tackled in his juvenile works,

but now depicted in an all-pervading and dazzling light.

In the middle of the fourth decade Canaletto painted another unquestioned masterpiece, *The Doge visiting the Church and Scuola di S. Rocco* in the National Gallery in London. The picture records the annual visit paid to the church of San Rocco by the doge on the saint's feast day — August 16 — a day when works by Venetian artists enroled in the Guild were put on show to the public in the square in front of the church. We do not know who commissioned the painting from Canaletto: the only clue that we have comes from the catalogue of an auction held in London in 1804, where the picture was described as coming "from the Vatican." This too is a *veduta* of exceptional luminosity, in which the figures of the doge, the ambassadors, and the senators are depicted with great clarity; the same is true of the architectural details, with even the hooks used to hang the festoons clearly visible. And yet none of the paintings hanging on the front of the school and the houses on the left can be identified, not even the one — the first on the right — that was mistakenly thought in the past to be a reproduction of the juvenile *veduta* of the *Campo dei Santi Giovanni e Paolo* by Canaletto himself, acquired by the Imperial ambassador and now in Dresden: it is as if Canaletto had scornfully refused to give space to other artists in his own painting.

In any case, Canaletto cannot have been a person with an easy-going character. Evidence for this is provided by a number of passages that crop up in letters written by people who had to deal with him. Owen McSwiney, for instance, wrote to the Duke of Richmond in 1727: "The fellow is very difficult and keeps on changing the price everyday; and if one wants to have a picture, then one has to be careful not to make it too obvious to him as one runs the risk of losing by it, in price as well as in quality." And in another letter written three years later to John Conduit: "He is a greedy and grasping man, and as he is famous people are happy to pay whatever he asks." Nor can his relationship with Smith have been wholly idyllic, given that on at least one occasion the Englishman complained to a correspondent about the painter's "impertinence." Count Tessin expressed himself in still harsher terms when, after a visit to Venice from Stockholm in 1736, he described Canaletto as miserly, pretentious, and even a bit of a cheat, while De Brosses, in 1739-40, placed the accent on his avidity, concluding bitterly that it was impossible to bargain with him.

Canaletto's splendid season of the thirties came to an end with numerous other masterpieces, of which it is worth mentioning at least *The Molo and the Riva degli Schiavoni: from the Bacino di S. Marco* now in the Toledo Museum of Art, datable to 1740. The painting was part of a group, subsequently dispersed, of thirteen *vedute* that were added, probably at different times during the eighteenth century, to the collection of the Princes of Liechtenstein in Vienna, and which also included the four juvenile canvases referred to above. The painting in Toledo is a wonderful example of Canaletto's mature style, with its extraordinary brilliance of color and superb clarity.

The *vedute* of *The Molo looking toward the Mint* and *The Riva degli Schiavoni: looking East* in a private collection in Rome are of almost the same quality and we prefer to date them to this period rather than to an earlier one as has been proposed in the past.

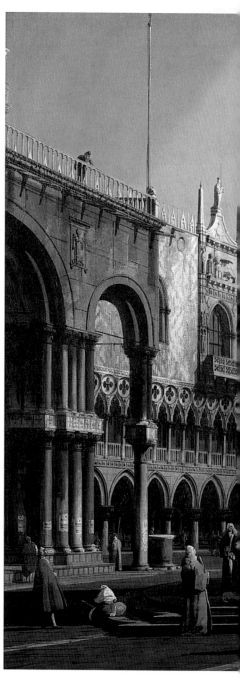

59. Canaletto
Capriccio with the Horses of the Basilica di S.
Marco set on the Piazzetta
108x129.5 cm
Windsor Castle, Royal Collections

60. Canaletto
London: seen from an
Arch of Westminster
Bridge
118x238 cm
Prague, Národní
Galerie

61. Canaletto
Old Walton Bridge
46.5x75 cm
London, Dulwich
College Picture Gallery

At the start of the fifth decade Canaletto's production seems to have passed through a peculiar stage: in the years from 1741 to 1744 he made the thirty-five etchings that, collected in a volume entitled *Vedute altre prese da i luoghi altre ideate*, would be published the same year as the coveted nomination of Joseph Smith to the post of British consul in Venice and with a dedication to him "in token of esteem and respect" on the title page. In 1742 he painted a long series of Roman *vedute*, much of them now in Windsor Castle, that were certainly based on the drawings made by his nephew Bernardo Bellotto during his stay in Rome. In the years immediately following he resumed his production of *capricci*, typical of his youth. The thirteen ornamental panels (of which only eleven have survived) that he

painted for Smith between 1742 and 1744 must be considered *capricci*, in which the painter broke down the reality of Venice and reassembled it to his own satisfaction: famous examples of this include the painting in which he places the team of horses set on the upper order of the facade of St Mark's on the ground in front of the church itself, and the one where he imagines, inserted neatly between the banks of the Carbon and the Vin, the Rialto Bridge as it had been designed in the late sixteenth century by Andrea Palladio but rejected at the time in favor of the one proposed by Antonio da Ponte.

This change of direction, this search for new themes and new means of expression, may have been the consequence of changing political conditions in Europe: the

62. Canaletto
*London: Westminster Abbey with a Procession of
the Knights of the Order of the Bath*
99x 101.5 cm
London, Westminster Abbey

outbreak of the Austrian War of Succession had drasti-
cally reduced the flow of tourists to Venice and this had
resulted in a diminution, if not the complete disappear-
ance, of the painter's profitable commissions from
abroad.

This was probably also the reason for Canaletto's decision to go to England, a direction in which he was in
any case naturally led by his still close ties with Smith.

Antonio reached London in May 1746, bearing a letter of recommendation written by Smith himself and addressed to Owen McSwiney, in which the consul asked
the Irishman to put the painter in touch with the Duke
of Richmond. Though the latter was absent, Canaletto
was fortunate enough to be introduced to Sir Hugh
Smithson, the future Duke of Northumberland, who became his first client in England, as well as his protector.

Notwithstanding this exalted patronage, the Venetian painter cannot have found his stay in the country
an easy one, partly owing to difficulties in his relations
with English artists. In fact they sought to discredit him,
by spreading the rumor that he was not the real Canaletto, but his nephew, Bernardo Bellotto, who by this time
had left Venice as well. Canaletto reacted to this slur

63. Canaletto
Capriccio: a Colonnade opening onto the
Courtyard of a Palace
131x93 cm
Venice, Gallerie dell'Accademia

64. Canaletto
Scala dei Giganti
42x29 cm
Mexico City, private collection

by placing an advertisement in the *Daily Advertiser* in
1749 and again in 1751, inviting art lovers to come and
watch him painting in his studio on Silver Street (now
Beak Street) near Regent Street in the heart of London.

In spite of this hostility, Canaletto received numerous commissions in London and painted about fifty large
vedute during his stay in England, some of them of the
highest quality. Works like *London: seen through an
Arch of Westminster Bridge*, painted in 1747 for the
Duke of Richmond, or the two *Views of the Thames*
produced at the same time for Prince Lobkowitz and
now in Prague, or the well-known *Old Walton Bridge*
in Dulwich Picture Gallery, painted for Thomas Hollis,
are hardly inferior to the luminous and lively Venetian
vedute. Canaletto paid particular attention to portraying daily life as well and in all his English paintings the

depiction of ceremonies is very precise (see for example *London: Westminster Abbey with a Procession of
the Knights of the Order of the Bath* of 1749, now in
Westminster Abbey), as is that of the uses and customs
of the country's inhabitants.

Canaletto remained in England until 1755, interrupting his stay in 1750 to go back to Venice for eight
months, so that he could invest the money he had
earned in London. On his definitive return to his native city, he went back to painting pictures for foreign
clients, who had started to turn up in Venice in large
numbers again with the improvement in the political situation in Europe. Yet his output in the last decade of
his life rarely reached the heights attained by his earlier
work: in fact paintings of really high quality were few
and far between. Among them, however, we have to
place the two extremely refined canvases now in the
National Gallery in London depicting the *Procuratie
Nuove at the Cafe Florian* and *Piazza S. Marco from
the Ascensione*, datable to no later than 1760, in which
the painter concentrates primarily on the capricious play
of light, and the series of four *vedute* painted between
1758 and 1763 for Sigismund Streit, now in Berlin. Of
these, the two night pieces representing the *Night Festival at San Pietro di Castello* and the *Festival on the
Eve of Sta. Marta* are particularly effective.

In 1765 Canaletto, who had only been admitted to
the Academy of Painting and Sculpture two years earlier
in the capacity of a painter of perspective, donated a
*Capriccio: a Colonnade opening onto the Courtyard
of a Palace* (now in the Galleries of the Accademia di
Venezia) to this institution. The arrangement of the
scene presents singular analogies with another contemporary *veduta*, this time painted from life, depicting the
Scala dei Giganti, now in a private collection in Mexico City, which is probably one of his last pictures of
Venice.

In fact Antonio died on April 18, 1768. Strangely,
the inventory of his possessions reveals that he was far
less well off than might have been expected, given his
universally proclaimed avarice and the enormous quantity of pictures he had painted. In reality, at the time
of his death, Canaletto possessed 2,150 ducats deposited with the Scuola dei Luganegheri, which would be
divided between the three sisters who survived him (Antonio had never married), 300 ducats in cash, a few
pieces of poor quality furniture, some jewelry of little
value, twenty-eight paintings that were left in his studio, and a modest wardrobe made up for the most part
of old and shabby clothes and cloaks.

A man of difficult character, Canaletto had no workshop, even though there is no doubt that he occasion-
ally made use of assistants. A number of painters, such
as Moretti, Tironi, or Fabris have been put forward in
the past as his pupils, but it is more likely that they were
simply imitators, and in any case of mediocre quality.

Bernardo Bellotto

The only painter who undoubtedly did work alongside Canaletto — although just for a short time — was the son of his sister Fiorenza, Bernardo Bellotto (Venice 1721 - Warsaw 1780). It can be deduced from the testimony of his contemporary Pietro Guarienti (1753) that Bernardo began to collaborate with his uncle at a very young age, around 1735. Nevertheless it is surprising to find that he was already enroled in the guild of Venetian painters in 1738, at the age of seventeen, which means that he must have already started to work independently. At least at the beginning, this would have consisted essentially in making copies of the paintings and drawings of his famous uncle. According to Guarienti, "he took to imitating him with much study and application." The same writer tells us of the various journeys made by Bernardo, to Rome and the principal cities of Northern Italy, where he executed numerous vedute and "painted many of those of Venice so diligently and so naturally, that it requires a very knowledgeable eye to distinguish them from those of his Uncle." This claim of Guarienti's is not without foundation, and the problem of distinguishing between the vedute of Bellotto and Canaletto is one that has thoroughly exercised the skills of modern critics.

According to the current state of studies, a limited number of vedute of Venice can be attributed with certainty to the young Bellotto, many of them previously regarded as the work of Canaletto. They include the four canvases, which originally formed a single group but are now split between the National Gallery in Ottawa and the Mills collection in Ringwood, in which that search for "objective" reality typical of Bellotto's later output, and so different from Canaletto's "virtual" reality, seems most clearly visible. Another is the View of the Rio dei Mendicanti and the Scuola Grande di San Marco in the Gallerie dell'Accademia in Venice, which is characterized by an intense contrast between the brightly lit parts of the scene and the extensive areas that are wrapped in deep and sharply defined shadow, and by the impasted paint, laid on in thick, parallel brush stro-

65. Bernardo Bellotto
View of the Rio dei Mendicanti and the Scuola Grande di San Marco
42x69 cm
Venice, Gallerie dell'Accademia

66. Bernardo Bellotto
A View of the Grand Canal at San Stae
70.5x126.5 cm
Milan, private collection

kes. Then there is the *View of the Grand Canal at San Stae* in a private collection, where cold tones of color predominate and it is easy to discern the unmistakable quality of Bellotto's lean figures, rendered with thick brush strokes and looking almost like caricatures. Lastly, there is the *View of the Campo dei Santi Giovanni e Paolo* in Springfield, based on the drawing signed and dated December 8, 1740, now in the Darmstadt Museum.

The same German Museum also has the preparatory drawing for the *View of Campo Santo Stefano* in Castle Howard, which is more or less the same view as the one painted by Canaletto for the Duke of Bedford in the thirties. A comparison between the two paintings is extremely useful in revealing the differences — subtle at this date — between Antonio and Bernardo, evident in Bellotto's use of a more marked contrast of light and shade between the sunlit areas and those in shadow, and in his typical way of painting elongated figures.

The journey to Rome, with stopovers in Florence and

Lucca, mentioned by Guarienti must have taken place in 1742, during the interval between Bernardo's marriage to Maria Elizabetta Pizzoni in November 1741 and the birth of their first son, Lorenzo, in October of the following year. Confirmation is provided by topographical details in the *vedute* he painted in the papal city, which are perfectly in keeping with this date.

At the time of his departure for Rome, however, Bellotto must have already established a reputation for himself in Venice, and four of his *vedute* — identified by some as the group now divided between Ottawa and Ringwood — had been acquired by Marshal Schulenburg in November 1740. In 1744 Bernardo left Venice again, heading for Lombardy and, the following year, Turin: it was at this time that he painted the splendid *vedute* of the Gazzada and the capital of the House of Savoy. His divergence from Canaletto's style is already evident in these works, and the difference was to become a gulf in the later *vedute* of Verona, where Bellotto went in 1746. This was the year that Canaletto left Venice for London. In July of the following year, Bernardo too left Italy, going to Dresden with his wife and children, a sign that he intended to be away from his native city for a long time. And in fact Bellotto was never to return to Venice, but stayed to work in the German states, in Saxony, Vienna, and Munich. In 1766 he went to Warsaw, where he died.

Michele Marieschi and Francesco Albotto

Another interesting *vedutista*, Michele Marieschi (Venice 1710-1743), was some ten years younger than Bellotto. His complex artistic personality still presents large areas of obscurity. What we do know is that Marieschi — like Canaletto before him — began his career in the field of theatrical scene painting, in the retinue of Gaspare Diziani, a figure painter from Belluno who was probably his patron, and that he married Angiola Fontana in 1737. There has been much debate over a journey that Michele made to Germany as a young man. There, according his contemporary Guarienti (1753), "the whimsicality and wealth of his ideas pleased many people, who employed him in large and small undertakings." Just what was involved in these "undertakings" is not certain: one clue is provided by the fact that Diziani had been in Germany from 1717 to 1719, where he also worked as a scene painter. So it is possible that it was the painter from Belluno who had pointed his young protege in the direction of the German world.

Marieschi's activity as a scene painter is recorded in a few engravings. One is by his own hand and represents a *Scenic View of a Large Courtyard* and was intended, as can be deduced from the inscription, as a set design. The other two, made from drawings of his that have been lost, were published to commemorate the funeral of Maria Clementina Sobiescki, Queen of Poland, held in Fano in 1735. The work of Giuseppe Camerata and Francesco Tasso, the two engravings depict the funeral decorations and *Castrum doloris* set up in the church of San Paterniano, clearly derived from the set designs of the Bibiena family. Other signs of the influence of the Bibiena can be found in Michele's paintings, especially in his numerous *capricci*, most of them organized around a single, central vanishing point on which the side scenes converge.

A large number of views of Venice are attributed to Marieschi, but there still seems to be a great deal of work to be done on the precise definition of his catalogue. In fact the recent revival of interest in the painter — who in the past, incredibly, was confused for a long time with the mediocre rococo figure painter Jacopo Marieschi — has sparked off considerable disagreement over at least two fundamental questions: on the one hand, the distinction between Michele's own works and those of his pupil and successor Francesco Albotto; on the other his disputed collaboration with other artists (the aforementioned Diziani, Francesco Fontebasso, Simonini, Antonio and Francesco Guardi, and Giambattista Tiepo-

67, 68. Michele Marieschi
View of the Basilica della Salute
124x213 cm
Paris, Louvre

lo are the names most often cited), who according to some critics were responsible for the main figures that appear in the paintings and engravings of Marieschi.

Michele's career as a painter in Venice was a short one, and can be limited to the years between 1735 and 1742: in January of the following year in fact, the painter, "burdened by illness," drew up his last will and testament and just a few days later, at the age of only thirty-two, concluded his brief life. A brief but highly industrious one, if we are to believe Guarienti's claim that "excessive application to toil and study caused his death."

As a consequence, his catalogue is fairly limited, in view of the fact that it was during this short period that he also executed the twenty-one large etchings published in 1741 under the title of *Magnificentiores Selectioresque Urbis Venetiarum Prospectus*, which constitutes one of the greatest masterpieces of Venetian eighteenth-century engraving.

There can be no doubt that Marieschi achieved considerable success as a painter in Venice: proof of this comes from the fact that as early as 1736 Marshall Schulenburg had purchased his *View of the Courtyard of the Doge's Palace* for the high price of 50 sequins. The work, which has recently surfaced on the British antiquarian market, is of remarkable quality, connoted by the scenic and unusual spaciousness bestowed on the impressive courtyard, the marked distinction be-

69, 70. Michele Marieschi
The Rialto Bridge with the Riva del Ferro
130x195.5 cm
St. Petersburg, Ermitage

tween the area shrouded in deep shade and the one flooded with dazzling light, which brings out every detail of the rich architectural decoration. In 1737 the Marshal bought another *veduta* by Marieschi, depicting the *Entry of the Patriarch Antonio Correr* (now the property of the British National Trust), which shows the procession made up of richly decked gondolas in the vicinity of the Rialto Bridge.

This view, in which the predilection for the expansion of spaces typical of Marieschi's training as a scene painter is still apparent, can profitably be compared with other famous paintings of his: for instance the *View of the Basilica of La Salute* in the Louvre or that of the *Rialto Bridge with the Riva del Ferro* in the Hermitage in St Petersburg. For a long time both of these spectacular works were attributed to Canaletto and it is only recent scholarship that has reassigned them to Marieschi's catalogue, of which they are perhaps the most refined examples. Characteristic of both is the "angled" point of view, which expands the breadth of the *veduta* enormously; typical, too, is the way that the works of architecture are painted with intersecting and

overlaid brush strokes, using thick paint laid on in lumps.

We do not know whom these pictures were painted for, but the names of several of Marieschi's foreign clients are known, a fact that demonstrated how Marieschi's fame had spread beyond the confines of the Republic of Venice. For example, three of his *vedute* were acquired in Venice in 1743 by the father of the first Earl of Malmesbury, James Harris. Another group of four views found its way to Castle Howard, the residence of those Earls of Carlisle whom we have already met in the guise of collectors of the works of Canaletto and Bellotto. The two *vedute* now in Berlin, on the other hand, come from the collections in the castle of Sans-Souci, having been purchased in Venice through the mediation of Francesco Algarotti.

It is not easy to establish a precise chronology for Marieschi's works, painted as they were over the space of a few years and therefore without any significant modification in his style. However in a large number of his masterpieces, such as the *View of the Rio di Cannaregio* in Buccleuch or the matching pictures that used to be in the Hallsborough collection in London depicting the *Grand Canal at San Geremia* and the *Grand Canal with the Fish Market*, the small figures in the foreground suggest the sparkling brushwork of Antonio Guardi.

At the time of Marieschi's death, at the beginning of 1743, he had a young apprentice, Francesco Albotto.

Pierre Mariette mentions him briefly in his *Abécédaire*, written before 1744, stating that he "paints views of Venice and landscapes adorned with works of architecture that are not badly handled" and that he called himself the "second Marieschi," having even married his widow. Since that time the artist faded out of the limelight, up until the time when, in 1972, a *View of the Doge's Palace from the Basin* turned up on the antiquarian market in New York, with the words "Francesco Albotto F. in Cale di Ca Loredan a San Luca" written on the back of the canvas, presumably in his own hand. Thorough investigation of the archives has recently brought to light further biographical information on this painter, who seems to have married Angiola Fontana, Marieschi's widow, on October 29, 1744, and to have been enroled in the guild of Venetian painters from 1750 to 1756. Albotto too died at the very early age of thirty-five, on January 13, 1757. This allows us to deduce that he was born in 1721 and was therefore about ten years younger than his master.

While considerable progress has been made in uncovering the details of Albotto's life, the same cannot be said as far as the tracing of works that were undoubtedly painted by him is concerned: in fact the only established painting of his remains the view of the Doge's Palace referred to above, and even this is only known to scholars through a black-and-white photograph, as the painting is in an inaccessible private collection.

However many other paintings have been attributed to him, essentially on the basis of their "inferior quality" with respect to those by Marieschi. In other words, one starts out from the presupposition that any painting "in the manner of Marieschi" but that does not attain the level reached by Marieschi, or that has topographical features indicating a date after 1742, must be the work of Albotto. This approach is not without its risks, given that it relies, for this painter as well, on the insidious method of attribution "by exclusion" that has yielded misleading results in other cases. Paradoxically, it is the same operation to which Marieschi's catalogue was subjected, around the middle of this century, with the inclusion of all the *vedute* of Venice of a certain quality that could not be attributed to Canaletto or Guardi.

Naturally, this does not mean that it is necessary to reject the labors of those who have been trying to build up a critical catalogue of Albotto's works exclusively on the basis of logical deductions that, although frequently persuasive, are, by their very nature as deductions, not absolute certainties. In fact it has to be remembered that there were a large number of painters active in Venice in the middle of the eighteenth century and that many of them were *vedutisti*. For example, what do we know of the paintings of Bernardo Zilotti, whose only surviving works are engravings even though the sources tell us he was a *veduta* and landscape painter? And what about Giovan Battista Grassi? And Tironi? Who can tell

71. *Michele Marieschi*
View of the Rio di Cannaregio
52x85 cm
Bowhill, Selkirk, Buccleuch Collection

72, 73. *Michele Marieschi*
The Grand Canal at San Geremia
54x82 cm
London, private collection

*74-76 Michele Marieschi
The Grand Canal with
the Fish Market
55x82 cm
London, private
collection*

77. Francesco Albotto
View of Campo Santi
Giovanni e Paolo
61x97 cm
Naples, Galleria
Nazionale di
Capodimonte

78. Francesco Albotto
San Giuseppe di
Castello
59.5x97 cm
Venice, private
collection

whether there is not another "second Marieschi" concealed among these and many other names of "painters without paintings?"

Emblematic of this is the case of the recent discovery of a painter to whom the critics have not yet been able to give a name. Another artist with a style similar to Marieschi's, he was the author of a group of thirteen views of Venice now in the Langmatt Foundation in Baden that seem to date, on the basis of the topographic features they contain, from 1743-4.

Nonetheless, it is still credible that Albotto painted the twelve *vedute* in the Capodimonte in Naples that had previously been attributed to Marieschi, but whose topographic features mean that they must date from a period later than 1742. Just as the process of deduction that has led to the assigning to Albotto, at a date subsequent to 1745, of the two fine *vedute* depicting the *Rio di Cannaregio with the Ponte dei Tre Archi* and the *Churches of San Nicolò and San Giuseppe di Castello* in a private collection in Venice, the second of which clearly derives from a model by Canaletto and not Marieschi, appears to be a logical one.

Francesco Guardi

The last great Venetian *veduta* painter, Francesco Guardi (Venice 1712-93) did not start painting views until the fifties. Before then, he worked in the field of figure painting. While it is not impossible that as a young man he collaborated with his elder brother Antonio, also a figure painter and the last great exponent of the Venetian rococo, who was certainly his first master at the end of the twenties, it appears that he soon broke away from his tutelage. He may already have done so by 1729, when Antonio passed on his job as painter to the Giovanelli family to Francesco in order to enter the service of Marshal Schulenburg. The Giovanelli owned many properties in Lombardy, Trentino, and Austria: the painters they employed were used for the most part to decorate the family's palaces, villas, and churches located in these areas. It is not unlikely, therefore that the young Francesco was sent to Austria by his patrons: this would explain the presence, in his juvenile paintings, of features that are more reminiscent of the works of artists like Maulbertsch or Unterperger than the airy *rocaille* lightness of Antonio.

On his return to Venice, probably after he had slackened his ties with the Giovanelli, Francesco must have decided to try out various new directions: this could be the reason why works like his various versions of the theme of the *Meeting* or *Place of Assembly* at first show the influence of Pietro Longhi, followed by the choice to devote himself to the *veduta* and landscape.

There has been much debate over just when he took this decision: the most recent criticism leans toward the hypothesis that his first venture into the genre of the *veduta* was made around the middle of the sixth decade, that is at a time when the influx of tourists to Venice began to revive after the end of the War of Austrian Succession and when Canaletto, who remained in London until 1755, was absent.

In an entry in his *Notatori* dated April 25, 1764, the nobleman Pietro Gradenigo wrote that "Francesco Guardi... a good Disciple of the renowned Canaletto, having had great success in using the *Camera Optica* to paint two canvases of a certain size, ordered by an English Visitor, with views of St Mark's Square looking toward the Church, and the Clock, and of the Rialto Bridge, to the left [of the] Fabbriche in the direction of Canareggio, put them on show today on the sides of the Procuratie Nove, and thereby procured universal approval." This brief, and well known, note by Gradenigo is the only mention of Francesco's activity to have been made by a contemporary writer and is fundamental to an understanding of the step that Guardi had taken in dedicating himself to the *veduta*.

79. Francesco Guardi
Nighttime Procession in Piazza S. Marco
48x85 cm
Oxford, Ashmolean Museum

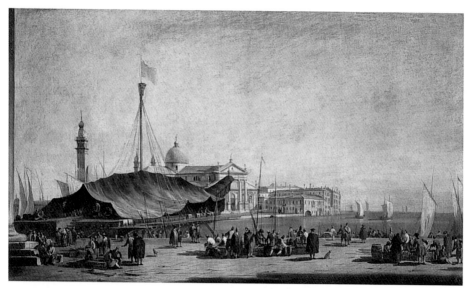

80. Francesco Guardi
The Piazzetta: looking toward San Giorgio Maggiore
49x83.5 cm
Treviso, Museo Civico

81. Francesco Guardi
The Lagoon with Boats, Gondolas, and Rafts
33x54 cm
Paris, Bentineck Collection

82. Francesco Guardi
The Giudecca Canal with the Zattere
72x120 cm
Edinburgh, formerly Buccleuch Collection

83. Francesco Guardi
The Lagoon: from the Fondamenta Nuove
72x120 cm
Edinburgh, formerly Buccleuch Collection

The fact that Gradenigo describes him as a "good Disciple" of Canaletto probably ought not to be taken in a literal sense, but as signifying that at the beginning of his career as a *vedutista* Francesco took his inspiration mainly from the work of the most celebrated artist in this particular field. In fact the views of Venice that are considered to be the earliest painted by Francesco, such as the one of *San Giorgio Maggiore* in the Museo Civico of Treviso, the signed, wide-angle *St Mark's Square* in the Stockholm Museum, or the *Nighttime Procession in Piazza S. Marco* in the Ashmolean Museum in Oxford (which records the celebrations of the election of the Venetian Carlo Rezzonico to the papal throne in 1758), reveal, in their adoption of a broadened perspective, precise description of the architecture, and even the typology of the little figures, the attention that the painter paid to the models of Canaletto, confirming the reliability of the information supplied by Gradenigo. In this period he also painted numerous *vedute* of the lagoon, in a manner that is strongly reminiscent, owing to the unusual breadth of the panorama, of the celebrated drawings by Canaletto in Windsor Castle dating from the forties and representing views of the lagoon from the Motta di Sant'Antonio. For example, the one in the Bentineck collection in Paris where the real protagonist is the silent expanse of water, traversed by a few cargo boats and delimited in the background by the distant view of low buildings; or the two *vedute* formerly in Buccleuch showing the *Giudecca Canal with the*

84. *Francesco Guardi*
The Rialto Bridge with the Palazzo dei Camerlenghi
60x91 cm
Edinburgh, formerly Buccleuch Collection

Zattere, dominated by the great marble bulk of the eighteenth-century church of the Gesuati, and the *Lagoon from the Fondamenta Nuove*, with the bluish vision of the foothills of the Alps in the background.

Francesco's Canalettian phase cannot have lasted long: in the *vedute* from the early part of the sixties, in fact, the signs of a change in direction are already apparent, evident above all in the way that the painter paid less attention to the description of architecture and in his use of an absolutely personal coloration, tending toward warm tones, while the small figures grew more and more generic, almost standardized in the typical way he outlined their "main points." He produced numerous masterpieces at this time, such as the series of six *vedute* in Buccleuch, in one of which — the view of the *Rialto Bridge with the Palazzo dei Camerlenghi* — the campanile of San Bartolomeo appears in the form that was given to it after 1754. Others are *The Rialto Bridge* in the Gulbenkian, the *vedute* now in Munich's Alte Pinakothek, the large canvases at Waddesdon Manor, and the *Campo Santi Giovanni e Paolo* in the Louvre, based on the exceptional preparatory drawing in the Budapest Museum.

85, 86. *Francesco Guardi*
Campo Santi Giovanni e Paolo
72x120 cm
Paris, Louvre

The two *vedute* in the Pinacoteca di Brera, depicting the *Grand Canal: looking toward the Rialto Bridge* and the *Grand Canal at the Fabbriche Nuove*, where the description of the buildings has become even more succinct, date from shortly afterward. During this period he also painted numerous views of St Mark's Square, outstanding examples of which are to be found in the National Gallery in London and the Accademia Carrara in Bergamo. They are characterized by a sharp division between the areas in shadow and the ones illuminated by a warm light, and by the low point of view, almost at the level of the square itself, which forces the painter to set figures in the foreground that are very large in proportion to the buildings.

This last characteristic had already vanished from the works produced at the beginning of the following decade, a time when Francesco painted numerous *capricci*, as well as *vedute* like the one depicting the *Bacino di S. Marco and the Island of San Giorgio* in the Gallerie dell'Accademia in Venice, which was certainly executed prior to 1774, the year when the campanile he shows as standing to the left of the church of San Giorgio collapsed. It was in the seventies that Guardi painted

629

another important group of works, the twelve scenes representing the celebrations for the election of Doge Alvise IV Mocenigo and based on engravings that Giambattista Brustolon had made from drawings by Canaletto and published in 1766. It seems likely that these pictures — now in the Louvre — had been painted for Doge Alvise Mocenigo himself, in office from 1763 to 1778, and were thus the first of a series of three official commissions received by Guardi in the latter part of his career. In any case, the dating of this series to the seventies is confirmed by the clothes worn by the figures, which are not slavish reproductions of those in Brustolon's engravings, but have been updated to match the fashion of the time.

There are stylistic resemblances between the canvases in the Louvre and some — the finest — of the numerous vedute by Guardi in the Gulbenkian Foundation in Lisbon: for instance, the ones representing *Piazza S. Marco* with the decorations designed by Maccaruzzi and set up for the Ascension Day Fair in 1777, and that of the *Grand Canal at Ca' Foscari* during a regatta.

Francesco received the other two public commissions in 1782, when he was asked to paint a series of pictures commemorating the visit to Venice of Paul Petrovitz — the future Tsar Paul I — and his wife Maria Feodorowna, whose identities were concealed under the pseudonym of the "Conti del Nord," and a second series celebrating the visit of Pope Pius VI.

The canvases that make up these two groups — a number of replicas exist of the second, perhaps made for private clients — are now dispersed among different collections: curiously, perhaps because the painter was unused to the requirements of documentation, some of them appear to be of poorer quality than others. But they do include several of Guardi's greatest masterpieces, such as *Pius VI giving his Blessing in Campo Santi Giovanni e Paolo* in the Ashmolean Museum in Oxford, which depicts the moment when the pope, standing on a temporary platform erected in front of the Scuola di San Marco, addresses the large crowd filling the square (in anticipation of the great influx of people the Rio dei Mendicanti had been covered with planks), depicted from behind in accordance with a custom that was to become recurrent in Francesco's late works (such as the *Ascent of Count Zambeccari's Montgolfier* in Berlin from 1784 or the two versions of the *Fire in the Oil Deposits of San Marcuola*, dating from 1789, in Munich and the Galleries of the Accademia di Venezia). Another masterpiece is the *Concert of Ladies in Honor of the Conti del Nord in the Sala dei Filarmonici*, now in Munich, where Francesco reaches new heights of poetry in the vibrant light that pervades the painting.

The *Meeting of Pius VI with the Doge on the Island of San Giorgio in Alga*, in a private collection in Milan, is also of the highest quality and appears to anticipate

the most famous works from the last years of Francesco's life, the *Outward Voyage of the Bucintoro to San Nicolò del Lido* and the *Return of the Bucintoro*, formerly in the Crespi collection, dating from the end of the eighties. Here the painter seems to go back, in the layout of the scenes, to the pictures of the lagoon he had painted at the end of the sixth decade or the start of the following one, at the beginning of his career as a vedutista. The buildings that border panoramas of "impossible" breadth are barely outlined, forming no more than a thin dividing line between the blue of the sky dotted with a few white clouds and the pale green of the water, furrowed by the countless gondolas accompanying the doge's ship. The whole is set amidst a shifting succession of small figures and boats, steeped in a light that literally eats away the edges of the forms.

Francesco attains similar heights of poetry in several more of his last works, such as the small *Rio dei Mendicanti* in the Accademia Carrara in Bergamo, where the architecture (see for example the detail of the sculpture on top of the church's tympanum, depicted with an "open" brush stroke, with no outlines) is depicted in a pictorial shorthand of exceptional charm.

And if it is true that these works, with the decomposition of their forms, were a sad omen of approaching death — Francesco was to die in the January of 1793 at the age of over eighty — then the disquieting *Gondola* in the Poldi Pezzoli, slipping alone through the silent lagoon close to the Fondamente Nuove, in front of the islands of San Cristoforo and San Michele, can be seen as the supreme symbol of a life drawing to its close. A difficult, almost poverty-stricken life, as can be deduced not only from the documents in the archives but also from what P. Edwards wrote to Antonio Canova on June 23, 1804: "You know however that this painter worked for his daily living, that he bought reject and very poorly primed canvases; and that to get by he used very greasy colors, and very often painted straight off. Anyone who bought his pictures had to resign himself to losing them within a short time, and I would not like to guarantee their lasting another ten years."

"He worked for his daily living": this was the destiny that Francesco left as his sole legacy to his son Giaco-

87. *Francesco Guardi*
The Grand Canal: looking toward the Rialto Bridge
56x75 cm
Milan, Pinacoteca di Brera

88. *Francesco Guardi*
The Grand Canal at the Fabbriche Nuove
56x75 cm
Milan, Pinacoteca di Brera

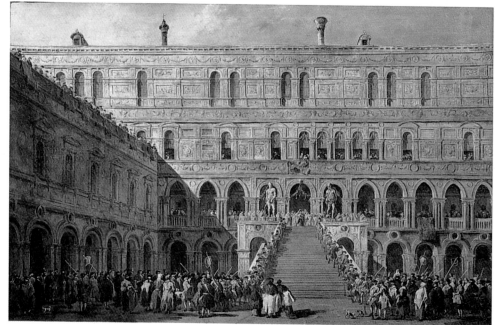

89. Francesco Guardi
Piazza S. Marco
62x96 cm
Bergamo, Accademia Carrara

90. Francesco Guardi
The Coronation of the Doge
66x101 cm
Paris, Louvre

91. Francesco Guardi
The Doge at the Basilica of La Salute
68x100 cm
Paris, Louvre

92. Francesco Guardi
Carnival Thursday on the Piazzetta
67x100 cm
Paris, Louvre

93. Francesco Guardi
The Bucintoro at San Nicolò del Lido
68x100 cm
Paris, Louvre

94. Francesco Guardi
The Outward Voyage of the Bucintoro to San
Nicolò del Lido
50x80 cm
Milan, private collection

95. Francesco Guardi
The Doge on the Bucintoro near the Riva di Sant'Elena, detail
66x100 cm
Paris, Louvre

96, 98. Francesco Guardi
Piazza S. Marco
61x91 cm
Lisbon, Gulbenkian Foundation

97. Francesco Guardi
Pius VI giving his Blessing in Campo Santi
Giovanni e Paolo
63.5x78.5 cm
Oxford, Ashmolean Museum

mo (Venice 1764-1835), who carried on his father's activity, but without either his instinctive poetic inspiration or his inimitable skill as a painter. And his sorry works — which can fairly be described as postcards of no artistic value — mark the inglorious end of an exceptional age, that of eighteenth-century Venetian vedutismo.

99. Francesco Guardi
Rio dei Mendicanti
19.5x15 cm
Bergamo, Accademia Carrara

100. Francesco Guardi
Gondola on the Lagoon
25x38 cm
Milan, Museo Poldi Pezzoli

The illustrations in this volume have been supplied by
the SCALA PICTURE LIBRARY,
the most important source of color transparencies
and digital images of the visual arts in the world.
The over 60,000 subjects visible on the site
www.scala.firenze.it
can be accessed through computerized procedures
that permit easy and rapid picture searches
of any complexity

e-mail archivio@scalagroup.com